Stephen Walther

ASP.NET
Kick Start

SAMS

800 East 96th Street, Indianapolis, Indiana 46240

ASP.NET Kick Start

International Standard Book Number: 0-672-32476-8

Library of Congress Catalog Card Number: 2002110542

Printed in the United States of America

First Printing: December 2002

05   04   10 9 8 7 6 5

Trademarks

All terms mentioned in this book that are known to be trademarks or service marks have been appropriately capitalized. Sams Publishing cannot attest to the accuracy of this information. Use of a term in this book should not be regarded as affecting the validity of any trademark or service mark.

Warning and Disclaimer

Every effort has been made to make this book as complete and as accurate as possible, but no warranty or fitness is implied. The information provided is on an "as is" basis. The author and the publisher shall have neither liability nor responsibility to any person or entity with respect to any loss or damages arising from the information contained in this book.

Bulk Sales

Sams Publishing offers excellent discounts on this book when ordered in quantity for bulk purchases or special sales. For more information, please contact

U.S. Corporate and Government Sales
1-800-382-3419
corpsales@pearsontechgroup.com

For sales outside of the U.S., please contact

International Sales
1-317-428-3341
international@pearsontechgroup.com

Associate Publisher
Michael Stephens

Acquisitions Editor
Neil Rowe

Development Editor
Rebecca Riordan

Managing Editor
Charlotte Clapp

Project Editor
Andy Beaster

Copy Editor
Pat Kinyon

Indexer
Tom Dinse

Proofreader
Mike Henry

Technical Editor
Mike Diehl

Team Coordinator
Lynne Williams

Interior Designer
Gary Adair

Cover Designer
Aren Howell

Page Layout
Joe Millay

Graphics
Oliver Jackson
Tammy Graham

Contents at a Glance

Introduction 1

Part I   **Building Web Form Pages**

1   Getting Familiar with the Development Environment 7

2   Using the Visual Studio .NET Designer...47

3   Creating Basic Web Form Pages 83

4   Validating Web Form Pages...117

5   Creating Web User Controls..139

6   Debugging Your Web Form Pages 153

Part II   **Working with Database Data**

7   Using the Visual Database Tools 177

8   Overview of ADO.NET...203

9   Saving Form Data 231

10   Using List Controls 261

11   Displaying Data with the `Repeater` Control.................................287

12   Displaying Data with the `DataList` Control.................................303

13   Displaying Data with the `DataGrid` Control................................327

Part III   **Working with ASP.NET Applications**

14   Improving Application Performance with Caching 373

15   Configuring Your Application...395

16   Securing Your Application...413

17   Maintaining Application State 439

18   Handling Application-Wide Events..455

19   Deploying Your Application...487

Part IV   **Components, Web Services, and Custom Controls**

20   Building Business Components...501

21   Building XML Web Services 533

22   Creating Custom Web Form Controls 557

Index 595

Table of Contents

Introduction   **1**

Part I   Building Web Form Pages

1   Getting Familiar with the Development Environment   7

Creating a Simple Web Forms Page...8
Working with Solutions and Projects..10
    Creating Projects 11
    Creating Solutions...12
    Accessing Project Files 13
Overview of Visual Studio .NET Windows..17
    Using Auto Hide 19
    Using the Start Page 20
    Using the Solution Explorer Window..21
    Displaying All Items in a Solution...23
    Copying a Project..23
    Using the Toolbox 24
    Using the Server Explorer..27
    Using the Properties Window 29
Using the Visual Studio .NET Designer...29
Using the Visual Studio .NET Code and Text Editor 30
    Taking Advantage of IntelliSense..30
    Navigating Code..33
    Outlining Code..35
    Customizing the Code Editor 36
    Using the Task List Window 39
Automatically Documenting Your Code..43
Summary...44

2   Using the Visual Studio .NET Designer   47

Creating a New HTML Page 48
    Previewing an HTML Page in a Browser...49
    Switching Between Design View and HTML View 49
    Setting the Target Schema Property...50

Working with HTML Pages in Design View...52
    Selecting Flow or Grid Layout Mode 53
    Adding HTML Elements to a Page 54
    Designing an HTML Page in Flow Layout Mode............................55
    Designing an HTML Page in Grid Layout Mode 56
    Mixing Flow and Grid Layout Modes...................................60
    Formatting Text...60
    Setting Background and Margin Properties 62
    Adding Images 63
    Adding Hypertext Links 64
    Adding Form Elements 66
    Adding Tables 69
    Adding Framesets 70
Working with HTML Pages in HTML View...73
    Taking Advantage of Automatic Statement Completion 73
    Enabling and Disabling Automatic Formatting..........................74
    Validating HTML Documents 76
Using the Document Outline...76
Adding Client-Side Scripts...77
Adding Style Sheets 79
    Adding Style Attributes Inline 79
    Adding a Style Block to a Page.......................................80
    Creating External Style Sheets 81
Summary...82

3   Creating Basic Web Form Pages   83

Overview of Web Form Pages...83
    Creating a Simple Web Form Page......................................84
    The Two Parts of a Web Form Page 86
    Compiling and Viewing Web Form Pages 87
Adding Server Controls 89
    Using HTML Controls 90
    Using Web Controls 92
    Adding Label Controls..94
    Adding Button Controls...94
    Adding TextBox Controls..96
    Adding List Controls 98
    Using the AutoPostBack Property......................................101
    Grouping Controls with Panels 103

     Formatting Web Controls 105
  Handling Events 107
     Handling Control Events 107
     Handling Page Events...111
  Summary..115

4 Validating Web Form Pages   117

  Overview of the Validation Controls..117
     Post Backs and Form Validation 118
     JavaScript and the Validation Controls 119
  Using Validation Controls..119
     Checking for Required Fields 119
     Validating a Range of Expressions 122
     Comparing Values 124
  Performing Data Type Checks...127
     Regular Expression Validation 129
  Performing Custom Validation 132
     Displaying a Summary of Validation Errors 136
  Summary..138

5 Creating Web User Controls   139

  Creating a Simple Web User Control..139
  Handling Events in a Web User Control...141
  Building Form Elements with Web User Controls.................................144
  Dynamically Loading Web User Controls..151
  Summary..152

6 Debugging Your Web Form Pages   153

  Building Your Project..153
     Building in Debug and Release Mode.............................155
     Explicit and Dynamic Compilation...............................156
     Displaying Errors in Your Application 157
  Using the Visual Studio .NET Debugger 158
     Adding Breakpoints..158
     Stepping Through Code 159
     Debugger Windows 160
     Adding Watches...161
     Debugging and Exceptions 162
     Debugging Client-Side Script 163

Debugging SQL...164
Page and Application Tracing..166
Using Page Tracing 166
Programmatically Enabling Tracing...170
Using Application Tracing...171
Summary...173

Part II   Working with Database Data

7   Using the Visual Database Tools   177

Visual Database Tools Support in Different Editions of
Visual Studio .NET...177
Working with Database Objects in Server Explorer...................................178
Browsing Database Objects with Server Explorer...........................179
Retrieving and Modifying Data with Server Explorer 180
Creating New Databases with Server Explorer 181
Creating New Database Tables with Server Explorer......................182
Creating New Database Views with Server Explorer 183
Creating New Stored Procedures with Server Explorer 185
Creating New Triggers with Server Explorer...................................187
Creating New Database Functions with Server Explorer................188
Designing Databases with Database Diagrams 191
Creating a New Database Diagram 192
Creating New Tables with Database Diagrams 193
Controlling How Tables Are Displayed..194
Visually Specifying Relationships 195
Adding Annotations to a Database Diagram 196
Controlling Page Breaks in a Database Diagram 196
Working with Database Projects 197
Creating a New Database Project...197
Creating Database References 198
Creating SQL Scripts..199
Creating SQL Queries 200
Summary...201

8   Overview of ADO.NET   203

The Three Dualities of ADO.NET 203
OleDb Versus SqlClient...204
DataSets Versus DataReaders..205
Relational Versus XML Views...205

Creating Database Connections..206
Using DataSets, DataAdapters, and DataViews.......................208
    Displaying Database Data with a DataSet..........................209
    Using DataViews..218
Using DataReaders and Commands..220
    Displaying Database Data with a DataReader 220
Caching Data for Better Performance 223
    Using the Cache Object 224
    Caching a DataSet in Memory 226
Summary...229

9   Saving Form Data   231
Overview of the Command Object 231
    Creating an SqlCommand Object 232
    Creating an OleDbCommand Object...................................235
Executing Commands with Parameters....................................237
    Using Parameters with the SqlCommand Object 238
    Using Parameters with the OleDbCommand Object.............241
Executing Commands with Stored Procedures.........................244
    Executing a Simple Stored Procedure 245
    Stored Procedures and Return Values 248
    Stored Procedures and Output Parameters 250
Creating a Pizza Order Form 253
Summary...259

10 Using List Controls   261
Overview of the List Controls...261
    Adding List Items with the ListItem Collection Editor.................262
    Adding List Items Programmatically 263
    Adding List Items with Databinding 265
    Retrieving the Selected List Item 267
    Enabling AutoPostBack 269
Displaying Database Data in a List Control............................271
Working with Multi-Select List Controls 275
Advanced List Control Topics 278
    Adding a Default List Item...279
    Displaying a Default List Item 281
    Creating Interactions Between List Controls....................282
Summary...285

11   Displaying Data with the `Repeater` Control   287

Binding the `Repeater` Control to Database Data 287

Using Templates with the `Repeater` Control...291

Formatting the Output of a Databinding Expression.............................292

Loading Templates from an External File 294

Adding Child Controls to the `Repeater` Control 297

Summary..302

12   Displaying Data with the `DataList` Control   303

Binding the `DataList` Control to Database Data 303

    Using Templates with the `DataList` Control................................306

Formatting the Appearance of a `DataList`..306

    Formatting the Borders in a `DataList` Control 307

    Using Auto Formatting with the `DataList` Control.......................308

    Creating a Multicolumn `DataList`...310

Creating a Menu with a `DataList` 312

    Using the `DataKeys` Collection 316

Creating a Single-Page Master/Detail Form 320

Summary..324

13   Displaying Data with the `DataGrid` Control   327

Automatically Displaying the Contents of a Database Table 327

Customizing the Appearance of the `DataGrid` Control.........................329

    Applying Auto Formatting to a DataGrid......................................330

    Specifying Columns in a DataGrid 331

    Displaying HyperLink Columns in a DataGrid 334

Sorting Data in a DataGrid..338

    Using Caching with Sorting..341

    Performing Ascending and Descending Sorts...............................342

Paging Through Records in a DataGrid 344

    Customizing the Paging User Interface 348

    Using Caching with Paging 349

Editing Database Records in a DataGrid 350

    Editing with Bound Columns 350

    Adding a Delete Button to the `DataGrid` Control......................357

    Using Smart Navigation with a DataGrid.....................................359

    Editing with Template Columns..359

Summary..369

Part III   Working with ASP.NET Applications

14   Improving Application Performance with Caching   373

Using Page Output Caching...373
    Using the `VaryByParam` Attribute 375
    Using Controls in a Cached Page 377
    Using the `VaryByHeader` Attribute 378
    Using the `VaryByCustom` Attribute 380
    Specifying the Cache Location 382
Using Partial Page Caching 382
    Using Controls in a Cached Web User Control 385
    Using Properties in a Cached User Control....................................386
Using Data Caching..386
    Adding and Removing Items from the Cache................................387
    Using File Dependencies 389
    Using Expiration Policies 392
    Setting Item Priorities...393
Summary...394

15   Configuring Your Application   395

Overview of the Machine.Config and Web.Config Files.........................395
Configuration Sections..396
    The `<configSections>` Section...397
    The `<appSettings>` Section...397
    The `<system.diagnostics>` Section...398
    The `<system.net>` Section 398
    The `<system.web>` Section 398
    The `<trace>` Element 398
    The `<globalization>` Element 398
    The `<httpRuntime>` Element 398
    The `<compilation>` Section...399
    The `<pages>` Element 399
    The `<customErrors>` Section...400
    The `<authentication>` Section 401
    The `<identity>` Element..401
    The `<authorization>` Section...401
    The `<machineKey>` Element 401
    The `<securityPolicy>` Section 402
    The `<sessionState>` Element 402
    The `<httpHandlers>` Section...402

The <httpModule> Section 403

The <processModel> Element 403

The <webControls> Element 404

The <clientTarget> Section...404

The <browserCaps> Section...404

The <webServices> Section 405

Adding Custom Configuration Information 405

Using the <appSettings> Section......................................405

Creating a Custom Section Handler 407

Advanced Configuration Topics...410

Applying Configuration Settings to a Particular File 410

Locking Configuration Settings 411

Summary...412

16   Securing Your Application   413

Overview of Forms Authentication..413

Authentication and Authorization 414

Enabling Forms Authentication 416

Creating a Simple Login Page 418

Retrieving the Username...421

Creating a Sign Out Link 422

Storing Usernames and Passwords in the Web.Config File 423

Storing Usernames and Passwords in a Database Table........................425

Adding a Registration Page 430

Implementing Custom Roles with Forms Authentication 434

Summary...437

17   Maintaining Application State   439

Using View State...439

How View State Really Works 441

Disabling View State...441

Adding Custom Information to View State....................................443

Protecting View State 444

Using Session State 445

Configuring Out-of-Process Session State..448

Enabling Cookieless Sessions 450

Using Application State 452

Summary...454

18   **Handling Application-Wide Events**   **455**

Using the Global.asax File 455

    Handling Application-Wide Errors 457

    Rewriting Page Requests 459

    Detecting the Start and End of a User Session 461

    Implementing Custom Caching 464

Using Custom HttpModules..466

    Creating the Cookieless Authentication Modules........................467

    Creating the Performance Logging Module 478

Summary..485

19   **Deploying Your Application**   **487**

Web Application Deployment Overview 487

    Things You Should Check Before Deployment 489

Creating Web Setup Projects 490

    Modifying Properties of a Web Setup Project..............................493

    Modifying the User Interface of the Web Setup Project 494

Summary..497

Part IV   **Components, Web Services, and Custom Controls**

20   **Building Business Components**   **501**

Why Use Components?..501

Components Versus Classes 503

Creating a Simple Component...506

    Creating Components with Static/Shared Methods......................508

    Adding Properties to a Component 510

Creating a Database Component 514

    Using DataReaders with Components...516

Creating Multi-Tiered Applications...518

Creating a Library of Components 522

    Adding Components to the Toolbox..526

Accessing the Current HttpContext in a Component............................527

Summary..531

21   Building XML Web Services   **533**

What Is a Web Service? 533
    ASP.NET Web Services 535
Creating a Simple ASP.NET Web Service 536
    Invoking a Web Service from a Web Form Page............................540
    Web Services and Namespaces...542
Exposing Database Data Through a Web Service 543
Exposing a Custom Object Through a Web Service 546
Advanced Web Service Topics 551
    Handling Errors When Calling Web Methods................................551
    Caching the Output of Web Methods 552
    Using Dynamic Discovery..553
Summary..555

22   Creating Custom Web Form Controls   **557**

Custom Web Form Controls Versus Web User Controls 557
Overview of Custom Web Form Controls...559
Creating a Simple Non-Composite Control..560
    Using the HtmlTextWriter Class..562
    Creating a Non-Composite Content Rotator Control....................565
Creating a Simple Composite Control...569
    Using the INamingContainer Interface...571
    Using Render with Composite Controls...572
    Composite Controls and Designer Support....................................575
    Creating a Composite Address Form Control 576
Adding Designer Support to a Custom Web Form Control 586
    Using Design-Time Attributes...586
    Controlling the Appearance of a Custom
      Control in the Toolbox..589
    Using the ControlDesigner Class...590
Summary..594

Index   **595**

About the Author

Stephen Walther—through his training company Superexpert AspWorkshops (www.AspWorkshops.com)—has taught workshops on building Web applications using Visual Studio .NET at NASA, Lockheed Martin, the National Science Foundation, the U.S. House of Representatives, Verizon, and others.

He is the author of the book *ASP.NET Unleashed* and a contributing author to *ASP.NET Tips, Tutorials, and Code.*

He got his start working with Active Server Pages by developing two large commercial Web sites. First, he created the Collegescape Web site, a Web site used by more than 200 colleges—including Harvard, Stanford, and M.I.T.—to accept online college applications (Collegescape was bought out by Petersons). Next, he created the CityAuction Web site, an auction site used by both Snap! and CitySearch (CityAuction was acquired by CitySearch).

He received his Bachelor of Arts from the University of California at Berkeley. He was a Ph.D. candidate in Linguistics and Philosophy at the Massachusetts Institute of Technology when he became involved with the World Wide Web.

Dedication

This book is dedicated to my sister, Sue Walther-Jones.

Acknowledgments

I want to thank my wife, Ruth Walther, for patiently enduring the time commitment of writing yet another book (especially when I had just sworn a month before that I wouldn't write another one for at least two years).

I also want to thank Scott Guthrie and Rob Howard at Microsoft for taking the time to meet with me and answering my questions about ASP.NET.

Finally, I want to thank Neil Rowe and Sondra Scott for all of the support and encouragement that they gave me while writing this book.

We Want to Hear from You!

As the reader of this book, *you* are our most important critic and commentator. We value your opinion and want to know what we're doing right, what we could do better, what areas you'd like to see us publish in, and any other words of wisdom you're willing to pass our way.

As an Associate Publisher for Sams, I welcome your comments. You can email or write me directly to let me know what you did or didn't like about this book—as well as what we can do to make our books better.

Please note that I cannot help you with technical problems related to the *topic* of this book. We do have a User Services group, however, where I will forward specific technical questions related to the book.

When you write, please be sure to include this book's title and author as well as your name, email address, and phone number. I will carefully review your comments and share them with the author and editors who worked on the book.

Email: feedback@samspublishing.com

Mail: Michael Stephens, Associate Publisher
            Sams Publishing
            800 East 96th Street
            Indianapolis, IN 46240 USA

For more information about this book or another Sams title, visit our Web site at www.samspublishing.com. Type the ISBN (excluding hyphens) or the title of a book in the Search field to find the page you're looking for.

Introduction

This is an introductory book on creating ASP.NET Web applications using Microsoft Visual Studio .NET. The focus of this book is the Visual Studio .NET development environment. You will learn how to take full advantage of the features of the Visual Studio .NET development environment to quickly develop professional Web applications.

The material in this book is organized around step-by-step walkthroughs of common programming tasks that you'll encounter when building Web applications. Each walkthrough was written to be detailed enough to stand on its own.

Each and every code sample in this book is presented in both C# and Visual Basic .NET. These are the two languages supported by Visual Studio .NET that are widely used when building Web applications. No preference is given to one language over another.

Who Should Read This Book?

This book was written for professional developers who need to quickly get started building Web applications using Visual Studio .NET. The intended audience includes two groups of developers.

First, the book was written for the developer who is migrating to ASP.NET from another technology, such as Java, Cold Fusion, PowerBuilder, or ASP Classic. If you are new to ASP.NET, you can use this book as an introduction to ASP.NET and the Microsoft .NET Framework. This book starts with the basics and works through to advanced features of the ASP.NET Framework.

Second, even if you are an existing ASP.NET developer, you can use this book to learn how to take advantage of the tools included in Visual Studio .NET for building Web applications. By fully taking advantage of the tools included in Visual Studio .NET, you can save yourself a substantial amount of development time.

How This Book Is Organized

This book is divided into four parts. The first part, "Building Web Form Pages," concentrates on the features in Visual Studio .NET for building individual Web Form Pages. You are provided with an overview of the Visual Studio .NET environment. You are introduced to the different types of Web Form controls that can be found in the Toolbox. Finally, the important topic of debugging your applications is discussed.

The second part of this book, "Working with Database Data," is devoted to the topic of creating database-driven Web Form Pages. In this part, you learn how to take full advantage of the tools included with Visual Studio .NET for working with databases, such as Microsoft SQL Server and Microsoft Access. For example, you learn how to use a DataGrid control to display, sort, and edit database data. You also learn how to save Form data to a database table.

The third part of this book, "Working with ASP.NET Applications," covers a variety of different topics. This part includes a chapter on improving the performance of your applications through caching. You also learn how to password-protect folders in your application with Forms Authentication. Finally, you learn several methods of deploying a completed application.

The final part of this book, "Components, Web Services, and Custom Controls," discusses three topics associated with creating custom classes. In this part, you learn how to create multi-tiered applications by separating your application logic into business components. You also learn how to take advantage of XML Web services to expose your business components to the Internet. The last chapter of this book discusses how you can extend the basic ASP.NET Framework by creating new Web Form controls.

What Do You Need to Know Before Reading This Book?

If you have experience with another programming language, such as Java, Visual Basic, or C++, you should have very little trouble understanding the code samples. Java and C++ developers will find C# code very familiar. Visual Basic and VBScript developers will find Visual Basic .NET very familiar. Every code sample is presented in both C# and Visual Basic .NET.

To get the most out of this book, you should also have some background in working with a database, such as Microsoft SQL Server or Microsoft Access. You'll need to know basic SQL to understand the database chapters.

Conventions Used in This Book

The following typographic conventions are used in this book:

- Code lines, commands, statements, variables, and any text you see onscreen appears in a mono typeface. **Bold mono** typeface is used to represent the user's input.

- Placeholders in syntax descriptions appear in an *italic mono* typeface. Replace the placeholder with the actual filename, parameter, or whatever element it represents.

- *Italics* highlight technical terms when they're being defined.

- The ➥ icon is used before a line of code that is really a continuation of the preceding line. Sometimes a line of code is too long to fit as a single line on the page. If you see ➥ before a line of code, remember that it's part of the line immediately above it.

- The book also contains Notes, Tips, and Cautions to help you spot important or useful information more quickly.

PART I

Building Web Form Pages

IN THIS PART

1 Getting Familiar with the Development Environment

2 Using the Visual Studio .NET Designer

3 Creating Basic Web Form Pages

4 Validating Web Form Pages

5 Creating Web User Controls

6 Debugging Your Web Form Pages

1

Getting Familiar with the Development Environment

IN THIS CHAPTER

- Creating a Simple Web Forms Page

- Working with Solutions and Projects

- Overview of Visual Studio .NET Windows

- Using the Visual Studio .NET Designer

- Using the Visual Studio .NET Code and Text Editor

- Automatically Documenting Your Code

In this chapter, you are introduced to the Visual Studio .NET integrated development environment. You start by creating a simple Web Form Page. Creating this page will introduce you to the process of creating new solutions and projects with Visual Studio .NET.

Next, you are given an overview of the main Visual Studio .NET windows. You learn how to work with the Solution Explorer window, the Properties window, the Server Explorer window, and the Toolbox.

The bulk of this chapter is devoted to a discussion of the two Visual Studio .NET interfaces that you'll use most often when building Web pages—the *Designer* and the *Code and Text Editor*. You'll learn how to take advantage of all the tools and features included with the Code and Text Editor to build Web pages.

In this chapter, you will learn

- How to create new ASP.NET Web Application projects with Visual Studio .NET

- How to use the Visual Studio .NET Designer

- How to use the Visual Studio .NET Code and Text Editor

Creating a Simple Web Forms Page

The best way to get familiar with the Visual Studio .NET environment is to build a simple Web Form Page. In this section, we'll create a page that dynamically displays the current date and time.

Whenever you start building an application with Visual Studio .NET, you should begin by creating a new project. Visual Studio .NET supports a number of different project types. When building Web Form Pages, you need to create an ASP.NET Web Application project. To do so, perform the following steps:

1. If you haven't already launched Visual Studio .NET, open it now by pointing to the Start button on the Microsoft Windows taskbar, pointing to Programs, and then clicking the Microsoft Visual Studio .NET icon.

2. After Visual Studio .NET opens, select New Project from the File menu. (Alternatively, you can click the New Project button from the Start Page.)

3. In the New Project dialog box, select either C# or VB.NET as the language for the project by selecting the Visual C# Projects folder or the Visual Basic Projects folder in the Project Types pane.

4. Select ASP.NET Web Application in the Templates pane.

5. Enter the path **http://localhost/myWebApp** in the Location text box.

6. Click OK.

After you complete these steps, your hard drive will make some noises as the necessary files for your project are created. When all the files are created, a new Web Form Page named WebForm1.aspx will appear.

Immediately after you create a new ASP.NET Web Application project, you are in Design View. While in Design View, you can visually design a Web Form Page by dragging and dropping elements onto the page from the Toolbox.

We'll add a Web Form Label to the page that we'll use to display the current date and time. To do so, perform the following steps:

1. Open the Toolbox by selecting Toolbox from the View menu.

2. In the Toolbox, click the tab labeled Web Forms.

3. From under the Web Forms tab, drag a Label onto the Designer surface (the main window) with your mouse.

Next, we need to add code to our Web Form Page that displays the current date and time in the Label. To add code, we need to switch to the Code Editor by doing the following:

C# Steps

1. Double-click the Designer surface (the main window) to switch to the Code Editor. (Alternatively, you can select Code from the View menu.)

2. Add the following code for the Page_Load() method:

```
private void Page_Load(object sender, System.EventArgs e)
{
  Label1.Text = DateTime.Now.ToString();
}
```

VB.NET Steps

1. Double-click the Designer surface (the main window) to switch to the Code Editor. (Alternatively, you can select Code from the View menu.)

2. Add the following code for the Page_Load() subroutine:

```
Private Sub Page_Load(ByVal sender As System.Object,
➥ByVal e As System.EventArgs) Handles MyBase.Load
  Label1.Text = DateTime.Now
End Sub
```

Finally, we can compile the project and open the Web Form Page in a browser by performing the following steps:

1. Switch back to the Design View of the Web Form Page by selecting the Designer from the View menu.

2. Enter the keyboard combination Ctrl+F8 to build and browse the page.

When the page opens in the browser integrated into Visual Studio .NET, you should see the page shown in Figure 1.1.

We moved pretty quickly through each of these steps. In the following sections of this chapter, you'll learn more about working with projects, the Visual Studio .NET windows, the Designer, and the Code Editor.

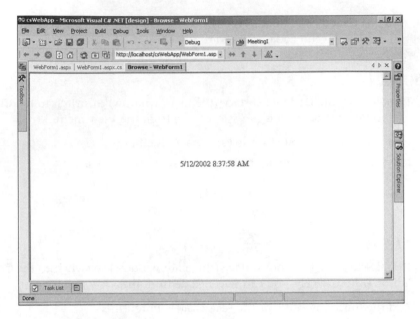

FIGURE 1.1   A simple Web Form Page.

Working with Solutions and Projects

When creating our simple Web Form Page in the previous section, the first thing we did was create a new project. A project contains all the files for a particular application.

You can create several different types of projects with Visual Studio .NET. For example

- *ASP.NET Web Application Project*—Contains files for creating an ASP.NET Web site

- *Windows Application Project*—Contains files for creating a desktop Windows application

- *ASP.NET Web Services Project*—Contains files for creating an XML Web service

- *Web Control Library Project*—Contains files for creating custom ASP.NET Web Forms controls

- *Class Library Project*—Contains files for creating classes that can be shared across multiple projects

For the most part, we'll be sticking to creating ASP.NET Web Applications in the first part of this book. We'll need to create other types of projects when building such things as components and custom controls.

Creating Projects

When you create a new ASP.NET Web Application, a new Web is created on your Web server. For example, when we created the myWebApp project in the first section of this chapter, a new Web was created in the wwwroot directory of the local machine.

You can develop a Web application on either your local machine or on a remote Web server. If you want to create a new project on a remote Web server, you'll need to provide the address of the remote Web server in the New Project dialog box when creating the project. So, instead of entering `http://localhost/myWebApp`, you would enter something like `http://somesite.com/myWebApp`.

When you create a new project, files for the project are automatically created in two places. One set of files is created on the Web server, and one set of files is created on the local machine.

First, a new folder containing the project files is created on your Web server (even when your Web server is located on the same machine as Visual Studio .NET). For example, if you enter `http://localhost/myWebApp` for the location of your project, a new folder named myWebApp is created in the root directory of your Web server (for example, `c:\inetpub\wwwroot\myWebApp`).

Second, a local copy of all the files in your project are kept by Visual Studio .NET in a special folder named VSWebCache. You can find the VSWebCache folder under the Documents and Settings folder (for example, `c:\Documents and Settings\user login\VSWebCache\machine name`).

Visual Studio .NET automatically creates two copies of a project so that you can efficiently work with project files even when you are working with a remote Web server. Normally, Visual Studio .NET takes care of all of the work of synchronizing the two sets of project files for you (but see the "Working with Projects Offline" section later in this chapter).

When a new project is created, two files are created on your Web server that contain information about your project. When creating a C# project, two files with the extensions .csproj and .csproj.webinfo are created. When you create a VB.NET project, two files with the extensions .vbproj and .vbproj.webinfo are created.

The .csproj or .vbproj file contains a list of all the items in your project along with some configuration information. The .csproj.webinfo or .vbproj.webinfo files contain the path to the .csproj or .vbproj file on the Web server.

If you want to open a project that you have previously created, you can open either the .csproj or .vbproj files. If the project is located on the local machine, you can open the project by opening the File menu, pointing to Open, and selecting Project. If the project is located on a remote server, you can select Project from Web on the Open submenu. However, you won't usually want to open a project directly. Typically, you will want to open a Solution that contains your project (see the next section, "Creating Solutions").

Creating Solutions

When you create a new project, a Solution is automatically created that contains the project. For example, when we created the myWebApp project in the first section of this chapter, a new Solution with the same name (myWebApp) was automatically created.

A Solution is a container for projects. It is not uncommon to need to work with multiple projects at the same time. For example, you might need to develop a custom Web Forms control while developing an ASP.NET Web Application. In that case, you would want to add both projects to the same Solution.

Information about a Solution is stored in two files with the extensions .sln and .suo. These files are not stored within a project. By default, they are stored on your local computer in the My Documents, Visual Studio Projects directory.

TIP

You can change the default location where your Solutions are stored by selecting Options from the Tools menu and clicking the Environment, Projects, or Solutions folder.

You can open a Solution that you have previously created by selecting Open Solution from the File menu. To open a Solution, browse to a .sln file and open it.

TIP

When you create a new project, a Solution with the same name is automatically created. If you want to control the name of a Solution, you need to create a Blank Solution and then add projects to it. To create a Blank Solution, open the File menu, point to New, and select Blank Solution.

Accessing Project Files

Visual Studio .NET supports two methods of accessing and modifying files located on a Web server. You can access project files by using FrontPage Server extensions, or you can access files directly through a file share.

The advantage of accessing project files through a file share is that this method is typically faster than using FrontPage extensions. However, to use file share access, your Web server must be located on the same local network as the computer running Visual Studio .NET. In other words, the file share method won't work when working with a Web server located at a remote ISP.

There are two ways of configuring project access. First, you can specify a default access method for all new projects by performing the following steps (see Figure 1.2):

1. Select Options from the Tools menu.

2. Select the folder labeled Projects.

3. Select Web Settings.

4. Choose either the File share or FrontPage Extensions option button.

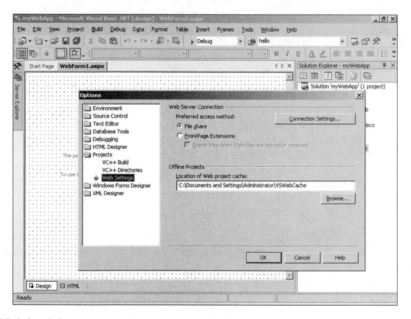

FIGURE 1.2   Selecting a project access method.

You can also change the project access method for an existing project by performing the following steps:

1. Right-click the project in the Solution Explorer window and select Properties.

2. Select the folder labeled Common Properties.

3. Display the Web Settings page.

4. Choose either File Share or FrontPage from the Web Access Mode drop-down list.

5. If you select File Share, you'll need to supply the path to the Web server directory in the Path text box.

6. Select Unload Project from the Project menu.

7. Select Reload Project from the Project menu.

If you want to use FrontPage Server Extensions to access files on a Web server, the Web server must be configured with FrontPage Server Extensions. Perform the following steps to launch the Server Extensions Configuration Wizard for Internet Information Server 5.0 on Windows 2000:

1. On the Web server on which you want to create your project, launch Internet Services Manager by clicking the Start button on the Microsoft Windows taskbar, pointing to Settings, Control Panel, Administrative Tools, and clicking Internet Services Manager.

2. In the tree menu, navigate to the node representing your default Web site.

3. From the Action menu, point to All Tasks, and select Configure Server Extensions. (If this option is unavailable, but the option Check Server Extensions is available, the FrontPage Server Extensions are already installed.)

After you complete the Server Extensions Configuration Wizard, you can create new projects on the Web server by using the FrontPage Extensions access method with Visual Studio .NET.

NOTE

To use FrontPage Extensions, you must have authentication enabled for your Web server. You can enable Windows authentication by opening the property sheet for your Web site in the Internet Services Manager, clicking the Directory Security tab, clicking the Edit button, and selecting the check box labeled Integrated Windows authentication.

Upgrading Existing Applications to Visual Studio .NET

Most likely, you have existing Web applications that you have developed with development environments other than Visual Studio .NET. For example, before upgrading to Visual Studio .NET, you might have used Microsoft's Visual InterDev or FrontPage, Macromedia's Dreamweaver or HomeSite, or even Notepad.

How do you take an existing Web application and use Visual Studio .NET to edit it? You have two choices—migrate or upgrade.

The first choice is to migrate an existing Web application to a new Visual Studio .NET application. In this case, you create a new Visual Studio .NET application on your Web server and then you copy existing files to the new application. To do this, perform the following steps:

1. Create a new ASP.NET Web Application project by opening the File menu, pointing to New, and selecting Project. In the New Project dialog box, select Visual C# Projects (or Visual Basic Projects) in the Project Types pane, and then select the ASP.NET Web Application template. Create a new path for your project on the Web server by entering the path in the Path text box (for example, `http://localhost/newApp`). Click OK.

2. Right-click the name of your new project in the Solution Explorer window, point to Add, and select Add Existing Item.

3. Navigate to the folder containing your old Web application.

4. Select All Files (*.*) from the Files of Type drop-down list. Selecting this option will display all files, including HTML files.

5. Select the files that you want to migrate. You can select multiple files at a time by holding down the Shift or Ctrl key when selecting files.

6. Click Open.

7. The old Web application files should now appear within the Solution Explorer window.

The advantage of using this first method of migrating an old application to a new Visual Studio .NET application is that you automatically get all the supporting ASP.NET Web application files. When you create a new project, all the configuration files are created for you.

The disadvantage of this first method is that it requires you to create a new location for your Web application. You must create a new folder on your Web server and migrate all of the old application files to it.

Instead of creating a new folder on your Web server, you can create a new project in an existing folder. To do this, perform the following steps:

1. Create a new project by opening the File menu, pointing to New, and selecting Project. In the New Project dialog box, select either C# or Visual Basic Projects in the Project Types pane and then select the New Project in Existing Folder template.

2. Enter the name `myApp` for the project and click OK. Next, enter the path to your existing application in the Folder location text box (for example, `http://localhost/oldApp`). Click OK.

3. Right-click the name of your new project in the Solution Explorer window, point to Add, and select Add Existing Item.

4. Navigate to the folder containing your old Web application.

5. Select All Files (*.*) from the Files of Type drop-down list. Selecting this option will display all files, including HTML files.

6. Select the files that you want to migrate. You can select multiple files at a time by holding down the Shift or Ctrl key when selecting files.

7. Click Open.

8. The old Web application files should now appear within the Solution Explorer window.

NOTE

The Standard Edition of Visual Studio .NET does not support the New Project in Existing Folder project template.

The disadvantage of using the New Project in Existing Folder template to upgrade an application is that it does not automatically create the supporting ASP.NET Web application configuration files for you. For example, if you need to use the Web.Config file, you need to manually add the file yourself.

NOTE

What about Visual InterDev Design Time Controls (DTCs)? These are no longer supported in Visual Studio .NET. You'll need to reproduce their functionality by using either Web server controls or Web User Controls.

Working with Projects Offline

Imagine that you are called to a meeting in Paris to demonstrate your newest Web application. You book a flight on the Concorde and get ready to go. Unfortunately, you remember at the last minute that your application has one little bug. What do you do?

Visual Studio .NET supports building Web applications offline. You can create a local copy of the files from a Web application on your local machine, modify the files, and then resynchronize the files with the Web server when you go online again. Consequently, you can leap on the Concorde with your laptop, make the modifications in the air, and update the Web server when you land in Paris.

To switch a project to offline mode, open the Project menu, point to Web Project, and select Work Offline (see Figure 1.3). When you do this, all the files from the Web server are copied to your computer. By default, the files are added to the VSWebCache folder on your computer.

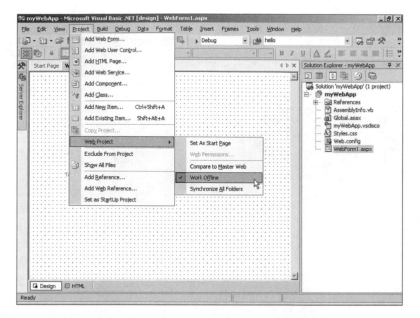

FIGURE 1.3   Selecting offline mode.

While working offline, you can continue to open the files in your application in a Web browser. You'll notice that the files are no longer served from your Web server. They are opened from an offline folder. To use offline mode, you need to have Internet Information Services running on your local computer.

After you have connected to the network, you can go back online by opening the Project menu, pointing to Web Project, and unchecking Work Offline. Your files should be automatically resynchronized with the files on the remote Web server. When you are back online, you can also manually resynchronize files by opening the Project menu, pointing to Web Project, and selecting Synchronize All Folders.

Overview of Visual Studio .NET Windows

In this section, you'll learn about the major user interface elements of the Visual Studio .NET environment. You'll receive a quick tour of the windows and objects that appear when you are working on a Web application project. For example, you'll learn how to create new files, use the Toolbox, and explore resources available on your network.

There are four main windows that you'll use when building projects in Visual Studio .NET (see Figure 1.4). By default, these windows are displayed when you first launch Visual Studio .NET:

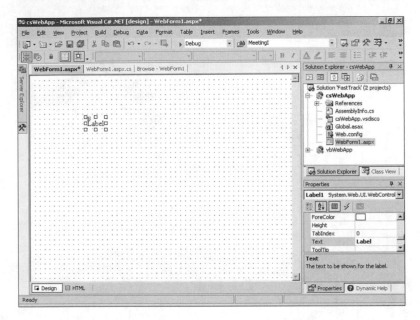

FIGURE 1.4   Visual Studio .NET windows.

- *Solution Explorer*—Displays all the projects and files contained within the current solution

- *Properties Window*—Displays a list of properties for the currently selected object

- *Toolbox*—Displays a list of items that you can add to a page

- *Server Explorer*—Displays server resources available on your local network, such as databases, event logs, and performance counters

You can open any of these windows by selecting the menu options located in the View menu. You can also open a particular window by clicking the corresponding icon for the window on the Standard Toolbar (located at the top-right of the screen).

TIP

You can reset Visual Studio .NET to its default window layout by selecting Options from the Tools menu and displaying the General page in the Environment folder. Click the button labeled Reset Window Layout.

Using Auto Hide

Before discussing the contents of each window, you should know about a new feature of Visual Studio .NET called auto hide. When auto hide is enabled for a window, the window is automatically minimized when you are not working with it.

Windows that support auto hide have a pushpin icon on their title menu. When the pushpin is oriented horizontally, auto hide is enabled. When the pushpin is oriented vertically, auto hide is disabled. To enable or disable auto hide for a window, simply click the pushpin.

TIP

You can enable auto hide for every window by selecting Auto Hide All from the Window menu. This is useful for instantly freeing up screen real estate.

When auto hide is enabled, the window is automatically hidden on the edge of the development environment when the mouse is not hovering over it. A tab represents the minimized window. To expand a hidden window, you can hover your mouse over the tab (see Figure 1.5).

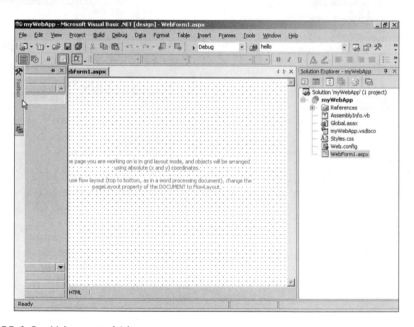

FIGURE 1.5   Using auto hide.

Using the Start Page

When you first launch Visual Studio .NET, you are presented with the Start Page (see Figure 1.6). The Start Page contains several sections that contain such information as the latest Visual Studio .NET headlines from Microsoft and links to various online resources. To get the most from the Start Page, you should open the page while connected to the Internet.

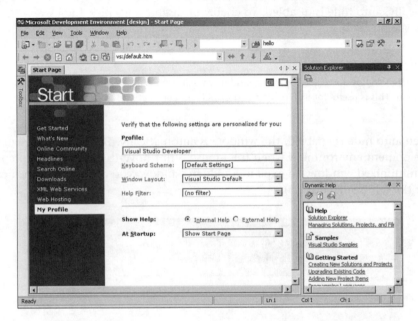

FIGURE 1.6   The Visual Studio .NET Start Page.

TIP

You can open the Start Page at any time by selecting Show Start Page from the Help menu.

You have a couple of options for customizing the Start Page. For example, if you don't want the Start Page to appear when you open Visual Studio .NET, you can have Visual Studio .NET automatically display the last opened solution at startup, display a dialog box for opening an existing project or creating a new project, or display an empty environment.

To modify the startup behavior of Visual Studio .NET, do the following:

1. Select Options from the Tools menu.

2. Select the Environment, General folder.

3. Select a startup option from the drop-down list labeled "At startup:"

You can also set a custom startup page. For example, you can have Visual Studio .NET display the home page for the www.Superexpert.com Web site whenever it first opens By doing the following:

1. Select Options from Tools menu.

2. Select the Environment folder.

3. Display the Web Browser page.

4. Next to Home Page, uncheck the Use Default check box.

5. Enter **http://www.Superexpert.com** in the Home page text box.

6. Click OK.

When you next open Visual Studio .NET, the home page of the Superexpert Web site will be displayed by default.

Using the Solution Explorer Window

The Solution Explorer is the main window for manipulating the files and folders in your application. By default, this window is located at the top-right of Visual Studio .NET.

If the Solution Explorer window is not open, you can open it by choosing Solution Explorer from the View menu. You can also open this window by clicking the Solution Explorer icon on the Toolbar (see Figure 1.7).

Adding Files and Folders to a Project

You can add files and folders to a project by right-clicking an existing project or folder in the Solution Explorer window and selecting a type of item to add. For example, to add a new folder to your Web application, you would right-click an existing project and choose Add, New Folder.

TIP

You can alternatively add new items to a project by selecting a new item to add from the Project menu.

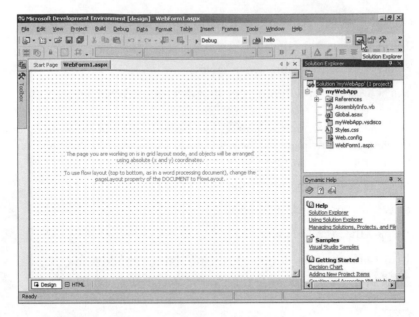

FIGURE 1.7   Displaying the Solution Explorer window.

You can also use Solution Explorer to add already existing items to a project. For example, if you want to add a cool GIF image that you created with Photoshop to your application, you would right-click the folder to which you want to add the image file and select Add, Add Existing Item. Next, you would browse to your image on your local hard drive, select it, and click OK to copy the image to the Web application.

An alternative method of adding existing items to Solution Explorer is to simply drag and drop the item from your desktop into the Solution Explorer window. If you prefer to not drag and drop the item, you can also right-click the item on your desktop, click Copy, right-click a folder in Solution Explorer, and click Paste.

Copying and Moving Items in a Project

Suppose that you need to move a file in your application from one folder to another. There are two ways that you can move items with Solution Explorer. First, you can simply drag and drop the item from one folder to another. To do this, just click the item, keep your mouse button pressed, and move your mouse until the mouse cursor hovers over the new folder. When you release the button, the item is copied.

Alternatively, you can right-click an item, choose Cut, right-click the new folder, and choose Paste. If you want to create a new copy of an item, simply choose Copy instead of Cut when selecting the item.

Displaying All Items in a Solution

By default, all the files and folders contained in a Solution are not displayed in the Solution Explorer window. To display all the items in Solution Explorer, choose Project, Show All Files.

When you show the hidden files, several new files and folders should appear in Solution Explorer. For example, both the Bin and Images directories appear. Also, the code-behind files for any Web Form Pages are explicitly displayed (see Figure 1.8).

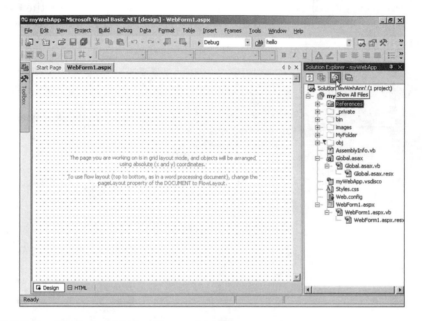

FIGURE 1.8   Displaying hidden files and folders.

You can also display and hide files by clicking the Show All Files icon on the Solution Explorer toolbar.

Copying a Project

You do not usually develop a Web application on a production Web server (unless your budget is extremely tight). Typically, you develop a Web application on a development server and then, when all the bugs are eliminated, you copy the finished application to the production server.

After you have completed a solution with Visual Studio .NET, you can copy the solution from your development server to your production server by using the Copy Project dialog box. You can open this dialog box by selecting Project, Copy Project.

You can also open the Copy Project dialog box by clicking the Copy Project icon located on the Solution Explorer toolbar.

Before you can copy a project, you need to supply a path to the destination server. You can supply any URL in the Destination Project Folder text box. If you are copying the project to a file share, you can enter the path to a file share.

The Copy Project dialog box enables you to select the particular files that you want to copy to the production server (see Figure 1.9). Normally, you do not want to copy the source code or project files to your production server. You can use the Copy Project dialog box to copy only those files that are needed for your Web application to execute.

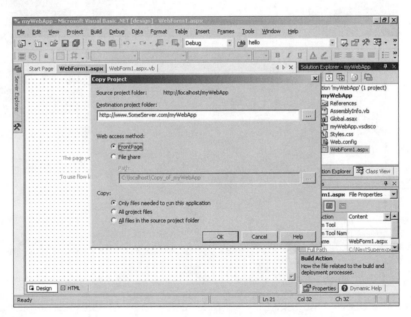

FIGURE 1.9   Copying a project to a new Web server.

Using the Toolbox

The Toolbox contains a set of commonly used controls, tags, and components that you can add to your applications. By default, the Toolbox is located on the left side of the Visual Studio .NET environment below the Server Explorer window.

If the Toolbox isn't visible, you can display it by selecting Toolbox from the View menu. Alternatively, you can open the Toolbox by clicking the Toolbox icon on the Toolbar (see Figure 1.10).

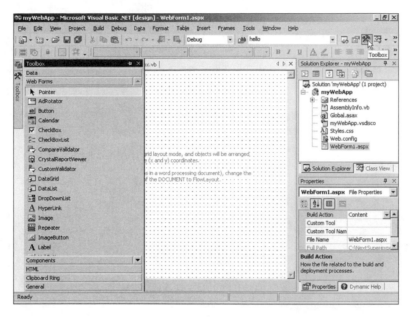

FIGURE 1.10   Opening the Toolbox.

The items in the Toolbox are organized under different tabs. The Toolbox displays different tabs depending on the type of application you are building. For an ASP.NET Web Application, the Toolbar contains the following tabs:

- *Data*—Contains classes related to data access. These Toolbar items are discussed in the second part of this book, "Working with Database Data."

- *Web Forms*—Contains the standard Web Form controls. These controls are discussed in Chapter 3, "Creating Basic Web Form Pages," and Chapter 4, "Validating Web Form Pages."

- *Components*—Contains components for performing advanced tasks, such as working with event logs and performance counters. These components are not discussed in this book.

- *HTML*—Contains items that represent the most common HTML tags. These items are discussed in the next chapter, "Using the Visual Studio .NET Designer."

- *Clipboard Ring*—Contains the last 12 items added to the system clipboard ring using the Copy or Cut command. For example, when you copy code from the Code Editor, it is automatically added to this tab.

- *General*—Contains any custom items or controls you want to add to your project.

Controlling How Toolbox Items Are Displayed

By default, the items under each tab in the Toolbox are displayed in a list. If you have a lot of items to display beneath a particular tab, you might want to disable list view (see Figure 1.11). To disable list view, right-click the Toolbox and uncheck List View.

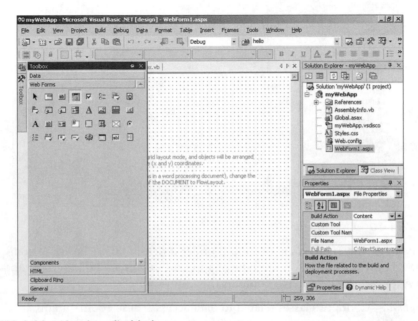

FIGURE 1.11   List view disabled.

You can also arrange the order in which the items in the Toolbar are displayed. If you simply want to display the items in alphabetical order, right-click the Toolbar and select Sort Items Alphabetically.

If you want more fine-grained control over the order of the items in a Toolbar, you can arrange each item individually. Right-click a particular item and select either Move Up or Move Down. You can also drag and drop an item from one position on the Toolbar to another.

Adding New Items to the Toolbox

You can add a variety of different items to the Toolbox including new Web Server controls, components, and even HTML content and code snippets.

For example, imagine that you have just downloaded a new Web server control that you want to use in your applications. You can add this control to the Toolbar by right-clicking the Toolbar and selecting Customize Toolbox (alternatively, you can select Customize Toolbox from the Tools menu).

When you select Customize Toolbox, the dialog box in Figure 1.12 appears. This dialog box contains two tabs—a tab for adding COM components and a tab for adding .NET Framework components. Choose the .NET Framework Components tab and click the Browse button to browse to the Web server control on your computer.

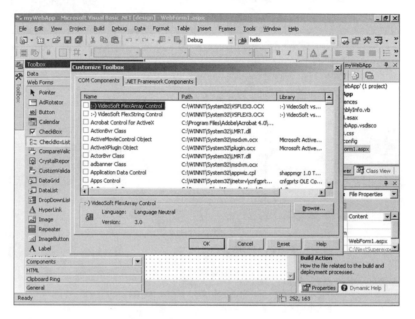

FIGURE 1.12   Customizing the Toolbox.

After you click Open, the control should appear in the list of .NET Framework components. Select the check box next to the component and click OK, the new control should now appear in the Toolbox, just like all the standard controls.

Adding New Tabs to the Toolbox

You can extend the Toolbox with your own custom tabs. For example, you might want to add a new tab named My Favorite Controls that contains only third-party Web server controls. To add a new tab, right-click the Toolbar and select Add Tab. Next, enter a name for the new tab.

You can remove a tab that you have added by right-clicking the tab in the Toolbar and selecting Delete Tab. You can also right-click the tab and select Move Up or Move Down to modify the order of the tabs in the Toolbar.

Using the Server Explorer

You can use the Server Explorer window to browse the servers and databases available on your network. By default, the Server Explorer window is located at the top left of the Visual Studio .NET environment (see Figure 1.13).

If the Server Explorer window is not visible, you can open it by selecting Server Explorer from the View menu. You can also display the Server Explorer window by clicking the Server Explorer icon on the Toolbar.

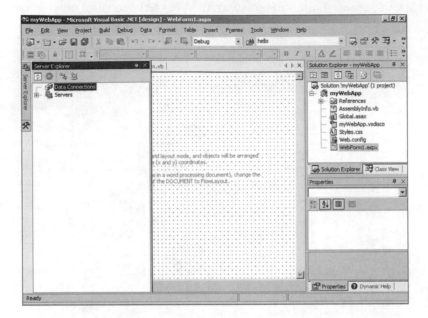

FIGURE 1.13   The Server Explorer window.

You can use Server Explorer to view information about all the servers located on your local network. For example, you can use Server Explorer to view server event logs, performance counters, message queues, and database servers.

NOTE

The Standard Edition of Visual Studio .NET does not support browsing server information. The Servers node does not appear in the Server Explorer window.

To add a new server to the Server Explorer window, perform the following steps:

1. Right-click Servers in the Server Explorer window and select Add Server.

2. Enter the name or IP address of the server to which you want to connect (sadly, you cannot enter a domain name for a server on the Internet).

3. Click OK.

After you complete these steps, a new server should appear under the Servers node in the Server Explorer window.

Using the Properties Window

You use the Properties window to set property values for the controls and components that you add to a page. When you first create an ASP.NET Web Application project, the Properties window displays all the properties for the `WebForm1.aspx` page.

You can use the drop-down list that appears at the top of the Properties window to select a particular object. For example, if you add a label to a page, you can use the drop-down list to select the Label and modify its properties.

Notice that there are several buttons that appear at the top of the Properties window. You can use the Alphabetic button to sort the properties that appear in the Properties window alphabetically. To sort the properties by category, click the Categorized button.

Using the Visual Studio .NET Designer

When you create a new page in Visual Studio .NET, the page opens in the Designer interface. You use the Designer when building the visual portion of your Web pages. The Designer supports two views—Design View and HTML View.

While in Design View, you can build a Web page by dragging and dropping elements from the Toolbox. For example, when building the simple Web Form Page at the beginning of this chapter, we added a Label to the page in Design View by dragging and dropping the Label from the Toolbox.

If you prefer to work directly with HTML tags, you can switch to HTML View. While working in HTML View, you can type HTML and ASP.NET tags directly into the HTML editor.

There are a number of ways to switch between the Design View and HTML View of a page:

- Click the Design View or HTML View tab that appears at the bottom left corner of the Designer interface.

- Press Ctrl+PgDn to switch back and forth between Design View and HTML View.

- Right-click the window and select View HTML Source or View Design.

- Select Design from the View menu, or select HTML Source from the View menu.

TIP

By default, when you open a new page, it appears in Design View. If you want new pages to automatically open in HTML View, select Options from the Tools menu. Navigate to the HTML Designer folder and display the General page. Finally, select HTML View for the page types that you want to open in HTML View.

We'll discuss how to build pages using both of the views available in the Designer in the following sections.

Using the Visual Studio .NET Code and Text Editor

You'll spend more than 50 percent of your time while developing applications with Visual Studio .NET working with the Code and Text Editor. You'll use the Code Editor to enter all of your C# or Visual Basic .NET code for your ASP.NET application. Because this is such an important tool, it's worth examining how to use it in detail.

To discuss the features of this editor, we'll need to open a code file in Visual Studio .NET. Perform the following steps:

1. If you don't already have an ASP.NET Web Application project open in Visual Studio .NET, create one. (For instructions on creating new projects, see the "Creating a Simple Web Form Page" section in the first part of this chapter.)

2. Select Add Web Form from the Project menu. Enter the name `TestCode.aspx` and click Open.

3. Switch to the Code and Text Editor by double-clicking the Designer surface.

After you complete these steps, the Code Editor should appear (see Figure 1.14). Don't worry about the actual code that appears in the Code Editor; we'll discuss the contents of the Code Editor later in this book in Chapter 3.

Taking Advantage of IntelliSense

When you use the Code and Text editor, you can take advantage of IntelliSense. IntelliSense encompasses a number of features that make it easier to enter code while you type (see Figure 1.15).

Some of the important features of IntelliSense include the following:

- *Automatic Statement Completion*—If you type the first part of a statement, the rest of the statement is completed for you.

- *View Class Members*—If you type the name of a class or the name of an instance of a class, followed by a period, all the methods and properties of the class are automatically listed in a drop-down list.

- *View Parameter Information*—If you type the name of a method or function, all of the possible parameters to the method or function are listed in a drop-down list.

- *View Variable Declarations*—If you hover your mouse over any variable, the declaration for the variable appears in a ToolTip.

- *Automatic Brace Matching*—If you type an opening brace such as a (, {, or [, the matching ending brace is displayed.

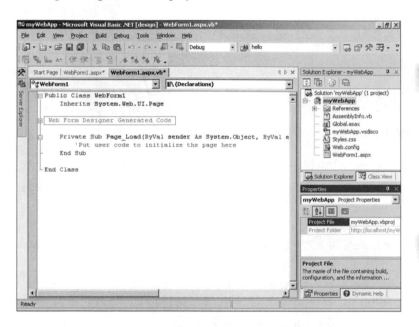

FIGURE 1.14   The Visual Studio .NET Code and Text Editor.

NOTE

You can disable IntelliSense statement completion by selecting Options from the Tools menu. Navigate to the Text Editor folder, and then the All Languages folder, and display the General page. In the Statement Completion section, uncheck the features that you don't want.

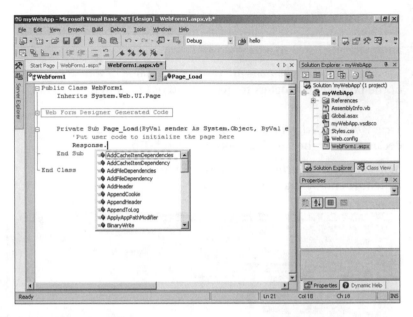

FIGURE 1.15   Using IntelliSense.

To practice using IntelliSense, perform the following steps:

1. In the Code Editor, find the comment Put User Code to Initialize the Page Here.

2. Enter a new line below the comment and enter the text **Response** followed by a single period. A list of all the methods and properties of the Response object should appear (see Figure 1.15).

3. Select the Write method from the drop-down list. You can select the Write method either by typing **W**, or you can use the up and down arrow keys.

4. If you press the Tab key, the text Response.Write is added to the Code Editor. Press the Tab key.

5. Next, enter an opening parenthesis (and a list of possible parameters should appear. You can use the up and down arrows to view all the possible parameters for the Write method.

You can use the following keyboard shortcuts with IntelliSense:

- Alt+Right Arrow—Invokes automatic statement completion after you type the first few letters of the statement

- Ctrl+J—Invokes the List Members feature listing all the methods and properties of a class

- Ctrl+Shift+Space—Invokes the Parameter Info features listing all the parameters for a method or function

- Ctrl+K+I—Invokes the Quick Info feature displaying the complete declaration for any variable

By taking advantage of IntelliSense, you can write code more efficiently. One of the major reasons that people use Visual Studio .NET is to take advantage of IntelliSense!

Navigating Code

The longer your code gets, the more difficult it is to find a particular section of code. Visual Studio .NET supplies a number of tools for quickly navigating to a particular section in the Code Editor.

Using the Navigation Bar

The Navigation Bar appears at the top of the Code Editor. It contains two drop-down lists that enable you to quickly navigate to a previously declared method in your code.

When working with a C# project, the top-left drop-down list contains a list of types in the current page. The top-right drop-down list contains a list of members. For example, you can quickly navigate to a method by selecting a method from the Members drop-down list.

In a VB.NET project, the top-left drop-down list is labeled Class Name and the top-right drop-down list is labeled Method Name. You can navigate to an existing function or subroutine or add a new one by selecting the appropriate method name from the top-right drop-down list.

Moving to a Line Number

If you receive an error when executing an application and you know the line number of the error, you will need to quickly get to the right line of code in the Code Editor. To do this, you can use the Edit, Go To menu option. A dialog box appears that enables you to enter a line number.

Moving to a Definition

You can right-click a variable, method, function, or subroutine and navigate directly to its declaration. To do this, right-click the item in the Code Editor and select Go to Definition.

Searching for Text

Visual Studio .NET supports both basic and advanced text searching features. You can use the Find command to simply perform a search for text in the current document. The Find command also supports several advanced features, such as the ability to search through multiple documents, support for regular expression matches, and support for incremental searches.

To perform a basic search, simply enter your search text in the Find text box on the toolbar. Press Enter and your document will be searched.

To perform more advanced searches, open the Edit menu, point to Find and Replace, and select Find (see Figure 1.16). To find text in external files, open the Edit menu, point to Find and Replace, and select Find in Files (you can also click the Find in Files icon on the toolbar).

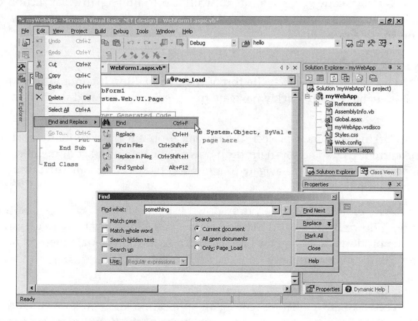

FIGURE 1.16   Opening the Find dialog box.

Finally, you can perform incremental searches. In an incremental search, text is matched as you type it. To perform an incremental search, open the Edit menu, point to Advanced, and choose Incremental Search. After you select this option, the cursor icon appears as a set of binoculars. If you enter text, the text is matched in the editor code document as you type.

Using Bookmarks

You can bookmark any location in a code document and return to it later. To add a bookmark, click the bookmark icon on the toolbar (it looks like a blue flag). After you add a bookmark, a light blue box appears next to the code line (see Figure 1.17).

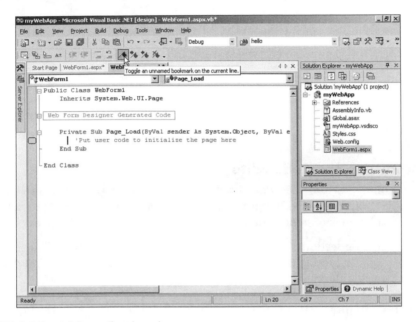

FIGURE 1.17   Adding a bookmark.

To return to a bookmark, you can use one of two additional bookmark icons on the toolbar. The Move the Caret to the Next Unnamed Bookmark icon navigates to the next bookmark in the document. The Move the Caret to the Previous Unnamed Bookmark icon navigates to the previous bookmark in the document.

Outlining Code

As you type methods, functions, and subroutines in the Code Editor, you might notice that plus and minus icons automatically appear on the left margin of the Code Editor. You can use these icons to collapse and expand particular areas of your document.

You can use this code outlining feature for any section of code. For example, you might write a long section of code that does some complicated text parsing. You might find it convenient to hide this section of code while you work on other sections of code in the document.

WARNING

Hiding sections of code works better with VB.NET than C#. Before you can hide a region of code with C#, you need to select Edit, Outlining, Stop Outlining. Be warned that selecting this option will disable all the automatic outlining.

To hide a section of code, perform the following steps:

1. Select the section of code you want to hide with the mouse.

2. Open the Edit menu, point to Outlining, and select Hide Selection.

After you hide a section of code, you can make it reappear by clicking the plus icon next to it.

Customizing the Code Editor

Visual Studio .NET provides you with several options for customizing the Code Editor. For example, if you happen to want to use a yellow script font on a blue background, you can modify the Code Editor to match your preferences.

In the following sections, you'll learn how to control how multiple Code editor windows appear, modify the Code Editor font, display line numbers, and display the Code Editor in full-screen mode.

Selecting Tab or Multiple Document Interface Mode

By default, when you open a new document to edit with the Code Editor, a new tab appears at the top of the Code Editor. You can switch between open windows by clicking the tabs. The default view mode for Visual Studio .NET is called *Tabbed Documents* mode.

If you prefer, you can use *Multiple Document Interface* (*MDI*) mode instead. When MDI mode is enabled, you can tile multiple windows on the screen at the same time (see Figure 1.18).

To switch from Tabbed Documents mode to MDI mode, perform the following steps:

1. Select Options from the Tools menu.

2. Navigate to the Environment folder and display the General page.

3. Under Settings, check the MDI Environment check box.

This change does not take effect until you shut down and restart Visual Studio .NET.

FIGURE 1.18   Viewing the Code Editor in MDI mode.

Modifying the Code Editor Font

You can use any font, foreground color, and background color with the Code Editor that you want. For example, Figure 1.19 shows the Code Editor with a blue background and a 24pt Script font.

To change the font and background color of the Code Editor window, perform the following steps:

1. Select Options from the Tools menu.

2. Navigate to the Environment folder.

3. Display the Fonts and Colors page.

4. Choose Text Editor in the Show Settings For drop-down list.

5. Pick any font and color options you want.

If you want to return these options to their default values, click the Use Defaults button.

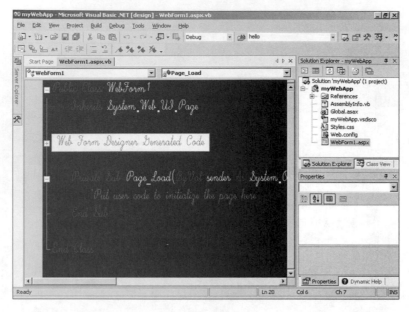

FIGURE 1.19 Customizing the Code Editor font.

Displaying Line Numbers

You can display line numbers in the left margin of the Code Editor (see Figure 1.20). To enable line numbering, perform the following steps:

1. Select Options from the Tools menu.

2. Navigate to the Text Editor folder.

3. Navigate to the All Languages folder.

4. Display the General page.

5. Check the Line Numbers check box.

After you complete these steps, line numbers will appear in the Code Editor window.

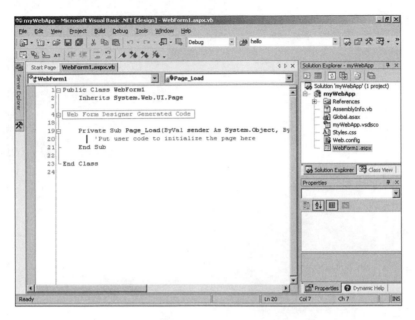

FIGURE 1.20 Displaying line numbers.

NOTE

Enabling line numbers does not cause line numbers to be printed when you print the code in the code window. There is a separate check box on the Page Setup dialog box (select Page Setup from the File menu) that enables or disables line numbers when printing.

Displaying the Code Editor in Full-Screen Mode

If you need to settle down and write a long page of code, it's nice to be able to switch to full screen mode. In full-screen mode, all the windows and toolbars are hidden except for the Code Editor window (see Figure 1.21).

To enable full-screen mode, press the key combination Alt+Shift+Enter. You can return to normal mode either by pressing Alt+Shift+Enter again or by clicking the full-screen icon in the full-screen window.

Using the Task List Window

In this section, you'll learn how to take advantage of the Task List window (see Figure 1.22). The Task List window can be used with the Code Editor to track several categories of tasks. For example, you can use the Task List to track errors in your code, track changes that still need to be made to your code, and to create shortcuts to lines of code.

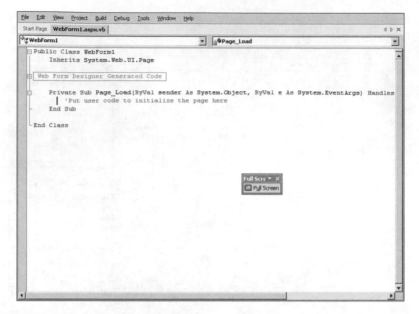

FIGURE 1.21   Using full-screen mode.

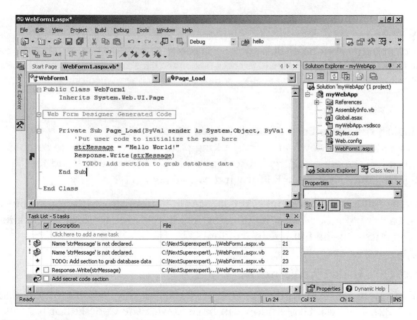

FIGURE 1.22   The Task List window.

There are several ways you can open the Task List window. If you want to open the Task List window and view every task entry, you can open the View menu, point to Show Tasks, and select All. You can also view particular categories of tasks under the View, Show Tasks menu:

- *Comment*—These entries are automatically added to the Task List when you use particular keywords in the comments in your code.

- *Build Errors*—These entries are automatically added to the Task List when your code contains errors.

- *User*—These entries are explicitly added by the user to the Task List.

- *Shortcut*—These entries are explicitly added by the user to the Task List as shortcuts to sections of code.

In the following sections, you'll learn how to work with each category of tasks.

Displaying Tasks for the Current File

By default, the Task List window displays tasks associated with all the files in a project. For example, if you have multiple Web Form Pages in a project, the tasks associated with all the pages appear in the Task List window. However, you might want to focus on only those tasks associated with the file currently opened in the Code Editor.

To display only those tasks associated with the current file displayed in the Code Editor, open the View menu, point to Show Tasks, and select Current File.

Adding Code Comments to the Task Lists

You can automatically add entries to the Task List by using particular keywords when adding comments to your code. For example, suppose that you add the following comment to your code:

C#

```
// TODO: Must add a subroutine here
```

VB.NET

```
' TODO: Must add a subroutine here
```

The special keyword TODO causes a new entry to automatically be added to the Task List. Notice that the TODO keyword appears in the context of a comment.

When you click the TODO entry in the Task List window, you are brought the correct line in the Code Editor window. To display all comment tasks, select View, Show Tasks, Comment.

You can add your own keywords that will automatically trigger the addition of tasks to the Task List. For example, you might want to add a keyword **SLOPPY** that indicates a sloppily written section of code.

To add a custom keyword, perform the following steps:

1. Select Options from the Tools menu.

2. Navigate to the Environment folder.

3. Display the Task List page.

4. Enter a name for the new task in the Name text box (for example, **SLOPPY**). The name is not case sensitive.

5. Enter a priority for the task.

6. Click Add.

7. Click OK.

After completing these steps, the comment will automatically appear in the Task List whenever you use the keyword SLOPPY.

Tracking Code Errors

When there are errors in your code, the errors are automatically added as tasks to the Task List window. Some errors are added to the Task List before the code is compiled. These errors are added to the Task List as you type. Other errors are added after the code is compiled.

For example, if you start using a variable named strMessage in your code and you neglect to declare it, an entry is automatically added to the Task List warning you of this fact.

You can view all the errors in the Task List by opening the View menu, pointing to Show Tasks, and selecting Build Errors, or by opening the View menu, pointing to Show Tasks, and selecting All. From the Task List window, you can click a particular error entry and navigate directly to the appropriate section of code.

Adding User Comments

You might want to add custom tasks to the Task List. For example, if you have a list of future changes that you plan to make to an application, you can add these proposed changes to the Task List.

To add a new user entry to the Task List, open the View menu, point to Show Tasks, and select User, or open the View menu, point to Show Tasks, and select All.

To add a new task, click the section of the Task List window that reads Click Here to Add a New Task. When you add a new task, you can specify the task priority and enter a description of the task.

After you complete the task, you can check the check box next to the task. Checking the check box next to a user task causes the task description to appear with a line through it (it strikes out the task).

Adding Shortcuts to the Task List

You can use the Task List window to maintain a list of shortcuts to sections of code. This works somewhat like adding a bookmark to your code. However, items added to the Task List are more permanent and they can have descriptions.

To open the Shortcut Task List window, open the View menu, point to Show Tasks, and select Shortcut, or open the View menu, point to Show Tasks, and select All.

To add a new shortcut to the Shortcut Task List window, right-click a line of code in the Code Editor and select the Add Task List Shortcut option. Alternatively, you can open the Edit menu, point to Bookmarks, and select Add Task List Shortcut.

After you add a shortcut to the Task List menu, you can navigate to the corresponding section of code in the Code Editor simply by double-clicking the shortcut.

Automatically Documenting Your Code

You can automatically generate documentation for a project or solution by selecting the Build Comment Web Pages from the Tools menu. Selecting this option generates a set of HTML pages that contain links to the pages in a project. Each page displays a list of the methods declared in the page (see Figure 1.23).

You can build Comment Web Pages when working with either a VB.NET or C# project. However, the C# language provides you with some additional options for commenting your code. When working with a C# project, you can add XML comments to your code by using the triple forward slash comment (///).

Consider the following code snippet:

```
public int AddNumbers( int val1, int val2 )
{
  return val1 + val2;
}
```

If you add an XML comment (a triple forward slash) before the code snippet in the Visual Studio .NET Code Editor, the following XML comment tags are automatically added.

```
/// <summary>
///
/// </summary>
/// <param name="val1"></param>
/// <param name="val2"></param>
/// <returns></returns>
public int AddNumbers( int val1, int val2 )
{
  return val1 + val2;
}
```

If you enter values for the *<summary>*, *<param>*, and *<returns>* tags, these values will appear when the Comment Web Pages are generated.

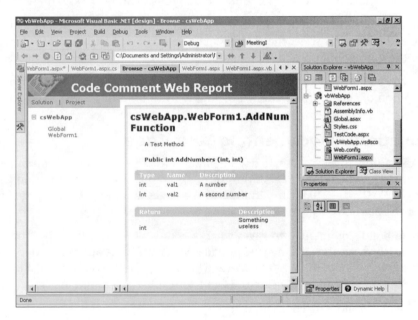

FIGURE 1.23   Building Comment Web Pages.

Summary

In this chapter, you were introduced to the major user interface features of the Visual Studio .NET development environment. In the first section of this chapter, you learned how to create a simple Web Form Page and add new solutions and projects to Visual Studio .NET.

Next, you received a quick tour of the windows that appear while working on an ASP.NET Web application. You learned the function of the Start Page, the Solution Explorer, the Toolbox, and the Server Explorer windows.

Finally, you learned how to customize the code and text editor to match your preferences. You discovered how you can modify the font and colors of the Code and Text editor. You also learned how to take advantage of the Task List window while working with the Code and Text editor.

2

Using the Visual Studio .NET Designer

IN THIS CHAPTER

- Creating a New HTML Page
- Working with HTML Pages in Design View
- Working with HTML Pages in HTML View
- Using the Document Outline
- Adding Client-Side Scripts
- Adding Style Sheets

Visual Studio .NET enables you to build Web pages with standard elements, such as forms, hypertext links, and tables. The development environment also provides advanced features, such as support for different browser versions, framesets, Cascading Style Sheets, and client-side scripts. In this chapter, you'll learn how to take advantage of these features to create the visual portion of the Web pages for your applications.

This chapter is divided into two parts, corresponding to the two methods that Visual Studio .NET supports for creating the visual interface for Web pages. If you prefer, you can build Web pages with Visual Studio .NET by using Design View. When you use Design View, you can quickly create a complicated Web page user interface by using a drag-and-drop interface.

If, on the other hand, you want to get your hands dirty and work directly with HTML code, you can take advantage of HTML View. When you work with HTML using HTML View, you have complete control over your HTML code. When using HTML View, you use the HTML editor that supports such advanced features as HTML validation and automatic formatting.

In this chapter, you will learn

- How to create Web pages in Design View
- How to create Web pages with the HTML Editor
- How to add advanced features to your pages, such as client-side scripts, style sheets, and framesets

Creating a New HTML Page

There are two situations in which you'll need to work with HTML in your Web applications. First, and most obvious, you'll need to work with HTML when creating static HTML pages. However, you'll also need to work with HTML when building Web Form Pages (Web Form Pages are described in detail in Chapter 3, "Creating Basic Web Form Pages").

You can use the methods for working with HTML described in this chapter when working with either static HTML pages or Web Form Pages. The only difference is that in this chapter you'll be working with files with the .htm extension rather than the .aspx extension. We'll be concentrating on static HTML pages in this chapter, but you'll need to use the same methods when building Web Form Pages in the remainder of this book.

To add a new static HTML page to a project, perform the following steps:

1. Select Add HTML Page from the Project menu.

2. Enter a name for the HTML page in the Name text box.

3. Click Open.

After the new HTML page is created, it will appear in the Solution Explorer window (see Figure 2.1).

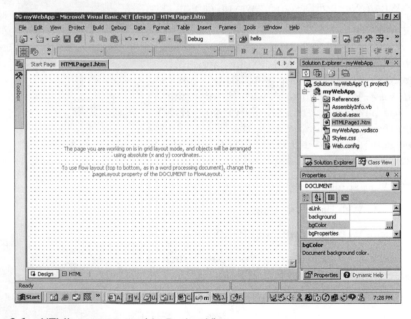

Figure 2.1   HTML page opened in Design View.

NOTE
You should add the HTML page to an open project. To learn how to create new projects with Visual Studio .NET, see the first section of Chapter 1, "Getting Familiar with the Development Environment."

Previewing an HTML Page in a Browser

While designing an HTML page, you can preview the page in a Web browser. To open an HTML page in a Web browser, right-click the HTML file in the Solution Explorer window and select View in Browser. A new tab will appear with the HTML output of the page.

Instead of previewing an HTML page in the default browser, you can open the page in another browser, such as Netscape Navigator. To open an HTML page in another browser, right-click the HTML page in the Solution Explorer window and select Browse With. A list of all the browsers configured on your machine will appear.

Finally, if you want to view the page using different resolutions, such as 640×480 or 800×400, you can select different browser window sizes in the Browse With dialog box.

Switching Between Design View and HTML View

Visual Studio .NET supplies two interfaces for editing HTML documents—Design View and HTML View. You can use any one of the following methods to switch between the two views:

- Click the Design or HTML tab at the bottom of the editor window.

- Select the menu option View, HTML Source in Design View or the menu option View, Design in HTML View.

- Right-click the editor window and select View HTML Source in Design View or View Design in HTML View.

- Use the keyboard shortcut Ctrl+PgDn to switch back and forth between Design View and HTML View.

Figure 2.2 illustrates how the editor appears in Design View, and Figure 2.3 illustrates how the editor appears in HTML View.

TIP
You can specify a default view to edit your HTML documents. For example, you might want all of your HTML documents to open in HTML View by default. To set the default view, do the following steps:

1. Select Tools, Options.

2. Select the folder labeled HTML Designer.

3. Select the General page.

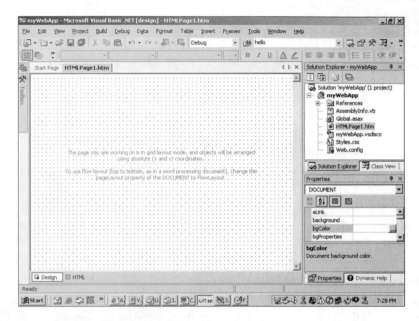

Figure 2.2   Viewing an HTML page in Design View.

Setting the Target Schema Property

Different browser types, such as Internet Explorer and Netscape Navigator, and different browser versions, such as Internet Explorer 3.0 and Internet Explorer 5.0, support different browser features. For example, support for Cascading Style Sheets varies wildly among different types of browsers and browser versions.

Within the Visual Studio .NET environment, you specify the target browser for an HTML document by using the targetSchema property. The targetSchema property determines, among other things, which HTML elements are available in the Toolbox, which properties are displayed for an HTML element, and which HTML attributes are displayed in the HTML editor when using automatic statement completion.

targetSchema can be set to any one of the following values:

- Internet Explorer 3.02/Navigator 3.0

- Navigator 4.0

- Internet Explorer 5.0

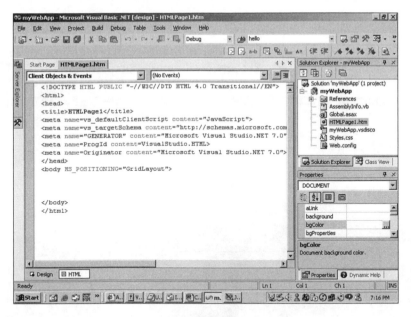

Figure 2.3   Viewing an HTML page in HTML View.

One of the most important features that the `targetSchema` property affects is support for Cascading Style Sheets. Unless the `targetSchema` is set to a browser that supports HTML 4.0 or later, support for Cascading Style Sheets is disabled.

The `targetSchema` property also affects whether support for client-side scripts is enabled or disabled. If the `targetSchema` is set below HTML 4.0, all support for client-side scripts is disabled.

NOTE

Modifying the `targetSchema` property alters the design features available in the Visual Studio .NET environment. It does not affect the behavior of Web Server controls. A Web Server control, such as `RequiredFieldValidator`, will use Cascading Style Sheets and client-side script with Internet Explorer 5.0, even when the `targetSchema` property is set to HTML 3.0 compatibility.

You can modify the `targetSchema` property for an HTML document by completing the following steps:

1. In Design View, right-click the main body of the HTML page and select Properties.

2. Click the General tab in the DOCUMENT Property Pages dialog box (see Figure 2.4).

3. Select a value in the Target Schema drop-down list.

Alternatively, you can select DOCUMENT from the drop-down list in the Property window and alter the targetSchema property from the property list.

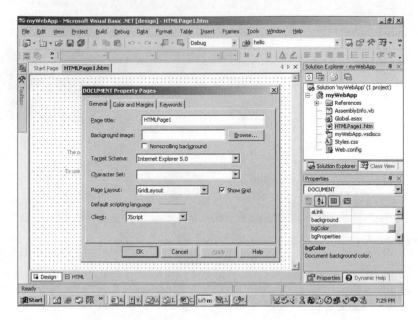

Figure 2.4   Viewing the DOCUMENT Property Pages dialog box.

Working with HTML Pages in Design View

When working with an HTML page in Design View, you can drag and drop your way to a fancy HTML page. Design View supports two methods of visually designing a page; you can add elements to a page by using Flow layout mode or Grid layout mode.

When you use Flow layout mode, you treat an HTML page just like a normal word processor document, such as Microsoft Word. You can type text directly onto the

HTML page. You can also use standard word processor formatting commands to align the text on the page.

Building an HTML page in Grid layout mode, on the other hand, is more like working with a graphic design program, such as Photoshop. In Grid layout mode, you can add elements to a page by using precise x and y coordinates. However, you cannot directly type text onto the page.

TIP

In the "Mixing Flow and Grid Layout Modes" section later in this chapter, you'll learn how to take advantage of the features of both layout modes in the same page.

In the following sections, you'll learn how to design pages by using both layout modes.

Selecting Flow or Grid Layout Mode

You can choose to design an HTML page by using either Flow or Grid layout mode by completing the following steps:

1. In the Properties window, select DOCUMENT from the drop-down list. If the Properties window is not visible, select Properties Window from the View menu.

2. In the Properties window, set the Page Layout property to either FlowLayout or GridLayout.

It's important to understand that you can design pages using either Flow or Grid layout modes that are compatible with any browser. In particular, you can design pages by using Grid layout mode that are compatible with browsers that do not support Cascading Style Sheets.

Visual Studio .NET uses different methods to implement Grid layout, depending on the value of the targetSchema property. If targetSchema is set to HTML 4.0 or later, elements are precisely positioned with Cascading Style Sheet style tags. If the targetSchema does not support Cascading Style Sheets, nested HTML tables are used to precisely position elements on the page.

Therefore, as long as you set the targetSchema property appropriately, you should not shy away from using Grid layout mode as a result of browser compatibility worries. Because almost all browsers support table tags, Grid layout is compatible with almost any browser.

> **NOTE**
>
> When you set the layout mode to Grid layout, a new `ms_positioning="GridLayout"`
> attribute is automatically added to the HTML document's `<body>` tag. If you switch back to
> Flow layout, this attribute is automatically removed.

Adding HTML Elements to a Page

After you add an HTML page to your project, you can add HTML elements to the
page from the HTML tab on the Toolbox. There are two ways that you can add items
from the Toolbox. First, you can double-click an item on the Toolbox, and the item
is added at the currently selected spot on the HTML page (the Designer surface). You
can also add an item from the Toolbox by dragging and dropping it onto the HTML
page.

For example, to add a Label to your HTML page, perform the following steps:

1. Select the HTML tab on the Toolbox. If the Toolbox is not visible, select the
   Toolbox from the View menu.

2. Left-click the Label icon on the Toolbox and drag the Label onto the Designer
   surface.

After you add the Label, the Designer surface should resemble Figure 2.5.

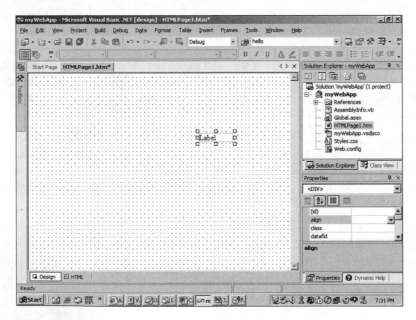

Figure 2.5   A Label on a page.

NOTE

Adding a Label to an HTML page adds a `<div>` tag to the page in the background.

After you add a Label to the page, you can modify the text that the Label displays by typing the text directly into the Label. Select the Label on the Designer surface and then click it again. (Be careful to wait a second before you perform the second click.) Now, you can type text into the Label.

NOTE

If you click a Label too quickly, you'll open the HTML design window and a client-side event handler will be added to your code. Don't worry, just click the Design tab at the bottom of the window and you'll be back where you started.

Notice that you can modify the size of the Label by clicking the Label and pulling on the square handles that appear on the edges of the Label. You can also change the position of the Label by dragging the Label on the page.

Designing an HTML Page in Flow Layout Mode

When Flow layout mode is enabled, you can create an HTML page just as you would create a normal word processing document. You can type text directly onto the Designer surface. When you type a carriage return, a paragraph break is automatically added.

TIP

You can view graphic symbols for paragraph breaks and other elements in Flow layout mode by selecting Details from the View menu.

In Flow layout mode, you can add HTML elements to the page from the Toolbox. However, you cannot precisely position the elements on the page. For example, if you add a Label control, the Label control is added inline with the rest of the text.

Flow layout mode supports a limited number of commands for aligning text. You can use the Align Left, Center, Align Right, and Justify commands.

The alignment commands are available by opening the Format menu and pointing to Justify. You can also access the alignment commands from the Formatting toolbar. If the Formatting toolbar isn't visible, open the View menu, point to Toolbars, and select Formatting.

Designing an HTML Page in Grid Layout Mode

When Grid layout mode is enabled, you can design an HTML page by providing precise x and y coordinates for all of its elements. In Grid layout mode, you cannot add text directly to an HTML page. Instead, you must add text to elements contained in the page, such as Labels.

In this section, you'll learn how to take advantage of the features that Visual Studio .NET provides for designing HTML pages in Grid layout mode. You'll learn how to display a grid and precisely position elements on a page.

Displaying a Grid

If you need to precisely position elements on a page, it's useful to have a visible grid against which to align elements. You can display a grid while working in Design mode by selecting Show Grid from the Format menu. You also can enable and disable this option by toggling the Show Grid icon on the toolbar.

> **NOTE**
>
> Displaying a grid adds a new meta tag to your document. When you display a grid, a vs_showGrid meta tag is automatically created.

By default, an 8-pixel by 8-pixel grid is displayed. To set the grid size to a new value, do the following:

1. Select Options from the Tools menu.

2. Navigate to the HTML Designer folder.

3. Display the Display page.

4. Enter a value for the horizontal and vertical spacing.

For example, Figure 2.6 illustrates how the HTML designer appears when the grid size is changed to a 50-pixel by 50-pixel grid.

Using Snap to Grid

When Snap to Grid is enabled, all elements added to the HTML designer are automatically moved so that their upper-left corners are aligned against the background grid (even when the grid is not visible). For example, if the grid size is set to 20-pixels by 20-pixels and Snap to Grid is enabled, you'll never have an element located 25 pixels from the left margin of the page.

To enable Snap to Grid for all new elements added to the page, select Snap to Grid from the Format menu. Alternatively, toggle the Snap to Grid icon on the toolbar. Enabling Snap to Grid does not cause existing page elements to be repositioned; it only applies to new elements.

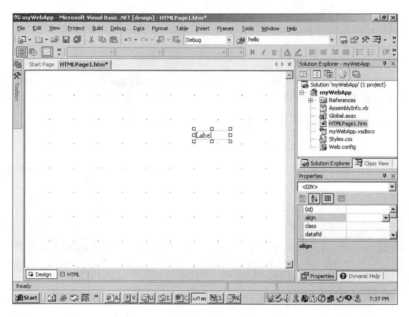

Figure 2.6   Modifying the grid size.

You also can apply Snap to Grid to a single element on a page without enabling Snap to Grid for the whole page. To snap a single element to the background grid, select the element with your mouse, open the Format menu, point to Align, and select Grid. Snap to Grid also affects the size of an element. When Snap to Grid is enabled and you resize an element on the page, the element is automatically resized to fit on grid lines.

You also can resize an element to fit the background grid when Snap to Grid is disabled. To do this, select an element on the page, open the Format menu, point to Make Same Size, and select Size to Grid.

Aligning Elements in Grid Layout Mode

Grid layout mode supports several commands for precisely aligning multiple elements on a page. You can use these commands to modify the relationship between two or more elements on a page.

To select multiple elements on a page, hold the Shift or Ctrl key while left-clicking the elements with the mouse. Alternatively, you can drag a selection box around the elements that you want to modify with the mouse.

TIP

To unselect one of the selected elements in a group, hold down the Shift key and click that element.

The following is a list of the alignment commands that you can use in Grid layout mode for controlling alignment:

- *Align Lefts*—Aligns the left edges of the elements
- *Align Centers*—Aligns the centers of the elements changing the horizontal positions of the elements
- *Align Rights*—Aligns the right edges of the elements
- *Align Tops*—Aligns the top edges of the elements
- *Align Middles*—Aligns the centers of the elements changing the vertical positions of the elements
- *Align Bottoms*—Aligns the bottom edges of the elements

You can also use the following commands to control the size of elements:

- *Make Same Width*—Modifies the elements to have the same width
- *Make Same Height*—Modifies the elements to have the same height
- *Make Same Size*—Modifies the elements to have the same width and height

The following commands enable you to control the horizontal spacing between elements:

- *Make Horizontal Spacing Equal*—When three or more elements are selected, each element is separated horizontally by the same number of spaces.
- *Increase Horizontal Spacing*—Increases the horizontal space between elements.
- *Decrease Horizontal Spacing*—Removes horizontal spaces between elements.
- *Remove Horizontal Spacing*—Removes all horizontal space between elements.

The following commands enable you to alter the vertical spacing between elements:

- *Make Vertical Space Equal*—When three or more elements are selected, each element is separated vertically by the same number of spaces.
- *Increase Vertical Spacing*—Increases the vertical space between elements.
- *Decrease Vertical Spacing*—Decreases the vertical spaces between elements.
- *Remove Vertical Spacing*—Removes all vertical spacing between elements.

All of these commands are available from the Format menu. They are also available on the Layout toolbar. (To open the Layout toolbar, open the View menu, point to Toolbars, and select Layout.)

When you select multiple elements, the last element selected is the dominant element. That means that when you select two elements and apply the Align Left command, the second selected element is aligned against the last selected element.

TIP

When aligning elements, you might want to lock one or more elements in place on the design surface. You can do this with the Lock Element command. This command is available by selecting Lock Element from the Format menu. (The command is also available from the Toolbar.)

Layering Elements in Grid Layout Mode

If the document `targetSchema` property is set to HTML 4.0 or later, you can layer elements on the design surface. In other words, you can place one element directly above or below another (this is also called z-ordering because you are arranging elements on the page's z-axis).

To layer one element on top of a second element, simply drag the first element over the second element. If you want to change the order of the elements, you can open the Format menu, point to Order, and then select either Bring to Front or Send to Back. Not all browsers support layering. If the `targetSchema` property is set to HTML 3.0, exclamation marks will appear when you attempt to layer elements (see Figure 2.7).

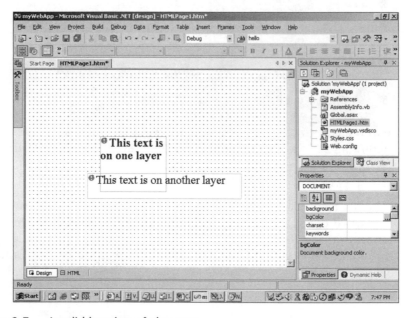

Figure 2.7 Invalid layering of elements.

Mixing Flow and Grid Layout Modes

You can combine the features of Flow and Grid layout mode in a single page by using the Flow Layout Panel and the Grid Layout Panel. Both the Flow Layout and Grid Layout Panels are available under the HTML tab on the Toolbox.

For example, suppose that you are working in Flow layout mode and need to precisely position form fields when constructing an HTML form. In that case, you can add a Grid Layout Panel to the page and add the form elements to the panel (see Figure 2.8).

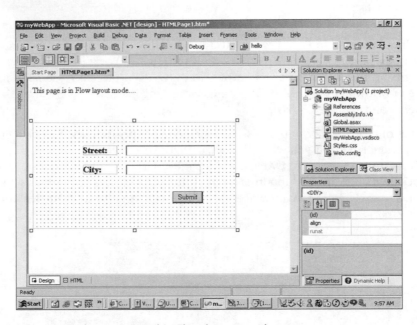

Figure 2.8   A Grid Layout Panel in Flow layout mode.

If you are working in Grid layout mode and discover that you need to add a considerable amount of text to a page, you can add a Flow Layout Panel (see Figure 2.9).

Formatting Text

Visual Studio .NET includes a variety of text formatting commands that you can use regardless of whether you are working in Flow or Grid layout mode. The formatting commands are available from the Format menu and the Formatting toolbar. (If the Formatting toolbar is not visible, open the View menu, point to Toolbars, and select Formatting.)

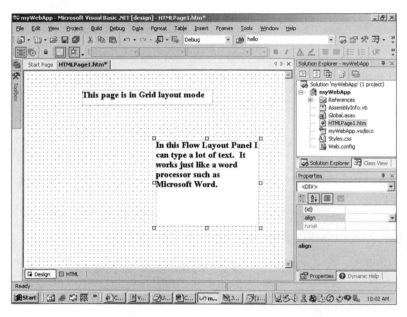

Figure 2.9   A Flow Layout Panel in Grid layout mode.

Visual Studio .NET contains all of the standard formatting commands, such as bold, italic, underline, superscript, and subscript. These commands are available by opening the Format menu and pointing to Font, and are also available on the toolbar.

You can also control text indentation by using the Increase Indent and Decrease Indent commands located from the Format menu or the toolbar.

The Formatting toolbar also includes a Font Name drop-down list for picking a typeface, a Font Size drop-down list for picking a font size, and foreground and background color pickers for choosing text foreground and background colors. (You can't use background color unless the document `targetSchema` property is set to a value equal or greater than HTML 4.0.)

Finally, the Formatting toolbar contains a drop-down list for the Block Format. Block Format options include the following:

- *Normal*—No formatting applied.

- *Formatted*—Text is preformatted with the HTML `<pre>` tag so that whitespace, such as carriage returns and spaces, is preserved.

- *Address*—Text is formatted with the HTML `<address>` tag to indicate a mailing address.

- *Heading*—Text is formatted with \<h1>, \<h2>, \<h3>, \<h4>, \<h5>, or \<h6> tags to create a page heading.

- *Numbered List*—Text is formatted with an HTML \<ol> tag to create a bulleted list with numbers.

- *Bulleted List*—Text is formatted with an HTML \<ul> tag to create a bulleted list without numbers.

- *Directory List*—Text is formatted with an HTML \<dir> tag to create a bulleted list appropriate for a directory listing.

- *Menu List*—Text is formatted with an HTML \<menu> tag to create a bulleted list appropriate for a menu.

- *Definition Term*—Text is formatted with an HTML \<dt> tag to create a particular definition in a definition list.

- *Definition*—Text is formatted with an HTML \<dl> tag to create a definition listing.

- *Paragraph*—Text is formatted with an HTML \<p> to enclose the text in a paragraph.

You can apply multiple Block Format commands to the same string of text. For example, you can apply Bulleted List formatting to text and change the Font Color to Red. If you want to remove all formatting from a string of text and start fresh, apply Normal formatting to the text.

Setting Background and Margin Properties

You can modify properties of an HTML document, such as its background color and margins, by opening the Property Pages for the document. There are two ways you can open the Property Pages:

- Right-click the Designer surface without clicking any elements that you have already added to the surface. Select Properties.

- In the Properties window, select DOCUMENT from the drop-down list and click the icon at the top of the Properties window labeled Property Pages.

Either method will open the dialog box displayed in Figure 2.10. The dialog box has three tabs labeled General, Colors and Margins, and Keywords.

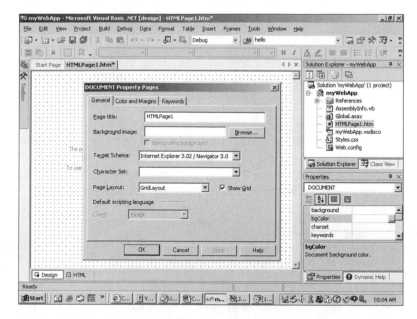

Figure 2.10   Opening DOCUMENT Property Pages.

The General tab enables you to set properties, such as the page title, page background color, and page background image. If the targetSchema is set to HTML 4.0 or later, this tab can also be used to specify the default client-side scripting language used for the page.

The Colors and Margins tab enables you to specify the default color for text and hypertext links. You can also use the options under this tab to set the top, left, right, and bottom margin sizes.

Finally, the Keywords tab enables you to supply the text used with the keywords meta tag. Some (but not all) search engines use the keywords meta tag when indexing HTML documents.

Adding Images

Adding an image to an HTML page requires the completion of two steps. First, you need to add the image file to your project:

1. Select Add Existing Item from the Project menu.

2. In the Add Existing Item dialog box, select All Files (*.*) to display image files.

3. Browse to the image on your hard drive.

4. Click Open.

After you add an image to your project, you can add the image to an HTML page by doing the following:

1. Select Image from the Insert menu.

2. Click the Browse button to navigate to the image in your project.

3. Click OK.

The Insert Image dialog box provides you with several options for the layout of the image. You can specify the image alignment, border thickness, and horizontal and vertical spacing around the image. Finally, you can supply alternative text for the image that will appear in browsers that do not support images.

NOTE

If you insert an image that is not part of your project, the image will not be deployed with your project when you deploy your project to a Web server.

After you add an image to a page, you can automatically add the width and height of the image to the HTML <img> tag by right-clicking the image and selecting Add Height/Width. In general, it's a good idea to add width and height attributes to an image to render the HTML page containing the image faster.

Adding Hypertext Links

If you want to link one HTML page to another enabling a user to navigate from the first page to the second, you need to create a hyperlink.

Before you can create a hyperlink, you must first select the text or image that you want to use as the label for the hyperlink. Select a string of text or an image with your mouse. Next, select Hyperlink from the Insert menu.

NOTE

In Grid layout mode, you'll need to select text that is contained within an HTML element, such as a Label, Flow Layout Panel, or Table element.

Selecting Hyperlink from the Insert menu causes the Hyperlink dialog box to appear (see Figure 2.11). You can use this dialog box to browse to a page to link to the current document.

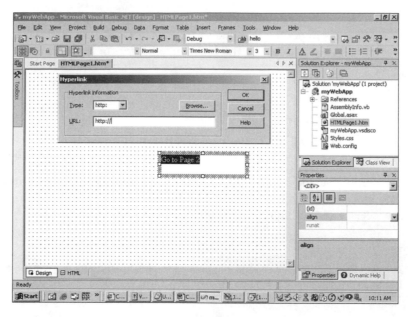

Figure 2.11   Opening the Hyperlink Dialog Box.

Adding a Bookmark

A bookmark, also known as a named anchor, enables you to name an area of a page. After you create a bookmark, you can create a hyperlink that navigates to the bookmark.

To create a bookmark, select some text on the Designer surface and select Bookmark from the Insert menu. Selecting this menu option opens a dialog box that enables you to enter a name for the bookmark. You can provide any name for a bookmark that you please.

After you create a bookmark, you can create a hyperlink that links to the bookmark by doing the following:

1. Select a string of text or an image on the HTML page.

2. Select Hyperlink from the Insert menu.

3. In the Hyperlink dialog box, choose (other) as the Type of the hyperlink.

4. In the URL text box, enter the name of a bookmark preceded by a pound sign (#). For example, #mybookmark.

5. Click OK.

You can also create a hyperlink that links to a bookmark on another page. For example, to create a hyperlink to a bookmark named mybookmark on a page named SomePage.htm, you would supply the following URL for the hyperlink:

```
/SomePage.htm#mybookmark
```

Adding Form Elements

You can drag and drop all of the standard HTML form elements—such as text fields, check boxes, and submit buttons—from the HTML Toolbox onto the design surface.

Typically, before you add form elements to an HTML page, you'll first want to add the HTML <form> tag itself to the page. To add opening and closing HTML <form> tags to a page, select FORM from the Insert menu.

> **NOTE**
>
> In Grid layout mode, the FORM command is available on the Insert menu only when you select an area in an HTML element, such as a Label or Flow Layout Panel.

You can view the locations of the opening and closing <form> tags by selecting Details from the View menu. You'll want to be careful to add any form elements between the opening and closing <form> tags.

Adding Text Fields

You can add a text field to a form by selecting a point within the opening and closing <form> tags and double-clicking the Text Field element in the HTML Toolbox. Adding a text field adds a single-line text box.

You can supply the following attributes for a text field:

- maxlength   The maximum number of characters that can be entered into the text field

- name   The name of the text field

- size   The width of the text field in characters

- value   The default value of the text field

Adding Password Fields

Password fields are similar to text fields, with the exception that the text in a password field is automatically hidden. Any text you enter into a password field is echoed with asterisks.

A password field supports the same attributes as a text field:

- `maxlength`   The maximum number of characters that can be entered into the password field
- `name`   The name of the password field
- `size`   The width of the password field in characters
- `value`   The default value of the password field

Adding Text Areas

A text area is a multi-line text box. To add a text area to a form, select a point within the opening and closing form tags and double-click the Text Area element in the HTML Toolbox.

After you add a text area to a form, you can supply values for the following attributes:

- `cols`   The width of the text area in characters.
- `name`   The name of the text area.
- `rows`   The height of the text area in characters.
- `wrap`   The wrap mode of the text area. To enable word wrapping, set wrap to either soft or hard. To disable word wrapping, set wrap to off.

NOTE

You can't supply a maximum length for a text area.

Adding Radio Buttons

Normally, you add radio buttons in groups. Only one radio button in a group of radio buttons can be checked at a time.

To add a radio button to a form, select an area within the opening and closing `<form>` tags and double-click the Radio Button element in the HTML Toolbox. You can supply values for the following properties of a radio button:

- `checked`   The default value of the radio button. If True, the radio button appears checked by default.
- `name`   The name of the radio button. Radio buttons with the same name are placed in the same group.
- `value`   The value submitted by the form when the radio button is checked.

Adding Check Boxes

Like radio buttons, you typically add check boxes to a form in groups. Unlike radio buttons, however, multiple check boxes can be checked at one time.

To add a check box to a form, select an area within the opening and closing <form> tags and double-click the Checkbox element in the HTML Toolbox. You can specify the following values for a check box:

- checked   The default value of the check box. If True, the check box appears checked by default.

- name   The name of the check box. Check boxes with the same name are placed in the same group.

- value   The value submitted by the form when the check box is checked.

Adding Drop-Down Lists and List Boxes

To add either a drop-down list or list box to a form, select a point between the opening and closing tags of the form and double-click either the DropDown or Listbox elements in the HTML Toolbox.

After you add a drop-down list or list box, you can add options to the element by right-clicking the element and selecting Properties. Selecting Properties opens a dialog box that enables you to insert a text and value for each option in the drop-down list or list box (see Figure 2.12).

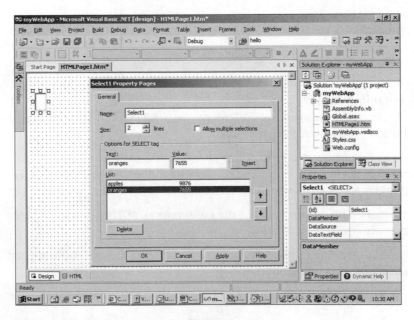

Figure 2.12   Adding list items to a list box.

Adding Buttons

There are three types of buttons that you can add to a form from the HTML Toolbox—Submit buttons, Reset buttons, and buttons. To add any of these three types of buttons to a form, select a point within the opening and closing `<form>` tags and double-click the Button element in the HTML Toolbox.

All three types of buttons support the following properties:

- `name`   The name of the button

- `size`   The width of the button in characters

- `value`   The text displayed on the button

Adding File Fields

A file field enables you to upload files from a client computer to the Web server. When you add a file field, a text box and Browse button are added to the form.

To add a file field to a form, select a point within the opening and closing `<form>` tags and double-click the File Field element in the HTML Toolbox.

Adding Hidden Fields

You can use a hidden field to pass additional information to the Web server when the form containing the hidden field is submitted. To add a hidden field to a form, select an area within the opening and closing form tags and double-click the Hidden Field element in the Toolbox.

Hidden fields support the following properties:

- `name`   The name of the hidden field

- `size`   The size in characters of the hidden field

- `value`   The text contained in the hidden field

Adding Tables

You can add an HTML table to a page by dragging and dropping the Table element from the HTML Toolbox. By default, a table added from the Toolbox contains three columns and three rows.

Alternatively, you can add a table by opening the Table menu, pointing to Insert, and selecting Table. Selecting this menu option provides you with more options for initially configuring the table (see Figure 2.13).

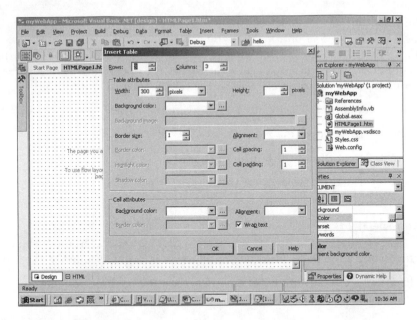

Figure 2.13   Setting Table options.

After you add a table, you can add and delete table columns, rows, and cells from the Table menu. For example, to add a new row to a table, select the table, open the Table menu, point to Insert, and select Row Below.

You can change properties of a table, such as the height, width, cell padding, cell spacing, and border colors of the table by opening the table's Property Pages. You open a table's Property Pages by right-clicking the table and selecting Properties.

TIP

You can display borders for tables that have invisible borders by selecting Visible Borders from the View menu.

You can also modify the properties of a particular column, row, or cell by selecting the column, row, or cell and selecting Select from the Table menu. After you select the table element, open the Property Pages for the element by right-clicking and selecting Properties.

Adding Framesets

Framesets enable you to display multiple HTML pages in a single window. Visual Studio .NET enables you to easily work with frames by supplying standard frameset templates.

To add a frameset to a project, do the following:

1. Select Add New Item from the File menu.

2. In the Add New Item dialog box, select the frameset template.

3. In the Name text box, specify a name for the frameset (for example,
    myFrameset.htm).

4. Click Open and the Select a Frameset Template dialog box appears (see Figure
    2.14).

5. Select a frameset template, such as Banner and Content or Horizontal Split,
    and click OK.

After completing these steps, the frameset will appear in Design View. Before you can
use the frameset, you'll need to assign files to each frame in the frameset.

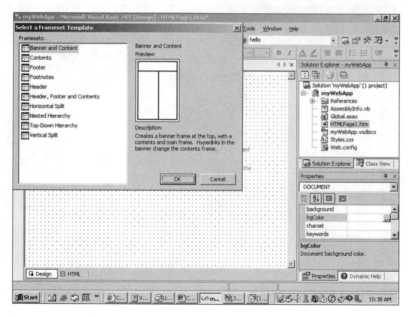

Figure 2.14   Selecting a frameset template.

Assigning Pages to Frames

After you create a frameset, you can assign existing files to the individual frames in
the frameset. For example, to assign a file named myPage.htm to a frame, do the
following:

1. Right-click inside a frame on the Designer surface.

2. Select Set Page for Frame, which opens the Select Page dialog box.

3. Enter the path to the myPage.htm file in the URL text box and click OK.

After you assign a file to a frame, the file will appear in the frame when you view the frameset in a browser.

Linking to a Page in a Frame

Framesets are commonly used for displaying both a menu and content page in the same window. For example, in a frameset with two frames, you might place a menu of links in the left frame that open pages in the right frame (see Figure 2.15). To open a page in a particular frame, you must include the name of the frame in the link.

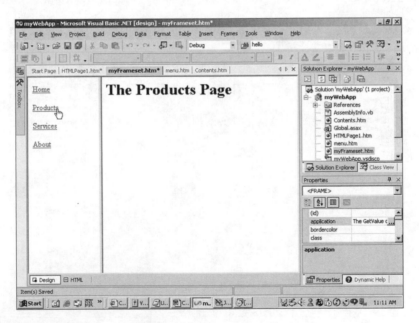

Figure 2.15   Displaying a menu and content page with a frameset.

To name a frame, perform the follow steps:

1. Left-click inside the frame.

2. In the property window, find the name property and supply a name (for example, contents).

After you name a frame, you can create a link to the frame by doing the following:

1. Select the HTML page that will contain the link.

2. Add a Label element to the HTML page by double-clicking the Label element on the HTML Toolbox.

3. Click inside the Label and type the text for the label (for example, **Products**).

4. Select the text by double-clicking the text with the left mouse button.

5. Select Hyperlink from the Insert menu.

6. Enter the path to the page that you want to open in the frame in the URL text box and click OK.

7. Click the link and find the target property in the Properties window.

8. For the target property, enter the name of the frame into which you want the link to open the page.

After you complete these steps, clicking the link will open a page into a new frame.

Modifying Frameset Properties

After you create a frameset, you can modify its properties by selecting options from the Frames menu. For example, selecting Seamless Join Between Frames hides the edges between frames.

You can also use the options under the Frames menu to delete and add frames to the current frameset. You'll need to use these options to create a frameset that is not included in the standard set of frameset templates.

Working with HTML Pages in HTML View

Visual Studio .NET provides you with a choice when building HTML pages. Some HTML developers prefer to work directly with the HTML source of a page rather than working in the context of a visual designer. If you want to work directly with the HTML content of a page, you need to switch to HTML View by clicking the HTML tab.

HTML is outside the scope of this book. In the following sections, you'll learn how to take advantage of the features of the HTML editor when writing HTML pages.

Taking Advantage of Automatic Statement Completion

When you start adding a new HTML tag in the HTML editor, a pop-up window appears that contains a list of valid HTML tags by default. If you select an HTML tag from the list, the tag is automatically added to the document.

Furthermore, if you select a tag that requires a closing tag, the closing tag is also added to the editor. For example, adding an opening <b> tag automatically adds a closing </b> tag.

You can also configure the HTML editor to automatically add quotation marks around the values that you assign to attributes in an HTML tag. This option is disabled by default.

You can disable or enable any of these options from the Options dialog box by doing the following

1. Select Options from the Tools menu.

2. Select the Text Editor folder.

3. Navigate to the HTML/XML folder.

4. Display the HTML Specific page.

From the HTML Specific page, you can modify the following options:

- To disable automatic HTML statement completion, uncheck the Auto pop-up HTML statement completion check box.

- To disable the automatic addition of HTML closing tags, uncheck the Close tag check box.

- To enable the automatic addition of quotes around attribute values, check the Attribute Value Quotes check box.

Enabling and Disabling Automatic Formatting

You can automatically format the source code of an HTML document by opening the Edit menu, pointing to Advanced, and selecting Format Document. You can also apply automatic formatting to a page by clicking the Format the Whole Document button on the HTML Editor toolbar. When you format a document, tags are automatically indented.

For example, if you start with HTML code that looks like the following:

```
<table><tr>
<td>Hello</td>
</tr>
</table>
```

After you apply automatic formatting, you get HTML code that looks like the following:

```
<table>
    <tr>
        <td>Hello</td>
    </tr>
</table>
```

You can control when automatic formatting is applied and particular automatic formatting options from the Format page in the Options dialog box (see Figure 2.16). To open the Format page, do the following:

1. Select Options from the Tools menu.

2. Navigate to the Text Editor folder.

3. Navigate to the HTML/XML folder.

4. Display the Format page.

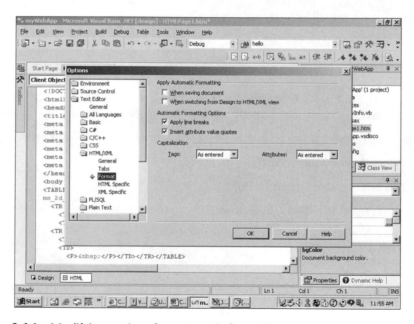

Figure 2.16   Modifying options for automatic formatting.

You can use the Format page to choose the circumstances under which automatic formatting is applied and the type of formatting that is applied. You can set the following options:

- *Apply Automatic Formatting When Saving Document*—Applies automatic formatting when the document is saved

- *Apply Automatic Formatting When switching from Design to HTML/XML View*—Applies automatic formatting when switching between Design and HTML View

- *Apply Line Breaks*—Add line breaks when applying automatic formatting

- *Insert Attribute Value Quotes*—Add quotation marks around HTML tag attribute values

You can also control capitalization for HTML tags and attributes. For example, you can indicate that you want all HTML tags added to a page to be lowercase and all HTML attributes to be uppercase.

Validating HTML Documents

When you add HTML tags to a page, the HTML is validated against the selected targetSchema by default. Any content that can't be validated appears with a red squiggly line beneath it. If you hover the mouse over the content, a ToolTip appears with an explanation for the validation failure.

For example, the following tags would raise a validation error:

```
<table><td>
```

Because you can't place a <td> tag directly within a <table> tag, the validation error "Per the active schema, the element 'td' cannot be nested within 'table'" appears.

You can turn off automatic validation by completing the following steps:

1. Select Options from the Tools menu.
2. Navigate to the Text Editor folder.
3. Navigate to the HTML/XML folder.
4. Display the HTML Specific page.
5. Uncheck the check box labeled Enable HTML validation.

You can also validate an HTML document at any time by clicking the Validate Document button on the HTML Editor toolbar.

Using the Document Outline

Regardless of whether you are building an HTML page in Design or HTML View, you can take advantage of the Document Outline to quickly navigate to particular elements in an HTML page. To display the Document Outline window, open the View menu, point to Other Windows, and select Document Outline.

You can use the Document Outline window to view either an outline of the HTML elements in a page or an outline of the scripts in a page. To switch between the two outlines, click either the HTML Outline or Script Outline button at the top of the Document Outline window.

Figure 2.17 illustrates the appearance of the Document Outline window when HTML Outline is selected. You can click any element to navigate directly to the element in the editor window.

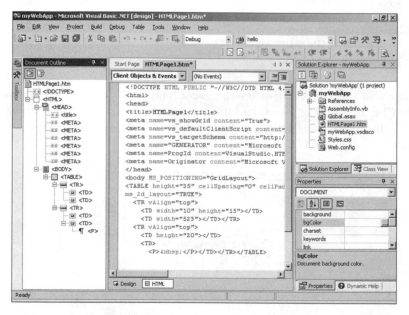

Figure 2.17   Displaying the Document Outline window.

Adding Client-Side Scripts

You can automatically add client-side script event handlers to an HTML page within the Visual Studio .NET environment. However, it is important to understand that different event handlers are available, depending on the value of the targetSchema property.

Another document property, the defaultClientScript property, determines the default client-side script language used with an HTML page. You can assign the value JScript or VBScript to this property.

There are two ways that you can automatically add client-side script event handlers to an HTML page. You can add a client event handler by using the Document Outline window or by using the Event drop-down list.

To add an event handler by using the Document Outline window, perform the following steps:

1. If the Document Outline window is not already open, open the View menu, point to Other Window, and select Document Outline.

2. Click the button labeled Script Outline at the top of the Document Outline window.

3. Expand an HTML element in the Document Outline window to see a list of events associated with the element.

4. Double-click the name of an event to automatically add a client-side script handler to the editor.

You can also add new client-side script event handlers to a page by taking advantage of the Client Objects & Events and the Events drop-down lists at the top of the HTML editor window. These drop-down lists are visible only when HTML View is enabled (see Figure 2.18).

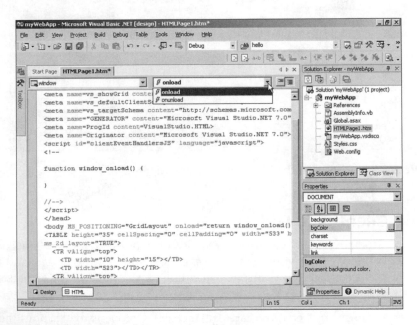

Figure 2.18   Adding client-side event handlers.

For example, to add an event-handler for the window_onload event, select Window from the Client Objects & Events drop-down list and onload from the Events drop-down list.

TIP

When working with client-side scripts in the HTML editor, you can hide all the HTML content in the page by clicking the Script Only View button at the top-right of the HTML editor window.

Adding Style Sheets

When the document targetSchema is set to the value HTML 4.0 or later, you can use Cascading Style Sheet attributes to format the elements of an HTML page. There are three ways that you can add style attributes to a page. You can add style attributes inline, within a <style> block on a page, or within an external style sheet.

Adding Style Attributes Inline

You can add style attributes to an individual HTML element in Design View. For example, suppose that you want to create a Button element with a red italic font and a blue background. To add these style attributes to a button, do the following:

1. Select the button in Design View.

2. Select Build Style from the Format menu (alternatively, right-click the button and select Build Style).

3. In the Style Builder dialog box (see Figure 2.19), select the Font icon and select the color Red and enable italics.

4. In the Style Builder dialog box, select the Background icon and select the color Blue.

You can modify the style attributes for an element at any time in the future by opening the Style Builder dialog box.

TIP

To apply style attributes to text in Design View, add either a DIV or SPAN element by selecting DIV or SPAN from the Insert menu. Next, apply the style attributes to the DIV or SPAN attribute.

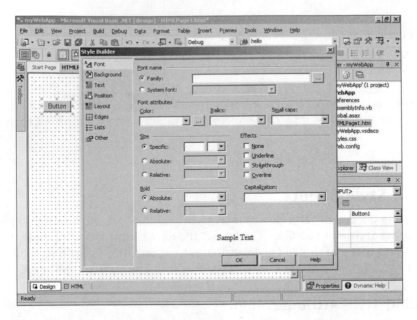

Figure 2.19   The Style Builder dialog box.

Adding a Style Block to a Page

Instead of adding style attributes to individual elements in an HTML page, you can add one <style> block that contains generalized style rules for the page. To add a <style> block to a page, follow these steps:

1. In Design View, select Document Styles from the Format menu.

2. In the Document Styles window, click the Add Style Sheet button.

Next, to select the element, class, or element ID to format with a style rule, do the following:

1. In the Document Styles window, click the Add Style Rule button.

2. In the Add Style Rule dialog box, select an HTML element, enter a classname, or enter an element ID.

Finally, you can specify the style rule to apply to the element, class, or element ID by performing the following steps:

1. Select an element, class, or element ID from the appropriate folder in the Document Styles window.

2. Click the Build Style button.

3. In the Style Builder dialog box, select the formatting for the element, class, or element ID.

Creating External Style Sheets

You can create a single external style sheet and apply the style sheet to multiple pages within a project. This is useful when you want to create a consistent look for all the pages in your application.

When you create a new ASP.NET Web Application, a single external style sheet file is created by default. You can work with this style sheet file or create a new one.

To create a new external style sheet, do the following:

1. Select Add New Item from the File menu.

2. Select the Style Sheet template in the Add New Item dialog box.

3. Name the style sheet anything you want by entering a name in the Name text box.

4. Click Open.

After you open an external style sheet file in the editor (see Figure 2.20), you can modify the style rules manually or with the Style Builder dialog box.

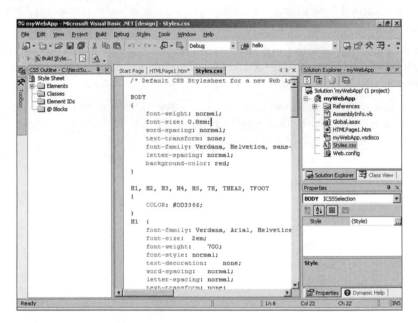

Figure 2.20 Editing an external style sheet.

To edit a style rule with the Style Builder dialog box, select an element in the CSS Outline window and select Build Option from the Styles menu. You can use the options in the Style Builder dialog box to specify the formatting associated with the element.

After you create an external style sheet, you can apply the style sheet to one or more HTML files by doing the following:

1. Open an HTML page in Design View.

2. Select Document Styles from the Format menu.

3. Click the Add Style Link button in the Document Styles dialog box.

4. Select the external style sheet that you want to link to the current HTML page from the Select Style Sheet dialog box.

Completing these steps adds a link tag to the HTML page that looks something like the following:

```
<LINK href="Styles.css" type=text/css rel=stylesheet>
```

Summary

In this chapter, you learned how to build HTML pages by using Visual Studio .NET. First, you learned how to create HTML pages in Design View. You learned how to design HTML pages by using either Flow layout or Grid layout mode.

Next, you learned how to work directly with HTML code by taking advantage of HTML View. You learned how to enable and disable various automatic formatting options available with the HTML editor.

Finally, you learned how to work with two advanced features of HTML pages. You learned how to add both client-side scripts and Cascading Style Sheets to an HTML page.

3

Creating Basic Web Form Pages

IN THIS CHAPTER

- Overview of Web Form Pages
- Adding Server Controls
- Handling Events

In this chapter, you learn how to build Web Form Pages. Web Form Pages, unlike standard static HTML pages, can contain dynamic content. You can use Web Form Pages to do such things as validate form data and display and edit database data. Web Form Pages are the most important part of any Web Application that you build with Visual Studio .NET.

In this chapter, you will learn

- How to create a simple Web Form Page
- How to add server controls to a Web Form Page
- How to handle events in a Web Form Page

Overview of Web Form Pages

Although Web Form Pages can contain dynamic content, the foundation of any Web Form Page is standard HTML. You create all the static portions of a Web Form Page by using the same methods that you learned about in Chapter 2, "Using the Visual Studio .NET Designer."

However, Web Form Pages can contain two things that cannot be included in static HTML pages. Web Form Pages can contain server controls and application logic.

You can think of server controls as server-side HTML tags. When you add a server control to a page, the control is executed on your Web server and it generates content that is sent to a Web browser.

The advantage of server controls over plain old HTML tags is that you can program server controls. Server controls have properties, methods, and events that you can manipulate in your code.

In this chapter, you'll be provided with an overview of the basic server controls for building form elements. For example, you'll learn how to add Textbox and Button controls to a Web Form Page.

A Web Form Page can also contain application logic. You can add programming code to a Web Form Page that executes whenever the page is requested. For example, you can write Visual Basic .NET code that retrieves data from a database table and displays the data in a server control.

In this chapter, you'll learn how to add application logic to a Web Form Page that handles different page events. For example, you'll learn how to display different messages on a page depending on the options that a user selects in a form.

Creating a Simple Web Form Page

We'll start with a simple Web Form Page. We'll create a page that randomly displays a fortune.

> **NOTE**
>
> You should add a Web Form Page to an existing ASP.NET project. To learn how to create a new project, see Chapter 1, "Getting Familiar with the Development Environment."

First, we need to add a Web Form to a project by doing the following:

1. Select Project, Add Web Form.

2. In the Add New Item dialog box, enter the name **Fortune.aspx** for the Web Form in the Name text box.

3. Click Open.

Now that you've created a Web Form Page, you can add server controls to the page from the Web Forms toolbox. We'll add a Label control to the page by performing the follow steps:

1. If the Toolbox window is not already open, select View, Toolbox.

2. Drag a Label control onto the Designer surface from under the Web Forms tab in the Toolbox.

After you add the Label control, your screen should resemble Figure 3.1.

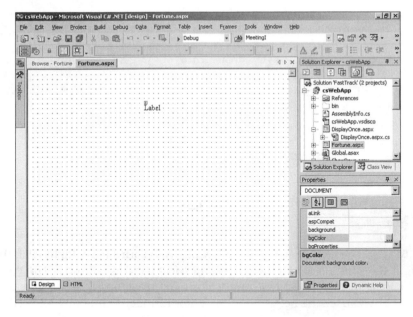

Figure 3.1   Adding a Label control to a Web Form Page.

The next step is to add some application logic to the page. We want to retrieve a random fortune from an ArrayList of fortunes and display the fortune in the Label control. To do this, perform the following steps:

1. Double-click the Designer surface to switch to the Code Editor.

2. Enter the following code for the Page_Load() method:

   C#

```csharp
private void Page_Load(object sender, System.EventArgs e)
{
  // Put user code to initialize the page here
  ArrayList colFortunes = new ArrayList();
  Random objRan = new Random();

  colFortunes.Add("Good things will happen!");
  colFortunes.Add("Future looks bright!");
  colFortunes.Add("Stay in bed!");

  Label1.Text = colFortunes[ objRan.Next( 3 ) ].ToString();
}
```

VB.NET

```
Private Sub Page_Load(ByVal sender As System.Object, ByVal e As
➡System.EventArgs) Handles MyBase.Load
  'Put user code to initialize the page here
  Dim colFortunes As New ArrayList()
  Dim objRan As New Random()

  colFortunes.Add("Good things will happen!")
  colFortunes.Add("Future looks bright!")
  colFortunes.Add("Stay in bed!")

  Label1.Text = colFortunes(objRan.Next(3))
End Sub
```

Finally, we are ready to compile and view our Web Forms page. Right-click the Web Form in the Solution Explorer window and select Build and Browse. The Web Form Page will be opened in a browser and you should see a fortune (see Figure 3.2). Whenever you click the Refresh button, a new fortune is randomly selected and displayed.

TIP

If you receive an error when building your code, select Build Solution from the Build menu. A list of errors in your code will pop up in the Task List window. You can double-click an error to go directly to the error in your code.

The Two Parts of a Web Form Page

When you create a Web Form Page, you typically need to work with the page by using three different interfaces. While designing the visual elements of a Web Form Page, you use either Design View or HTML View with the Designer. While developing the application logic for a Web Form Page, you use the Code Editor.

In reality, a Web Form Page consists of two files. One file, the presentation page, contains all the user interface elements of the Web Form, such as HTML tags and Web server controls. This file must end with the extension .aspx. This is the page that you actually request when opening the page in your Web browser.

A Web Form also uses a second file, called the *code-behind file*, which contains all the application logic for the page. By default, the code-behind file does not appear in the Solution Explorer window. To see this file, you must select Show All Files from the Project menu. The code-behind file has the same name as the presentation page with the addition of the extension .cs or .vb. The code-behind file ends with the extension .cs or .vb because it is a C# or VB.NET class file.

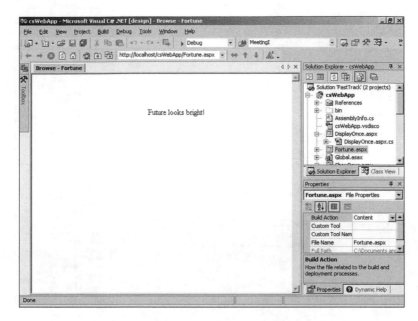

Figure 3.2   A Web Form Page displaying a random fortune.

While working with the user interface elements of a Web Form, you use either Design or HTML View in the Designer window. To add application logic to a page, you work with the Code Editor. You can switch between the Designer and Code Editor by using any of the following methods:

- Double-click the Designer surface to switch to the Code Editor.

- Select Code from the View menu to switch to the Code Editor or select Design from the View menu to switch to the Designer window.

- Use the keyboard shortcuts Shift+F7 and F7.

- In the Designer window, right-click the page and select View Code.

- In the Solution Explorer window, right-click the page and select either View Code or View Designer.

Compiling and Viewing Web Form Pages

Because one part of a Web Form Page is a C# or Visual Basic .NET class file, you must compile a Web Form Page before you can view it in a Web browser. If you don't compile a Web Form before opening the page in a browser, you'll receive the error displayed in Figure 3.3.

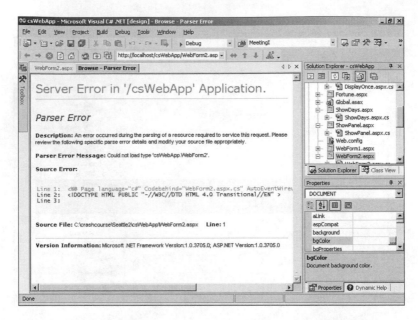

Figure 3.3   Error from viewing a Web Form Page without compiling it.

You can compile all the files in a project and view the output of a particular Web Form Page by right-clicking the page in the Solution Explorer window and selecting Build and Browse. The page is compiled and displayed in the default Visual Studio .NET Web browser. This will be the preferred method of compiling and viewing pages used in this book.

TIP

If you prefer to use the keyboard, you can build and browse the current page by pressing Ctrl+F8.

It is important to understand that there is no way to build only a single page in a project. When you do a build, all files contained in the project are compiled. This means that when you have any errors in any page in a project, you cannot build any other page.

TIP

You can temporarily exclude a page from a project by right-clicking the page in Solution Explorer and selecting Exclude From Project. You'll need to do this when the page has an error but you want to work on another page before fixing it. You can recover the excluded page by selecting Show All Files from the Project menu and then right-clicking the filename and selecting Include In Project.

Alternatively, you can build all the files in a solution or project without opening a page in a Web browser. You can select any one of the following options from the Build menu:

- *Build Solution*—Compiles all files in all projects contained in the current solution that have been modified since the Build command was last executed

- *Rebuild Solution*—Compiles all files in all projects contained in the current solution, regardless of whether the files have been modified since the Build command was last executed

- *Build Project Name*—Compiles all files in a particular project that have been modified since the Build command was last executed

- *Rebuild Project Name*—Compiles all files in a particular project that have been modified since the Build command was last executed

When you compile the files in a project using any of these methods, an Output window opens that displays messages generated during compilation. At the end of compilation, the Output window should display the number of files that were successfully built.

If any errors are encountered while building a project or solution, the Task window will open and display a list of the errors. You can double-click any error in the Task List to go directly to the page containing the error.

NOTE

You also can compile the files in your application by using the options located under the Debug menu. Debugging is discussed in detail in Chapter 6, "Debugging Your Web Form Pages."

Adding Server Controls

Unlike standard HTML pages, Web Form Pages can contain Web server controls. Web server controls represent the user interface elements in a page. Unlike normal HTML tags, server controls have properties, methods, and events that you can access within your code.

There are two types of server controls that you can add to a Web Form Page—HTML controls or Web Forms controls.

The HTML controls directly reflect existing HTML tags. For example, there is an HTML control that represents an HTML <form> tag, an HTML control that represents an HTML <table> tag, and so on. You can take an existing HTML document and quickly convert the HTML elements contained in the document into server controls by taking advantage of the HTML controls.

There are more Web controls than HTML controls. The Web controls do not directly reflect existing HTML tags. For example, the DataGrid Web control enables you to display and edit database data and the Calendar control enables you to display an interactive calendar.

In the following sections, you learn how to add both HTML and Web controls to your Web Form Pages.

Using HTML Controls

Within Design View, you can convert any HTML element in a page to an HTML control. To convert an element, right-click the element within Design View and select Run As Server Control. After you convert an HTML element to a server control, it will appear with a green glyph that looks something like a VCR play button (see Figure 3.4).

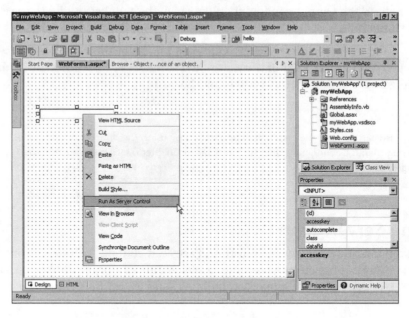

Figure 3.4   Converting an HTML text field to a server control.

For example, to convert an HTML text field into an HTML control, do the following:

1. Add a Web Form Page to your project and switch to Design View.

2. Add a text field to your Web Form Page by double-clicking the Text Field element under the HTML tab on the Toolbox.

3. Right-click the text field on the Designer surface and select Run As Server Control.

When you added the text field to the Web Form Page in step 2, the following HTML tag was added to the page (you can see this tag by switching to HTML View):

```
<INPUT type="text">
```

After you convert the text field to an HTML control, the tag is converted to look like the following:

```
<INPUT type="text" id=Text1 name=Text1 runat="server">
```

You should notice that three new attributes are added to the HTML tag: id, name, and runat. The id attribute provides the control with a unique identifier for the page. The name attribute provides the control with a name for the form. Finally, and most importantly, the runat="server" attribute marks the HTML tag as a server control.

When you convert an HTML tag into an HTML control, the tag is automatically converted to one of the following HTML controls:

- HtmlAnchor   Represents a hyperlink tag

- HtmlButton   Represents a button tag

- HtmlForm   Represents a form tag

- HtmlGenericControl   Represents any HTML tag not explicitly represented by another HTML control

- HtmlImage   Represents an image tag

- HtmlInputButton   Represents a submit or reset button

- HtmlInputCheckbox   Represents a check box tag

- HtmlInputFile   Represents a file upload button

- HtmlInputHidden   Represents a hidden form field

- HtmlInputImage   Represents an image button

- HtmlInputRadioButton   Represents a radio button

- HtmlInputText   Represents a text field or password field

- HtmlSelect   Represents a select tag (a drop-down list or list box)

- HtmlTable   Represents a table tag

- HtmlTableCell   Represents a table cell tag

- HtmlTableRow   Represents a table row tag

- HtmlTextArea   Represents a text area

If you convert an image into an HTML control, the image tag is converted into an HtmlImage control. If you convert a tag that does not have a corresponding control, the tag is converted into an HtmlGenericControl. For example, if you convert a <span> tag into a control, the control is represented by the HtmlGenericControl control.

Using Web Controls

Unlike HTML controls, Web Forms controls do not directly correspond to existing HTML controls. You can find all of the Web Forms controls under the Web Forms tab on the toolbar.

The Web Forms controls can be divided into three groups. The first group of Web controls represents basic form and page elements:

- CheckBox   Represents a single check box

- CheckBoxList   Represents a group of multiple check boxes

- DropDownList   Represents a drop-down list of items

- Hyperlink   Represents a hyperlink to a new page

- Image   Represents an image

- ImageButton   Represents an image button

- Label   Represents a label

- LinkButton   Represents a hyperlink that submits a form to the same page

- Listbox   Represents a list box of items

- Literal   Represents static text or HTML in a page

- Panel   Represents a container other controls

- Placeholder   Represents a spot on the page where other controls can be added

- RadioButton   Represents a single radio button

- RadioButtonList   Represents a group of multiple radio buttons

- Table   Represents an HTML table

- TextBox   Represents a single-line, multi-line, or password text box

You'll learn how to use many of the controls in this first group in the following sections of this chapter.

There's also a second group of Web controls that enable you to perform form validation. The following is a list of the controls in this group:

- CompareValidator   Enables you to validate the data in a form field against a fixed value or other form field

- CustomValidator   Enables you to validate the data in a form field by using a custom subroutine

- RangeValidator   Enables you to validate the data in a form field against a minimum and maximum value

- RegularExpressionValidator   Enables you to validate the data in a form field against a regular expression

- RequiredFieldValidator   Enables you to validate the data in a form field by checking whether the form field contains a value

- ValidationSummary   Enables you to display a summary of validation error messages on a page

You'll learn how to validate forms with the validation controls in Chapter 4, "Validating Web Form Pages."

There's a third group of controls that enable you to format, display, and edit data:

- Repeater   Enables you to format items from a data source

- DataList   Enables you to format items from a data source in multiple columns and create interactive menus

- DataGrid   Enables you to format, sort, page through, and edit items from a data source

You'll learn how to take advantage of the data controls in the second part of this book, "Working with Database Data."

Finally, the members of the last group of controls are harder to categorize. The Web controls in this group enable you to perform more specialized tasks:

- AdRotator   Can be used to randomly display banner advertisements

- Calendar   Can be used to display an interactive calendar

- CrystalReportViewer   Can be used to display reports with Crystal Reports

- Xml   Can be used to display XML documents

Adding Label Controls

There are two types of labels that you can add from the Toolbox. You can add an HTML label from the HTML tab or a Label Web Forms control from the Web Forms tab. It's important to not confuse these two types of labels.

A Web Forms Label control, unlike a standard HTML label, enables you to dynamically assign content to an area of a page. For example, you can use a Label control to display the current time, display the number of records in a database table, or display an error when validating a form.

A Label control has one important property—the Text property. In your code, you can assign any text to the Text property that you want. For example, earlier in this chapter, in the "Creating a Simple Web Form Page" section, you assigned a random fortune to a Label control with a line of code that looks like the following:

C#

```
Label1.Text = colFortunes[ objRan.Next( 3 ) ].ToString();
```

VB.NET

```
Label1.Text = colFortunes(objRan.Next(3))
```

One potentially confusing thing about a Web Forms Label control is that you cannot assign text to it in the same way as you can assign text to an HTML label. If you want to assign text to an HTML label, you can simply double-click the label and type the text. When using a Web Forms Label control, on the other hand, you need to explicitly set the value of the Text property.

For example, suppose that you want to add a Label control to a page that, by default, displays the text "Hello World!". To do so, perform the following steps:

1. Double-click the Label control under the Web Forms tab to add a Label control to a page.

2. Select the label from the drop-down list in the Properties window.

3. Find the Text property in the Properties window and enter the value `"Hello World!"`.

After you complete these steps, the label should display the text "Hello World!".

Adding Button Controls

There are three types of button controls that you can add to a Web Form Page:

- Button   Displays the normal form submit pushbutton

- ImageButton   Displays an image for the button

- LinkButton   Displays a hypertext link for a button

All three types of buttons submit a form and any information it contains back to the Web server. The buttons differ only in their appearance.

For example, suppose that you want to create a page that displays the current time. However, you want to add a button to the page that enables you to refresh the current time whenever it is clicked.

First, you need to add the necessary controls to the Designer surface:

1. Select Add Web Form from the Project menu. Enter the name **RefreshTime.aspx** for the page and click Open.

2. Add a Web Forms Label control to the page by dragging the Label control from under the Web Forms tab on the toolbar onto the Designer surface.

3. Add a Button control to the page by dragging the Button control from under the Web Forms tab on the toolbar onto the Designer surface.

Next, you need to add code to the Code Editor that executes whenever you click the button:

1. Double-click the Button control on the Designer surface. Double-clicking the button should switch you to the Code Editor and the cursor should automatically appear within a method named Button1_Click().

2. Within the Button1_Click() method, enter the following line of code:

   C#

   ```
   Label1.Text = DateTime.Now.ToString();
   ```

   VB.NET

   ```
   Label1.Text = DateTime.Now
   ```

3. Right-click the Web Form Page in the Solution Explorer window and select Build and Browse.

When you have completed these steps, a page similar to the one in Figure 3.5 should be displayed.

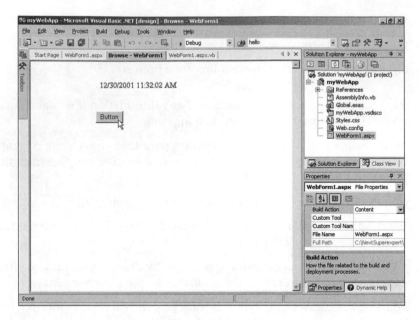

Figure 3.5   Adding a Button control to a Web Form Page.

Adding TextBox Controls

A TextBox Web control represents an HTML text field. However, unlike a standard HTML text field, a TextBox control has properties, methods, and events that you can manipulate in your code.

The most important property of a text box is the Text property. You can use the Text property to assign a default value to a text box in your code. You can also use the Text property to read a value that a user has entered into the text box.

For example, suppse that you want to create a Web Form Page with Label, TextBox, and Button controls. When someone enters text into the text box and clicks the button, the text is copied from the TextBox control to the Label control.

Perform the following steps to add the necessary controls:

1. Create a new Web Form Page named **CopyField.aspx** by selecting Add Web Form from the Project menu.

2. Add a Label control to the page by double-clicking the Label control under the Web Forms tab on the toolbar.

3. Add a TextBox control to the page by double-clicking the TextBox control under the Web Forms tab on the toolbar.

4. Add a `Button` control to the page by double-clicking the `Button` control under the Web Forms tab on the toolbar.

Next, you need to add the code that executes when you click the `Button` control:

1. Double-click the `Button` control on the Designer surface. Double-clicking the button should switch you to the Code Editor and the cursor should automatically appear within a method named `Button1_Click()`.

2. Within the `Button1_Click()` method, enter the following line of code:

C#

```
Label1.Text = TextBox1.Text;
```

VB.NET

```
Label1.Text = TextBox1.Text
```

3. Right-click the Web Form Page in the Solution Explorer window and select Build and Browse.

If you enter text into the `TextBox` control and click the button, the text should be copied to the `Label` control (see Figure 3.6).

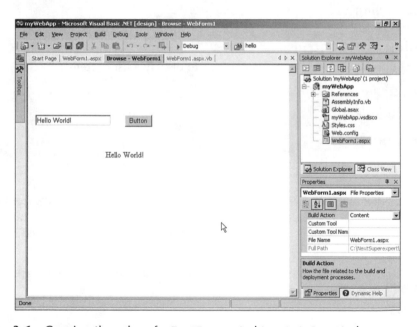

Figure 3.6   Copying the value of a `TextBox` control to a `Label` control.

A TextBox control can represent a single-line, multi-line, or a password field. To display different types of fields with a TextBox control, you assign different values to the TextBox control's TextMode property. (You can modify the TextMode property in the Properties window.)

By default, the TextMode property has the value SingleLine and a single-line text field is displayed. You specify the width of a single-line text box by assigning a value to the control's Columns property. You can indicate a maximum length for a single-line text box with the MaxLength property. (The maximum length is specified in characters.)

If you assign the value Password to the TextMode property, the text box displays a password field. A password text box works in exactly the same way as a single-line text box except for the fact that any characters entered into the text box are hidden (characters are echoed with asterisks).

Finally, if you assign the value MultiLine to the TextMode property, the text box renders a text area. When creating a multi-line text box, you can assign values to the both the Columns and Rows properties. However, any value assigned to the MaxLength property is ignored.

You can also assign a value to the Wrap property when working with a multi-line text box. When Wrap has the value True, text automatically word wraps within the text box. When Wrap is False, text continues scrolling to the right until you enter a carriage return.

Adding List Controls

You can use any of the following controls to display a list of items:

- ListBox
- DropDownList
- RadioButtonList
- CheckBoxList

All of the list controls share common properties because they all derive from the base ListControl class. One of the most important of these properties is the Items property. The Items property represents the individual list items displayed by the control.

Suppose, for example, that you want to display a list of products in a ListBox control. Perform the following steps to do so:

1. Double-click the `ListBox` control in the Web Forms tab on the Toolbox.

2. In the Properties window, click the ellipsis that appears next to the `Items` property.

3. Click the Add button in the ListItem Collection Editor (see Figure 3.7).

4. Enter **Shaving Cream** for the value of the `Text` property in the ListItem Properties pane of the ListItem Collection Editor.

5. Click the Add button.

6. Enter **Shampoo** for the value of the `Text` property in the ListItem Properties pane of the ListItem Collection Editor.

7. Click OK.

8. Right-click the Web Form Page in the Solution Explorer window and select Build and Browse.

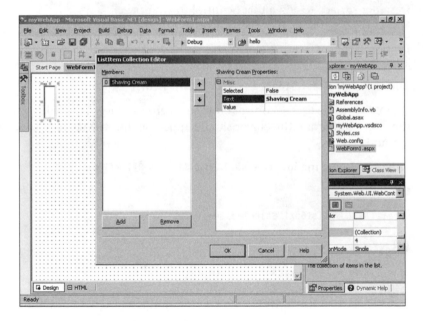

Figure 3.7   The ListItem Collection Editor.

After you complete these steps, the list box will display the two products: Shaving Cream and Shampoo.

All the list controls have a property named `SelectedItem` that represents the currently selected list item in the list control. You can use `SelectedItem.Text` to return the `Text` property of a list item and `SelectedItem.Value` to return the `Value` property of a list item. The `Text` property represents the text that the list control displays, and the `Value` property represents a hidden value associated with the list item.

Suppose that, after creating a list box that displays a list of products, you want to show the selected item from the list box in a `Label` control.

Perform the following steps to add the necessary controls:

1. Create a new Web Form Page named **ShowList.aspx** by selecting Add Web Form from the Project menu.

2. Drag the `ListBox` control from under the Web Forms tab on the Toolbox onto the Designer surface.

3. Add a couple list items to the `ListBox` by selecting `ListBox` in the Properties window and clicking the ellipsis next to the `Items` property.

4. Drag the `Label` control from under the Web Forms tab on the Toolbox onto the Designer surface to add a `Label` control to your page.

5. Drag the `Button` control under the Web Forms tab on the Toolbox onto the Designer surface to add a `Button` control to your page.

Next, add the code that displays the selected list item:

1. Double-click the `Button` control on the Designer surface. This will switch you to the Code Editor and the cursor should appear within the `Button1_Click()` method.

2. Enter the following line of code in the `Button1_Click()` method:

   C#

   ```
   Label1.Text = ListBox1.SelectedItem.Text;
   ```

   VB.NET

   ```
   Label1.Text = ListBox1.SelectedItem.Text
   ```

3. Right-click the Web Form Page in the Solution Explorer window and select Build and Browse.

If you select an item in the list box and click the button, the text of the selected item will appear in the `Label` control (see Figure 3.8).

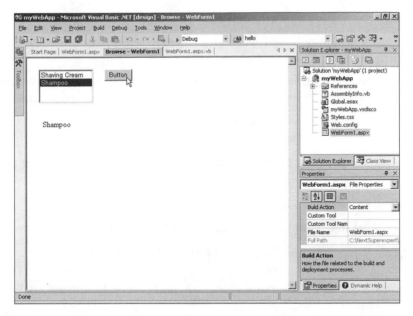

Figure 3.8 Displaying the `SelectedItem` from a `ListBox` control.

Using the `AutoPostBack` Property

Several of the Web controls that represent form elements, such as the list controls and the `TextBox` control, have a special property called the `AutoPostBack` property. When `AutoPostBack` has the value `True`, any change to the control causes the form that contains the control to be automatically posted back to the server.

> **WARNING**
>
> The `AutoPostBack` property uses client-side JavaScript. Older browsers do not support JavaScript, and the `AutoPostBack` property will fail to function correctly with these browsers.

For example, one common user interface element found in Web applications is a drop-down list used as a navigation menu. When you pick an option in the drop-down list, you are automatically brought to a new page without even clicking a button. Changing the selected item is enough to cause the page to be automatically posted back to the server.

You can create a `DropDownList` control that automatically posts back to the server by performing the following steps.

First, you need to add the necessary Web Forms controls:

1. Create a new Web Form Page named **AutoPostForm.aspx** by selecting Add Web Form from the Project menu.

2. Drag the DropDownList control from under the Web Forms tab on the Toolbox onto the Designer surface to add a DropDownList control to your page.

3. In the Properties window, select the DropDownList control and assign the value True to the AutoPostBack property.

4. In the Properties window open the ListItem Collection Editor dialog box by clicking the ellipsis next to the Items property.

5. Add a list item with the text **Home** and the value home.aspx.

6. Add a list item with the text **Products** and the value products.aspx.

7. Click OK to close the ListItem Collection Editor dialog box.

Next, you need to add code that executes whenever a new item is selected in the DropDownList control:

1. Double-click the DropDownList control on the Designer surface. Doing this will switch you to the Code Editor and add a new method named DropDownList1_SelectedIndexChanged().

2. Type the following lines of code in the DropDownList1_SelectedIndexChanged() method:

   C#

   ```
   Response.Redirect(DropDownList1.SelectedItem.Value);
   ```

   VB.NET

   ```
   Response.Redirect(DropDownList1.SelectedItem.Value)
   ```

3. In the Solution Explorer window, right-click the Web Form Page and select Build and Browse.

If you change the selected item in the DropDownList control to **Products**, the Products.aspx page will automatically load. (You'll receive a 404 Not Found error if the Products.aspx page has not been added to your project.)

Grouping Controls with Panels

You can group controls together on a page by using the Panel control. The advantage of grouping controls within Panel controls is that you can hide or display the controls as a single group.

The Panel control has a property named Visible. When the Visible property is assigned the value False, all elements contained in the panel are hidden.

For example, suppose that you want to display one or another set of questions in an HTML form, depending on the answer a user enters for a previous form question. You can place the two separate sets of questions in two Panel controls. You can then selectively hide or display the contents of each Panel control by modifying the Panel control's Visible property.

To hide or display the contents of a Panel control when a Button control is clicked, do the following:

First, you need to add the necessary controls to the page:

1. Create a new Web Form Page named **ShowPanel.aspx** by selecting Add Web Form from the Project menu.

2. Add a Panel control to the Web Form Page by dragging the Panel control located under the Web Forms tab on the Toolbox onto the Designer surface.

3. Click the Panel control twice on the Designer surface and erase the text "Panel."

4. Stretch the Panel control on the Designer surface by pulling the handles that appear around the control with your mouse.

5. Add an HTML label to the Panel control by selecting the label element located under the HTML tab on the Toolbox and dragging the element onto the Panel control on the Designer surface.

6. Click the HTML Label control on the Designer surface and enter the text **"Hello World!"**.

7. Add a Button control to the Web Form Page by dragging the Button control located under the Web Forms tab on the Toolbox onto the Designer surface.

Next, you need to add the code that hides or displays the contents of the panel:

1. Double-click the Button control on the Designer surface. This will switch you to the Code Editor and add a new method named Button1_Click().

2. Enter the following line of code in the Button1_Click() method:

C#

```
Panel1.Visible = !Panel1.Visible;
```

VB.NET

```
Panel1.Visible = Not Panel1.Visible
```

3. In the Solution Explorer window, right-click the Web Form Page and select Build and Browse.

When you click the button, the text "Hello World!" should disappear. When you click the button again, the text should reappear (see Figure 3.9).

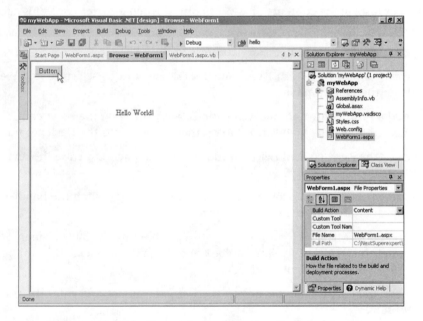

Figure 3.9   Hiding and displaying controls with a Panel control.

NOTE

A Panel control uses flow layout. Consequently, you cannot precisely position elements within a Panel control. You can, however, add a Grid Layout Panel or a Table to a Panel control when you want to have more control over the layout of the elements within a panel.

In this case, we simply added an HTML `Label` control to a single panel on a page. However, you can use the same technique to add multiple `Panel` controls to a page that contain multiple elements, such as `TextBox` and `DropDownList` controls.

Formatting Web Controls

All the Web controls share a common set of formatting properties (all the Web controls derive from the base `WebControl` class). You can use these properties to modify such properties as the font and color of the controls. You can modify the following properties in the Properties window for each control:

- `AccessKey`   A keyboard shortcut to the control. For example, if you enter the letter A, you can navigate to the control by pressing Alt+A on your keyboard.

- `BackColor`   The background color displayed behind the control. Modifying this property opens the Color Dialog box that enables you to pick Custom, Web, or System colors.

- `BorderColor`   The color used for the border of the control. Modifying this property opens the Color Dialog box that enables you to pick Custom, Web, or System colors.

- `BorderStyle`   The border style used for the control. Possible values include `Solid`, `Dashed`, and `Groove`.

- `BorderWidth`   The size of the control's border. This value can be specified in pixels or, in the case of more recent browsers, you can specify other units.

- `CssClass`   The Cascading Style Sheet class to associate with the control.

- `Enabled`   The state of the control. When `Enabled` is `False`, the control appears ghosted on certain browsers such as Microsoft Internet Explorer version 4.0 or later.

- `Font`   The font used with the control. You can select the name (typeface) and size of the font and whether the font appears in bold, italic, overline, strikeout, or underline.

- `ForeColor`   The foreground color used with the control. Modifying this property opens the Color Dialog box that enables you to pick Custom, Web, or System colors.

- `Height`   The height of the control in pixels or, in the case of more recent browsers, you can specify other units.

- `TabIndex`   The tab index of the control in a group of controls. Modifies the tab order of controls in a form when used with Internet Explorer 4.0 or later.

- ToolTip   The pop-up text message displayed above a control when you hover the mouse over it.

- Width   The width of the control in pixels or, in the case of more recent browsers, you can specify other units.

For example, you can use these properties to create a Panel control with a dashed red border, and a pink background (see Figure 3.10).

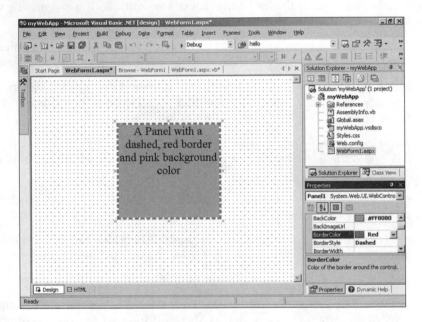

Figure 3.10   Using formatting properties.

You should understand that not all of these properties work with all controls. For example, modifying an ImageButton control's Font property is both harmless and meaningless. Furthermore, many of these properties, such as the AccessKey and TabIndex properties, only work with Internet Explorer version 4.0 and later (these properties are ignored on other browsers).

The values of several of these properties, such as the Width and Height properties, are specified in units. The default unit for these properties is the pixel. For example, if you enter 120 for the width, this value will be interpreted as 120 pixels.

More recent browsers support the following additional units of measurements (Internet Explorer 5.0 and later supports all of these units):

- *cm*—Centimeters.

- *em*—Size relative to parent element's size. For example, 2em is twice the size of the parent element.

- *ex*—Font size relative to the size of the parent font's lowercase x. For example, a font with the size 2ex is twice the size of the lowercase x in the parent font.

- *in*—Inches.

- *mm*—Millimeters.

- *%*—Percentage.

- *pc*—A pica represents 12 points.

- *px*—Pixels (the default value).

- *pt*—Points (1/72 of an inch).

Again, not all properties support all units. Furthermore, not all browsers support all these units.

Handling Events

As you've seen in previous sections, controls in a Web Form Page can raise events. For example, when you click a button, the Button control raises a Click event. Or, when you select a new list item in a ListBox control, the control raises a SelectedIndexChanged event.

A Web Form Page itself can raise events. For example, you can use page events to perform certain actions whenever the page is requested by a browser.

In the following sections, you'll learn how to handle both control and page events.

Handling Control Events

If you want to perform some action whenever an event is raised by a control, you need to add an event handler to your code. An *event handler* is a method or subroutine that executes when a certain event is raised.

There are two ways you can add event handlers to your code. First, you can double-click a control on the Designer surface. Double-clicking a control will automatically switch you to the Code Editor and add an event handler for the control's default event.

If you need to add an event handler for something other than a control's default event, you'll need to perform different steps, depending on whether you are working with C# or VB.NET.

To add an event handler with C#, you need to select the control from the drop-down list in the Properties window. Next, click the icon at the top of the Properties windows labeled events (the lightning bolt). Clicking the events button will display a list of all the events associated with the control. You can double-click any of the events listed in the properties window to add an event handler for that event.

To add an event handler when working with VB.NET, you need to switch to the Code Editor (select Code from the View menu). Select a control from the Classname drop-down list that appears at the top-left of the Code Editor. If you select an event from the Method Name drop-down list that appears at the top-right of the Code Editor, the corresponding event handler will be automatically added to your code (see Figure 3.11).

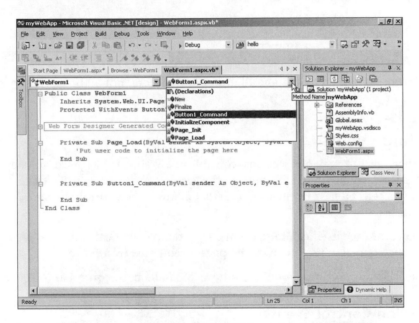

Figure 3.11   Adding an event handler in VB.NET from the Code Editor.

In most cases, the default event is the one with which you'll want to work. For example, if you add a Button control named **Button1** to a page and you double-click the button on the Designer surface, the following event handler is added to the Code Editor:

C#

```
private void Button1_Click(object sender, System.EventArgs e)
{
}
```

VB.NET

```
Private Sub Button1_Click(ByVal sender As Object,
➥ByVal e As System.EventArgs) Handles Button1.Click

End Sub
```

An event handler always accepts two parameters—an `Object` parameter and an `EventArgs` parameter. All event handlers, regardless of the nature of the event, have the same two parameters.

The `Object` parameter represents the control that raised the event. You might want to associate multiple controls with the same event-handling subroutine. In that case, you could use the `Object` parameter to identify the control that raised the event.

The `System.EventArgs` parameter contains additional information about the event that was raised. This parameter is useless in the case of a simple `Button` control because there is no additional event information to pass to the event-handling subroutine.

An example of a control with a more interesting `EventArgs` parameter is the `ImageButton` control. The event handler for an `ImageButton` `Click` event looks like the following:

C#

```
private void ImageButton1_Click(object sender,
➥System.Web.UI.ImageClickEventArgs e)
{
}
```

VB.NET

```
Private Sub ImageButton1_Click(ByVal sender As System.Object,
➥ByVal e As System.Web.UI.ImageClickEventArgs) Handles ImageButton1.Click

End Sub
```

Notice that the second parameter passed to this event handler is a `System.Web.UI.ImageClickEventArgs` parameter. This parameter has two properties that you can read in your code—an `X` property that represents the x coordinate of location where the user clicked and a `Y` property that represents the y coordinate of where the user clicked.

For example, you can display the values of the `X` and `Y` properties by using a `Label` control as shown in the following:

C#

```csharp
private void ImageButton1_Click(object sender, System.Web.UI.ImageClickEventArgs e)
{
  Label1.Text = "You clicked at the following coordinates:";
  Label1.Text += e.X;
  Label1.Text += " and ";
  Label1.Text += e.Y;

}
```

VB.NET

```vbnet
Private Sub ImageButton1_Click(ByVal sender As System.Object,
➥ByVal e As System.Web.UI.ImageClickEventArgs) Handles ImageButton1.Click
  Label1.Text = "You clicked at the following coordinates:"
  Label1.Text &= e.X
  Label1.Text &= " and "
  Label1.Text &= e.Y
End Sub
```

If you add this event handler to your Web Form Page and click the image displayed by the ImageButton, the page in Figure 3.12 is displayed.

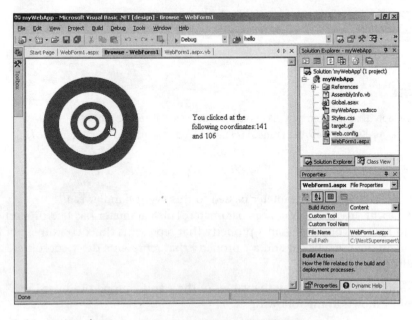

Figure 3.12 Using the ImageClickEventArgs parameter.

Handling Page Events

A Web Form Page itself has several events that you can handle in your code. The most important of these events is the Page_Load event.

When you create a Web Form Page, Visual Studio .NET automatically creates a Page_Load event handler to handle the Page_Load event for you. You can view this event handler by switching to the Code Editor:

C#

```
private void Page_Load(object sender, System.EventArgs e)
{
  // Put user code to initialize the page here
}
```

VB.NET

```
Private Sub Page_Load(ByVal sender As System.Object,
➥ByVal e As System.EventArgs) Handles MyBase.Load
  'Put user code to initialize the page here
End Sub
```

This Page_Load subroutine is executed every time someone requests the Web Form Page. The Page_Load subroutine is used most often for initializing variables and controls contained in the Web Form Page.

For example, suppose that you want to display the number of days, hours, minutes, and seconds until the new millennium (the year 3001) in a Label control every time a page is requested (see Figure 3.13).

First, you need to create the necessary controls:

1. Create a new Web Form Page named **ShowDays.aspx** by selecting Project, Add Web Form.

2. Add a Label control to the Web Form Page by dragging the Label control located under the Web Forms tab on the Toolbox onto the Designer surface.

Next, you need to add the code that displays the number of days, hours, minutes, and seconds to the next millennium:

1. Switch to the Code Editor by double-clicking the Designer surface.

2. Enter the following code for the Page_Load method:

C#

```csharp
private void Page_Load(object sender, System.EventArgs e)
{
  TimeSpan objSpan =
    DateTime.Parse( "1/1/3001" ) - DateTime.Now;
  Label1.Text = String.Format(
    "Only {0} days, {1} hours, {2} minutes, {3} seconds left!",
    objSpan.Days,
    objSpan.Hours,
    objSpan.Minutes,
    objSpan.Seconds);
}
```

VB.NET

```vbnet
Private Sub Page_Load(ByVal sender As System.Object,
➥ByVal e As System.EventArgs) Handles MyBase.Load
  Dim objSpan As TimeSpan

  objSpan = _
    DateTime.op_Subtraction(#1/1/3001#, DateTime.Now)
  Label1.Text = String.Format( _
    "Only {0} days, {1} hours, {2} minutes, {3} seconds left!", _
    objSpan.Days, _
    objSpan.Hours, _
    objSpan.Minutes, _
    objSpan.Seconds)
End Sub
```

3. Right-click the page in the Solution Explorer window and select Build and Browse.

After you create this Web Form Page, a countdown to the new millennium is displayed in the Label control every time you refresh the page (click the Refresh button). The countdown is updated within the Page_Load event handler.

The IsPostBack Property

Code located in the Page_Load subroutine executes each and every time a page is requested. Often, this is not what you want. In many cases, you want to execute code only when the page is first requested.

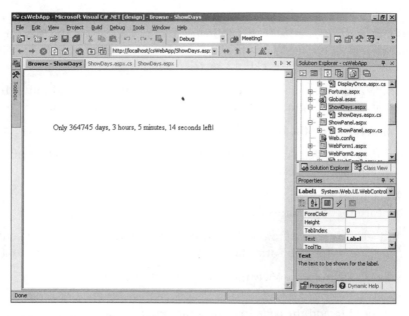

Figure 3.13   Displaying the number of days until the millennium.

All controls, both HTML controls and Web controls, retain their values between posts back to the same page on the Web server. For example, if you assign text to a Label control and click a Button control to reload the page, the Label control will retain the text when the page is redisplayed.

> **NOTE**
>
> The ability of controls to retain their values between posts back to the same page is called *view state*.

The Data controls, such as the Repeater and DataGrid controls, also retain their values between post backs to the server. For example, if you grab data from a database in the Page_Load event handler and assign the data to a DataGrid control, the DataGrid control will automatically retain the data, even if you repeatedly reload the page by clicking a Button control.

Because controls automatically retain their values between post backs to the server, you typically do not need to assign values to the controls each and every time the page is requested. Typically, you want to assign the value only when the page is first requested.

You can detect whether a page is being requested for the first time by using the IsPostBack property. The IsPostBack property has the value False the first time a page is requested and the value True if the page has been submitted back to the server at least once (for example, by clicking a Button or LinkButton control).

For example, suppose that you want to display the current date and time when the page is first requested, but not when the page is posted back to itself.

First, you need to add the necessary controls:

1. Create a new Web Form Page named **DisplayOnce.aspx** by selecting Add Web Form from the Project menu.

2. Add a Label control to the Web Form Page by dragging the Label control from beneath the Web Forms tab on the Toolbox onto the Designer surface.

3. Add a Button control to the Web Form Page by dragging the Button control from under the Web Forms tab on the Toolbox onto the Designer surface.

4. Select Code from the View menu to switch to the Code Editor.

Next, you need to add the code to display the current time:

1. Double-click the Designer surface to switch to the Code Editor.

2. Enter the following code for the Page_Load() method:

C#

```csharp
private void Page_Load(object sender, System.EventArgs e)
{
  if (!IsPostBack)
    Label1.Text = DateTime.Now.ToString();
}
```

VB.NET

```vbnet
Private Sub Page_Load(ByVal sender As System.Object,
➥ByVal e As System.EventArgs) Handles MyBase.Load
  If Not IsPostBack Then
    Label1.Text = DateTime.Now
  End If
End Sub
```

3. In the Solution Explorer window, right-click the Web Form Page and select Build and Browse.

When the page is first opened, the current date and time is displayed (see Figure 3.14). However, if you click the Button control, the current date and time are not updated. The IsPostBack property is used in the Page_Load event handler to prevent the Label control from being updated when the page is posted back to the server.

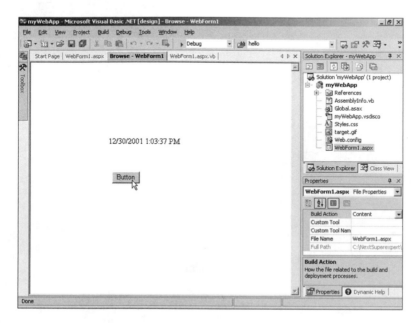

Figure 3.14   Using the IsPostBack property.

Summary

In this chapter, you learned how to create basic Web Form Pages. First, you were provided with an overview of how Web Form Pages work. You learned how to add a new Web Form Page to a project and compile it.

Next, you were given an overview of HTML and Web controls. You learned how to add each type of control to your project.

Finally, you explored the important topic of event-handling in Web Form Pages. You learned how to handle both control and page events by adding event handlers to your code.

4

Validating Web Form Pages

IN THIS CHAPTER

• Overview of the Validation Controls

• Using Validation Controls

• Performing Data Type Checks

• Performing Custom Validation

If you want to collect information from the users of your application, you'll most likely need to implement some type of form validation. For example, you'll need a way to make certain form fields required and prevent users from entering the wrong type of information into them.

Fortunately, Visual Studio .NET makes it easy to validate form data. You can add a variety of Validation controls to your Web Form Page to prevent the wrong type of data from being submitted.

In this chapter, you'll learn

- How to use the common properties shared by all Validation controls

- How to use the Validation controls to check for required fields, check for the correct data type, or perform custom validation tasks

- How to display a summary of validation errors in a Web Form Page

Overview of the Validation Controls

There are five standard Validation Web controls that you can add to a Web Form Page to validate form data:

- `CompareValidator`   Enables you to validate the data in a form field against a fixed value or other form field

- `CustomValidator`   Enables you to validate the data in a form field by using a custom subroutine

- RangeValidator   Enables you to validate the data in a form field against a minimum and maximum value

- RegularExpressionValidator   Enables you to validate the data in a form field against a regular expression

- RequiredFieldValidator   Enables you to validate the data in a form field by checking whether the form field contains a value

All of the Validation controls support three properties—the ControlToValidate property, Text property, and IsValid property. All the Validation controls derive from the BaseValidator class.

The ControlToValidate property contains the ID of the form control that you want to validate. For example, suppose that you want to create a text box in a Web Form Page named txtPassword and you don't want a user to be able to submit the form without entering a value for the TextBox control. In that case, you would add a RequiredFieldValidator control to the page and assign the value txtPassword to the RequiredFieldValidator control's ControlToValidate property.

The second property that all Validation controls share is the Text property. You assign the error message that you want the Validation control to display to the Text property. For example, you might assign the value You must enter a password! to the Text property of a RequiredFieldValidator control. Whatever error message you assign to the Text property appears at the same location as the Validation control on a page.

Finally, all Validation controls have an IsValid property. The IsValid property has the value True when the control indicated by the ControlToValidate property passes the validation test. Otherwise, this property has the value False. You can use this property to determine the nature of the particular validation errors contained in a Web Form Page.

Post Backs and Form Validation

If you have worked with HTML forms in the past, you are probably used to creating forms that post to a new page. To take advantage of Validation controls in a Web Form Page, however, you cannot post the form information to a new page. Instead, you must post the Web Form Page back to the same page on the Web server.

For example, suppose that you want to add two Web Form Pages to a project—a page named Register.aspx and a page named ThankYou.aspx. The Register.aspx page contains a registration form and the ThankYou.aspx page contains a thank you message for registering.

When designing your project, you might be tempted to have the Register.aspx page post the form to the ThankYou.aspx page. The user fills out the registration form, submits it, and receives a thank you message. However, you can't take advantage of Validation controls in the Register.aspx page when you post a form to a new page.

Instead, the Register.aspx page should post back to itself. This way, you can display error messages with any Validation controls that you have added to the form. When there are no validation errors in the Register.aspx page, you can explicitly redirect the user to the ThankYou.aspx page.

By default, Web Form Pages automatically post back to themselves. However, you must explicitly add the code to the Web Form to redirect the user to a new page when there are no validation errors in the page. You'll see several examples of how to do this when we discuss the individual Validation controls.

JavaScript and the Validation Controls

When you use the Validation controls with Microsoft Internet Explorer 4.0 or later, the Validation controls will automatically use client-side JavaScript. This means that the Validation controls can immediately display error messages on the browser while the user is in the process of completing a form. If there are any validation errors in a page, the client-side JavaScript will prevent the user from submitting the form back to the server.

If you are not using Microsoft Internet Explorer 4.0 or later, you can still use the Validation controls. The Validation controls will "fall back" to performing validation on the server after the form is submitted to the Web server. Validation error messages won't be displayed immediately, but they will appear after the page is posted back to the Web server.

Using Validation Controls

All the Validation controls can be found under the Web Forms tab in the Toolbox. Because these controls are Web controls, you can add them only to Web Form Pages and not to other types of pages, such as HTML pages.

Furthermore, the Validation controls only work with server controls, such as the TextBox control. You cannot use the Validation controls with standard HTML text fields.

In the following sections, you'll learn how to take advantage of each of the Validation controls to perform common form validation tasks.

Checking for Required Fields

You can use the RequiredFieldValidator control to automatically display an error message when you submit a form with an empty form field. For example, you can use the RequiredFieldValidator control with a login form to prevent users from submitting the form when values have not been entered for the username and password form fields.

The RequiredFieldValidator has two important properties that you need to set:

- ControlToValidate   The form field to validate
- Text   The error message to display

To create a login form with a required username form field, complete the following steps.

First, you need to create the necessary form elements:

1. Create a new Web Form Page named **Login.aspx**.

2. Add an HTML Label to the Web Form Page and assign it the text **Username**.

3. Add a TextBox control to the Web Form Page.

4. Add a RequiredFieldValidator control to the Web Form. Assign the following two properties to the control:

Property	Value
Text	**Required!**
ControlToValidate	**TextBox1**

5. Add a Button control to the Web Form Page.

Next, you need to add the code that executes when you click the Button control:

1. Add a Button1_Click() method to the Web Form Page by double-clicking the Button control on the Designer surface. This will switch you to the Code Editor.

2. Enter the following code for the Button1_Click() method:

C#

```
private void Button1_Click(object sender, System.EventArgs e)
{
  if (Page.IsValid)
    Response.Redirect( "success.aspx" );
}
```

VB.NET

```
Private Sub Button1_Click(ByVal sender As System.Object,
➥ByVal e As System.EventArgs) Handles Button1.Click
  If IsValid Then
    Response.Redirect("Success.aspx")
  End If
End Sub
```

Finally, you need to add the success page to your project and compile the pages:

1. Add a new Web Form Page to your project named **Success.aspx**.

2. Add an HTML Label to the Success.aspx page and enter the text **Thank you for completing the form!** into the label.

3. Right-click the Login.aspx page in the Solution Explorer window and select Build and Browse.

If you attempt to submit the Login.aspx page by clicking the Button control and you don't enter a username, the error message in Figure 4.1 is displayed. However, if you enter a value into the username text box and submit the form, you are automatically redirected to the Success.aspx page.

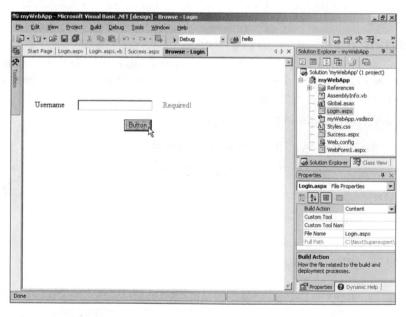

Figure 4.1   Using the RequiredFieldValidator control.

When you click the `Button` control, the `Button1_Click` event handler executes. This subroutine contains the following code:

C#

```
private void Button1_Click(object sender, System.EventArgs e)
{
  if (Page.IsValid)
    Response.Redirect( "success.aspx" );
}
```

VB.NET

```
Private Sub Button1_Click(ByVal sender As System.Object,
➥ByVal e As System.EventArgs) Handles Button1.Click
  If IsValid Then
    Response.Redirect("Success.aspx")
  End If
End Sub
```

The `IsValid` property has the value `True` when there are no validation errors in the form. If there are no validation errors, the `Response.Redirect` method is used to automatically redirect the user to the Success.aspx page. Otherwise, the Login.aspx page is redisplayed and the user can see any validation error messages.

Validating a Range of Expressions

You can use the `RangeValidator` control to specify a minimum and maximum value for a `TextBox` control. You can use this control to check for a range of integers, currency amounts, dates, strings, or doubles.

The `RangeValidator` control has five important properties:

- `ControlToValidate`   The form field to validate
- `MinimumValue`   The minimum valid value in the range of values
- `MaximumValue`   The maximum valid value in the range of values
- `Text`   The error message to display
- `Type`   The type of comparison to perform (possible values are `String`, `Integer`, `Double`, `Date`, `Currency`)

For example, suppose that you want to add an Age text box to a Web Form Page. In that case, you might want to prevent a user from entering an age less than 2 or greater than 120.

To use the `RangeValidator` control with an Age text box, perform the following steps. First, you need to add the necessary controls to the page:

1. Create a new Web Form Page named **Register.aspx**.

2. Add an HTML `Label` to the Web Form Page and enter the text **Age**.

3. Add a `TextBox` control to the Web Form Page.

4. Add a `RangeValidator` control to the Web Form Page and assign the following properties to it:

Property	Value
Text	**Out of Range!**
ControlToValidate	**TextBox1**
MinimumValue	**2**
MaximumValue	**120**
Type	**Integer**

5. Add a `Button` control to the Web Form Page.

Next, you need to add the code that executes when you click the `Button` control:

1. Add a `Button1_Click()` method to the Web Form Page by double-clicking the `Button` control on the Designer surface. This will switch you to the Code Editor.

2. Enter the following code for the `Button1_Click()` method:

C#

```
private void Button1_Click(object sender, System.EventArgs e)
{
  if (Page.IsValid)
    Response.Redirect( "success.aspx" );
}
```

VB.NET

```
Private Sub Button1_Click(ByVal sender As System.Object,
➥ByVal e As System.EventArgs) Handles Button1.Click
  If IsValid Then
    Response.Redirect("Success.aspx")
  End If
End Sub
```

3. Right-click the Register.aspx page in the Solution Explorer window and select Build and Browse.

If you enter a value less than 2 or greater than 120 into the Age text box and submit the form, an error message will be displayed by the RangeValidator (see Figure 4.2). Otherwise, the Button1_Click event handler will execute and redirect you to the Success.aspx page (we created the Success.aspx page in the previous section).

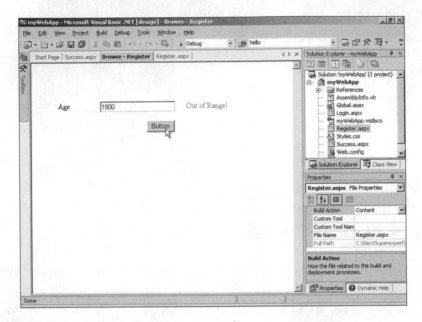

Figure 4.2   Using the RangeValidator control.

Comparing Values

You can use the CompareValidator to compare the value of one control to another control or to compare the value of one control to a fixed value. The CompareValidator has six important properties:

- ControlToValidate   The form field to validate

- ControlToCompare   The form field to perform the comparison against

- Operator   The operator used for the comparison (possible values are Equal, NotEqual, GreaterThan, GreaterThanEqual, LessThan, LessThanEqual, and DataTypeCheck)

- Text   The error message to display
- Type   The type of comparison to perform (possible values are String, Integer, Double, Date, Currency)
- ValueToCompare   The fixed value to compare

For example, suppose that you are building a Web application to schedule meetings. The form might contain a field for entering the starting time of the meeting and a second field for entering the ending time of the meeting. You could use the CompareValidator to ensure that the time entered into the second field occurs after the time entered into the first field.

Or, suppose that you have only one form field for entering a meeting date. In that case, you might want to check that the date entered into the field occurs after the current date and time (you can't retroactively schedule meetings).

To use the CompareValidator to check whether a value entered into a field occurs after the current date and time, perform the following steps.

First, you need to add the necessary controls to the page:

1. Create a new Web Form Page named **Schedule.aspx**.

2. Add an HTML Label to the Web Form Page and enter the text **Meeting Date** into the label.

3. Add a TextBox control to the Web Form Page.

4. Add a CompareValidator control to the Web Form Page and assign the following values to its properties:

Property	Value
Text	**Bad Date!**
ControlToValidate	**TextBox1**
Operator	**GreaterThan**
Type	**Date**

5. Add a Button control to the Web Form Page.

Next, you need to add the necessary code for both the Page_Load and Button_Click event handlers:

1. Add a Button1_Click() method to the Web Form Page by double-clicking the Button control on the Designer surface. This will switch you to the Code Editor.

2. Enter the following code for the Button1_Click() method:

   C#

```
private void Button1_Click(object sender, System.EventArgs e)
{
  if (Page.IsValid)
    Response.Redirect( "success.aspx" );
}
```

   VB.NET

```
Private Sub Button1_Click(ByVal sender As System.Object,
➥ByVal e As System.EventArgs) Handles Button1.Click
  If IsValid Then
    Response.Redirect("Success.aspx")
  End If
End Sub
```

3. Enter the following code for the Page_Load() method:

   C#

```
private void Page_Load(object sender, System.EventArgs e)
{
  CompareValidator1.ValueToCompare = DateTime.Now.ToString("d");
}
```

   VB.NET

```
Private Sub Page_Load(ByVal sender As System.Object,
➥ByVal e As System.EventArgs) Handles MyBase.Load
  CompareValidator1.ValueToCompare = DateTime.Now
End Sub
```

4. Right-click the Schedule.aspx page in the Solution Explorer window and select Build and Browse.

The current date is assigned to the CompareValidator control's ValueToCompare property within the Page_Load event handler. If you enter a date that is not greater than the current date into the text box and submit the form, you'll receive the error message displayed in Figure 4.3.

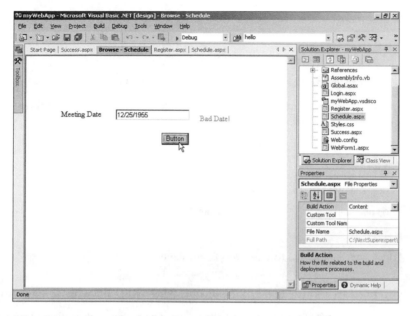

Figure 4.3   Comparing values with the `CompareValidator` control.

TIP

Like the `RangeValidator`, if you don't enter a value into the text box and submit the form, the `CompareValidator` control will not display an error message. If you want to require a value for a control, you must add both a `CompareValidator` and `RequiredFieldValidator` control to the Web Form Page.

Performing Data Type Checks

One common validation task involves checking whether the right type of data was entered into a form field. For example, you do not want users entering the text "apple" into a form field labeled Birth Date.

You can use the `CompareValidator` to perform data type checks by assigning the value `DataTypeCheck` to the `CompareValidator` control's `Operator` property.

To prevent a user from entering the wrong type of value into a Birth Date field, perform the following steps.

First, you need to add the necessary controls to the page:

1. Create a new Web Form Page named **Survey.aspx**.

2. Add an HTML Label to the Web Form Page and enter the text **Birth Date** into the Label.

3. Add a TextBox control to the Web Form Page.

4. Add a CompareValidator control to the Web Form Page.

5. In the Properties window, select the CompareValidator control and assign the following values to its properties:

Property	Value
Text	**Invalid Date!**
ControlToValidate	**TextBox1**
Operator	**DataTypeCheck**
Type	**Date**

6. Add a Button control to the Web Form Page.

Next, you need to add the code that executes when you click the Button control:

1. Add a Button1_Click() method to the Web Form Page by double-clicking the Button control on the Designer surface. This will switch you to the Code Editor.

2. Enter the following code for the Button1_Click() method:

C#

```
private void Button1_Click(object sender, System.EventArgs e)
{
  if (Page.IsValid)
    Response.Redirect( "success.aspx" );
}
```

VB.NET

```
Private Sub Button1_Click(ByVal sender As System.Object,
➥ByVal e As System.EventArgs) Handles Button1.Click
  If IsValid Then
    Response.Redirect("Success.aspx")
  End If
End Sub
```

After you complete these steps, you'll receive an error if you attempt to enter anything except a date into the Birth Date form field (see Figure 4.4).

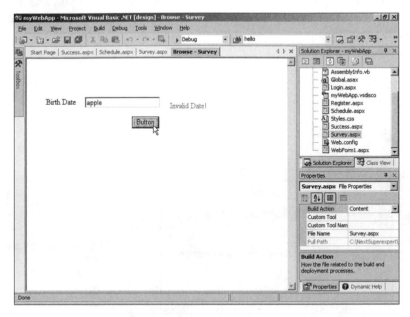

Figure 4.4   Checking the data type of a form field.

The CompareValidator is very picky about the format of acceptable dates. You are allowed to enter dates by using a short date format, such as 12/25/1966. Other date formats, such as December 12, 1966, will fail.

Regular Expression Validation

You can use the RegularExpressionValidator to check whether the value of a form field matches a specified pattern. For example, you can use this Validation control to validate Social Security numbers, postal codes, phone numbers, and email addresses.

Regular expressions are a complex topic that falls outside the scope of this book. Fortunately, however, you don't need to understand regular expressions to take advantage of the RegularExpressionValidator. Visual Studio .NET provides you with several prewritten regular expressions.

The RegularExpressionValidator has three important properties:

- ControlToValidate   The form field to validate

- Text   The error message to display

- ValidationExpression   The regular expression pattern to match

You can supply any regular expression pattern that you want for the
ValidationExpression property. Alternatively, you can use one of the predefined
regular expression patterns supplied with Visual Studio .NET. If you add a
RegularExpressionValidator control to a page and click the ellipses next to the
ValidationExpression property, the Regular Expression Editor dialog box in Figure 4.5
appears.

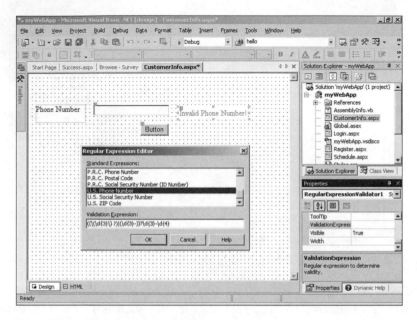

Figure 4.5   The Regular Expression Editor.

For example, suppose that you need to validate a Phone Number form field by using
the RegularExpressionValidator. To do so, perform the following steps:

1. Create a new Web Form Page named **CustomerInfo.aspx**.

2. Add an HTML Label to the Web Form Page and enter the text **Phone Number** into
    the label.

3. Add a TextBox control to the Web Form Page.

4. Add a RegularExpressionValidator control to the Web Form Page and assign the
    following values to its properties:

Property	Value
Text	**Invalid Phone Number!**
ControlToValidate	**TextBox1**

5. In the Properties window, click the ellipsis next to the `ValidationExpression` property to open the Regular Expression Editor dialog box.

6. In the Regular Expression dialog box, click U.S. Phone Number and click OK.

7. Add a `Button` control to the Web Form Page.

Next, you need to add the code that executes when you click the `Button` control:

1. Add a `Button1_Click()` method to the Web Form Page by double-clicking the `Button` control on the Designer surface. This will switch you to the Code Editor.

2. Enter the following code for the `Button1_Click()` method:

   C#

   ```
   private void Button1_Click(object sender, System.EventArgs e)
   {
     if (Page.IsValid)
       Response.Redirect( "success.aspx" );
   }
   ```

   VB.NET

   ```
   Private Sub Button1_Click(ByVal sender As System.Object,
   ➥ByVal e As System.EventArgs) Handles Button1.Click
     If IsValid Then
       Response.Redirect("Success.aspx")
     End If
   End Sub
   ```

3. Right-click the CustomerInfo.aspx page in the Solution Explorer window and select Build and Browse.

If you attempt to enter a phone number that has an invalid pattern into the text box, you'll receive the error displayed in Figure 4.6.

TIP

Like the other Validation controls, if you don't enter a value into the text box and submit the form, the `RegularExpressionValidator` control will not display an error message. If you want to require a value for a control, you must add both a `RegularExpressionValidator` and `RequiredFieldValidator` control to the Web Form Page.

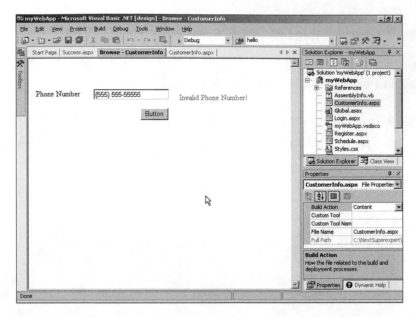

Figure 4.6   Using the `RegularExpressionValidator` control.

Performing Custom Validation

If you need to validate a form field and none of the standard Validation controls perform the necessary type of validation, you can use the `CustomValidator` control to perform any type of validation that you might desire.

You can associate the `CustomValidator` control with a custom event handler. The custom validation event handler contains your validation logic.

For example, suppose that you don't want users to enter more than 10 characters in a multi-line text box. In that case, you can associate an event handler with the `CustomValidator` control that returns an error when the `TextBox` control contains too many characters. To do so, perform the following steps:

> **NOTE**
>
> You cannot use the `MaxLength` property to limit the number of characters that a user can enter into a multi-line text box because the `MaxLength` property does not work with a multi-line text box.

1. Create a new Web Form Page named **ShortForm.aspx**.

2. Add an HTML `Label` to the Web Form Page and enter the text **Comments** into the label.

3. Add a `TextBox` control to the Web Form Page and assign the value **MultiLine** to the control's `TextMode` property.

4. Add a `CustomValidator` control to the Web Form Page and assign the following values to its properties:

Property	Value
Text	**Comments Too Long!**
ControlToValidate	**TextBox1**

Next, you need to add the custom validation function by adding an event handler for the `CustomValidator` control:

1. Add a `CustomValidator1_ServerValidate()` method by double-clicking the `CustomValidator` control on the Designer surface. This will switch you to the Code Editor.

2. Enter the following code for the `CustomValidator1_ServerValidate()` subroutine:

C#

```csharp
private void CustomValidator1_ServerValidate(object source,
➥ System.Web.UI.WebControls.ServerValidateEventArgs args)
{
  if (args.Value.Length > 10)
    args.IsValid = false;
  else
    args.IsValid = true;
}
```

VB.NET

```vbnet
Private Sub CustomValidator1_ServerValidate(ByVal source As System.Object,
➥ByVal args As System.Web.UI.WebControls.ServerValidateEventArgs)
➥Handles CustomValidator1.ServerValidate
If args.Value.Length > 10 Then
    args.IsValid = False
  Else
    args.IsValid = True
  End If
End Sub
```

Next, you need to add a Button control and an event handler for the Button control:

1. Switch back to the Designer by selecting View, Designer.

2. Add a Button1_Click() method to the Web Form Page by double-clicking the Button control on the Designer surface. This will switch you to the Code Editor.

3. Enter the following code for the Button1_Click() method:

   C#

   ```csharp
   private void Button1_Click(object sender, System.EventArgs e)
   {
     if (Page.IsValid)
       Response.Redirect( "success.aspx" );
   }
   ```

   VB.NET

   ```vbnet
   Private Sub Button1_Click(ByVal sender As System.Object,
   ➥ByVal e As System.EventArgs) Handles Button1.Click
     If IsValid Then
       Response.Redirect("Success.aspx")
     End If
   End Sub
   ```

4. Right-click the ShortForm.aspx page in the Solution Explorer window and select Build and Browse.

If you attempt to add more than 10 characters to the text box, and you submit the form, the error in Figure 4.7 will be displayed.

The custom validation subroutine looks like the following:

C#

```csharp
private void CustomValidator1_ServerValidate(object source,
➥ System.Web.UI.WebControls.ServerValidateEventArgs args)
{
  if (args.Value.Length > 10)
    args.IsValid = false;
  else
    args.IsValid = true;
}
```

VB.NET

```
Private Sub CustomValidator1_ServerValidate(ByVal source As System.Object,
➥ByVal args As System.Web.UI.WebControls.ServerValidateEventArgs)
➥Handles CustomValidator1.ServerValidate
If args.Value.Length > 10 Then
    args.IsValid = False
  Else
    args.IsValid = True
  End If
End Sub
```

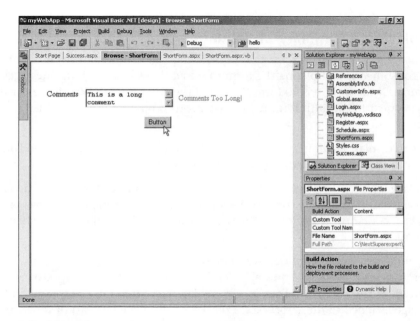

Figure 4.7   Using the `CustomValidator` control.

The second parameter passed to the `ServerValidate` subroutine has two properties—the `Value` property and `IsValid` property. The `Value` property contains whatever text was entered into the control being validated. In our custom validation handler, we check the length of the `Value` property to check whether more than 10 characters were entered into the multi-line text box.

You use the `IsValid` property to indicate whether or not the validation check was successful. If you assign the value `False` to the `IsValid` property, the `CustomValidator` control will display an error message.

WARNING

The `CustomValidator` that we created in this section uses a server-side validation subroutine. The subroutine will not execute until the form is posted back to the server. If the form contains other Validation controls that use client-side validation, such as the `RequiredFieldValidator`, the error message displayed by the `CustomValidator` will not be displayed until all the other validation errors in the Web Form Page are fixed.

Displaying a Summary of Validation Errors

If you are creating a long form that uses several Validation controls, it might be difficult for someone completing the form to see all the validation error messages. For example, if the form has 50 form fields and there is a single validation error that appears next to the 48th form field, the person completing the form may never see it.

You can display a summary of all the validation error messages for a Web Form Page in a single location by using the `ValidationSummary` control.

To take advantage of the `ValidationSummary` control, you need to provide a value for the `ErrorMessage` property for each Validation control on a page. The `ErrorMessage` property contains the error that the `ValidationSummary` control displays when there is an error.

It is important to not confuse a Validation control's `Text` property with its `ErrorMessage` property. The message assigned to the `Text` property appears at the same location on the Web Form Page as the Validation control. On the other hand, the message assigned to the `ErrorMessage` property is displayed as part of the summary displayed by the `ValidationSummary` control.

Typically, you'll want to supply a different error message for the `Text` and `ErrorMessage` properties. For example, for the text property, you might assign the message "First name is required!" for the `ErrorMessage` property.

For example, suppose that you need to create a simple pizza order form with two required form fields—the customer name and customer phone number. Additionally, suppose that you want to display a summary of validation errors at the top of the pizza order form. To do so, perform the following steps:

1. Create a new Web Form Page named **PizzaOrder.aspx**.

2. Add an HTML Label to the Web Form Page and enter the text **Customer Name** into the label.

3. Add a TextBox control to the Web Form Page.

4. Add a RequiredFieldValidator control to the Web Form Page and enter the following values for its properties:

Property	Value
ControlToValidate	**TextBox1**
Text	**Required!**
ErrorMessage	**Customer Name is Required!**

5. Add a second HTML Label to the Web Form Page and enter the text **Customer Phone Number** into the label.

6. Add a second TextBox control to the Web Form Page.

7. Add a second RequiredFieldValidator control to the Web Form Page and enter the following values for its properties:

Property	Value
ControlToValidate	**TextBox2**
Text	**Required!**
ErrorMessage	**Customer Phone Number is Required!**

8. Add a ValidationSummary control to the top of the Web Form Page.

9. Add a Button control to the Web Form Page.

10. Right-click the PizzaOrder.aspx page in the Solution Explorer window and select Build and Browse.

If you attempt to submit the form in the PizzaOrder.aspx page without entering a value for the Customer Name and Customer Phone number fields, validation errors will appear in two places. Each of the two RequiredFieldValidator controls will display the error message Required!. Furthermore, the ValidationSummary control will display the error messages Customer Name is Required! and Customer Phone Number is Required! (see Figure 4.8).

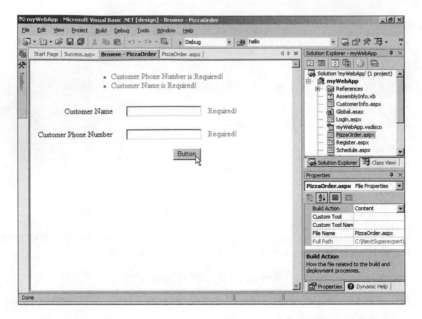

Figure 4.8   Using the ValidationSummary control.

Summary

In this chapter, you learned how to validate the form fields contained in a Web Form Page. First you were provided with an overview of the common properties shared by all the standard Validation controls. You also learned how the Validation controls support client-side JavaScript when used with Internet Explorer 4.0 or later.

Next, you created pages that use each of the Validation controls. You learned how to use the RequiredFieldValidator control to check for required fields, the RangeValidator control to check for a minimum and maximum value, the CompareValidator control to compare values, the RegularExpressionValidator control to validate email addresses and phone numbers, and the CustomValidator control to execute a custom validation subroutine.

Finally, you learned how to display a summary of validation error messages in a page by taking advantage of the ValidationSummary control.

5

Creating Web User Controls

IN THIS CHAPTER

- Creating a Simple Web User Control

- Handling Events in a Web User Control

- Building Form Elements with Web User Controls

- Dynamically Loading Web User Controls

Web User Controls enable you to reuse the same visual elements in multiple pages. You can use Web User Controls to create standard page elements, such as standard headers or footers, navigation bars, and menus. You also can use Web User Controls to compose new controls out of multiple existing controls. For example, you can use a Web User Control to create an address form that can be used on multiple pages.

In this chapter, you will learn

- How to create a standard page header

- How to build an address form from other controls

- How to dynamically load Web User Controls

Creating a Simple Web User Control

Imagine that you need to display the same header on all the Web Form Pages in your application. You want to display the very same company logo and text at the top of every page. This is a good situation in which to create a Web User Control.

We'll create a Web User Control that acts as a standard page header.

1. Add a new Web User Control to your project by selecting Add Web User Control from the Project menu. Enter the name **Header.ascx** for the name of the User Control and click Open.

2. Type the text **Standard Company Header** at the top of the Web User Control. Select the text with your mouse, select Font from the Format menu, and select Bold.

3. Add a horizontal rule to the Web User Control by double-clicking the Horizontal Rule element located under the HTML tab in the Toolbox.

You should notice that the process of creating a Web User Control is very similar to the process of creating a standard Web Form Page. You can design a Web User Control by dragging-and-dropping elements from the Toolbox, or you can switch to HTML view and add the HTML content manually.

Now that we've created the User Control, we can test it in a Web Form Page.

1. Add a new Web Form Page to your project named **Home.aspx**.

2. Drag and drop the Header.ascx file from the Solution Explorer window onto the Home.aspx page (see Figure 5.1).

3. Right-click Home.aspx in the Solution Explorer window and select Build and Browse.

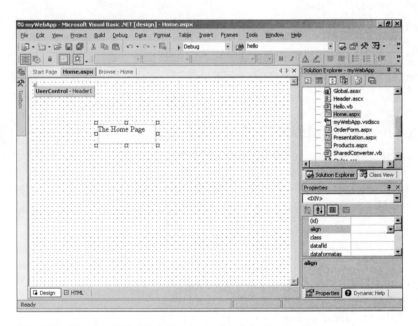

Figure 5.1   The Header Web User Control added to the Designer surface.

When you display the Home.aspx page, the contents of the Header Web User Control should appear at the top of the page (see Figure 5.2). You can use the same Header Web User Control in multiple Web Form Pages in your application.

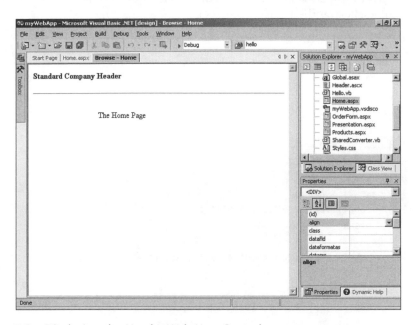

Figure 5.2   Displaying the Header Web User Control.

Handling Events in a Web User Control

As you saw in the previous section, a Web User Control is very similar to a standard Web Form Page. In fact, you can add the same event handling subroutines to a Web User Control as you can add to a Web Form Page.

You can use a Web User Control to handle control events, such as the Button Click event. You can even handle events such as Page_Load in a Web User Control.

For example, suppose that you want to randomly display a featured product on each page contained in your project. We'll create a simple ContentRotator Web User Control that randomly displays one item from a list of items.

1. Add a new Web User Control to your project named **ContentRotator.ascx** and click Open.

2. Add a Label control to the Web User Control by double-clicking the Label control located under the Web Forms tab in the Toolbox.

3. Switch to the Code Editor by selecting Code from the View menu (or by double-clicking the Designer surface).

4. Enter the following code for the Page_Load() method:

C#

```csharp
private void Page_Load(object sender, System.EventArgs e)
{
  Random objRan = new Random();
  switch (objRan.Next(3))
  {
    case 0:
      Label1.Text = "Hats on sale!";
      break;
    case 1:
      Label1.Text = "Discount on all electronics!";
      break;
    case 2:
      Label1.Text = "Buy stuff cheap!";
      break;
  }
}
```

VB.NET

```vbnet
Private Sub Page_Load(ByVal sender As System.Object,
➥ByVal e As System.EventArgs) Handles MyBase.Load
  Select Case Int(Rnd() * 3)
    Case 0
      Label1.Text = "Hats on sale!"
    Case 1
      Label1.Text = "Discount on all electronics!"
    Case 2
      Label1.Text = "Buy stuff cheap!"
  End Select
End Sub
```

The ContentRotator Web User Control displays a random message every time it is loaded. In the control's Page_Load subroutine, a random message is assigned to a Label control.

The Page_Load method in a Web User Control executes separately from the Page_Load method in the page that contains the control. First the containing page's Page_Load method executes, and then the Web User Control's Page_Load method executes.

To test the ContentRotator control in a Web Form Page, do the following:

1. Add a new Web Form Page to your project named **Products.aspx**.

2. Add a Grid Layout Panel control to the Web Form Page by dragging the control from the Toolbox onto the Designer surface.

3. Drag and drop the ContentRotator.ascx file from the Solution Explorer window onto the Grid Layout Panel on the Designer surface.

4. Right-click Products.aspx in the Solution Explorer window and select Build and Browse.

Every time you refresh the Products.aspx page (by selecting Refresh from the View menu), a random message is displayed (see Figure 5.3).

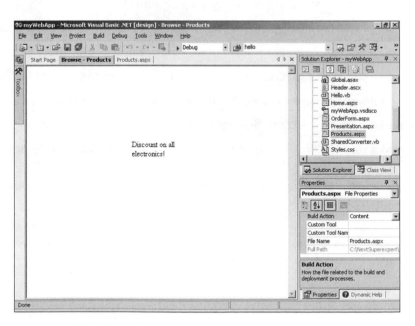

Figure 5.3   Using the ContentRotator Web User Control.

Notice that we did not add the ContentRotator control directly to the Web Form Page. Instead, we first added a Grid Layout Panel control and then we added the ContentRotator control to the Grid Layout Panel control. Because we added the Web User Control to the Grid Layout Panel, we can precisely position the Web User Control on the page.

Building Form Elements with Web User Controls

You can add items from the Toolbox, such as HTML elements and server controls, to the body of a Web User Control. For example, you can build a Web User Control from TextBox and other form controls.

For example, suppose that you need to display an address form within multiple Web Pages. You might even need to display the same address form twice within the same page to retrieve a customer's shipping and billing address. Instead of re-creating the address form over and over again, you can encapsulate it in a Web User Control.

Perform the following steps to create a basic address Web User Control:

1. Add a new Web User Control to your project named **Address.ascx** and click Open.

2. Add a Grid Layout Panel to the Web User Control.

3. Add an HTML Label element with the text **Street** to the Grid Layout Panel.

4. Add a TextBox control to the Web User Control next to the Street label.

5. Add a second HTML Label element with the text **City** to the Grid Layout Panel.

6. Add a second TextBox control to the Web User Control next to the City label.

7. Add a third HTML Label element with the text **State** to the Grid Layout Panel.

8. Add a second TextBox control to the Web User Control next to the State label.

After you add the HTML and form elements to the Address control, the Designer surface should resemble Figure 5.4.

If you want to be able to read the contents of the Street, City, and State TextBox controls from a Web Form Page that contains the Address control, you need to expose the TextBox controls through properties of the Address control.

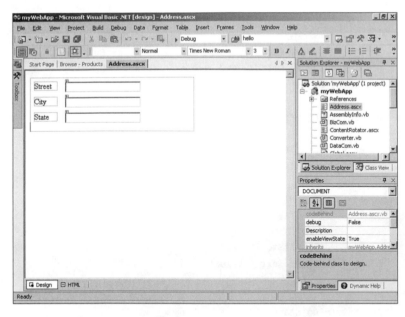

Figure 5.4   The Address Web User Control.

1. Switch to the Code Editor by selecting Code from the View menu.

2. Add three properties to the Web User Control by entering the following code:

C#

```
namespace myApp
{
  using System;
  using System.Data;
  using System.Drawing;
  using System.Web;
  using System.Web.UI.WebControls;
  using System.Web.UI.HtmlControls;

  /// <summary>
  ///  Summary description for Address.
  /// </summary>
```

146

CHAPTER 5   Creating Web User Controls

```csharp
public abstract class Address : System.Web.UI.UserControl
{
  protected System.Web.UI.WebControls.TextBox TextBox1;
  protected System.Web.UI.WebControls.TextBox TextBox2;
  protected System.Web.UI.WebControls.TextBox TextBox3;

  public string Street
  {
    get { return TextBox1.Text; }
    set { TextBox1.Text = value; }
  }

  public string City
  {
    get { return TextBox2.Text; }
    set { TextBox2.Text = value; }
  }

  public string State
  {
    get { return TextBox3.Text; }
    set { TextBox3.Text = value; }
  }

  private void Page_Load(object sender, System.EventArgs e)
  {
    // Put user code to initialize the page here
  }

}
}
```

VB.NET

```vb
Public MustInherit Class Address
    Inherits System.Web.UI.UserControl
    Protected WithEvents TextBox1 As System.Web.UI.WebControls.TextBox
    Protected WithEvents TextBox2 As System.Web.UI.WebControls.TextBox
    Protected WithEvents TextBox3 As System.Web.UI.WebControls.TextBox

    Public Property Street() As String
        Get
```

```
                  Return TextBox1.Text
            End Get
            Set(ByVal Value As String)
                  TextBox1.Text = Value
            End Set
      End Property

      Public Property City() As String
            Get
                  Return TextBox2.Text
            End Get
            Set(ByVal Value As String)
                  TextBox2.Text = Value
            End Set
      End Property

      Public Property State() As String
            Get
                  Return TextBox3.Text
            End Get
            Set(ByVal Value As String)
                  TextBox3.Text = Value
            End Set
      End Property

      Private Sub Page_Load(ByVal sender As System.Object,
➥ByVal e As System.EventArgs) Handles MyBase.Load
            'Put user code to initialize the page here
      End Sub

End Class
```

Now that you've added a Street, City, and State property to the Web User Control, you can access the values of the TextBox controls contained in the User Control from within a Web Form Page.

Let's go ahead and create an order form that contains areas for customers to enter both a shipping and a mailing address.

1. Add a new Web Form Page to your project named **OrderForm.aspx**.

2. Add an HTML Label with the text Shipping Address to the Web Form Page.

3. Add a Flow Layout Panel control to the Web Form Page by dragging the control from the Toolbox onto the Designer surface beneath the Shipping Address label.

4. Drag and drop the Address.ascx file from the Solution Explorer window onto the Flow Layout Panel.

5. Add a second HTML Label with the text **Billing Address** to the Web Form Page beneath the Flow Layout Panel.

6. Add a second Flow Layout Panel control to the Web Form Page by dragging the control from the Toolbox onto the Designer surface beneath the Billing Address label.

7. Drag and drop the Address.ascx file, a second time, from the Solution Explorer window onto the Flow Layout Panel.

8. Right-click OrderForm.aspx in the Solution Explorer window and select Build and Browse.

After you complete these steps, you should see the page in Figure 5.5. Notice that the same Address form fields appear twice—for the Billing Address and the Shipping Address.

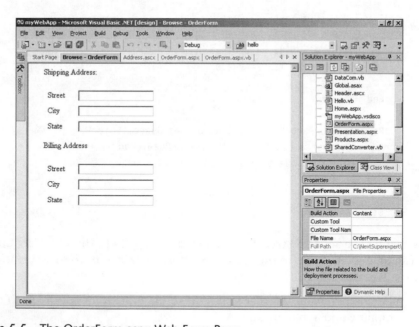

Figure 5.5   The OrderForm.aspx Web Form Page.

In a real-world project, you'll need to retrieve the values entered into the address form fields and save the data to a database. We'll discuss database access in detail in the second part of this book, "Working with Database Data." Here, we'll simply retrieve all the values entered into the Shipping and Billing address form fields and display the values in a Label control.

Before we can access any properties of the Web User Control within our Web Form Page, we need to declare each instance of the Address control in the page.

1. Open the OrderForm.aspx in the Code Editor by selecting Code from the View menu.

2. Enter the following two lines of code at the top of the OrderForm class declaration:

   C#

   ```
   protected Address Address1;
   protected Address Address2;
   ```

   VB.NET

   ```
   Protected WithEvents Address1 As Address
   Protected WithEvents Address2 As Address
   ```

Normal Web Form controls, such as the TextBox and Label controls, are automatically declared in the code-behind file when you drag the controls from the Toolbox. Because a Web User Control is added from the Server Explorer window, you must add the declarations to the code-behind file manually.

Next, we'll add a Button and Label control to the OrderForm.aspx page.

1. Switch back to the Designer by selecting Designer from the View menu.

2. Add a Label control to the OrderForm.aspx page by dragging the control from under the Web Forms tab in the Toolbox onto the Designer surface. Place the Label control on the right side of the page.

3. Add a Button control to the OrderForm.aspx page by dragging the control from under the Web Forms tab in the Toolbox onto the Designer surface.

4. Double-click the Button control. This will switch you to the Code Editor.

5. Enter the following code for the Button1_Click subroutine:

C#

```csharp
private void Button1_Click(object sender, System.EventArgs e)
{
  Label1.Text = "Shipping Address:"
    + "<li>" + Address1.Street
    + "<li>" + Address1.City
    + "<li>" + Address1.State
    + "<p>Billing Address:"
    + "<li>" + Address2.Street
    + "<li>" + Address2.City
    + "<li>" + Address2.State;
}
```

VB.NET

```vb
Private Sub Button1_Click(ByVal sender As System.Object,
➥ByVal e As System.EventArgs) Handles Button1.Click
  With Label1
    .Text = "Shipping Address:"
    .Text &= "<li>" & Address1.Street
    .Text &= "<li>" & Address1.City
    .Text &= "<li>" & Address1.State
    .Text &= "<p>Billing Address:"
    .Text &= "<li>" & Address2.Street
    .Text &= "<li>" & Address2.City
    .Text &= "<li>" & Address2.State
  End With
End Sub
```

6. Right-click OrderForm.aspx in the Solution Explorer window and select Build and Browse.

If you enter values into the Address form fields and click the Button control, the contents of the form fields will appear in the Label control (see Figure 5.6). The contents of the Address form fields are retrieved in the Button1_Click subroutine. Address1 represents the first instance of the Address control, the Shipping Address, and Address2 represents the second instance, the Billing Address.

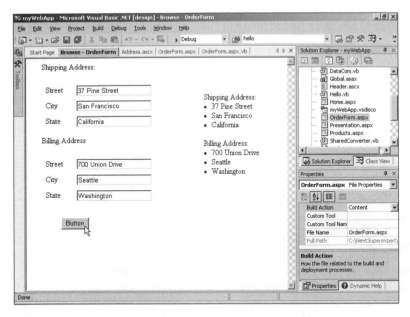

Figure 5.6   Displaying the contents of the Address control.

Dynamically Loading Web User Controls

You can programmatically add Web User Controls to a page. This is useful when you need to change the layout of a page to fit different circumstances.

For example, suppose that you want to randomly display one of a group of featured product descriptions on a Web page. Furthermore, suppose that you want each featured description to be stored in separate Web User Controls.

1. Create a new Web User Control named **Featured1.ascx**.

2. Type the text **Apples on Sale!** onto the Designer surface.

3. Create a second Web User Control named **Featured2.ascx**.

4. Type the text **Books on Sale!** onto the Designer surface.

5. Create a new Web Form page named **ShowFeatured.aspx**.

6. Add a PlaceHolder control to the page.

7. Double-click the Designer surface to switch to the Code Editor and enter the following code for the Page_Load() method:

C#

```
private void Page_Load(object sender, System.EventArgs e)
{
```

```
Control ctlFeatured = null;
Random objRan = new Random();
switch (objRan.Next(2) )
{
  case 0:
    ctlFeatured = LoadControl( "Featured1.ascx" );
    break;
  case 1:
    ctlFeatured = LoadControl( "Featured2.ascx" );
    break;
}
PlaceHolder1.Controls.Add( ctlFeatured );
}
```

VB.NET

```
Private Sub Page_Load(ByVal sender As System.Object,
➥ByVal e As System.EventArgs) Handles MyBase.Load
  Dim ctlFeatured As Control
  Select Case Int(Rnd() * 2)
    Case 0
      ctlFeatured = LoadControl("Featured1.ascx")
    Case 1
      ctlFeatured = LoadControl("Featured2.ascx")
  End Select
  PlaceHolder1.Controls.Add(ctlFeatured)
End Sub
```

8. Right-click the ShowFeatured.aspx page in the Solution Explorer window and select Build and Browse.

Each time you open the ShowFeatured.aspx page, one of the two Web User Controls is randomly loaded into the page by calling the LoadControl() method of the Page class. The Web User Control is inserted into the PlaceHolder control.

Summary

In this chapter, you learned how to build Web User Controls to create reusable user interface elements. For example, you learned how to create a standard header for all the Web Form Pages in your project by building a header Web User Control. You also learned how to create Web User Controls that display dynamic content and contain form elements. Finally, you looked at how you could dynamically load Web User Controls from the hard drive.

6

Debugging Your Web Form Pages

IN THIS CHAPTER

- Buildling Your Project
- Using the Visual Studio .NET Debugger
- Page and Application Tracing

This chapter tackles the three related topics of building, debugging, and tracing your Web projects. The first section examines in detail what happens when you build a project. We'll also discuss the different types of errors that can occur in an application.

Next, we look at the integrated Visual Studio .NET debugger. You'll learn how to use the debugger to set breakpoints and step through your code.

Finally, you learn how to take advantage of both page and application tracing. You can use both types of tracing to view debugging information from a live application.

In this chapter, you will learn

- How to build your application in both debug and release modes

- The different categories of errors in your application

- How to use the Visual Studio .NET debugger

- How to trace the execution of a single page or all pages in an application

Building Your Project

Visual Studio .NET supports three methods for compiling and executing your Web Forms application:

- Build and Browse

- Start

- Start without Debugging

First, you can perform a Build and Browse. This option is available from the File menu and is also available when you right-click a page in Solution Explorer. Finally, you can perform a Build and Browse by using the keyboard combination Ctrl+F8.

When you select a page and perform a Build and Browse, all the pages in the same project as the selected page are compiled. Pages in other (independent) projects are not compiled. After the project is compiled, the selected page appears in a browser window that opens in Visual Studio .NET.

> **NOTE**
>
> I'm oversimplifying a bit in this section because building one project might cause other *dependent* projects to be built (even when using the Build command rather than the Build Solution command). For example, building an ASP.NET Web Application project that depends on a Web Control Library project will cause both projects to be built. You can view project dependencies by selecting Project Dependencies from the Project menu.

A second method of compiling pages is by using the Start menu option. You can start an application from the Debug menu by clicking the Start icon on the toolbar (the VCR run button) or by using the F5 keyboard shortcut.

Before you can use the Start option, you need to specify a start page and, if you have multiple projects in your solution, a startup project. You specify a start page by right-clicking a file in the Solution Explorer window and selecting Set As Start Page. You specify a startup project by right-clicking a project in Solution Explorer and selecting Set As Startup Project.

When you start an application, the application builds the project in a solution and opens an external browser that displays the startup page. You must close this external window before you can return to editing the files in the solution.

> **TIP**
>
> If you don't need to use the debugger, performing a Build and Browse is the fastest way to compile and view a page.

Finally, you can compile an application by using the Start without Debugging menu option. This menu option is available under the Debug menu. You can also start an application without debugging by using the keyboard combination Ctrl+F5. The Start without Debugging command also opens an external browser, so it can be slower than doing a Build and Browse.

Building in Debug and Release Mode

Regardless of the method you use to build an application, the application is compiled in debug mode by default. This is bad. Building an application in debug mode can have a severe impact on performance.

Before you release an application into production, you'll need to modify two configuration settings. First, select Release from the Solution Configurations drop-down list (see Figure 6.1). After you select Release, make sure that you build your application one more time.

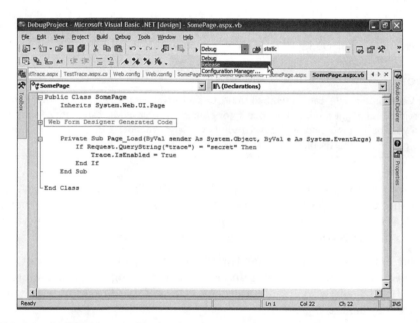

FIGURE 6.1   Building an application in release mode.

Second, you'll need to modify your application's Web.Config file. Open the Web.Config file from Solution Explorer. Find the <compilation> section and assign the value false to the debug attribute.

When developing an application, you normally need to develop the application in debug mode. If you don't develop the application in debug mode, you cannot view runtime errors and you cannot use the integrated Visual Studio .NET debugger.

When you build an application in debug mode, the /debug and /optimize compiler options are sent to the C# or VB.NET compiler. The /debug option causes the compiler to generate a programmer database (.pdb) file. Without a .pdb file, Visual Studio .NET cannot display runtime errors. The .pdb file contains a mapping between MSIL code and source code.

The /optimize compiler option tells the compiler to perform automatic optimizations on your code. However, because the compiler may optimize your code by rearranging it, enabling optimization can prevent debugging from working.

Explicit and Dynamic Compilation

A Web Form Page consists of two files—the presentation page and the code-behind file. The two parts of a Web Form Page are compiled in different ways.

The code-behind file must be explicitly compiled. When you compile a project in Visual Studio .NET, you are compiling the code-behind files in the project. All the code-behind files are compiled into a single assembly (.dll file) that has the same name as your project. This assembly is placed in the /bin folder of your application.

> **NOTE**
>
> If Visual Studio .NET cannot write to the /bin directory, it won't be able to compile your project. You might run into this issue if, for example, you have Microsoft Index Server running on your development computer. Microsoft Index Server can lock a directory while indexing. To get around this problem, disable Index Server.

You can view this assembly in a project by selecting Show All Files from the Project menu and expanding the Bin folder in the Solution Explorer window. When a project is compiled in Debug mode, this folder will contain a .dll file and a .pdb file. When a project is compiled in release mode, it will contain only the .dll file.

The presentation part of your Web Form Pages—the .aspx files—also must be compiled. However, you are not responsible for compiling the presentation pages. The ASP.NET Framework handles the compilation of these pages for you in a process known as *dynamic compilation*.

The ASP.NET Framework automatically compiles any .aspx page when the page is first requested. The compiled assembly that corresponds to the requested page is stored in the following folder:

```
\WINNT\Microsoft.NET\Framework\Framework Version\
➥Temporary ASP.NET Files\Project Name\
```

If you look in this folder, you'll find folders and files with strange names like 1e994b and 892323.dll. The .dll files correspond to the compiled presentation pages. If you are really curious, you can open these files with ILDasm, the Intermediate Language Dissassembler, and view their contents.

When the presentation pages in an application are compiled in debug mode (in other words, <compilation debug=true /> in the Web.Config file), a bunch of additional files are added to the folder. For example, you should see files with the extensions .cmdline, .cs, and .vb. The .cmdline files contain the actual statement that was sent to the compiler to dynamically compile a presentation page. The .cs and .vb files contain the source code for the presentation page class file.

Displaying Errors in Your Application

There are four types of errors that might prevent a Web Form Page from executing:

- *Configuration Errors*—These are caused by errors in the Web.Config file (for example, if you have an opening tag without a matching closing tag).

- *Parser Errors*—These are caused by problems in a Web Form Page (for example, if you attempt to use the non-existent `<asp:DoesNotExist>` control).

- *Compilation Errors*—These errors are language specific and can be caught at compile time (for example, assigning a value of the wrong data type to a property).

- *Runtime Errors*—There are errors that could not be caught by the compiler. Examples include null reference and division by zero exceptions. These are the nastiest errors because they are the most difficult to debug.

There are two configuration settings that determine how errors are displayed. First, you need to enable debugging for both the code-behind files and the presentation pages in your application to view detailed runtime error information. Unless debugging is enabled, .pdb files are not generated and the source of the error cannot be displayed (both of these options are enabled by default).

Second, by default, errors are not displayed on a remote computer for security reasons. If you are developing an application on a remote Web server, you'll need to disable custom errors to see error messages. Open the Web.Config file from the Solution Explorer window, find the `<customErrors>` tag and assign the value Off to the mode attribute. Disabling custom errors will cause errors to be displayed on a remote computer. For this reason, you need to be careful to re-enable custom errors when you are ready to deploy your Web application.

After you have made these configuration changes, you can view error information in two places. When you compile the code-behind pages in a project, you can view any compilation errors by opening the Task List window (Select Show Tasks from the View menu and open Build Errors). All other errors will appear in the Web Form Page itself when it is displayed in a browser.

NOTE

The Task List window also displays Intellisense code validation errors. For example, if you attempt to nest a `<ul>` tag directly beneath a `<table>` tag in a presentation page, an error will appear in the Task List window with a red squiggly line. These errors do not prevent your project from being compiled.

Using the Visual Studio .NET Debugger

You can use the integrated Visual Studio .NET debugger to step through an executing ASP.NET application line-by-line and view the values of any variables. The debugger is an invaluable tool for tracking down problems in your code.

In the following sections, you'll learn how to set breakpoints, create watches, handle exceptions, and debug client-side scripts and SQL stored procedures.

Adding Breakpoints

Before you can debug an application, you need to set one or more breakpoints. A *breakpoint* is a point in your code where you want the execution of your application to temporarily stop. After you stop your application at a breakpoint, you can step through your code and view the values of variables.

You set a breakpoint by clicking on the left margin of the Code Editor. A breakpoint is represented with a filled red circle (see Figure 6.2).

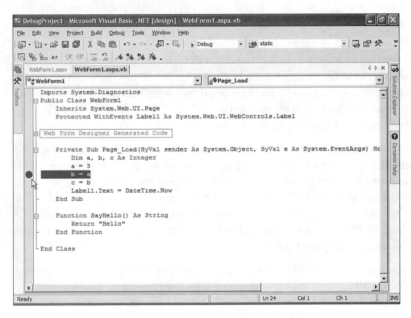

FIGURE 6.2   Adding a breakpoint.

After you add a breakpoint, start your application by selecting Start from the Debug menu (you'll need to specify the Startup Page and Startup Project in the Solution Explorer window). The Web Form Page that was selected as the start page will stop executing when the breakpoint is hit.

TIP

As an alternative to setting a breakpoint, you can use the Run to Cursor command. Right-click anywhere within the Code Editor and select Run to Cursor.

Stepping Through Code

After your code has hit a breakpoint, you can step through your code line-by-line by using the commands from the Debug toolbar. From the Debug toolbar, the Debug menu, or by using special keys, you can:

- *Continue*—Resumes execution of the application until the next breakpoint is hit or the application terminates (use F5 from the keyboard).

- *Break All*—Enables you to manually break the execution of an application. Clicking Break All when an application is running will cause the application to stop in the same way as if a breakpoint were hit (use Ctrl+Alt+Break from the keyboard).

- *Stop Debugging*—Disables continued debugging for the application. Causes all future breakpoints to be ignored (use Shift+F5 from the keyboard).

- *Restart*—Restarts the application and stops at the first breakpoint (use Ctrl+Shift+F5 from the keyboard).

- *Show Next Statement*—Displays the next statement that will be executed (not available from the Debug menu).

- *Step Into*—Executes the next line of code stepping into methods, functions, and subroutines (use F11 from the keyboard).

- *Step Over*—Executes the next line of code stepping over methods, functions, and subroutines (use F10 from the keyboard).

- *Step Out*—Executes the next line of code that is outside the current method, function, or subroutine (use Shift+F11 from the keyboard).

The Step Into and Step Over commands require additional explanation. The only difference between Step Over and Step Out is when the next statement to be executed is a method, function, or subroutine. If you use Step Into, the debugger steps into the function, executes the first statement in the function, and then stops execution. If you use Step Over, the debugger executes the entire function and stops execution at the next line.

NOTE

If you have used earlier versions of Visual Studio, you might have different keyboard shortcuts ingrained into your fingertips for stepping through code. You can change any keyboard shortcut by selecting Options from the Tools menu and selecting the Environment, Keyboard folder. In this case, you'll want to change the shortcuts for the `Debug.StepInto` and `Debug.StepOut` commands.

Alternatively, you can change keyboard shortcuts by changing your profile. Select Show Start Page from the Help menu and click My Profile.

You can also control execution by dragging the yellow arrow that appears at the margin of the Code Editor. For example, if you drag the yellow arrow down, the intervening code will be skipped.

Debugger Windows

There are a number of windows that appear when you are using the debugger. You can use these windows to monitor the current state of your application when your application is running. Not all of these windows appear automatically, but you can open any of them by selecting Windows from the Debug menu.

- *Breakpoints*—Displays information about all the current breakpoints.

- *Running Documents*—Displays all the open documents. This window is useful when you are performing client-side script debugging.

- *Watch*—Displays Watch windows for viewing the current state of selected variables.

- *Autos*—Displays the values of selected variables automatically. When used with C#, this automatically displays the values of variables located in the current statement and previous statement. When used with VB.NET, it displays the values of variables in current statement, the previous three statements, and next three statements.

- *Locals*—Displays the values of all variables in the current context. For example, it displays the values of all variables contained in the current method, function, or subroutine.

- *This/Me*—Displays all the properties of the current object, (for example, the window displays all the properties of the current Web Form Page).

- *Immediate*—Enables you to view and modify the values of variables directly. You can print the values of variables and assign new values to variables from this window.

NOTE

This is not a complete list of all the windows available while debugging. Some of the windows are pretty specialized. For example, you can view the assembly code that corresponds to the currently executing code by opening the Disassembly window.

Adding Watches

A watch enables you to see the current state of a variable. The Visual Studio .NET debugger supports two types of watches—Watches and QuickWatches.

> **TIP**
>
> You can also view the current value of any variable by hovering your mouse over the variable in the Code Editor. Its current value will appear in a Tooltip.

You can open up to four Watch windows from the Debug, Windows menu. After you open a Watch window, you can add as many variables to the window as you want. There are several ways that you can add an individual variable to the Watch window:

- Select the variable in the Code Editor and drag it onto the Watch window.
- Select the variable in the Code Editor, right-click, and select Add Watch.
- Type the name of the variable in the Watch window.

As you step through your code, the values of variables in the Watch windows are automatically updated (see Figure 6.3). You can even modify the values of variables directly in the Watch window. Modifying the values of variables modifies their values in the executing code.

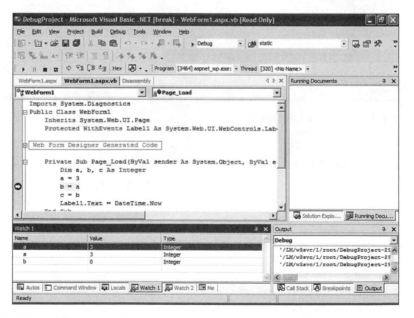

FIGURE 6.3   Adding a watch.

The second type of watch is a QuickWatch. You can open a QuickWatch window by selecting QuickWatch from the Debug menu or by right-clicking in the Code Editor and selecting QuickWatch. If you select a variable in the Code Editor before opening the QuickWatch window, the variable and its current value will automatically appear in the QuickWatch window.

You can use the QuickWatch window for more than just viewing the values of variables. You can also use the window to evaluate expressions and get the return values of methods and functions. After you enter an expression, click Recalculate to see the expression's value (see Figure 6.4).

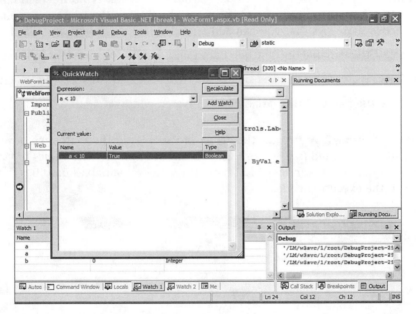

FIGURE 6.4   Using a QuickWatch.

Debugging and Exceptions

All errors in the .NET Framework are represented by exceptions (instances of the Exception class or a derived class). For example, a division by zero error is represented by the DivideByZeroException class.

You can configure the debugger so that when an exception is thrown in your application, the application will automatically switch back to the debugger in the same way as if it hit a breakpoint. That way, you can examine the values of all the variables at the point when the exception was hit. You can even decide to continue the execution of the application after the exception.

You configure how the debugger handles exceptions by selecting Exceptions from the Debug menu. The Exception dialog box enables you to specify responses to two different conditions. First, you can indicate that your code should break into the debugger as soon as there is an exception. You also can indicate that your code should switch to the debugger when an exception is not handled by your code.

These options enable you to handle two different scenarios. You might want to debug an exception even when it is being handled by your code in a Try...Catch block. Alternatively, you might want to break to the debugger only in the case of unhandled exceptions.

Unfortunately, these options can be confusing in the case of Web Form Pages. All exceptions in a Web Form Page are automatically handled by the ASP.NET Framework. Therefore, the only meaningful option when debugging a Web Form Page is to select the option to break into the debugger when the exception is thrown.

You can select this option by selecting Common Language Runtime Exceptions and selecting Break Into the Debugger in the When the Exception Is Thrown panel. After you select this option, a red ball with an X should appear next to Common Language Runtime Exceptions (see Figure 6.5).

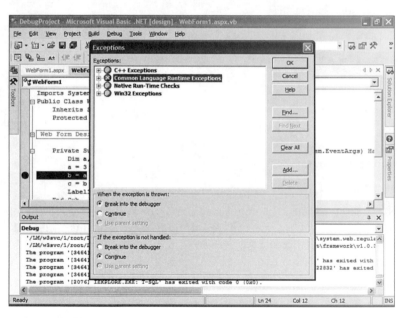

FIGURE 6.5   Handling exceptions in the debugger.

Debugging Client-Side Script

You can use the debugger to debug client-side script in your Web Form Pages. The debugger can be used with both VBScript and JavaScript client-side code.

The first step in enabling client-side script debugging is to enable debugging in Internet Explorer:

1. In Internet Explorer, Select Internet Options from the Tools menu.

2. Click the Advanced tab.

3. Make sure that Disable Script Debugging is unchecked (this option is located under the Browsing category).

Unfortunately, you can't set breakpoints in the same way for client-side script as you can for normal server-side code. Instead of setting a breakpoint in the Code Editor, you need to use either the debugger statement (in the case of JavaScript) or the Stop statement (in the case of VBScript).

For example, the following client-side JavaScript script will break into the debugger when the debugger statement is hit:

```
function window_onload() {
  var someVar = 23;
  debugger;
  document.write( someVar );
}
```

When debugging VBScript scripts, you need to use the Stop statement:

```
Sub window_onload
  Dim someVar

  someVar = 23
  Stop
  Document.write(someVar)
End Sub
```

When the debugger or Stop statement is reached, the Web Form Page will break into the debugger. At that point, you can step through the client-side code and create new breakpoints in the normal way.

Debugging SQL

You can use the debugger to debug SQL stored procedures, functions, and triggers. You can debug these objects directly or in the context of executing an application.

For example, if you want to step through a stored procedure statement-by-statement, you can simply right-click the stored procedure in the Server Explorer window and select Step Into Stored Procedure. You can also step through a stored procedure when the stored procedure is open in the Code Editor by right-clicking the Code Editor and selecting Step Into Stored Procedure (see Figure 6.6).

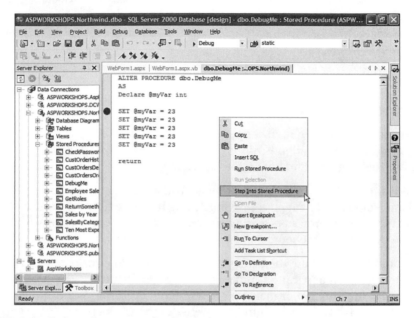

FIGURE 6.6 Debugging a stored procedure.

The more interesting case is when you want to debug a stored procedure in the context of an executing ASP.NET Web application. Before you can do this, you must enable SQL debugging for the application:

1. Right-click the name of your project in the Solution Explorer window and select Properties.

2. In the Properties dialog box, select the Configuration Properties folder and select the Debugging node.

3. Check the SQL Server Debugging check box.

After you complete these steps, you can place a breakpoint in a stored procedure and stop an executing ASP.NET application at that breakpoint. The debugger can move seamlessly between your ASP.NET code and the SQL statements in the stored procedure.

NOTE

I'm assuming in this section that you are debugging an SQL stored procedure located on the same server as Visual Studio .NET and your Web server. There are additional configuration steps that you must complete to debug stored procedures located on a remote SQL Server. See the following section in the Visual Studio .NET documentation:

Visual Studio .NET, Developing with Visual Studio .NET, Building, Debugging and Testing, Debugging, Debugging SQL

Page and Application Tracing

Tracing enables you to output the values of variables, or other debugging information, while your application is running. You can use tracing as an alternative to using the debugger to find bugs while developing an application.

One advantage of tracing over the debugger is that you can use tracing with a "live" Web site. For example, suppose that something has gone horribly wrong with your Products.aspx page. You start getting customer service reports of errors in this page, but you don't know the source of the errors.

You wouldn't want to use the debugger to track down an error on a live Web site because placing an application in debug mode carries with it a severe performance penalty. In this situation, it makes more sense to use tracing. You can use tracing to find out what is happening behind the scenes in the Products.aspx page without the rest of the world knowing that you are debugging the page.

The ASP.NET Framework supports two types of tracing—page and application tracing. We'll examine both types of tracing in the following sections.

Using Page Tracing

In the old days, you would track down errors in an ASP page by using the `Response.Write()` statement. If you weren't sure about the current value of a variable at a certain point in your code, you would `Response.Write()` the value of the variable to the browser window.

The `Response.Write()` statement, used as a debugging tool, has some serious drawbacks. First, if you forget to remove a `Response.Write()` statement before you move your application into production, the whole world will see your debugging information. Second, you can't use `Response.Write()` on a "live" Web application because, once again, everyone in the world will see your debugging information.

Instead of using `Response.Write()`, you can use the `Trace.Warn()` statement. Unlike the `Response.Write()` statement, you can hide the output of every `Trace.Warn()` statement in a page with a single switch. Furthermore, unlike the `Response.Write()` statement, the output of the Trace.Warn() statement only shows up on the local machine by default. That way, the rest of the world does not see your debugging information.

Perform the following steps to enable page-level tracing:

1. Create a new Web Form Page named **TestTrace.aspx**.

2. In the Properties window, select DOCUMENT and assign the value FlowLayout to the pageLayout property and the value True to the trace property.

3. Add TextBox, Calendar, and DataGrid controls to the page by dragging these controls from the Toolbox onto the Designer surface.

4. Double-click the Designer surface to switch to the Code Editor and enter the following code for the Page_Load handler:

C#

```
private void Page_Load(object sender, System.EventArgs e)
{
  Trace.Warn( "A message from me!" );
}
```

VB.NET

```
Private Sub Page_Load(ByVal sender As System.Object,
➥ByVal e As System.EventArgs) Handles MyBase.Load
  Trace.Warn("A message from me!")
End Sub
```

5. Right-click the TestTrace.aspx page in the Solution Explorer window and select Build and Browse.

When the TestTrace.aspx page opens, you should see the page in Figure 6.7. Notice that additional information has been automatically appended to the bottom of the page.

WARNING

Page-level tracing does not work well with pages in Grid Layout mode. The problem with Grid Layout mode is that it absolutely positions elements on a page so the tracing information tends to get hidden behind the page content.

The two most useful sections appended to the page are the Trace Information and Control Tree sections. The Trace Information section displays information about the Page Init, PreRender, SaveViewState, and Render events. It also displays any custom trace information that you outputted with the Trace.Warn() statement, so your custom message "A message from me!" appears in this section.

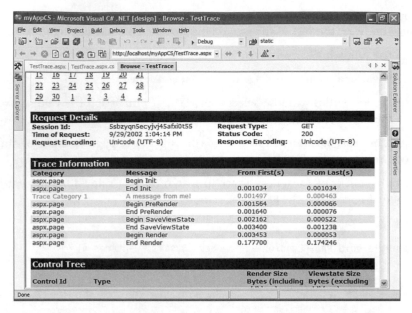

FIGURE 6.7 Using page tracing.

The Trace Information section displays execution speed statistics for each entry. It displays the time in seconds between the execution of the first entry and the current entry. It also displays the time in seconds between the previous entry and the current entry. You can use these statistics to identify slow code.

The Control Tree section shows all the controls contained in the current page. If you look in the control tree, you should see the TextBox, DataGrid, and Calendar controls that you added to the page. The Control Tree section displays the Render and View State size for each control.

> **TIP**
>
> The View State information is valuable when you want to determine which controls in a page are consuming the most View State. For example, if you are using a DataGrid control only to display information, you should disable View State for this control by assigning the value False to the control's EnableViewState property (to learn more about View State see Chapter 17, "Maintaining Application State").

By default, the trace information appears only when the page is opened on the same server as the Web server. This is both good and bad. It means that the rest of the world will not see your trace information when you are debugging a live Web application. However, it also means that you won't see the trace information when developing an application on a remote machine.

You can configure your application to show trace information remotely by modifying the Web.Config file:

1. Open the root Web.Config file from the Solution Explorer window.

2. Find the <trace> section.

3. Assign the value false to the localOnly attribute (be careful, this file is case sensitive!).

4. Save the Web.Config file.

NOTE

You can use the Trace.Write() statement instead of the Trace.Warn() statement. The two statements behave identically except for the fact that the Trace.Warn() statement outputs messages in red and the Trace.Write() statement outputs messages in black. I typically use the Trace.Warn() statement because it is easier to see the output.

Placing Trace Messages in Different Categories

If you need to output a significant number of trace messages from a page, you might want to group the trace messages into categories. You can assign a trace message to a category by passing an additional parameter to the Trace.Warn() method:

C#

```
Trace.Warn("Trace Category 1", "A message from me!" );
```

VB.NET

```
Trace.Warn("Trace Category 1", "A message from me!" )
```

The category can be any string. It shows up in the left column of the Trace Information section when tracing is enabled.

By default, the messages in the Trace Information section appear in order of execution. If you are using categories, it is more useful to group related trace messages by their category. You can do this by modifying the traceMode property of the DOCUMENT in the Properties window. This property accepts the two values SortByTime (the default) and SortByCategory.

Tracing and Exceptions

Trace information appears even when there is a runtime error in the page. This means that you can use tracing to output the values of variables in statements leading up to the exception. The exception information is automatically appended to the Trace Information section.

You can also explicitly write out an exception. This is useful when you are handling exceptions in your code with `Try...Catch` blocks. For example, the following code will output the division by zero exception to the Trace Information section even though it was handled:

C#

```csharp
int zero = 0;
int results;

try
{
  results = 12 / zero;
}
catch (Exception ex)
{
  Trace.Warn("Exceptions", "An Error!", ex);
}
```

VB.NET

```vbnet
Dim zero As Integer = 0
Dim results As Integer

Try
  results = 12 / zero
Catch ex As Exception
  Trace.Warn("Exceptions", "An Error!", ex)
End Try
```

In this code, three parameters are passed to the `Trace.Warn()` statement. The first parameter represents the trace category, the second parameter represents a custom message, and the final parameter represents the exception. Because the exception was handled, the exception information will only appear in the Trace Information and not on the page.

Programmatically Enabling Tracing

In a production application, you don't want page tracing information to be displayed. However, if something has gone wrong with a page, you might want an easy way to display the trace information. For example, when a certain secret string is passed in the query string, you want the trace information to be displayed.

You can programmatically enable or disable page tracing with the `Trace.IsEnabled` property. You can use the following `Page_Load` method to enable tracing only when the query string `trace=secret` is passed to the page:

C#

```csharp
private void Page_Load(object sender, System.EventArgs e)
{
  if (Request.QueryString[ "trace" ] == "secret")
    Trace.IsEnabled = true;
}
```

VB.NET

```vbnet
Private Sub Page_Load(ByVal sender As System.Object,
➥ByVal e As System.EventArgs) Handles MyBase.Load
  If Request.QueryString("trace") = "secret" Then
    Trace.IsEnabled = True
  End If
End Sub
```

For security reasons, you'll want to be careful to use a closely guarded password instead of `secret`. Remember that it is possible to steal database passwords and other sensitive data when tracing is enabled.

Using Application Tracing

Application tracing enables you to gather trace information for every page running in an application. When you enable application tracing, you can view trace information in a special page named Trace.axd.

If you open the Trace.axd page in your browser, you'll receive an error. For security reasons, application tracing is disabled by default. Before you can use application tracing, you need to modify the Web.Config file:

1. Open the Web.Config file from the Solution Explorer window.

2. Find the <trace> section.

3. Assign the value `true` to the `enabled` property.

After you complete these steps, open the Trace.axd page in a Web browser. You should see the page in Figure 6.8.

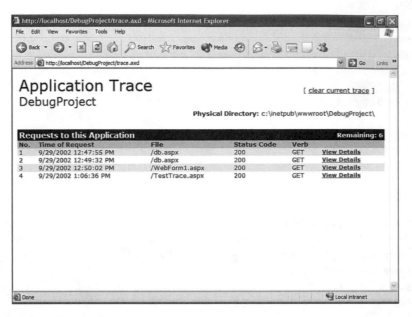

FIGURE 6.8   Using application tracing.

The Trace.axd page shows tracinginformation for 10 requests. After 10 requests, you must flush the current trace information by clicking the Clear Current Trace link at the top-right of the page.

> **NOTE**
>
> You can control how many pages are tracked in the Trace.axd page by changing the requestLimit attribute in the <trace> section of the Web.Config file.

If you open another page in the Web browser—for example, the TestTrace.aspx page that we created in the previous section—and return to the Trace.axd page, you'll see a new entry that corresponds to the page that you requested. If you click View Details, you'll see all the trace information generated for that page.

It's important to note that the trace information will contain any custom trace messages that were created with the Trace.Warn() statement. This means that you can disable page tracing for a page but still be able to see your custom trace information for the page by opening the Trace.axd page.

Summary

In this chapter, you learned how to build, debug, and trace your ASP.NET Web applications. In the first section, you looked at the topic of building applications in detail. You learned how to build an application in both debug and release mode. You also learned about the different types of errors that can be raised when building a Web application.

Next, you learned how to use the integrated Visual Studio .NET debugger. You learned how to set breakpoints and add watches. You also learned how to debug client-side script and SQL stored procedures, triggers, and functions.

Finally, you examined the topic of tracing. You learned how to output custom trace information by taking advantage of both page and application tracing.

PART II

Working with Database Data

IN THIS PART

7 Using the Visual Database Tools

8 Overview of ADO.NET

9 Saving Form Data

10 Using List Controls

11 Displaying Data with the `Repeater` Control

12 Displaying Data with the `DataList` Control

13 Displaying Data with the `DataGrid` Control

7

Using the Visual Database Tools

IN THIS CHAPTER

- Visual Database Tools Support in Different Editions of Visual Studio .NET

- Working with Database Objects in Server Explorer

- Designing Databases with Database Diagrams

- Working with Database Projects

Visual Studio .NET includes a rich set of tools for browsing and creating database objects, such as database tables and stored procedures. You can use these tools to make changes to a database without leaving the Visual Studio .NET development environment.

In this chapter, you'll learn how to take advantage of these tools to

- Browse and create database objects in the Server Explorer window

- Interactively create database tables and define the relationship between tables by using database diagrams

- Build reusable queries and other SQL scripts by creating a Database Project

Visual Database Tools Support in Different Editions of Visual Studio .NET

First, the bad news. Different editions of Visual Studio .NET have varying support for the Visual Database Tools. So, many of the features of the Visual Database Tools discussed in this chapter might not be available to you, depending on the particular edition of Visual Studio .NET that you have installed on your machine.

If you have the Enterprise edition of Visual Studio .NET (either the Enterprise Developer or Enterprise Architect edition), you can take advantage of all of the features of the Visual Database Tools. You can browse tables, execute stored procedures, and view data on any database on your network. You can also use the Visual Database Tools to visually design new tables and other objects for Microsoft SQL Server and Oracle databases.

The Professional edition of Visual Studio .NET also enables you to browse tables, execute stored procedures, and view data on any database on your network. However, you can design new tables and other objects only when working with the Desktop edition of Microsoft SQL Server. In particular, you cannot design new database objects for the full edition of Microsoft SQL Server.

Finally, if you have the standard edition of Visual Studio .NET, you can only access the Desktop edition of Microsoft SQL Server or a Microsoft Access database. You cannot visually design new database objects; you can only browse existing objects and data.

Because this book assumes that you are using (at least) Visual Studio .NET Professional, it also assumes that you will be working with the Desktop edition of Microsoft SQL Server. Fortunately, an instance of the Desktop edition named NETSDK is automatically installed on your computer when you install Visual Studio .NET. We'll be using this instance when discussing the Visual Database Tools in this chapter.

NOTE

If you have Visual Studio .NET Professional Edition and the Desktop Edition of Microsoft SQL Server is not installed, you can install it by re-executing the Visual Studio .NET setup program. Click the Start button on the Toolbar. Point to Settings and then the Control Panel. Launch the Add/Remove Programs applet. You'll need to select the component labeled SQL Server Desktop Engine for installation.

It is important to understand that the Desktop edition of SQL Server is simply a hobbled version of the full edition of Microsoft SQL Server. It is missing some advanced functionality and it is not designed to efficiently handle more than a handful of concurrent users. However, you can use the Desktop edition of SQL Server to design a database and, when you are finished, you can import the finished database objects to the full version of SQL Server.

Working with Database Objects in Server Explorer

You can use the Server Explorer window to browse existing database objects and create new ones. In the following sections, you'll learn how to use Server Explorer to create new databases, database tables, database views, stored procedures, triggers, and database functions.

Browsing Database Objects with Server Explorer

The Server Explorer window contains two nodes—Data Connections and Servers (see Figure 7.1). If you expand the Data Connections folder, you'll see a list of existing database connections. If you expand the Servers folder, you'll see a list of servers on your network.

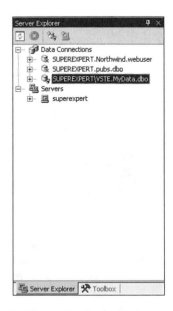

FIGURE 7.1   Working with the Server Explorer window.

You can use either the Data Connections or Servers node to browse the contents of a database. You can expand a database to view its tables, views, stored procedures, and functions. If you expand a table, you can view all of the table's columns. If you expand a view, stored procedure, or function, you can view all of its parameters (see Figure 7.2).

You can control which database objects appear in Server Explorer from the Options dialog box. You can hide or display system objects and you can hide or display objects owned by other users by doing the following:

1. Open the Options dialog box by selecting Options from the Tools menu.

2. Select the Database Tools folder.

3. Select the Server Explorer page.

4. Enable or disable the Show System Objects or Show Objects Owned by Any User check boxes.

5. Click OK.

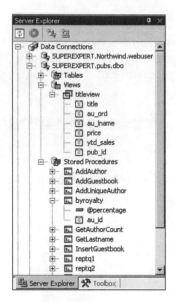

FIGURE 7.2   Browsing columns and parameters in Server Explorer.

Database system objects contain the tables that hold information that SQL Server needs to function correctly. Typically, it is not a good idea to display database system objects. Modifying a system object can corrupt your database.

Retrieving and Modifying Data with Server Explorer

If you right-click the name of a database table in Server Explorer, you have the option to Retrieve Data from Table. Selecting this option retrieves all the rows from the table and displays the rows in a grid (see Figure 7.3). You can also invoke this command simply by double-clicking the name of the table.

> **WARNING**
>
> The Retrieve Data from Table command retrieves every row from a database table. So, if you have a database table with 2 billion records, you might have a very long wait to see the results.

After you retrieve the contents of a database table, you can edit the data. Simply select a cell in the grid and modify the cell's value. As soon as you leave the cell, the data is automatically updated in the underlying database.

You also can use the grid to add a new row to a database table. Enter the new row at the bottom of the grid (it's marked with an asterisk). After you leave the new row, the row is automatically added to the underlying database table.

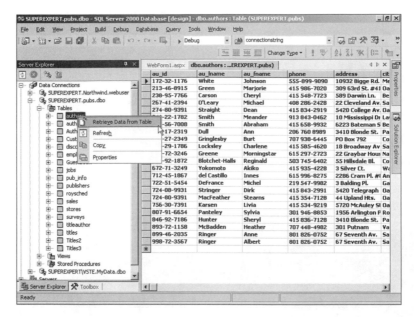

FIGURE 7.3   Retrieving database records.

Finally, you can delete a row of data by selecting the row and selecting Delete from the Edit menu.

Creating New Databases with Server Explorer

When you start building a new database-driven Web application, you might need to create a new database. You can use Server Explorer to add a new database to an existing Microsoft SQL Server database server.

You can add a new database in two places within Server Explorer. If you right-click the Data Connections node and select Create New SQL Server Database, you can add both a new database to your database server and a new connection to the database to the Server Explorer window. Alternatively, you can expand the Servers node, and then the SQL Servers folder, right-click a database server, and select New Database. Either method of creating a new database opens the Create Database dialog box (see Figure 7.4).

WARNING

When creating a new database for the Desktop edition of Microsoft SQL Server, you might receive the error Could Not Obtain Exclusive Lock on Database. If you receive this error, you should restart the database server to clear away any existing connections and locks.

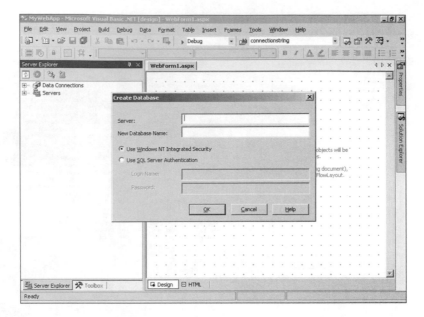

FIGURE 7.4   The Create Database dialog box.

Creating New Database Tables with Server Explorer

You can use the Server Explorer window to create new database tables. To add a new database table, expand a database in the Server Explorer window, right-click the Tables node and select New Table. Selecting New Table will open the Table Designer (see Figure 7.5).

> **NOTE**
>
> Visual Studio .NET Professional Edition enables you to create and modify database tables only when working with the Desktop edition of SQL Server. For example, you can create a new table in the NETSDK database. However, you cannot create new tables for the full edition of Microsoft SQL Server (you need the Enterprise Edition of Visual Studio .NET to do that).

You can use the Table Designer to create a new database table by specifying the properties for the table's columns. In the top part of the Table Designer window, you can list the name, data type, length, and nullability of each column.

The bottom part of the Table Designer window enables you to specify additional properties for a column, such as whether the column is an identity column.

When you are finished designing a database table, select Save *Table Name* from the File menu. The Choose Name dialog box appears enabling you to enter a name for the new table.

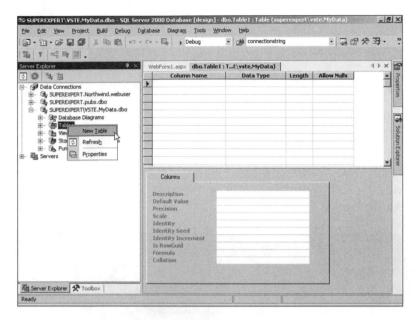

FIGURE 7.5   Opening the Table Designer.

TIP

While designing a table, you can specify relationships, indexes, keys, and check constraints. Select these options from the View menu.

After you create a table, you can modify the design of the table any time in the future by right-clicking the name of the table in the Server Explorer window and selecting Design Table. This opens the same Table Designer that you used to initially create the table.

Creating New Database Views with Server Explorer

A database view enables you to create a virtual table from other tables and views. You can use views to simplify your database queries. For example, if you discover that you commonly need to combine the results of two tables when performing queries, you can represent the contents of the two tables in a single view, or you can use a view to represent a subset of data in a database table.

You create a view by supplying a single SQL Select statement. For example, to create a view that represents all the seafood products from the Products table, you would execute the following `Create View` statement:

```
Create View SeafoodProducts
As
Select * From Products
Where CategoryID = 8
```

After you create a view, you can treat it just like a table. For example, you can retrieve all the rows from the view as follows:

```
Select * from SeafoodProducts
```

To create a new view with the Server Explorer window, right-click the Views node and select New View. When you create a new view, the Query and View Designer opens (see Figure 7.6).

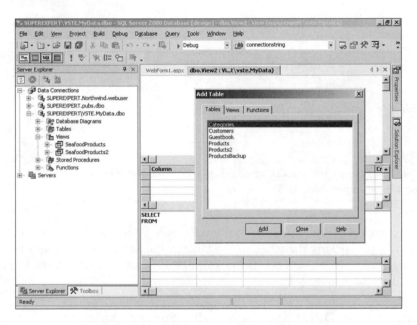

FIGURE 7.6   The Query and View Designer.

When you first open the Query and View Designer, the Add Table dialog box appears. You can use this dialog box to indicate the tables, views, and functions that you need to reference in your view. When you are finished with the Add Table dialog box, click Close.

The Query and View Designer contains four panes:

- *Diagram Pane*—Enables you to graphically specify a query by representing tables and joins between tables

- *Grid Pane*—Enables you to specify a query through a spreadsheet-like grid

- *SQL Pane*—Enables you to enter the raw SQL command for a query

- *Results Pane*—Displays the results of executing a query

TIP

You can hide and display individual panes by selecting Panes from the View menu or from the toolbar.

The Diagram, Grid, and SQL panes provide you with three alternatives for designing a query. Changes that you make to a query in one pane are automatically reflected in the other two panes.

The Results pane enables you to test your query while you are building it. To execute the query, select Run from the Query menu (you can also click the red exclamation mark on the Toolbar).

When you are finished designing a view, select Save *View Name* from the File menu. When you save the view, you are provided with the opportunity to name the view.

After you create a view, you can modify it at any time in the future by right-clicking the view and selecting Design View. You can also test the view by selecting the menu option Retrieve Data from View.

Creating New Stored Procedures with Server Explorer

You can use a stored procedure to package one or more SQL commands into a single statement. A stored procedure is similar to a subroutine in that it enables you to reuse a set of statements.

You can create a new stored procedure in Server Explorer by right-clicking the Stored Procedures node and selecting New Stored Procedure. Selecting this menu option opens a page that contains the following Create Procedure script:

```
CREATE PROCEDURE dbo.StoredProcedure1
/*
    (
        @parameter1 datatype = default value,
        @parameter2 datatype OUTPUT
    )
*/
AS
    /* SET NOCOUNT ON */
    RETURN
```

You can use this script as the skeleton for your stored procedure. For example, to create a stored procedure that adds a new entry into the Products table, you would enter the following code:

```
Create Procedure AddProduct
(
  @ProductName Varchar( 40 ),
  @UnitPrice Money,
  @Discontinued BIT
)
As
Insert Products
(
  ProductName,
  UnitPrice,
  Discontinued
) Values (
  @ProductName,
  @UnitPrice,
  @Discontinued
)
```

After you save a stored procedure, the stored procedure appears under the Stored Procedures node in the Server Explorer window. Furthermore, the code for the stored procedure is automatically updated in the editor. An Alter Procedure statement appears instead of a Create Procedure statement.

While building a stored procedure in the editor, you can take advantage of the Query and View Designer. For example, to add a new query to the body of a stored procedure, right-click the editor surface and select Insert SQL. This option will open the Query and View Designer.

When you are finished designing a query with the Query and View Designer, save the query and close the window. The query will appear in the stored procedure editor with a blue box around it (see Figure 7.7). If you want to modify the query, you can right-click within the blue box and select Design SQL Block.

After you create a stored procedure, you can execute it by right-clicking the stored procedure in the Server Explorer window and selecting Run Stored Procedure. If the stored procedure requires input parameters, a dialog box appears that enables you to enter values for the parameters.

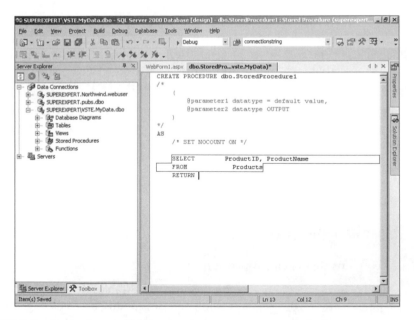

FIGURE 7.7   Designing a stored procedure.

Creating New Triggers with Server Explorer

A *trigger* is a stored procedure that executes whenever the contents of a database table are changed. You can create triggers that execute whenever a row is inserted, updated, or deleted.

For example, suppose that you want to create an audit table that keeps track of every record that has been deleted from the Products table. Whenever a record is deleted from the Products table, a copy of the record is added to the ProductsAudit table. To copy deleted rows from one table to the other, you would create a trigger on the Products table that looks like the following:

```
CREATE TRIGGER Products_Audit
ON dbo.Products
FOR DELETE
AS
Insert ProductsAudit ( ProductName, UnitPrice, Discontinued )
Select ProductName, UnitPrice, Discontinued
From Deleted
```

This code declares a Delete trigger. The Insert statement executes whenever a row is deleted from the Products table. Notice that the Insert statement refers to a table named Deleted. In the context of a trigger, the Deleted table contains any rows deleted from the table associated with the trigger. Within a trigger, you can also use the inserted table to retrieve the new values added to the table.

You create triggers in the Server Explorer window by right-clicking the name of a table and selecting New Trigger. After you select this option, the following code appears in the editor window:

```
CREATE TRIGGER Products_Trigger1
ON dbo.Products
FOR /* INSERT, UPDATE, DELETE */
AS
    /* IF UPDATE (column_name) ...*/
```

This code contains the schema for creating a trigger.

When you save a trigger, the trigger appears under the Tables node of a database (triggers appear with a lightning bolt icon). You can modify a saved trigger by right-clicking the name of the trigger and selecting Edit Trigger.

TIP

When designing an SQL statement for a trigger within the Query and View Designer, use the Change Type command on the Query menu to modify the type of SQL statement. For example, you can use this menu option to create Insert or Update statements.

While creating or editing a trigger, you can use the Query and View Designer. Right-click the editor surface and select Insert SQL. SQL statements appear within the editor surrounded by a blue box. You can right-click within the blue box, select Design SQL Block, and modify an SQL statement with the Query and View Designer.

Creating New Database Functions with Server Explorer

User-defined functions, new with SQL Server 2000, enable you to create procedures that return either a single value or a table. For example, you can define a function that performs a standard tax calculation and use the function in your Select statements, or you can create functions that build a new table from multiple tables.

There are three types of user-defined functions:

- *Scalar-valued Functions*—Return a single value such as an Integer, Money, or Varchar value

- *Inline Functions*—Return a table from a single Select statement

- *Table-valued Functions*—Return a table built from executing multiple `Select` statements

Scalar-valued functions are useful when you need to perform a calculation. For example, the following `Create Function` statement creates a function that multiplies a parameter by the fixed value .03:

```
CREATE FUNCTION dbo.CalculateTax
(
  @UnitPrice Money
)
RETURNS Money
AS
BEGIN
  RETURN @UnitPrice * .03
END
```

After you create this function, you can use it within your queries. For example, the following query returns the UnitPrice and tax amount for each product in the Products table:

```
Select UnitPrice, dbo.CalculateTax( UnitPrice ) As Tax
From Products
```

Because functions can return tables, you can create functions as an alternative to creating database views. A database view can contain only a single SQL Select statement, and a view cannot contain any parameters. On the other hand, a function can contain multiple statements and it can accept multiple parameters.

For example, imagine that you need to work with different subsets of the rows contained in the Products table. Sometimes you want to display all the seafood products and other times you want to display all the produce products. In this case, you'll need to create a function instead of a view because you need to return subsets of rows based on a parameter.

You can create the necessary function with the following `Create Function` statement:

```
Create FUNCTION dbo.SubProducts
    (
    @CategoryName NVarchar( 15 )
    )
RETURNS TABLE
AS
```

```
RETURN
Select Products.*
From Products, Categories
Where Products.CategoryID = Categories.CategoryID
And Categories.CategoryName = @CategoryName
```

This statement declares an inline function. This function is an inline function because the function returns a table based on a single Select statement.

After you create this function, you can retrieve all the seafood products by executing a Select statement like the following:

```
Select * From SubProducts( 'seafood' )
```

Because the function is an inline function, you can also use it in statements other than a Select statement. For example, if you want to double the price of all the produce products, you can execute the following statement:

```
Update SubProducts( 'produce' )
Set UnitPrice = UnitPrice * 2
```

Finally, a table-valued function, like an inline function, returns a table. However, a table-valued function contains multiple Select statements.

For example, suppose that product information is stored in two database tables named Products1 and Products2 in your database. You can treat these tables as a single table by creating the following table-valued function:

```
CREATE FUNCTION dbo.CombineProducts
()
RETURNS
@CombineProductsTable TABLE
(
  ProductName Varchar( 40 ),
  UnitPrice Money
)
AS
BEGIN
INSERT INTO @CombineProductsTable
Select ProductName, UnitPrice from Products1

INSERT INTO @CombineProductsTable
Select ProductName, UnitPrice from Products2
RETURN
END
```

After you create this function, you can retrieve a list of products from both the Products1 and Products2 tables by executing the following Select statement:

```
Select * from CombineProducts()
```

Because this function retrieves data from multiple tables, you cannot use this function in an Update or Insert statement. Table-valued functions cannot be updated.

You can create new user-defined functions within the Server Explorer window by right-clicking the Functions node and selecting New Scalar-valued Function, New Inline Function, or New Table-valued Function. Each option will automatically create the skeleton for the necessary function.

When creating or editing a function, you can use the Query and View Designer to visually create SQL statements. To launch the Designer, right-click the editor surface and select Insert SQL. SQL statements appear in the editor window surrounded by a blue box. You can edit any SQL statement by right-clicking within the blue box and selecting Design SQL Block.

After you build a function, you can test it by right-clicking the name of the function in the Server Explorer window and selecting Run Scalar-valued Function, Run Inline Function, or Run Table-valued Function. If a function has parameters, you'll be prompted in a dialog box to enter values for the parameters.

You can return to a function and edit it at any time by right-clicking the name of the function in Server Explorer and selecting Edit Scalar-valued Function, Edit Inline Function, or Edit Table-valued Function.

Designing Databases with Database Diagrams

You can use database diagrams to perform two tasks. First, you can use database diagrams to graphically document the structure of your database. You can use a database diagram to document the properties of the tables in a database and document the relationship between the tables. After you add one or more tables to a database diagram, you can annotate and print the diagram.

A second and perhaps more important use for database diagrams is for designing the structure of your database. In the previous section, you learned how to create tables with the Visual Table Designer. However, the Table Designer only enables you to work with one table at a time. Instead of using the Table Designer to create new tables, you can create new tables by using database diagrams.

The advantage of creating tables with database diagrams is that you can view and modify the properties of multiple tables in the context of a single diagram. In other words, if you need to build several database tables and define relationships between the tables, you should consider using database diagrams instead of the Table Designer.

In the following sections, you'll learn to take advantage of database diagrams to add existing tables to a database diagram, create new tables, and define the relationship between tables.

Creating a New Database Diagram

You create new database diagrams within the Server Explorer window. You can create database diagrams under either the Data Connections or the Servers nodes.

> **NOTE**
>
> Visual Studio .NET Professional Edition enables you to create database diagrams only when working with Microsoft SQL Server Desktop Edition databases. In particular, you cannot create database diagrams for the full edition of Microsoft SQL Server. To do this, you need to buy the Enterprise Edition of Visual Studio .NET.

In either case, expand a database, right-click the Database Diagrams node, and select New Diagram.

When you create a new database diagram, you are prompted with the Add Table dialog box to add one or more existing tables to the diagram. For example, Figure 7.8 illustrates a database diagram that contains the Categories and Products database tables.

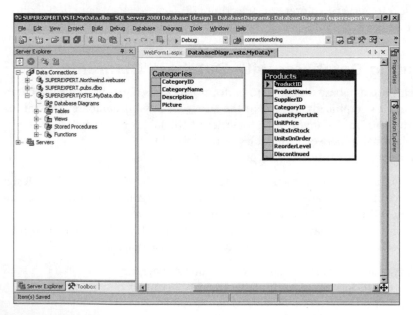

FIGURE 7.8   Creating a new database diagram.

After you open a database diagram, you can add additional existing tables to the diagram by selecting Add Table from the Diagram menu.

Creating New Tables with Database Diagrams

As already mentioned, you can use database diagrams not only when working with existing tables but also to create new tables. To create a new table in a database diagram, select New Table from the Diagram menu. When you add a new table, you'll be prompted for the name of the new table. Next, the table will appear in the diagram.

You can add columns to the new table by supplying the column name, data type, length, and specifying whether the column allows Null values. You can enter these column properties directly onto the Designer surface.

> **NOTE**
>
> To add columns to a table within a database diagram, the table's view must be set to either Standard or Custom. For more information on table views, see the next section, "Controlling How Tables Are Displayed."

If you need to set more advanced column properties, such as a column's default value or whether a column is an identity column, you must open the property pages for the table. You can open a table's property pages by selecting Property Pages from the View menu or by right-clicking the table and selecting Property Pages.

The Property Pages dialog box contains five tabs (see Figure 7.9):

- *Tables*—Enables you to select a table to modify and provide values for its properties, such as the table's name, identity or ROWGUID column, description, and file group.

- *Columns*—Enables you to select a column and provide values for its properties, such as the column's description and default value.

- *Relationships*—Enables you to define relationships between tables. You can use this tab to create a new relationship and specify the primary key and foreign key table used in the relationship.

- *Indexes/Keys*—Enables you to add both clustered and non-clustered indexes and unique constraints to a table.

- *Check Constraints*—Enables you to add a constraint condition to a table.

Finally, you can specify the primary key for a table by selecting a column and choosing Set Primary Key from the Diagram menu. When you add a primary key, a key symbol appears next to the column in the database diagram.

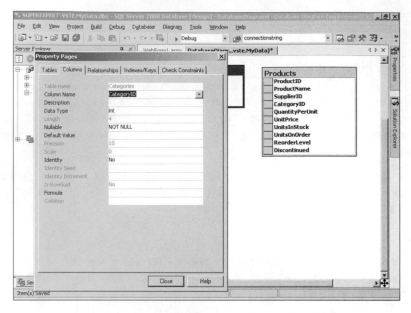

FIGURE 7.9   Opening a table's property pages.

Until you save your changes to the table, the name of the table will appear followed by an asterisk character. You can save your changes by saving the current selection or saving the entire database diagram. Both options are available from the File menu.

Controlling How Tables Are Displayed

You can modify how tables are displayed in a database diagram by selecting Table View from the Diagram menu. You can select from the following options:

- *Standard*—Displays column name, data type, length, and nullability for each column

- *Column Names*—Displays only column names

- *Keys*—Displays only key columns

- *Name Only*—Displays only the name of the table

- *Custom*—Displays a custom set of properties

For example, Figure 7.10 illustrates how the Categories table appears with each of the first four options.

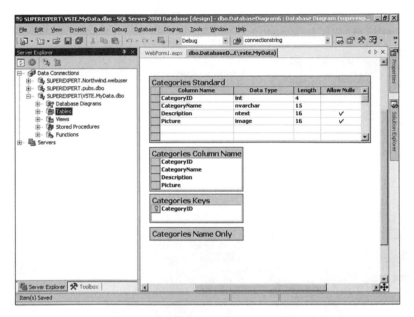

FIGURE 7.10 Different table views of the Categories table.

Notice that the last table view option enables you to specify a custom view. You indicate the column properties that you want displayed in a custom view by opening the Diagram menu, pointing to Table View, and selecting Modify Custom.

You should also notice that there are a couple of other options for controlling how tables are displayed under the Diagram menu. If you select one or more tables and select Autosize Selected Tables from the Diagram menu, the selected tables are automatically resized to fit their content. If you select Arrange Tables from the Diagram menu, the tables are rearranged in an orderly manner on the diagram surface.

Visually Specifying Relationships

You can visually specify relationships between the columns of tables within a database diagram. You can create one-to-many relationships, one-to-one relationships, and many-to-many relationships.

For example, to specify a one-to-many relationship between the Categories and Products table in the Northwind database (see Figure 7.11), do the following:

1. Right-click the CategoryID column in the Categories table and select Set Primary Key.

2. Left-click the CategoryID column in the Categories table and drag the mouse on top of the CategoryID column in the Products table (the Create Relationship dialog box will appear).

3. Click OK to create the new table relationship.

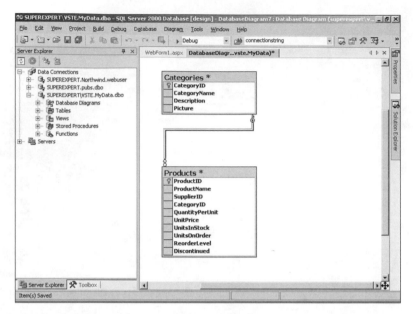

FIGURE 7.11   Creating a one-to-many relationship.

By default, the names of the relationships are not displayed in the database diagram. If you want the names of the relationships to appear, you should select Show Relationship Labels from the Diagram menu.

Adding Annotations to a Database Diagram

You can add text annotations to a database diagram. Text annotations can be used to add any text you want to a diagram. For example, you can use text annotations to document the purpose of a group of tables.

To add a text annotation, open the Diagram menu, point to New, and select Text Annotation. This menu option adds a label to the diagram that you can resize and drag across the diagram surface (see Figure 7.12). You can specify the font to use with the annotation by selecting Diagram, Set Text Annotation Font.

Controlling Page Breaks in a Database Diagram

Because one purpose of a database diagram is for documenting the structure of a database, being able to control how a diagram is printed is important. You don't want page breaks appearing in the wrong places.

FIGURE 7.12   Adding a text annotation.

There are two menu options that you can use to handle page breaks in a database diagram. The Recalculate Page Breaks option on the View menu enables you to recalculate page breaks after you have rearranged tables in a diagram. The View Page Breaks option, also on the View menu, enables you to see page breaks on the designer surface. This option also displays line numbers and the right margin of the page.

Working with Database Projects

You can use a Database Project to create and store a set of queries or SQL scripts. After you create the queries or scripts, you can execute them over and over again against the same or different databases.

In the following sections, you'll learn how to create a new Database Project, add database references to a Database Project, and create queries and SQL scripts.

Creating a New Database Project

Typically, you add a Database Project to an existing Solution. For example, if you are developing a database-driven Web site, you would create a solution that contains both an ASP.NET Web Application Project and a Database Project.

To add a Database Project to an existing solution, perform the following steps:

1. Open the File menu, point to New, and select Project.

2. In the Project Types pane, expand the Other Projects folder and select Database Projects (see Figure 7.13).

3. Enter a name for the Database Project (for example, `MyDBProject`).

4. Select the Add to Solution radio button.

5. Click OK.

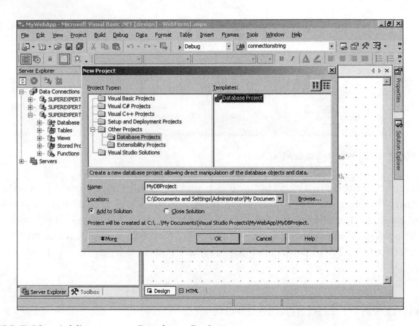

FIGURE 7.13   Adding a new Database Project.

After you complete these steps, the new Database Project will appear in the Solution Explorer window. When the Database Project is first created, it contains three folders—Change Scripts, Queries, and Database References.

Creating Database References

Before you can execute the SQL scripts that you create in a database project, you first need to create a database reference. A database reference contains connection information to a database.

A database reference is similar to the database connections that appear in the Server Explorer window. However, unlike a database connection, a database reference is stored in a particular project and is saved with the solution.

To create a new database reference, do the following:

1. Right-click the Database References folder in Solution Explorer and select New Database Reference.

2. In the Add Database Reference dialog box, you can select an existing database connection to use for creating the database reference, or you can create a new database connection.

3. After selecting or creating a database connection, click OK.

After you complete these steps, the new database reference appears under the Database References folder in Solution Explorer. You can add as many database references to this folder as you want.

You can set the default database reference for an entire Database Project by right-clicking a database reference and selecting Set as Project Default. The icon for the default database reference will appear in red.

You can also set the default database reference for particular folders in a Database Project. When you specify a default database reference for a folder, all SQL scripts and queries contained in the folder will execute against the database reference by default. To set a default database reference for a particular folder, right-click the folder and select Set Default Reference.

Creating SQL Scripts

You create new SQL scripts in a Database Project by right-clicking a folder and selecting Add SQL Script. You can add any of the following types of scripts:

- *SQL Script*—Opens a blank page that enables you to enter any SQL script

- *Database Query*—Opens a page that contains a template for creating an SQL script for retrieving database data

- *Stored Procedure Script*—Opens a page that contains a template for creating an SQL stored procedure

- *Table Script*—Opens a page that contains a template for creating a new database table

- *Trigger Script*—Opens a page that contains a template for creating a new database trigger

- *View Script*—Opens a page that contains a template for creating a new database views

---

NOTE

You can modify the SQL script templates. All the SQL script templates can be found in the following directory:

```
\Program Files\Microsoft Visual Studio .NET\Common7\
➥Tools\Templates\Database Project Items
```

After you create a script, you can execute it in one of three ways. You can right-click the name of the script in the Solution Explorer window and select Run. Selecting Run will execute the script using the default database reference.

If you want to execute the script against a database other than the one indicated by the default database reference, you can right-click the script and select Run On. The Run On command will open a dialog box that enables you to select a particular database reference or database connection.

Finally, you can simply drag and drop a script onto a particular database reference in the Solution Explorer window. When you drop a script onto a reference, the script will execute against the database represented by the reference.

Creating SQL Queries

If you prefer to use the Query and View Designer to build your database commands (see Figure 7.14), you can add a query to a Database Project. To add a query to a Database Project, right-click a folder and select Add Query.

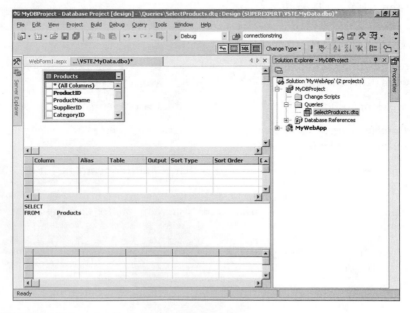

FIGURE 7.14   Using the Query and View Designer.

When you create a query, the default database reference is used to retrieve a list of tables that you can use while building your query. Consequently, you should check that the default database reference is set appropriately for a folder before adding a new query to the folder.

When you are ready to test a query, you can execute the query directly from the Query and View Designer. Select Run from the Query menu. Alternatively, you can click the Run Query button (the red exclamation mark) on the Toolbar.

Summary

In this chapter, you were provided with an overview of the Visual Database Tools included with Visual Studio .NET. In the first section, you learned how to create database objects—such as tables and stored procedures—in the Server Explorer window.

Next, you learned how to design the structure of an entire database by taking advantage of database diagrams. You learned how to create new tables in a database diagram and visually specify the relationship between tables.

Finally, you learned to create and use Database Projects. You learned how you can add SQL scripts and queries to a database project and execute the scripts by using database references.

8

Overview of ADO.NET

IN THIS CHAPTER

- The Three Dualities of ADO.NET

- Creating Database Connections

- Using DataSets, DataAdapters, and DataViews

- Using DataReaders and Commands

- Caching Data for Better Performance

In this chapter, you are introduced to ADO.NET, the data access technology included with the .NET Framework. You are provided with an overview of the objects in ADO.NET that can be used to access a database. You can use these objects to update and retrieve data from a variety of databases, including Microsoft SQL Server, Oracle, and Microsoft Access.

In this chapter, you will learn

- How to create database connections

- How to represent database data with DataSets

- How to represent database data with DataReaders

- How to improve database access performance through data caching

The Three Dualities of ADO.NET

ADO.NET is the next generation of Microsoft's ActiveX Data Objects (ADO). You use the classes in the ADO.NET Framework to retrieve and update database data whenever you create an application by using the .NET Framework. You use the same set of classes, regardless of whether you are building an ASP.NET, Windows Forms, or console application.

The classes in the ADO.NET Framework are extremely flexible. You can use the classes in the ADO.NET Framework to connect to different types of databases, represent data by using different data access models, and work with both relational and XML data.

There are five main classes in the ADO.NET Framework:

- `Connection`   Represents a connection to a data source

- `Command`   Represents a command that can be executed against a data source

- `DataAdapter`   Represents a set of commands that can be executed against a data source

- `DataReader`   Represents a set of records using a connected model of data access

- `DataSet`   Represents a set of records using a disconnected model of data access

OleDb Versus SqlClient

Most of the classes in the ADO.NET Framework have two versions. One version is designed to work with databases using OLE DB providers, and one version is designed to work specifically with Microsoft SQL Server (version 7.0 or later).

For example, there are actually two `Connection` classes in the ADO.NET Framework. There is an `OleDbConnection` class that is used for connecting to a database that has an OLE DB provider and a `SqlConnection` class for connecting to Microsoft SQL Server.

The OleDb classes can be used with any database that has a native OLE DB provider. Most major databases—including Microsoft Access, Oracle, and Microsoft SQL Server—have an OLE DB provider.

The SqlClient classes can be used only with Microsoft SQL Server (version 7.0 or later). These classes are optimized for SQL Server. They work directly at the network protocol layer and do not use any intermediate layers, such as OLE DB or ODBC to communicate with a database. The SqlClient classes represent the fastest database access technology that Microsoft has ever developed.

So, if you are building an application that is designed to work specifically with Microsoft SQL Server, you should use the SqlClient classes. On the other hand, if you need to communicate with another type of database or there is a possibility that you will need to work with another type of database in the future, you should use the OleDb classes.

NOTE

There are additional sets of ADO.NET classes for working with other types of databases or for using alternative types of connections. For example, there is a specialized set of ADO.NET classes that is designed to communicate with a database by using ODBC drivers. There's also a set of classes designed specifically for communicating with Oracle databases.

These classes are not included with the .NET Framework by default. If you need to use these classes, you'll need to download them from the Microsoft Web site.

DataSets Versus DataReaders

The classes in the ADO.NET Framework support two different data access models. You can use the ADO.NET classes to represent data by using a DataSet or a DataReader.

A DataSet represents an in-memory database. When you represent database data with a DataSet, you copy the data from the physical database to the in-memory database represented by a DataSet.

A DataReader, on the other hand, represents only a single record from a database at a time. When you use a DataReader, you loop through the records from the database to retrieve the records into your application.

There are two primary advantages that DataSets have over DataReaders. First, the Visual Studio .NET development environment better supports DataSets. You can use the tools provided by Visual Studio .NET to generate and work with DataSets.

Second, DataSets, unlike DataReaders, can be cached in memory. You can store a single DataSet in your server's memory and reuse the same DataSet across multiple requests to the same or different pages. Caching data in memory can significantly improve the performance of your application.

However, DataSets also have two significant disadvantages. First, when you represent database records with a DataSet, all the records must be copied into the Web server's memory. If you need to represent a database table with two billion records, all two billion records must be copied into memory. In contrast, because a DataReader only represents a single record at a time, you can use a DataReader to work more efficiently with large sets of records.

A second, and perhaps more important, disadvantage of DataSets is that they are significantly slower than DataReaders. If you simply need to display the contents of a database table one time, retrieving database data with a DataSet can be significantly slower than retrieving the same data with a DataReader.

Relational Versus XML Views

You can use the classes in the ADO.NET Framework to represent data by using a relational or XML model. In a relational model, data is represented as rows in a table. In an XML model, data is represented as nodes in a tree.

For example, you can copy the contents of a database table into a DataSet and represent the database data in an XML document. Alternatively, you can load the contents of an XML document into a DataSet and represent the contents of the document as rows in a table.

Creating Database Connections

Before you can do anything else with a database in your application, you need to open a connection to it. You open a database connection by using the Connection class.

There are two versions of the Connection class. You use the SqlConnection class to represent a connection to a Microsoft SQL Server (version 7.0 or later) database, and you use the OleDbConnection class to represent a connection to other types of databases, such as Microsoft Access or Oracle.

There are two ways that you can add a connection to a Web Form Page. You can create a new connection by using the Server Explorer window or by dragging the SqlConnection or OleDbConnection object from the Toolbox.

Using the Server Explorer window is the easier method of creating a connection because you can use the Server Explorer window to provide the connection information only once and create the same connection on multiple Web Form Pages.

To create add a new connection to a SQL Server database to a Web Form Page, do the following:

1. Open the Server Explorer window by selecting Server Explorer from the View menu.

2. In the Server Explorer window, right-click Data Connections and select Add Connection. This will open the Data Link Properties dialog box.

3. In the Data Link Properties dialog box, select the Provider tab and select the Microsoft OLE DB Provider for SQL Server.

4. In the Data Link Properties dialog box, select the Connection tab.

5. Enter the name of your SQL database server. (If the database server is located on the local machine, you can enter **Localhost**.)

6. Choose either Windows NT Security or SQL Server security. If you select SQL Server security by entering your username and password, make sure that you check the Allow Saving Password check box.

7. Select a database from your database server (for example, Pubs or Northwind).

8. Click OK to close the Data Link Properties dialog box.

9. In the Server Explorer window, select the new connection from under Data Connections and drag the connection onto your Web Form Page.

NOTE

If you check the Allow Saving Password option when creating the data connection, you'll get a warning dialog box when you finish adding the connection. Don't let the warning scare you. You are simply being warned that your database password will be saved by Visual Studio .NET so that it can be automatically used when you add the data connection to a Web Form Page.

When you drag the connection from the Server Explorer window onto the Web Form Page, a new `SqlConnection` object should be added to the Designer window (see Figure 8.1).

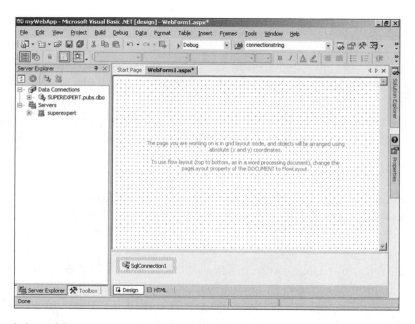

Figure 8.1   Adding a connection with Server Explorer.

The process of creating a connection to other types of databases is very similar. For example, to create a connection to a Microsoft Access database, you would choose the Microsoft JET 4.0 OLE DB Provider and provide the path to the Access database file (the .MDB file) on your hard drive.

When creating a connection to an Oracle database, you would select the Microsoft OLE DB Provider for Oracle and specify the name of the database server and login and password information.

When you create a connection to a database other than Microsoft SQL Server (version 7.0 or later), an `OleDbConnection` object is created instead of an `SqlConnection` object.

NOTE

Notice that we created a connection using the `SqlConnection` object by selecting an OLE DB provider in the Data Link Properties dialog box. This is confusing, but it's how Visual Studio .NET works.

Using DataSets, DataAdapters, and DataViews

You can use a DataSet to represent a set of database records in your Web server's memory. For example, you can copy the contents of a database table into a DataSet and then display the contents of the DataSet on a Web Form Page.

When you work with a DataSet, you need to work (at a minimum) with the following three objects:

- Connection—Represents a connection to a database. When working with Microsoft SQL Server, you use the `SqlConnection` object and when working with other databases, you use the `OleDbConnection` object.

- DataAdapter—Represents the SQL commands used to populate the DataSet with database data or update the database with changes in the DataSet.

- DataSet—Represents a container for data

You should think of a DataSet as an in-memory database. You can add multiple DataTables to a DataSet that represent different sets of database records. Whereas a DataSet is an in-memory database, a DataTable is an in-memory database table.

A DataSet is data source agnostic. You can use a DataSet to represent records from different types of databases, such as Microsoft SQL Server and Oracle. You can also load XML files into a DataSet. You can even combine records from multiple data sources in a single DataSet. For example, you can create a DataSet that contains mixed data from an Oracle and SQL Server database and an XML file.

A DataAdapter represents the bridge between a DataSet and a physical database. You use the DataAdapter to copy records from a physical database to a DataSet. You can also use a DataAdapter to copy records back from a DataSet to a physical database.

There are two versions of the DataAdapter. The `SqlDataAdapter` is used to create DataSets by copying records from a Microsoft SQL Server database. The `OleDbDataAdapter` is used to create DataSets by copying records from other types of databases.

Displaying Database Data with a DataSet

In this section, you will learn how to add the Authors database table to a DataSet and display the contents of the DataSet with the DataGrid control.

> **NOTE**
>
> We'll discuss the DataGrid control in detail later in this book (see Chapter 13, "Displaying Data with the DataGrid Control"). For now, we'll just take advantage of the DataGrid as a convenient mechanism to display database records quickly.

To create and display a DataSet, you'll need to complete each of the following tasks:

1. Create a connection to the Pubs database.

2. Create a DataAdapter to retrieve the data from the Authors database table.

3. Create a DataSet that contains the Authors database table.

4. Use the DataAdapter to fill the DataSet with records from the Authors database table.

5. Create a DataGrid that is bound to the DataSet.

If you haven't already created a connection to the Pubs database in the Server Explorer window, you'll need to create one before doing anything else by doing the following:

1. In the Server Explorer window, right-click Data Connections and select Add Connection. This will open the Data Link Properties dialog box.

2. Select the Provider tab and select Microsoft OLE DB Provider for SQL Server.

3. Select the Connection tab and enter the name of your database server, credential information, and select the Pubs database.

4. Make sure that you have the Allow Saving Password check box checked.

5. Click OK to close the Data Link Properties dialog box.

After you complete these steps, a new connection to the Pubs database is added to the Server Explorer window.

Next, you need to create the DataAdapter by performing the following steps. The DataAdapter is used to retrieve the data from the Authors database table.

1. Add a new Web Form Page named **DisplayAuthors.aspx** to your project.

2. Add an `SqlDataAdapter` to the Web Form Page by double-clicking the `SqlDataAdapter` object located under the Data tab in the Toolbox. This will launch the Data Adapter Configuration Wizard.

3. Click Next to start the wizard.

4. Select the connection to the Pubs database and click Next.

5. Check the Use SQL Statements check box and click Next.

6. Enter the statement `Select * From Authors` into the text box and click Next.

7. Click Finish to close the Data Adapter Configuration Wizard.

The DataAdapter retrieves all the records from the Authors database table.

NOTE

If you want to create a DataAdapter that retrieves data from a database other than Microsoft SQL Server, you need to add an `OleDbDataAdapter` rather than an `SqlDataAdapter`.

Next, you need to create the DataSet and fill the DataSet with data from the Authors database table by using the DataAdapter by doing the following:

1. Add a DataSet to the Web Form Page by double-clicking the `DataSet` object located under the Data tab in the Toolbox. This will open the Add Dataset dialog box.

2. In the Add Dataset dialog box, select Untyped DataSet and click OK.

3. Switch to the Code Editor by selecting View, Code (or double-click the Designer surface).

4. Enter the following code for the `Page_Load` event handler:

C#

```
private void Page_Load(object sender, System.EventArgs e)
{
    sqlDataAdapter1.Fill( dataSet1 );
}
```

VB.NET

```
Private Sub Page_Load(ByVal sender As System.Object,
➥ByVal e As System.EventArgs) Handles MyBase.Load
  SqlDataAdapter1.Fill(DataSet1)
End Sub
```

In the `Page_Load` event handler, the `SqlDataAdapter`'s `Fill()` method is called to fill the DataSet1 DataSet with records from the Authors table.

The final step is to display the DataSet in a DataGrid control. (The DataGrid control is discussed in detail in Chapter 13.) To do so, perform the following steps:

1. Switch to the Designer window by selecting Designer from the View menu.

2. Add a DataGrid control to the Web Form Page by dragging the DataGrid control located under the Web Forms tab in the Toolbox onto the Designer surface.

3. Switch to the Code Editor by selecting Code from the View menu (or double-clicking the Designer surface).

4. Modify the Page_Load event handler by adding the necessary code to bind the DataSet to the DataGrid. The final Page_Load subroutine should look like the following:

C#

```
private void Page_Load(object sender, System.EventArgs e)
{
    sqlDataAdapter1.Fill( dataSet1 );
    DataGrid1.DataSource = dataSet1;
    DataGrid1.DataBind();
}
```

VB.NET

```
Private Sub Page_Load(ByVal sender As System.Object,
➥ByVal e As System.EventArgs) Handles MyBase.Load
  SqlDataAdapter1.Fill(DataSet1)
  DataGrid1.DataSource = DataSet1
  DataGrid1.DataBind()
End Sub
```

5. Right-click the DisplayAuthors.aspx page in the Solution Explorer window and select Build and Browse.

When the DisplayAuthors.aspx page is opened, all the rows from the Authors database table should be displayed (see Figure 8.2). The DataGrid control displays the contents of the DataSet.

Displaying All Rows with a DataSet

In the previous section, you created a DataSet by dragging a DataAdapter from the Toolbox and completing the DataAdapter Configuration Wizard. There is an easier method of adding a DataAdapter to a page. You can simply drag a table from beneath a data connection in the Server Explorer window to create the DataAdapter automatically.

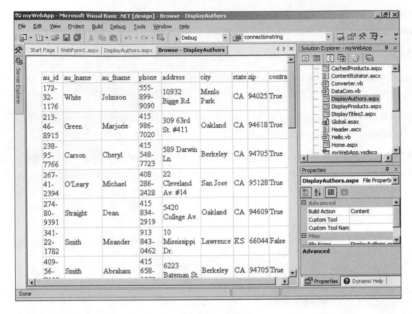

Figure 8.2   Displaying the Authors database table.

If you drag a table from Server Explorer onto the Designer surface, a DataAdapter is created that retrieves all the columns and all the rows from the table. Perform the following steps to quickly create a page that displays the contents of the Titles table.

First, you need to add the necessary objects and controls to the Web Form Page:

1. Create a Web Form Page named **ShowTitles.aspx**.

2. In the Server Explorer window, expand the Data Connection to the Pubs database.

3. Drag the Titles table onto the Designer surface. Completing this step will automatically add a SqlConnection and SqlDataAdapter to the page.

4. In the Toolbox, select the DataSet from under the Data tab and drag it onto the Designer surface. When the Add DataSet dialog box appears, check Untyped Dataset and click OK.

5. In the Toolbox, select the DataGrid control from under the Web Forms tab and drag it onto the Designer surface.

Next, you need to add the code to the page to fill the DataSet and bind the DataSet to the DataGrid:

1. Switch to the Code Editor by double-clicking the Designer surface.

2. Enter the following code for the Page_Load() method:

   C#

   ```
   private void Page_Load(object sender, System.EventArgs e)
   {
       sqlDataAdapter1.Fill( dataSet1 );
       DataGrid1.DataSource = dataSet1;
       DataGrid1.DataBind();
   }
   ```

   VB.NET

   ```
   Private Sub Page_Load(ByVal sender As System.Object,
   ➥ByVal e As System.EventArgs) Handles MyBase.Load
       SqlDataAdapter1.Fill( DataSet1 )
       DataGrid1.DataSource = DataSet1
       DataGrid1.DataBind()
   End Sub
   ```

3. Right-click the ShowTitles.aspx page in the Solution Explorer window and select Build and Browse.

After you complete these steps, the entire contents of the Titles database table will appear in the DataGrid control.

If you expand a table in the Server Explorer window, you can view the columns associated with the table. If you select one or more columns from the table and drag the columns onto the Designer surface, a DataAdapter is created that contains only those columns (and the primary key column).

Using a Typed DataSet

In the previous section, we created something called an Untyped DataSet. Instead of using an Untyped DataSet, you can use a Typed DataSet. The tables and columns contained in a DataSet are represented in different ways in a Typed and Untyped DataSet.

The tables and columns in an Untyped DataSet are represented as collections. In contrast, the tables and columns in a Typed DataSet are represented as strongly typed properties.

For example, to refer to the Authors DataTable in an Untyped DataSet, you would use the following expression:

C# Code

```
dataSet1.Tables["Authors"]
```

VB.NET Code

```
DataSet1.Tables("Authors")
```

To refer to the Authors DataTable in a Typed DataSet, in contrast, you can use the following expression:

C# Code

```
dataSet1.Authors
```

VB.NET Code

```
DataSet1.Authors.
```

One advantage of a Typed DataSet is that it supports Visual Studio .NET IntelliSense. Because tables and columns are exposed as strongly typed properties of a typed DataSet, Visual Studio .NET can display statement auto-completion options as you type.

Another advantage of Typed DataSets is that errors can be caught by Visual Studio .NET at compile time rather than runtime. If you attempt to assign the string `"apple"` to a decimal column in a Typed DataSet, this error can be detected when the Web Form Page is compiled.

A final advantage of Typed DataSets is better support by the Visual Studio .NET Designer. For example, when using a Typed DataSet, you can add columns to a DataGrid by name. The list of column names from the DataSet appears in the Property Pages for the DataGrid.

When you create a Typed DataSet, you add two extra objects to your project—an XML Schema and a .NET class. The XML Schema provides information about the data type of each of the columns in a DataSet. The Schema is used to generate a .NET class that derives from the DataSet class. The .NET class exposes the collections in a DataSet as strongly typed properties.

In this section, we'll create a Typed DataSet that represents the Titles database table. We'll display the contents of the typed DataSet in a DataGrid. The following is an overview of the steps that we'll need to perform:

1. Create a connection to the Pubs database.

2. Create a DataAdapter to retrieve the data from the Titles database table.

3. Add a Typed DataSet to the project that represents the Titles database table.

4. Add an instance of the Typed DataSet to a Web Form Page.

5. Use the DataAdapter to fill the instance of the Typed DataSet.

6. Create a DataGrid that is bound to the instance of the Typed DataSet.

If you haven't already created a connection to the Pubs database, you need to create this connection before doing anything else by doing the following:

1. In the Server Explorer window, right-click Data Connections and select Add Connection. This will open the Data Link Properties dialog box.

2. Select the Provider tab and select Microsoft OLE DB Provider for SQL Server.

3. Select the Connection tab and enter the name of your database server, credential information, and select the Pubs database.

4. Make sure that you check the Allow Saving Password check box.

5. Click OK to close the Data Link Properties dialog box.

After you complete these steps, a new connection to the Pubs database is added to the Server Explorer window.

Next, you need to create the DataAdapter. The DataAdapter will be used for two tasks. You'll use the DataAdapter to create the Typed DataSet and to fill the typed DataSet with records from the Titles table. To create the DataAdapter, perform the following steps:

1. Add a new Web Form Page named **ShowTypedTitles.aspx** to your project.

2. Drag the Titles table from the Pubs Data Connection onto the Designer surface. This will add both a new `SqlConnection` and an `SqlDataAdapter` object to the page.

Next, we need to generate the Typed DataSet by performing the following steps. Creating the Typed DataSet will add an XML Schema and .NET class to your project.

1. Select Generate Dataset from the Data menu. This opens the Generate Dataset dialog box.

2. Under Choose a Dataset, select the New radio button and enter the name **TitlesDS**.

3. Make sure that the Titles table is checked and the Add This DataSet to Designer check box is checked.

4. Click OK to generate the Typed DataSet.

When you add the Typed DataSet to your project, a new file named TitlesDS.xsd is added to your project. A .NET class file is also added to your project. To see this file, select Show All Files from the Project menu.

Because you checked the Add This DataSet to Designer check box, an instance of the typed DataSet is added automatically to your Web Form Page. The instance of the Typed DataSet added to the Web Form Page is named TitlesDS1.

Next, you need to fill the instance of the Typed DataSet with the records from the Titles database table, by doing the following:

1. Switch to the Code Editor by selecting View, Code (or by double-clicking the Designer surface).

2. Enter the following code for the `Page_Load()` method:

   C#

   ```
   private void Page_Load(object sender, System.EventArgs e)
   {
       sqlDataAdapter1.Fill(TitlesDS1);
   }
   ```

   VB.NET

   ```
   Private Sub Page_Load(ByVal sender As System.Object,
   ➥ByVal e As System.EventArgs) Handles MyBase.Load
       SqlDataAdapter1.Fill(TitlesDS1)
   End Sub
   ```

Finally, to display the typed DataSet in a DataGrid, you need to add a `DataGrid` control to the Web Form Page and bind the DataGrid to the DataSet. To do so, do the following:

1. Switch to the Designer window by selecting Designer from the View menu.

2. Add a `DataGrid` control to the Web Form Page.

3. Switch to the Code Editor by selecting Code from the View menu (or double-click the Designer surface).

4. Add two additional statements to the `Page_Load` event handler to bind the Typed DataSet to the DataGrid. The final `Page_Load` event handler should look like the following:

C#

```csharp
private void Page_Load(object sender, System.EventArgs e)
{
    sqlDataAdapter1.Fill(TitlesDS1);
    DataGrid1.DataSource = dataSet1;
    DataGrid1.DataBind();
}
```

VB.NET

```vbnet
Private Sub Page_Load(ByVal sender As System.Object,
➥ByVal e As System.EventArgs) Handles MyBase.Load
  SqlDataAdapter1.Fill(TitlesDS1)
  DataGrid1.DataSource = DataSet1
  DataGrid1.DataBind()
End Sub
```

5. Right-click the ShowTypedTitles.aspx page in the Solution Explorer window and select Build and Browse.

When the ShowTypedTitles.aspx page is opened, all the rows from the Titles database table are displayed in the DataGrid control.

After you create one Typed DataSet in a project, you can add an instance of the Typed DataSet to multiple Web Form Pages in the project. For example, to add an instance of the TitlesDS Typed DataSet to another page named DisplayTypedTitles2.aspx by doing the following:

1. Add a new Web Form Page named **DisplayTypedTitles2.aspx** to your project.

2. Add a DataSet to the Web Form Page by double-clicking the DataSet object under the Data tab in the Toolbox. This will open the Add Dataset dialog box.

3. In the Add Dataset dialog box, check the Typed DataSet radio button and select TitlesDS from the drop-down list.

4. Click OK to close the Add Dataset dialog box.

Before you can use the instance of the Typed DataSet in the new page, you still need to fill the DataSet by using the DataAdapter. Follow the same procedure to create the DataAdapter for this new page as you did for the DisplayTitles.aspx page.

Using DataViews

A DataView provides you with a particular view of the data contained in a DataSet. You can use a DataView to represent the records in a DataSet sorted in a particular order, or you can use a DataView to represent the records in a DataSet filtered by a particular criterion (or both).

A DataView has two important properties:

- `Sort`   The name of the column or columns that specify the sort order of the rows in the DataView (for example, `Title DESC`).

- `RowFilter`   An expression that filters rows in the DataView (for example, `price > 10.00`).

For example, suppose that you want to display a list of records from the Titles database table. However, suppose that you want to display the rows sorted by the publication date, and that you don't want to display any book that costs less than $10.00.

> **NOTE**
>
> I want to emphasize that the example in this section is for illustrative purposes only. A better way to display the rows from the Titles table with a certain sort order and selection criteria would be to build these requirements into the original SQL `Select` statement that you created when building the DataAdapter. We'll come across more realistic situations in which the DataView object can be employed on Chapter 13.

First, let's create a new Web Form Page that contains all the necessary database objects and controls:

1. Create a new Web Form Page named **TitlesDataView.aspx**.

2. In the Server Explorer window, expand the Data Connections folder, expand the Data Connection to the Pubs database, expand the Tables folder, and drag the Titles table onto the Designer surface. Completing this step will add an `SqlConnection` and an `SqlDataAdapter` to your page.

3. Under the Data tab in the Toolbox, drag the `DataSet` object onto the Web Form Page. When the Add Dataset dialog box appears, select Untyped Dataset and click OK.

4. From the Web Forms tab in the Toolbox, drag the `DataGrid` control onto the Web Form Page.

Previously, we've bound the DataGrid directly to a DataSet. This time, however, we want to bind the DataGrid to a DataView so that we can sort and filter the contents of the DataSet by doing the following:

1. Under the Data tab in the Toolbox, drag the DataView object onto the Web Form Page.

Finally, we need to add the necessary code to the page to sort and filter the DataView and bind the DataGrid to the DataView. We do this by performing the following:

1. Switch to the Code Editor by selecting View, Code (or double-click the Designer surface).

2. Enter the following code for the Page_Load() handler:

C#

```csharp
private void Page_Load(object sender, System.EventArgs e)
{
  sqlDataAdapter1.Fill(dataSet1);
  dataView1 = dataSet1.Tables[0].DefaultView;
  dataView1.Sort = "pubdate";
  dataView1.RowFilter = "price > 10.00";
  DataGrid1.DataSource = dataView1;
  DataGrid1.DataBind();
}
```

VB.NET

```vbnet
Private Sub Page_Load(ByVal sender As System.Object,
➥ByVal e As System.EventArgs) Handles MyBase.Load
  SqlDataAdapter1.Fill(DataSet1)
  DataView1 = DataSet1.Tables(0).DefaultView
  DataView1.Sort = "pubdate"
  DataView1.RowFilter = "price > 10.00"
  DataGrid1.DataSource = DataView1
  DataGrid1.DataBind()
End Sub
```

3. Right-click the page in the Solution Explorer window and select Build and Browse.

When the page opens, the titles should appear in order of the publication date. Furthermore, you shouldn't see any book that costs less than $10.00 (see Figure 8.3).

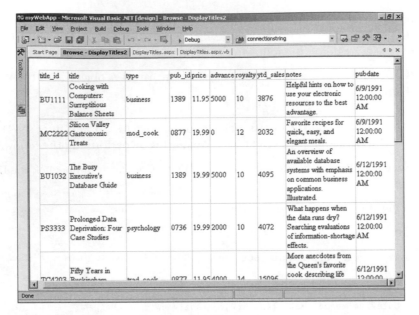

Figure 8.3   Displaying records with a DataView.

Using DataReaders and Commands

To this point, we have examined only one set of classes included with ADO.NET for representing data. In previous sections, you learned how to use the DataSet class to represent a set of database records. However, instead of using a DataSet, you can use a DataReader.

A DataReader is about twice as fast as a DataSet. If you need to display a set of records from a database table in the quickest possible way, you should use a DataReader.

Unfortunately, the Visual Studio .NET development environment does not support DataReaders as well as it supports DataSets. This doesn't mean that you can't use DataReaders when building applications with Visual Studio .NET. It just means that, when working with a DataReader, you'll need to spend more time working in the Code Editor.

Displaying Database Data with a DataReader

When representing database data with a DataReader, you need to work with the following three objects:

- Connection—Represents a connection to a database

- Command—Represents a database command

- DataReader—Represents the set of records returned by the command

Like the majority of the other ADO.NET objects, there are two versions of each of these objects. There is an SQL version for working with Microsoft SQL Server (version 7.0 or later) and an OleDb version, for working with any database that has a native OLE DB Provider (all major databases including Oracle and Microsoft Access). For example, there is both a SqlDataReader and an OleDbDataReader.

Perform the following steps to add the database objects that you'll need to create a SqlDataReader that represents the records from the Titles database table:

1. Add a new Web Form page named **TestDataReader.aspx** to your project.

2. Add an SqlConnection object to the Web Form Page by dragging a database connection from the Server Explorer window onto the Designer surface. (If you don't have any existing connections in the Server Explorer window, see the "Creating Database Connections" section earlier in this chapter.)

3. Add an SqlCommand object to the Web Form Page by double-clicking the SqlCommand object located under the Data tab in the Toolbox.

4. In the Properties window, select the SqlCommand object. Assign the value **SqlConnection1** to the Connection property and assign the text **Select * From Titles** to the CommandText property.

5. Modifying the CommandText property will cause a dialog box to appear asking you whether you want to regenerate the parameters collection for the command. Click No.

Next, we can create the SqlDataReader in the Code Editor by doing the following:

1. Switch to the Code Editor by selecting View, Code (or by double-clicking the Designer surface).

2. Enter the following code for the Page_Load() handler:

C#

```
private void Page_Load(object sender, System.EventArgs e)
{
  System.Data.SqlClient.SqlDataReader dtrTitles;
  sqlConnection1.Open();
  dtrTitles = sqlCommand1.ExecuteReader();
  sqlConnection1.Close();
}
```

VB.NET

```
Private Sub Page_Load(ByVal sender As System.Object,
➥ByVal e As System.EventArgs) Handles MyBase.Load
  Dim dtrTitles As System.Data.SqlClient.SqlDataReader
  SqlConnection1.Open()
  dtrTitles = SqlCommand1.ExecuteReader()
  SqlConnection1.Close()
End Sub
```

The Page_Load() handler creates a SqlDataReader by calling the ExecuteReader()
method of the SqlCommand object. Notice that the database connection, represented
by the SqlConnection object, must be explicitly opened before the ExecuteReader
method is called.

To test our SqlDataReader, we'll display its contents in a DataGrid control. (The
DataGrid control is covered in detail in Chapter 13.) First we add the DataGrid:

1. Switch back to the Designer by selecting Designer from the View menu.

2. Add a DataGrid control to the TestDataReader.aspx page by dragging the control
   from the Toolbox onto the Designer surface.

Next, we can bind the DataGrid to the DataReader:

1. Switch to the Code Editor by selecting View, Code (or by double-clicking the
   Designer surface).

2. Modify the Page_Load() method so that it contains the following code:

   C#

```
private void Page_Load(object sender, System.EventArgs e)
{
  System.Data.SqlClient.SqlDataReader dtrTitles;
  sqlConnection1.Open();
  dtrTitles = sqlCommand1.ExecuteReader();
  DataGrid1.DataSource = dtrTitles;
  DataGrid1.DataBind();
  sqlConnection1.Close();
}
```

   VB.NET

```
Private Sub Page_Load(ByVal sender As System.Object,
➥ByVal e As System.EventArgs) Handles MyBase.Load
```

```
    Dim dtrTitles As System.Data.SqlClient.SqlDataReader
    SqlConnection1.Open()
    dtrTitles = SqlCommand1.ExecuteReader()
    DataGrid1.DataSource = dtrTitles
    DataGrid1.DataBind()
    SqlConnection1.Close()
End Sub
```

3. In the Solution Explorer window, right-click the TestDataReader.aspx page and select Build and Browse.

The additional statements in the Page_Load() handler copy the contents of the SqlDataReader into the DataGrid control. When the page is opened, all the records from the Titles database table are displayed in the DataGrid control (see Figure 8.4).

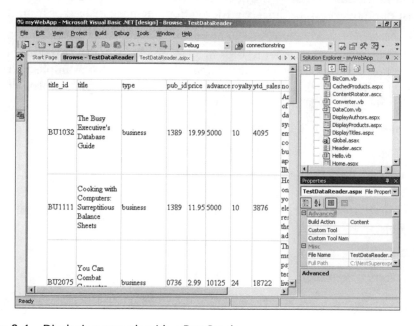

Figure 8.4   Displaying records with a DataReader.

Caching Data for Better Performance

Accessing a database is one of the slowest operations that you can perform in a Web application. Whenever possible, you should avoid opening a connection to a database and retrieving records. One good way to avoid accessing a database is to cache database data in your server's memory. Although access to the data in a database is slow, access to data in memory is lightning fast.

In this section, you'll learn how to take advantage of the Cache object to store a DataSet in memory so that you can use the same DataSet across multiple page requests.

Using the Cache Object

If you add an item to the Cache object in a Web Form Page, the item remains in the cache across multiple page requests. By taking advantage of the Cache object, you need to retrieve a set of records from the database only once.

For example, suppose that you are building an online store that sells a couple thousand products. You could load the list of products into a DataSet and store the DataSet in the Cache. That way, whenever someone wants to view a list of products, the list of products can be quickly retrieved from memory instead of from the database.

Because you can sort and filter records in a DataSet, by using the DataView object, you can even present different views of the items in the Cache. For example, you can display all the products related to Beanie Babies on one page and display all the products related to TeleTubbies on another.

The Cache object has two important methods:

- Insert   Inserts a new item into the Cache

- Remove   Removes an item from the Cache

For example, you would use the following code to add the string Hello World! to the Cache object:

C# Code

```
Cache.Insert( "myString", "Hello World!" );
```

VB.NET Code

```
Cache.Insert( "myString", "Hello World!" )
```

This statement adds a new item to the cache named myString that has the value Hello World!. You can abbreviate the previous Insert statement as follows:

C# Code

```
Cache[ "myString" ] = "Hello World!";
```

VB.NET Code

```
Cache( "myString" ) = "Hello World!"
```

You would use the following statement to remove the myString item from the Cache:

C# Code

```
Cache.Remove( "myString" );
```

VB.NET Code

```
Cache.Remove( "myString" )
```

There are two important warnings that you must heed that concern the Cache object. First, the Cache object is case sensitive (even in VB.NET). Consequently, adding an item named Item1 to the Cache is different than adding an item named ITEM1.

Second, items that you add to the Cache are not guaranteed to be there when you attempt to retrieve them. The Cache object automatically drops items from the cache when your Web server's memory gets too low.

For this reason, you should always check to make sure that an item still exists after you retrieve it from the Cache. You can check whether something exists by comparing it to the value null when using C# or the keyword Nothing when using Visual Basic .NET.

Typically, when you want to retrieve an item from the Cache, you use logic that looks like the following:

C# Code

```
string strMessage = "";

strMessage = (string)Cache["message"];
if (strMessage == null)
{
  strMessage = "Hello World!";
  Cache["message"] = strMessage;
}
Response.Write(strMessage);
```

VB.NET Code

```
Dim strMessage As String
```

```
strMessage = Cache("message")
If strMessage = Nothing Then
  strMessage = "Hello World!"
  Cache("message") = strMessage
End If
Response.Write(strMessage)
```

In this example, an item named message is stored in the Cache. After the item is retrieved from the Cache, the item is compared against either null or Nothing. If the item doesn't have a value, the item is recreated and added to the Cache. In either case, the value of the item is displayed.

In this case, we added a string to the Cache. However, you'll use the same logic with any item, such as a DataSet, that you might add to the Cache.

Caching a DataSet in Memory

In this section, you will learn how to store the Products database table in the Cache object. You will load the Products database into a DataSet and add the DataSet to the Cache.

You'll create a page that displays the cached Products table in a DataGrid. To create this page, you'll need to complete the following steps:

1. Create a connection to the Northwind database.

2. Create a DataSet that represents the Products database table.

3. Cache the contents of the DataSet in the Cache object.

4. Create a DataGrid that is bound to the cached DataSet.

The first step is to create the connection to the Northwind database. The Northwind database is a sample database that is automatically created when you install SQL Server. Perform the following steps to create the connection:

1. In the Server Explorer window, right-click Data Connections and select Add Connection. This will open the Data Link Properties dialog box.

2. Select the Provider tab and select Microsoft OLE DB Provider for SQL Server.

3. Select the Connection tab and enter the name of your database server, credential information, and select the Northwind database.

4. Make sure that you check the Allow Saving Password check box.

5. Click OK to close the Data Link Properties dialog box.

Completing these steps will add a new connection to the Server Explorer window.

Next, we need to create a new Web Form Page and add the necessary database objects and controls to the page by doing the following:

1. Create a new Web Form Page named **CachedProducts.aspx**.

2. In the Server Explorer window, expand the Data Connection to the Northwind database and expand the Tables folder. Drag the Products database table onto the Designer surface.

3. Under the Data tab in the Toolbox, find the `DataSet` object and drag it onto the Designer surface. When the Add Dataset dialog box appears, select Untyped DataSet and click OK.

4. Under the Web Forms tab in the Toolbox, find the `DataGrid` control and drag it onto the Designer surface.

5. Under the Web Forms tab in the Toolbox, find the `Label` control and drag it onto the Designer surface.

Finally, we need to fill the DataSet with data from the Products database table by using the DataAdapter, add the DataSet to the Cache, and display the cached data in a DataGrid.

1. Switch to the Code Editor by selecting View, Code (or by double-clicking the Designer surface).

2. Modify the `Page_Load()` method so that it contains the following code:

C#

```
private void Page_Load(object sender, System.EventArgs e)
{
  dataSet1 = (DataSet)Cache[ "Products" ];
  if (dataSet1 == null)
  {
    Label1.Text = "Retrieving data from database!";
    dataSet1 = new DataSet();
    sqlDataAdapter1.Fill( dataSet1 );
    Cache[ "Products" ] = dataSet1;
  }
  DataGrid1.DataSource = dataSet1;
  DataGrid1.DataBind();
}
```

VB.NET

```vb
Private Sub Page_Load(ByVal sender As System.Object,
➥ByVal e As System.EventArgs) Handles MyBase.Load
  DataSet1 = Cache("Products")
  If DataSet1 Is Nothing Then
    Label1.Text = "Retrieving data from database!"
    DataSet1 = New DataSet()
    SqlDataAdapter1.Fill(DataSet1)
    Cache("Products") = DataSet1
  End If
  DataGrid1.DataSource = DataSet1
  DataGrid1.DataBind()
End Sub
```

3. In the Solution Explorer window, right-click the CachedProducts.aspx page and select Build and Browse.

The first time you open the CachedProducts.aspx page, the Products database table will be retrieved from the database and the message "Retrieving data from database!" will appear in the Label control (see Figure 8.5). However, if you refresh the page (by selecting Refresh from the View menu), the Products table will be retrieved from the Cache object instead of the database.

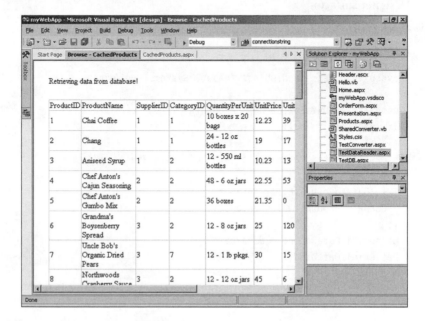

Figure 8.5   Displaying cached records.

Summary

In this chapter, you were introduced to the most important classes for working with database data. In the first part of this chapter, you learned how to work with both Untyped and Typed DataSets to represent and display database data. You learned how to take advantage of DataAdapters to copy a set of records into a DataSet.

Next, you learned an alternative, and faster, method of representing database data with a DataReader. You used a Command object with a DataReader to quickly retrieve and display records from a database table.

Finally, you discovered how to improve the performance of database access in a Web Form Page by using the Cache object. You used the Cache object to store a DataSet in the Web server's memory so that the same cached data can be used across multiple page requests.

9

Saving Form Data

IN THIS CHAPTER

- Overview of the Command Object

- Executing Commands with Parameters

- Executing Commands with Stored Procedures

- Creating a Pizza Order Form

One of the most important tasks that you'll need to perform when building a database-driven application is saving form data to a database table. For example, if your Web site includes a pizza order form, you'll need some method of saving the pizza orders to a database table.

In this chapter, we'll focus on methods for saving data to a database. You'll learn

- How to represent and execute SQL commands with the Command object

- How to use parameters when executing an SQL command

- How to optimize your application by using SQL stored procedures with the Command object

- How to create a pizza order form that saves form data to a database table

Overview of the Command Object

The ADO.NET Command object represents a database command. It can represent a Select, Insert, Update, or Delete command. Or, for that matter, it can represent any valid command that can be executed against a database.

There are actually two versions of the Command object. The SqlCommand object can be used when executing commands against a Microsoft SQL Server database (version 7.0 or later). On the other hand, the OleDbCommand object can be used with any database that has a native OLE DB provider, such as Microsoft Access or Oracle.

The `SqlCommand` and `OleDbCommand` objects share the same methods and properties. So, if you understand how to use one `Command` object, you understand how to use both.

Creating an `SqlCommand` **Object**

You can use the `SqlCommand` object to insert new records into a Microsoft SQL Server database. Imagine, for example, that you want to create a Web Form Page that adds a new category to the Categories table in the Northwind database.

> **NOTE**
>
> You should add new Web Form Pages to an existing ASP.NET Web Application project. For information on creating new projects see Chapter 1, "Getting Familiar with the Development Environment."

To do so, perform the following steps:

1. Create a new Web Form Page named **AddCategory.aspx**.

2. From the Server Explorer window, drag and drop a database connection to the Northwind database onto the Designer surface (adding the connection will add an instance of the `SqlConnection` object named sqlConnection1).

3. Drag and drop an `SqlCommand` object from beneath the Data tab in the Toolbox onto the Designer surface. Adding the `SqlCommand` object will create a new SqlCommand named sqlCommand1 (SqlCommand1 in the case of VB.NET).

4. In the Properties window, select the sqlCommand1 object and assign the value sqlConnection1 to its `Connection` property.

5. In the Properties window, assign the following SQL command to the `CommandText` property of the `SqlCommand1` object:

   ```
   Insert Into Categories (CategoryName) Values ('Books')
   ```

   After you enter the value for the `CommandText` property, the Regenerate Parameters dialog box appears. Click No to close the dialog box.

Completing these steps initializes both an `SqlConnection` and `SqlCommand` object (see Figure 9.1). However, we need to add three more lines of code to the code-behind file for the page to actually execute the `SqlCommand` and insert the data.

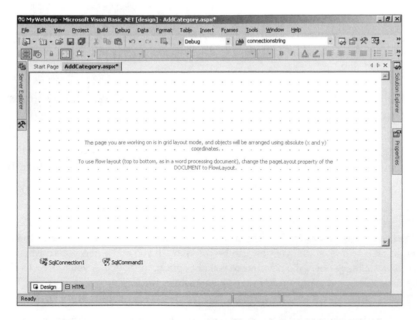

FIGURE 9.1   Adding an SqlConnection and SqlCommand object to a page.

Perform the following steps to add a Button control that will execute the command:

1. Add a Button control to the AddCategories.aspx page.

2. Double-click the Button control. This will switch you to the code-behind file for AddCategories.aspx.

Next, do the following to add the code for the Button Click event handler:

1. Enter the following code for the Button1_Click() handler:

   C#

   ```csharp
   private void Button1_Click(object sender, System.EventArgs e)
   {
     sqlConnection1.Open();
     sqlCommand1.ExecuteNonQuery();
     sqlConnection1.Close();
   }
   ```

   VB.NET

   ```vbnet
   Private Sub Button1_Click(ByVal sender As System.Object,
   ➥ByVal e As System.EventArgs) Handles Button1.Click
   ```

```
        SqlConnection1.Open()
        SqlCommand1.ExecuteNonQuery()
        SqlConnection1.Close()
    End Sub
```

2. Right-click AddCategories.aspx in the Solution Explorer window and select
   Build and Browse.

After you complete these steps, a new record is added to the Categories table
every time you click the button. You can verify that a new record is added by
double-clicking the Categories table in the Server Explorer window (see Figure 9.2).

WARNING

When you double-click a table in the Server Explorer window, you get a list of all the records
in that table. However, this window can be confusing. If you add a new record when the
window is already open, the new record will not appear. In that case, you'll need to requery
the database by selecting Run from the Query menu.

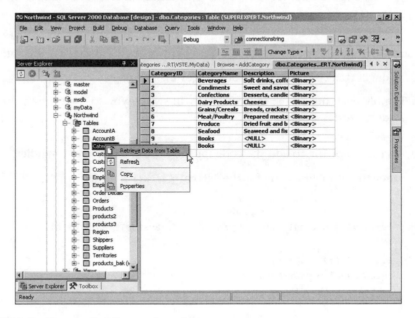

FIGURE 9.2   Data in the Categories table.

The SqlCommand is actually executed when you call the ExecuteNonQuery() method in
the code-behind file. Notice that you need to explicitly open the Connection object
before executing the SqlCommand and close it afterwards.

Creating an `OleDbCommand` Object

You can use the `SqlCommand` object only when working with Microsoft SQL Server (version 7.0 or later). If you need to work with another database server, such as Microsoft Access, Oracle, or an earlier version of SQL Server, you'll need to use the `OleDbCommand` object.

Suppose that you have a Microsoft Access database named MyDB.mdb and the database contains a table named Categories. Additionally, suppose that you want to add a new record to the Categories table within a Web Form Page.

> **WARNING**
>
> Make sure that the Access database is not open exclusively in any other application (including Microsoft Access) or you will not be able to access it in the Web Form Page.

You can do so by performing the following steps:

1. Create a new Web Form Page named **AddCategoryAccess.aspx**.

2. From the Server Explorer window, drag and drop a database connection to the MyDB.mdb database onto the Designer surface. Adding the connection will add an instance of the `OleDbConnection` object named oleDbConnection1 (OleDbConnection1 in VB.NET). If a database connection to the MyDB.mdb database does not already exist, create one by right-clicking the Database Connections folder in the Server Explorer window and selecting Add Connection.

3. Drag and drop an `OleDbCommand` object from beneath the Data tab on the Toolbox onto the Designer surface. Adding the `OleDbCommand` object will create a new `OleDbCommand` named oleDbCommand1 (OleDbCommand1 in VB.NET).

4. In the Properties window, select the oleDbCommand1 object and assign the value oleDbConnection1 to its `Connection` property.

5. In the Properties window, assign the following SQL command to the `CommandText` property of the oleDbCommand1 object:

```
Insert Into Categories (CategoryName) Values ('Books')
```

After you enter the value for the `CommandText` property, the Regenerate Parameters dialog box appears. Click No to close the dialog box.

Now that you've set up both the `OleDbConnection` and `OleDbCommand` objects (see Figure 9.3), you can execute the SQL command.

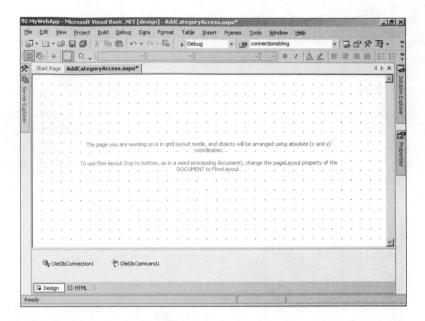

FIGURE 9.3   Adding an `OleDbConnection` and `OleDbCommand` object to a page.

To execute the SQL command, do the following:

1. Add a `Button` control to AddCategoriesAccess.aspx.

2. Double-click the `Button` control. This will switch you to the code-behind file.

3. Enter the following code for the `Button1_Click` handler:

   C#

   ```
   private void Button1_Click(object sender, System.EventArgs e)
   {
     oleDbConnection1.Open();
     oleDbCommand1.ExecuteNonQuery();
     oleDbConnection1.Close();
   }
   ```

   VB.NET

   ```
   Private Sub Button1_Click(ByVal sender As System.Object,
   ➥ByVal e As System.EventArgs) Handles Button1.Click
           OleDbConnection1.Open()
           OleDbCommand1.ExecuteNonQuery()
           OleDbConnection1.Close()
       End Sub
   ```

4. Right-click AddCategoriesAccess.aspx in the Solution Explorer window and select Build and Browse.

Each time you click the button on the Web Form Page, the new category Books is added to the Categories table. You can confirm this by double-clicking the Categories table in the Server Explorer window.

Executing Commands with Parameters

In the previous section, we used the Command object to execute an SQL command that did not contain any parameters. The Command inserts exactly the same data into the database each and every time you execute it. In this section, you'll learn how to use parameters with the Command object.

Parameters are represented by the Parameter object—the SqlParameter object in the case of Microsoft SQL Server and the OleDbParameter object in the case of other databases. When you create a parameter, you can specify values for the following properties:

> **NOTE**
>
> This isn't a full list of the properties of the Parameter object. To view information on all the properties, look up either the SqlParameter or OleDbParameter class in the .NET Framework SDK documentation.

- Direction   Specifies whether the parameter is an input, output, input/output, or return value.

- Precision   Used with decimal (numeric) values to specify the maximum number of digits for the parameter's values. (The number 12.125 has a precision of 5.)

- Scale   Used with decimal (numeric) values to indicate the number of digits to represent on the right of the decimal point for the parameter's value. (The number 12.125 has a scale of 3.)

- Size   Specifies the maximum size of the parameter (for strings, size is measured in characters and for binary data, size is measured in bytes).

- SourceColumn   Used with DataSets to specify the name of the column corresponding to the parameter in the underlying database table.

- SourceVersion   Used with DataSets to specify the version of the parameter value in various editing stages.

- `SqlDbType/DBType`   Specifies the database type of the parameter.

- `Value`   Specifies or contains the value of the parameter.

- `ParameterName`   Specifies the name of the parameter.

Fortunately, the Visual Studio .NET environment automatically assigns the proper values to the majority of these properties for you. The development environment automatically generates `Parameter` objects when you create a new command.

In the following sections, you learn how to use parameters with both the `SqlCommand` and `OleDbCommand` objects.

Using Parameters with the `SqlCommand` Object

Suppose that you need to create a survey form for your Web site (see Figure 9.4). You want to ask users to enter their names and provide some comments about your Web site. In this section, you'll create an `SqlCommand` object that saves data from a survey form to a database table.

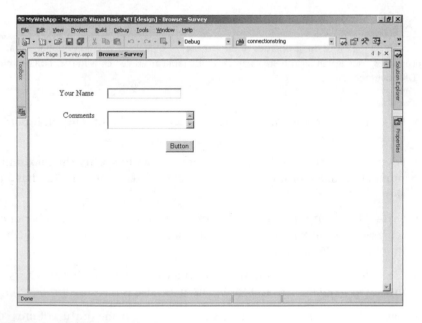

FIGURE 9.4   Creating a survey form.

Before you can create the survey form, you first need to create a database table to store the form information:

1. Create a new database table named **Survey**. Select a database (for example, Northwind) in the Server Explorer window and expand the database folder. Right-click the Tables folder and select New Table. Add the following columns to the table:

Column Name	Data Type	Length	Allow Nulls
survey_id	int	4	No
survey_name	varchar	100	No
survey_comments	text	16	Yes

2. When you create the survey_id column, mark the column as an Identity column by assigning the value Yes to the column's Identity property.

3. Save the table with the name **Survey** (click the icon of the floppy on the toolbar).

Now that we have our database table, we can create a Web Form Page that contains a form for inserting data into the table.

1. Create a new Web Form Page named **Survey.aspx**.

2. Add two HTML Label controls to the page by dragging them from under the HTML tab in the Toolbox onto the Designer surface. Enter the text **Your Name** for the first label and the text **Comments** for the second label.

3. Add a TextBox control to the page and assign the value **txtUsername** to its ID property.

4. Add a second TextBox control to the page and assign the value **txtComments** to its ID property and the value **MultiLine** to its TextMode property.

5. Add a Button control to the page.

Next, we need to add an SqlConnection and SqlCommand object to the page and initialize the SqlCommand object's parameters collection.

1. Add a data connection to the database that contains the Survey table to the Web Form Page. Drag the data connection from the Server Explorer window onto the Designer surface. Adding the data connection automatically creates an instance of the SqlConnection object.

2. Add an SqlCommand object to the page by dragging the SqlCommand object from beneath the Data tab in the Toolbox onto the Designer surface. Adding the SqlCommand creates an instance of the SqlCommand object named sqlCommand1 (SqlCommand1 in VB.NET).

3. Associate the SqlCommand object with the SqlConnection object. In the Properties window, assign the value **sqlConnection1** to the SqlCommand object's Connection property.

4. Assign the following value to the SqlCommand object's CommandText property:

Insert Into Survey (survey_name,survey_comments) values (@survey_name, @survey_comments)

After you modify the CommandText property, the Regenerate Parameters dialog box appears. Click Yes to create the necessary parameters.

In the last step, the SqlParameter objects were automatically generated for you when you specified the value of the CommandText property. If you switch to the code-behind file for the page and expand the Web Form Designer Generated Code region, you'll notice that the following statements were automatically added to the file:

C#

```
this.sqlCommand1.Parameters.Add(new
➥System.Data.SqlClient.SqlParameter("@survey_name",
➥System.Data.SqlDbType.VarChar, 100, "survey_name"));

this.sqlCommand1.Parameters.Add(new
➥System.Data.SqlClient.SqlParameter("@survey_comments",
➥System.Data.SqlDbType.VarChar, 2147483647, "survey_comments"));
```

VB.NET

```
Me.SqlCommand1.Parameters.Add(New
➥System.Data.SqlClient.SqlParameter("@survey_name",
➥System.Data.SqlDbType.VarChar, 100, "survey_name"))

Me.SqlCommand1.Parameters.Add(New
➥System.Data.SqlClient.SqlParameter("@survey_comments",
➥System.Data.SqlDbType.VarChar, 2147483647, "survey_comments"))
```

The first statement initializes the SqlParameter object for the @survey_name parameter, and the second statement initializes the @survey_comments parameter.

There's one last step that you must complete to get the survey form to work correctly. You must associate the TextBox controls with the SqlParameter objects and execute the SQL command.

1. Double-click the `Button` control. This will switch you to the Code editor.

2. Enter the following code for the `Button1_Click` handler:

   C#

   ```
   private void Button1_Click(object sender, System.EventArgs e)
   {
     sqlCommand1.Parameters["@survey_name"].Value = txtUsername.Text;
     sqlCommand1.Parameters["@survey_comments"].Value = txtComments.Text;
     sqlConnection1.Open();
     sqlCommand1.ExecuteNonQuery();
     sqlConnection1.Close();
   }
   ```

   VB.NET

   ```
   Private Sub Button1_Click(ByVal sender As System.Object,
   ➥ByVal e As System.EventArgs) Handles Button1.Click
     SqlCommand1.Parameters("@survey_name").Value = txtUsername.Text
     SqlCommand1.Parameters("@survey_comments").Value = txtComments.Text
     SqlConnection1.Open()
     SqlCommand1.ExecuteNonQuery()
     SqlConnection1.Close()
   End Sub
   ```

3. Right-click the Survey.aspx page in the Solution Explorer window and select Build and Browse.

If you complete the survey form and click the button, the values you enter are added to the Survey database table. You can check whether the new data is being successfully added by double-clicking the Survey table in the Server Explorer window.

Using Parameters with the `OleDbCommand` Object

In the previous section, you created a survey form by using the `SqlCommand` object and `SqlParameter` objects. If you want to work with databases other than Microsoft SQL Server, such as Microsoft Access, you'll need to use the `OleDbCommand` object with `OleDbParameter` objects. In this section, you'll rewrite the survey form to work with a Microsoft Access database table.

First, you'll need to create the Microsoft Access database. If a database named MyDB.mdb does not already exist, create it. Next, add a table named Survey to the MyDB.mdb database. The Survey table should have the following columns:

Field Name	Data Type
survey_id	AutoNumber
survey_name	Text
survey_comments	Memo

Now that we have our database table, we can create a Web Form Page that contains a form for inserting data into the table.

1. Create a new Web Form Page named **SurveyAccess.aspx**.

2. Add two HTML Label controls to the page and enter the text **Your Name** for the first label and the text **Comments** for the second label.

3. Add a TextBox control to the page and assign the value **txtUsername** to its ID property.

4. Add a second TextBox control to the page and assign the value **txtComments** to its ID property and the value **MultiLine** to its TextMode property.

5. Add a Button control to the page.

Next, we need to add an OleDbConnection and OleDbCommand object to the page and initialize the OleDbCommand object's parameters collection.

1. Create a new data connection to the MyDB.mdb database by right-clicking the Data Connections folder in the Server Explorer window and selecting Add Connection. Enter the connection information for the MyDB.mdb database and click OK.

2. Drag the new database connection from the Server Explorer window onto the Designer surface. Adding the data connection automatically creates an instance of the OleDbConnection object.

3. Add an OleDbCommand object to the page by dragging the OleDbCommand object from beneath the Data tab in the Toolbox onto the Designer surface. Adding the OleDbCommand creates an instance of the OleDbCommand object named oleDbCommand1 (OleDbCommand1 in VB.NET).

4. Associate the OleDbCommand object with the OleDbConnection object. In the Properties window, assign the value **oleDbConnection1** to the OleDbCommand object's Connection property.

5. Assign the following value to the OleDbCommand object's CommandText property:

```
Insert Into Survey (survey_name,survey_comments) values (?,?)
```

After you modify the CommandText property, the Regenerate Parameters dialog box appears. Click Yes to create the necessary parameters.

Notice that you do not use named parameters in the Insert Into statement as you did in the case of SqlParameter objects. Instead, you use question marks as placeholders for each parameter.

In the previous step 5, the OleDbParameter objects were automatically generated when you specified the value of the CommandText property. If you switch to the code-behind file for the page and expand the Web Form Designer Generated Code region, you'll notice that the following statements were automatically added to the file:

C#

```
this.oleDbCommand1.Parameters.Add(new
➥System.Data.OleDb.OleDbParameter("survey_name",
➥System.Data.OleDb.OleDbType.VarWChar, 50, "survey_name"));

this.oleDbCommand1.Parameters.Add(new
➥System.Data.OleDb.OleDbParameter("survey_comments",
➥System.Data.OleDb.OleDbType.VarWChar, 0, "survey_comments"));
```

VB.NET

```
Me.OleDbCommand1.Parameters.Add(New
➥System.Data.OleDb.OleDbParameter("survey_name",
➥System.Data.OleDb.OleDbType.VarChar, 50, "survey_name"))

Me.OleDbCommand1.Parameters.Add(New
➥System.Data.OleDb.OleDbParameter("survey_comments",
➥System.Data.OleDb.OleDbType.VarChar, 0, "survey_comments"))
```

The first statement initializes the OleDbParameter object for the survey_name column, and the second statement initializes the OleDbParameter for the survey_comments column.

There's one last step that you must complete to get the survey form to work correctly. You must associate the TextBox controls with the OleDbParameter objects and execute the SQL command.

1. Double-click the Button control. This will switch you to the Code editor.

2. Enter the following code for the Button1_Click handler:

C#

```csharp
private void Button1_Click(object sender, System.EventArgs e)
{
  oleDbCommand1.Parameters["survey_name"].Value = txtUsername.Text;
  oleDbCommand1.Parameters["survey_comments"].Value = txtComments.Text;
  oleDbConnection1.Open();
  oleDbCommand1.ExecuteNonQuery();
  oleDbConnection1.Close();
}
```

VB.NET

```vbnet
Private Sub Button1_Click(ByVal sender As System.Object,
➥ByVal e As System.EventArgs) Handles Button1.Click
  OleDbCommand1.Parameters("survey_name").Value = txtUsername.Text
  OleDbCommand1.Parameters("survey_comments").Value = txtComments.Text
  OleDbConnection1.Open()
  OleDbCommand1.ExecuteNonQuery()
  OleDbConnection1.Close()
End Sub
```

3. Right-click the SurveyAccess.aspx page in the Solution Explorer window and select Build and Browse.

If you enter values for the form fields in the survey form and submit the form, the values you enter are added to the Survey database table. You can check whether the new data is being successfully added by double-clicking the Survey table in the Server Explorer window.

Executing Commands with Stored Procedures

To this point, we have using the Command object to execute SQL commands by representing the SQL command with a string. Normally, this is not the best practice. Instead, you should use SQL stored procedures.

A *stored procedure* is a package of one or more SQL commands that are stored in the database server. It can include both input and output parameters. A stored procedure is the database equivalent of a C# method or Visual Basic subroutine.

There are several benefits derived from using SQL stored procedures. First, and most importantly, using stored procedures can have a significant impact on the performance of a database-driven application. A string representing a SQL command must be parsed and compiled each and every time it is sent to the database. In contrast, a stored procedure typically needs to be parsed and compiled only once.

A second important benefit of stored procedures is that they make your code more modular. You can call the same stored procedure from multiple Web Form Pages. For example, you can write a standard stored procedure for inserting data into the Products table. If your requirements change and you need to modify the logic for inserting the data, you can modify the logic in one place—within the stored procedure—without modifying all the pages that call the stored procedure.

Finally, stored procedures make it easier to perform complex operations against a database. For example, suppose that you need to insert a new row into a database table and return the Identity value for the new row. Retrieving the Identity value when inserting data with SQL strings is difficult. On the other hand, retrieving the Identity value when using a stored procedure is easy (see the "Stored Procedures and Return Values" section later in this chapter).

WARNING

There's a bug in the current version of Visual Studio .NET that prevents it from displaying informative error messages when you attempt to save a new stored procedure using the Visual Database Tools. To view an informative error message, you need to close the window containing the stored procedure instead of saving the stored procedure.

Executing a Simple Stored Procedure

Let's start by creating a simple stored procedure that inserts new records into a database table named Books. You'll create a Web Form Page that enables users to enter a title and price for the book and submit the data to the database table (see Figure 9.5).

First, we'll need to create the Books database table.

1. Create a new database table named Books. In the Server Explorer window, select a database (for example, Northwind), right-click the Tables folder, and select New Table. Enter the following columns for the Books table:

Column Name	Data Type	Length	Allow Nulls
book_id	int	4	No
book_title	varchar	50	No
book_price	money	8	No

2. Make the book_id column an identity column by assigning the value Yes to its Identity property.

3. Save the table with the name **Books**.

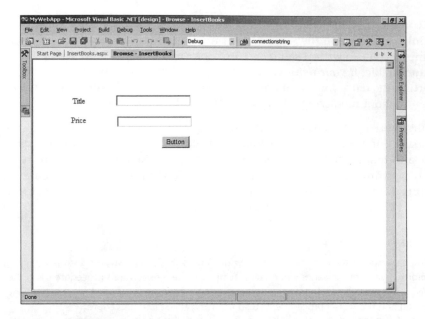

FIGURE 9.5   Form for inserting books into the Books table.

Next, we need to create the stored procedure that inserts the new records into the Books table.

1. Right-click the Stored Procedures folder in the database that contains the Books table and select New Stored Procedure (see Figure 9.6).

2. Enter the following code for the stored procedure:

```
Create PROCEDURE dbo.InsertBooks
    (
        @title varchar(50),
        @price money
    )
AS
Insert Books
(
  book_title,
  book_price
) Values (
  @title,
  @price
)
```

3. Save the new stored procedure by selecting File, Save StoredProcedure1.

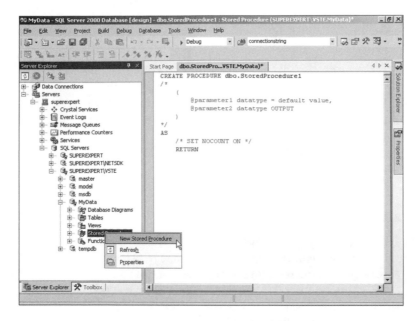

FIGURE 9.6   Adding a new stored procedure.

Next, we need to create the Web Form Page that will call the InsertBooks stored procedure.

1. Create a new Web Form Page named **InsertBooks.aspx**.

2. Add two HTML labels to the InsertBooks.aspx page and enter the text **Title** into the first label and the text **Price** into the second label.

3. Add a TextBox control to the page and assign the value **txtTitle** to its ID property.

4. Add a second TextBox control to the page and assign the value **txtPrice** to its ID property.

5. Add a Button control to the page.

Now, we are ready to add an SqlCommand object to the page that represents the InsertBooks stored procedure. This part is easy. Drag the InsertBooks stored procedure from the Server Explorer window onto the Designer surface. Adding the stored procedure automatically creates a new SqlConnection object and SqlCommand object.

Finally, we need to tie the TextBox controls to the SqlCommand object's parameters.

1. Double-click the Button control. This will switch you to the Code editor.

2. Enter the following code for the `Button1_Click` handler:

C#

```csharp
private void Button1_Click(object sender, System.EventArgs e)
{
  sqlCommand1.Parameters["@title"].Value = txtTitle.Text;
  sqlCommand1.Parameters["@price"].Value = txtPrice.Text;
  sqlConnection1.Open();
  sqlCommand1.ExecuteNonQuery();
  sqlConnection1.Close();
}
```

VB.NET

```vbnet
Private Sub Button1_Click(ByVal sender As System.Object,
➥ByVal e As System.EventArgs) Handles Button1.Click
  SqlCommand1.Parameters("@title").Value = txtTitle.Text
  SqlCommand1.Parameters("@price").Value = txtPrice.Text
  SqlConnection1.Open()
  SqlCommand1.ExecuteNonQuery()
  SqlConnection1.Close()
End Sub
```

3. Right-click the InsertBooks.aspx page in the Solution Explorer window and select Build and Browse.

After you complete these steps, you'll have a form that you can use to add new records to the Books database table. You can test whether records are actually being added by double-clicking the Books table in the Server Explorer window.

Stored Procedures and Return Values

All stored procedures return a value after they are executed. By default, a stored procedure returns a value of 0. However, you can return any other integer value that you want.

For example, return values are commonly used to return the Identity value of a new row inserted into a database table. In the previous section, we created a stored procedure named InsertBooks that inserts a new book record into the Books database table. In this section, we'll modify the InsertBooks stored procedure so that it returns the Identity of the new row inserted.

First, we need to modify the InsertBooks stored procedure.

1. Right-click the `InsertBooks` stored procedure in the Server Explorer window and select Edit Stored Procedure. Modify the procedure by adding the following `Return` statement:

```
ALTER PROCEDURE dbo.InsertBooks
    (
       @title varchar(50),
       @price money
    )
AS
Insert Books
(
  book_title,
  book_price
) Values (
  @title,
  @price
)

Return @@Identity
```

2. Save the `InsertBooks` stored procedure by selecting Save InsertBooks from the File menu.

Next, we need to modify the InsertBooks.aspx page so that it displays the identity value returned by the return value.

1. Add a `Label` control to the InsertBooks.aspx page and clear its `Text` property to an empty string.

2. Switch to the code-behind file for InsertBooks.aspx by double-clicking the `Button` control.

3. Modify the `Button1_Click` handler by assigning the return value to the `Label` control as follows:

C#

```
private void Button1_Click(object sender, System.EventArgs e)
{
  sqlCommand1.Parameters["@title"].Value = txtTitle.Text;
  sqlCommand1.Parameters["@price"].Value = txtPrice.Text;
  sqlConnection1.Open();
  sqlCommand1.ExecuteNonQuery();
  Label1.Text = sqlCommand1.Parameters["@RETURN_VALUE"].Value.ToString();
  sqlConnection1.Close();
}
```

VB.NET

```
Private Sub Button1_Click(ByVal sender As System.Object,
➥ByVal e As System.EventArgs) Handles Button1.Click
  SqlCommand1.Parameters("@title").Value = txtTitle.Text
  SqlCommand1.Parameters("@price").Value = txtPrice.Text
  SqlConnection1.Open()
  SqlCommand1.ExecuteNonQuery()
  Label1.Text = SqlCommand1.Parameters("@RETURN_VALUE").Value
  SqlConnection1.Close()
End Sub
```

4. Right-click the InsertBooks.aspx page in the Solution Explorer window and select Build and Browse.

After you complete these steps, the identity value of new records added to the Books table will be displayed in the Label control (see Figure 9.7).

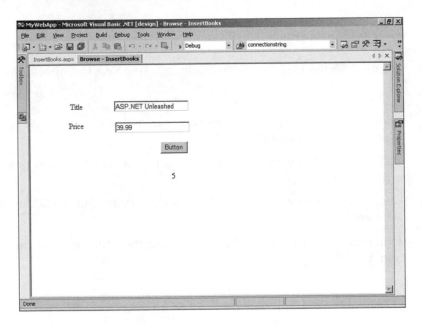

FIGURE 9.7   Returning the identity value from a stored procedure.

Stored Procedures and Output Parameters

The problem with return values is that you can use them to return only one type of value—integer values. Also, you can only return a single return value in a stored procedure. If you need to return different types of values or multiple values from a stored procedure, you need to use output parameters.

For example, suppose that you need to create a page that enables a user to display the title and price of a book given the book's ID (see Figure 9.8). In that case, it makes sense to create a stored procedure that accepts one input parameter—the book's ID—and returns two output parameters—the book's title and price.

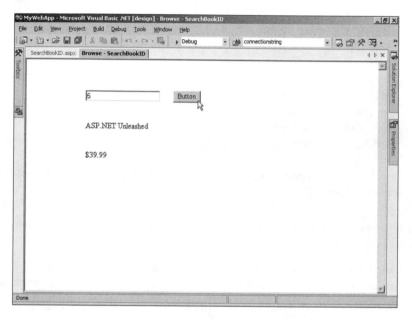

FIGURE 9.8   Retrieving book information.

First, let's create the Web Form Page that contains the form for retrieving book information:

1. Create a new Web Form Page named **SearchBookID.aspx**.

2. Add a TextBox control to the page.

3. Add a Button control to the page.

4. Add two Label controls to the page. Set the EnableViewState property of both Label controls to the value **False**, and set the Text property of both Label controls to an empty string.

Next, we need to create the stored procedure that does the actual lookup on the book ID:

1. Right-click the Stored Procedures folder beneath your database in the Server Explorer window and select New Stored Procedure.

2. Enter the following code for the body of the stored procedure:

```
CREATE PROCEDURE dbo.SearchBookID
    (
        @bookID int,
        @title varchar(50) OUTPUT,
        @price money OUTPUT
    )
AS
Select
  @title = book_title,
  @price = book_price
From Books
Where book_id = @bookID
```

3. Save the SearchBookID stored procedure by selecting Save StoredProcedure1 from the File menu.

Finally, we need to wire-up the SearchBookID stored procedure with the SearchBookID Web Form Page.

1. Drag the SearchBookID stored procedure from the Server Explorer window onto the Designer surface. This will create an SqlConnection and SqlCommand object.

2. Double-click the Button control. This will switch you to the code-behind file for the SearchBookID.aspx page.

3. Enter the following code for the Button1_Click handler:

C#

```
private void Button1_Click(object sender, System.EventArgs e)
{
  if (TextBox1.Text != String.Empty)
  {
    sqlCommand1.Parameters["@BookID"].Value = TextBox1.Text;
    sqlConnection1.Open();
    sqlCommand1.ExecuteNonQuery();
    if (sqlCommand1.Parameters["@title"].Value != DBNull.Value )
    {
      Label1.Text = (string)sqlCommand1.Parameters["@title"].Value;
      Label2.Text = String.Format("{0:c}",
```

```
sqlCommand1.Parameters["@price"].Value);
    }
    sqlConnection1.Close();
  }
}
```

VB.NET

```
Private Sub Button1_Click(ByVal sender As System.Object, ByVal e As
System.EventArgs) Handles Button1.Click
  If TextBox1.Text <> String.Empty Then
    SqlCommand1.Parameters("@BookID").Value = TextBox1.Text
    SqlConnection1.Open()
    SqlCommand1.ExecuteNonQuery()
    If Not IsDBNull(SqlCommand1.Parameters("@title").Value) Then
      Label1.Text = SqlCommand1.Parameters("@title").Value
      Label2.Text = String.Format("{0:c}",
SqlCommand1.Parameters("@price").Value)
    End If
    SqlConnection1.Close()
  End If
End Sub
```

4. Right-click the SearchBookID.aspx page in the Solution Explorer window and select Build and Browse.

After you create the SearchBookID.aspx page, you can enter a book ID and return the title and price of the book. The SearchBookID stored procedure uses two output parameters—@title and @price—to return the title and price information from the Books database table.

NOTE

To keep the code simple, we did not add any validation to the SearchBookID.aspx page. So, if you enter something other than a number in the TextBox control, you'll receive an error. You can fix this by adding a CompareValidator control to the page (see Chapter 4, "Validating Web Form Pages").

Creating a Pizza Order Form

In this final section of this chapter, you'll learn how to create a pizza order form (see Figure 9.9). To this point, for the sake of clarity, all the sample code in this chapter has been oversimplified. In this final section, however, you'll learn how to include all the elements necessary for creating a polished form.

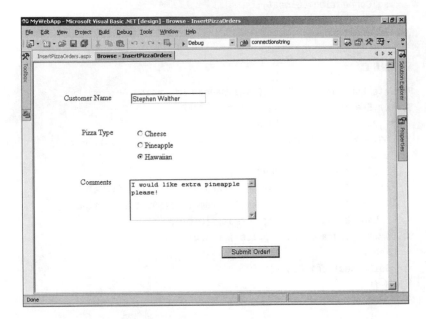

FIGURE 9.9   The pizza order form.

We'll start by creating a new database table to contain the pizza orders. We'll create a Microsoft SQL Server database table.

1. Expand a database in the Server Explorer window (for example, Northwind). Right-click the Tables folder, select New Table, and enter the following columns for the new table:

Column Name	Data Type	Length	Allow Nulls
po_id	int	4	No
po_customer	varchar	100	No
po_pizzatype	tinyint	1	No
po_comments	text	16	Yes

2. Mark the po_id column as an identity column by assigning the value Yes to its Identity property.

3. Save the table with the name **PizzaOrders**.

Next, we need to create the stored procedure for inserting new records into the PizzaOrders table.

1. Right-click the Stored Procedures folder beneath the MyData database and select New Stored Procedure.

2. Enter the following code for the new stored procedure:

```
CREATE PROCEDURE dbo.InsertPizzaOrders
    (
      @customer varchar( 100 ),
      @pizzatype tinyint,
      @comments text
    )
AS
Insert PizzaOrders
(
  po_customer,
  po_pizzatype,
  po_comments
) Values (
  @customer,
  @pizzatype,
  @comments
)
```

3. Save the stored procedure with the name **InsertPizzaOrders**.

Next, we need to create the InsertPizzaOrders form.

1. Create a new Web Form Page named InsertPizzaOrders.aspx.

2. Add three HTML Label controls to the page and enter the text **Customer Name** for the first label, the text **Pizza Type** for the second label, and the text **Comments** for the third label.

3. Add a TextBox control next to the Customer Name Label and assign the following values to the control in the Properties window:

Property	Value
ID	txtCustomer
MaxLength	100

4. Add a RadioButtonList control to the page and assign the value **radlPizzaType** to the control's ID value.

5. In the Properties window, click the ellipses that appear next to the Items property. This will open the ListItem Collection Editor. Enter the following ListItems in the editor:

Text	Value	Selected
Cheese	0	True
Pineapple	1	False
Hawaiian	2	False

Click the OK button to close the ListItem Collection Editor.

6. Add a second TextBox control next to the Comments Label and assign the following values to the control in the Properties window:

Property	Value
ID	txtComments
TextMode	MultiLine
Columns	30
Rows	5

7. Add a Button control to the page and assign the value **Submit Order!** to the Button control's Text property.

At this point, the InsertPizzaOrders.aspx form should resemble the form in Figure 10.

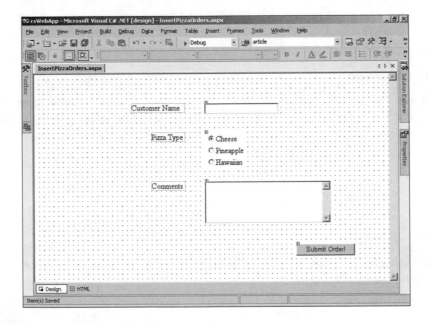

FIGURE 9.10   Partially completed InsertPizzaOrders.aspx page.

Because we are adding all the necessary bells and whistles to this form, we next need to add validation to the form (for more information on the Validation controls, see Chapter 4).

1. Add a `RequiredFieldValidator` control next to the `txtCustomer` TextBox.

2. Set the following properties of the `RequiredFieldValidator` control:

Property	Value
ControlToValidate	txtCustomer
Text	Required!

Next, we are ready to wire-up the InsertPizzaOrders.aspx Web Form Page with the `InsertPizzaOrders` stored procedure.

1. Drag the `InsertPizzaOrders` stored procedure from the Server Explorer window onto the Designer surface. This will add a new `SqlConnection` and `SqlCommand` object to the page.

2. Double-click the Button control on the Designer surface. This will switch you to the Code editor. Enter the following code for the `Button1_Click` handler:

C#

```csharp
private void Button1_Click(object sender, System.EventArgs e)
{
  if (IsValid)
  {
  sqlCommand1.Parameters["@customer"].Value = txtCustomer.Text;
  sqlCommand1.Parameters["@pizzatype"].Value =
radlPizzaType.SelectedItem.Value;
  sqlCommand1.Parameters["@comments"].Value = txtComments.Text;
  sqlConnection1.Open();
  sqlCommand1.ExecuteNonQuery();
  sqlConnection1.Close();
  Response.Redirect("Success.aspx");
  }
}
```

VB.NET

```vbnet
Private Sub Button1_Click(ByVal sender As System.Object,
➥ByVal e As System.EventArgs) Handles Button1.Click
  If IsValid Then
    SqlCommand1.Parameters("@customer").Value = txtCustomer.Text
    SqlCommand1.Parameters("@pizzatype").Value =
radlPizzaType.SelectedItem.Value
    SqlCommand1.Parameters("@comments").Value = txtComments.Text
```

```
        SqlConnection1.Open()
        SqlCommand1.ExecuteNonQuery()
        SqlConnection1.Close()
        Response.Redirect("Success.aspx")
    End If
End Sub
```

Notice that we have coded the `Button1_Click` handler so that it redirects the user to a page named Success.aspx after the user successfully submits an order. This page contains a simple Thank You message (see Figure 9.11). Perform the following steps to create the Success.aspx page:

1. Create a new Web Form Page named Success.aspx.

2. Add an HTML `Label` to the page and enter the text **Thank you for placing your order!**

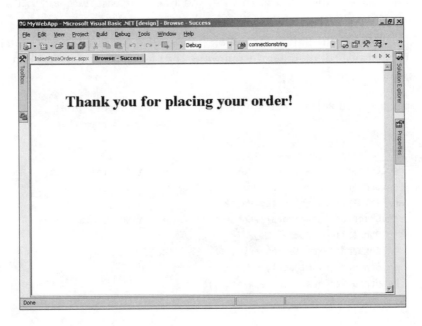

FIGURE 9.11   The Success.aspx page.

That's it! Finally, we are ready to compile and view the InsertPizzaOrders.aspx page. Right-click the page in the Solution Explorer window and select Build and Browse. If you attempt to submit a pizza order without entering a customer name, you'll receive a validation error. When you successfully enter a pizza order, the order is inserted into the PizzaOrders database table and you are redirected to the Success.aspx page.

Summary

In this chapter, you learned how to submit form data to a database table. In the first part of this chapter, you were provided with an overview of the `Command` object and you learned how to execute simple SQL commands by using both the `SqlCommand` and `OleDbCommand` objects.

Next, you learned how to work with parameters when executing a command. You learned how to create input, return value, and output parameters.

Finally, you learned how to use SQL stored procedures with the `SqlCommand` object. In the final section of this chapter, you learned how to create a pizza order form that enables you to add orders to a database table with the help of an SQL stored procedure.

10

Using List Controls

IN THIS CHAPTER

- Overview of the List Controls

- Displaying Database Data in a List Control

- Working with Multi-Select List Controls

- Advanced List Control Topics

In this chapter, you'll learn how to work with the ASP.NET list controls. In particular, you'll learn how to use the list controls to display database data. For example, you'll learn how to display a set of database records that represent book titles in a DropDownList control.

By the end of this chapter, you'll know how to

- Bind database data to the list controls

- Work with multi-select list controls

- Assign default values to a list control

- Copy list items from one list control to another

Overview of the List Controls

You can use any of the list controls to enable users to select one or more items from a list of items. For example, in a registration form, you might want to display a list of countries displayed in a drop-down list.

The ASP.NET Framework includes the following list controls:

- DropDownList   Enables you to select one item from a drop-down list of list items

- ListBox   Enables you to select one or more items from a box of list items

- RadioButtonList   Enables you to select one item from a list of mutually exclusive radio buttons

- CheckBoxList   Enables you to select one or more items from a list of check boxes

All of the list controls inherit from the base .NET Framework `ListControl` class. That means that if you understand how to use one list control, you understand how to use all the list controls because they all share the same base methods and properties.

You can add list items to any of the list controls in one of three ways: by using the ListItem Collection Editor, by adding list items programmatically, or by using data-binding. In the following sections, you are provided with examples of each method of populating a list control.

Adding List Items with the ListItem Collection Editor

If you need to add a small number of list items to a list control, and the list of items will remain relatively stable, then you can take advantage of the Visual Studio .NET ListItem Collection Editor (see Figure 10.1).

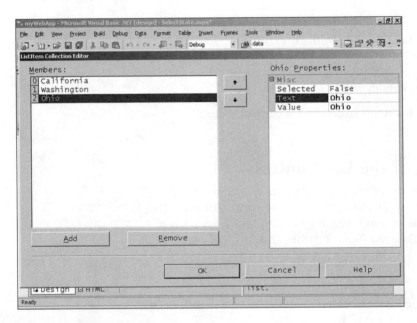

FIGURE 10.1   Using the ListItem Collection Editor.

For example, perform the following these steps to add a `ListBox` control to a form that contains three list items labeled California, Washington, and Ohio:

1. Add a Web Form Page to your project named **SelectState.aspx**.

2. Drag a `ListBox` control from under the Web Forms tab in the Toolbox onto the Designer surface.

3. Select the `ListBox` control in the Properties window and select the `Items` property.

4. Clicking the ellipsis next to the `Items` property opens the ListItem Collection Editor.

5. Add three list items to the editor with the `Text` values **California**, **Washington**, and **Ohio**.

6. Click OK to close the ListItem Collection Editor.

After you complete these steps, the `ListBox` will appear on the Designer surface with the new list items that you added.

Adding List Items Programmatically

Instead of using the ListItem Collection Editor, you can add list items directly to the Items collection of a list control. This is useful, for example, when you need to generate the list items in your code.

For example, suppose that you want to display a list of one hundred options labeled option 1, option 2, and so on.

1. Add a Web Form Page to your project named **SelectOption.aspx**.

2. Add a `ListBox` control to the page.

3. Switch to the code-behind page for the SelectOption.aspx page by selecting Code from the View menu.

4. Enter the following code for the `Page_Load` handler:

C#

```
private void Page_Load(object sender, System.EventArgs e)
{
  if (!Page.IsPostBack )
  {
    for ( int intCounter = 1;intCounter < 101;intCounter++)
    {
      ListBox1.Items.Add("option " + intCounter);
    }
  }
}
```

VB.NET

```
Private Sub Page_Load(ByVal sender As System.Object,
➥ByVal e As System.EventArgs) Handles MyBase.Load
```

```
Dim intCounter As Integer

If Not Page.IsPostBack Then
  For intCounter = 1 To 100
    ListBox1.Items.Add("option " & intCounter)
  Next
End If
End Sub
```

5. Right-click the SelectOption.aspx page in the Solution Explorer window and select Build and Browse.

When the SelectOption.aspx page appears, a list of 100 options will appear (see Figure 10.2).

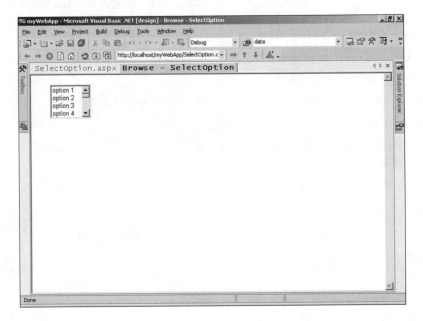

FIGURE 10.2   Adding list items programmatically.

When adding items programmatically, you might want to specify different text and value properties for the list items. For example, you might want to display a list of product names in a list box, but retrieve a product code when someone selects an item in the list box.

The ListItem class has both a Text and Value property. The Text property contains what is actually displayed in the list control. The Value property contains a hidden value for the list item.

You can programmatically add items to a list control by explicitly creating a ListItem and adding the ListItem to the control's Items collection. For example, the following code creates a ListItem with the text Stereo and the value P788:

C#

```
ListBox1.Items.Add(new ListItem("Stereo", "P788"));
```

VB.NET

```
ListBox1.Items.Add(New ListItem("Stereo", "P788"))
```

Adding List Items with Databinding

Finally, you can add list items to a list control by taking advantage of databinding. You can bind several different types of data to a list control including DataSets, DataReaders, collections, and enumerations.

For example, suppose that you want to display a drop-down list of colors. Included in the .NET Framework class library, in the System.Drawing namespace, is an enumeration named the KnownColor enumeration. Perform the following steps to bind the KnownColor enumeration to a DropDownList:

1. Add a Web Form Page to your project named **SelectColor.aspx**.

2. Add a DropDownList control to the page.

3. Switch to the code-behind page for the SelectColor.aspx page by selecting Code from the View menu.

4. Enter the following code for the Page_Load subroutine:

   C#

   ```
   private void Page_Load(object sender, System.EventArgs e)
   {
     if (!Page.IsPostBack)
     {
       DropDownList1.DataSource =
         System.Enum.GetNames(typeof(System.Drawing.KnownColor));
       DropDownList1.DataBind();
     }

   }
   ```

VB.NET

```
Private Sub Page_Load(ByVal sender As System.Object,
➥ByVal e As System.EventArgs) Handles MyBase.Load
  If Not Page.IsPostBack Then
    DropDownList1.DataSource = _
      System.Enum.GetNames(GetType(System.Drawing.KnownColor))
    DropDownList1.DataBind()
  End If
End Sub
```

5. Right-click the SelectColor.aspx page in the Solution Explorer window and select Build and Browse.

When the page opens, all the colors included in the KnownColor enumeration are displayed in the DropDownList box (see Figure 10.3).

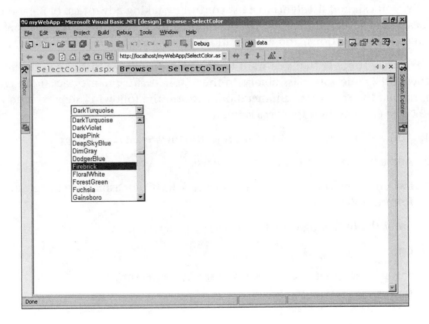

FIGURE 10.3   Adding list items with databinding.

You bind data to a control by using one property and one method. First, you use the DataSource property to indicate the source of the data. In the previous example, the data source was the KnownColor enumeration. However, it could have been a variety of different data sources including database data or an array list of country names.

Next, you need to call the DataBind() method to retrieve the items from the data source into the control. When the DataBind() method is called in the previous example, the items from the KnownColor enumeration are copied into the DropDownList control.

Later, you'll learn how to bind database data to a list control by taking advantage of the DataSource property and the DataBind() method.

Retrieving the Selected List Item

Regardless of the method you use to add list items to a list control, you can determine the text and value of the currently selected item in the list control with the SelectedItem property. For example, you can display the text of the selected list item in a Label control as follows:

C#

```
Label1.Text = ListBox1.SelectedItem.Text;
```

VB.NET

```
Label1.Text = ListBox1.SelectedItem.Text
```

And you can display the value of the currently selected item in a list control as follows:

C#

```
Label1.Text = ListBox1.SelectedItem.Value;
```

VB.NET

```
Label1.Text = ListBox1.SelectedItem.Value
```

Suppose that you want to display a list of products in a ListBox control and you want to display the currently selected item in a Label control.

1. Add a Web Form Page to your project named **SelectProduct.aspx**.

2. Add a ListBox control to the page.

3. Add a Button control to the page.

4. Add a Label control to the page.

5. Double-click the Button control on the Designer surface. This will switch you to the Code Editor.

6. Enter the following code for the `Button1_Click` subroutine:

   C#

   ```csharp
   private void Button1_Click(object sender, System.EventArgs e)
   {
     Label1.Text = ListBox1.SelectedItem.Text;
   }
   ```

   VB.NET

   ```vbnet
   Private Sub Button1_Click(ByVal sender As System.Object,
   ➥ByVal e As System.EventArgs) Handles Button1.Click
     Label1.Text = ListBox1.SelectedItem.Text
   End Sub
   ```

7. Enter the following code for the `Page_Load` handler:

   C#

   ```csharp
   private void Page_Load(object sender, System.EventArgs e)
   {
     if (!IsPostBack )
     {
       ArrayList colProducts = new ArrayList();
       colProducts.Add("Apples");
       colProducts.Add("Oranges");
       colProducts.Add("Strawberries");
       ListBox1.DataSource = colProducts;
       ListBox1.DataBind();
     }
   }
   ```

   VB.NET

   ```vbnet
   Private Sub Page_Load(ByVal sender As System.Object,
   ➥ByVal e As System.EventArgs) Handles MyBase.Load
     Dim colProducts As ArrayList

     If Not IsPostBack Then
       colProducts = New ArrayList()
       colProducts.Add("Apples")
       colProducts.Add("Oranges")
       colProducts.Add("Strawberries")
       ListBox1.DataSource = colProducts
       ListBox1.DataBind()
     End If
   End Sub
   ```

8. Right-click the SelectProduct.aspx page in the Solution Explorer window and select Build and Browse.

The ListBox contained in SelectProduct.aspx is bound to an ArrayList in the Page_Load handler. The colProducts ArrayList is assigned to the ListBox control's DataSource property. When the DataBind() method is called, the items from the ArrayList are copied into the ListBox and, when the page is rendered, the items are displayed in the Web Form Page.

When you select a list item in the ListBox control and click the Button control, the Button1_Click handler executes. This method assigns the value of the Text property of the selected list item to a Label control (see Figure 10.4).

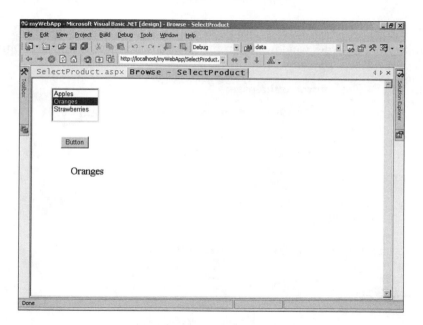

FIGURE 10.4   Using the SelectedItem property.

Enabling AutoPostBack

If you assign the value True to a list control's AutoPostBack property, the form containing the list control will be automatically posted back to the server whenever a new item is selected in the list control. In other words, when you enable the AutoPostBack property, you do not need to add a Button control to the form because the form will post automatically whenever a new selection is made.

> **WARNING**
>
> The `AutoPostBack` property assumes that a Web browser supports client-side JavaScript. Because not all Web browsers support client-side JavaScript, you must be careful when using this property. If you attempt to use `AutoPostBack` with a downlevel browser, nothing will happen when you select a new item.

For example, you can create a `DropDownList` control that automatically posts to the server whenever you select a new item in a drop-down list. Follow these steps to enable the `AutoPostBack` property with a `DropDownList` control that contains a list of names of famous philosophers:

1. Add a Web Form Page named **SelectPhilosopher.aspx** to your project.

2. Add a `DropDownList` control to the page.

3. In the Properties window, assign the value `True` to the `DropDownList` control's `AutoPostBack` property.

4. Add a `Label` control to the page.

5. Double-click the `DropDownList` control on the Designer surface. This will switch you to the Code Editor.

6. Enter the following code for the `DropDownList1_SelectedIndexChanged` handler:

    C#

    ```csharp
    private void DropDownList1_SelectedIndexChanged(object sender,
    ➥System.EventArgs e)
    {
      Label1.Text = DropDownList1.SelectedItem.Text;
    }
    ```

    VB.NET

    ```vbnet
    Private Sub DropDownList1_SelectedIndexChanged(ByVal
    ➥sender As System.Object, ByVal e As System.EventArgs)
    ➥Handles DropDownList1.SelectedIndexChanged
      Label1.Text = DropDownList1.SelectedItem.Text
    End Sub
    ```

7. Enter the following code for the `Page_Load` handler:

    C#

    ```csharp
    private void Page_Load(object sender, System.EventArgs e)
    {
      if (!Page.IsPostBack)
      {
    ```

```
    ArrayList colPhilosophers = new ArrayList();
    colPhilosophers.Add("Frege");
    colPhilosophers.Add("Russell");
    colPhilosophers.Add("Quine");

    DropDownList1.DataSource = colPhilosophers;
    DropDownList1.DataBind();
  }
}
```

VB.NET

```
Private Sub Page_Load(ByVal sender As System.Object,
➥ByVal e As System.EventArgs) Handles MyBase.Load
  Dim colPhilosophers As ArrayList

  If Not Page.IsPostBack Then
    colPhilosophers = New ArrayList()
    colPhilosophers.Add("Frege")
    colPhilosophers.Add("Russell")
    colPhilosophers.Add("Quine")

    DropDownList1.DataSource = colPhilosophers
    DropDownList1.DataBind()
  End If
End Sub
```

8. Right-click the SelectPhilosopher.aspx page in the Solution Explorer window
   and select Build and Browse.

When you select a new philosopher in the DropDownList control, the form is automatically posted back to the server and the name of the new philosopher appears in the Label control.

Notice that we did not place the logic for assigning the name of the philosopher to the Label control within the Button1_Click handler. Because there is no longer a Button control on the page, we need to perform this operation within the DropDownList1_SelectedIndexChanged handler. This handler is executed whenever a new item is selected in the DropDownList control.

Displaying Database Data in a List Control

In the previous section, you learned how to bind a data source—such as a collection or enumeration—to a list control. In this section, you'll learn how to bind database data to a list control.

Suppose, for example, that you want to display a list of book titles from the Titles database table in a drop-down list. First, we need to create a DataSet that represents the contents of the database table.

1. Add a Web Form Page named **SelectTitle.aspx** to your project.

2. In the Server Explorer window, under the Data Connections tab, navigate to the Titles database table located under the Pubs data connection. (If you don't already have an existing data connection to the Pubs database, you'll need to create one.)

3. Drag and drop the Titles database table from the Server Explorer window onto the Designer surface. This will add an SqlConnection and SqlDataAdapter object to your Web Form Page.

4. Add a DataSet to the page by dragging the DataSet object from under the Data tab on the Toolbox onto the Designer surface.

5. When the Add DataSet dialog box appears, select the Untyped Dataset option and click OK.

After you complete these steps, you will have the necessary objects to represent the contents of the Titles database table. Next, you need to bind the Titles database table to a DropDownList control.

1. Add a DropDownList control to the SelectTitle.aspx page.

2. Switch to the code-behind file for the SelectTitle.aspx page by selecting Code from the View menu.

3. Enter the following code for the Page_Load handler:

C#

```
private void Page_Load(object sender, System.EventArgs e)
{
  if (!Page.IsPostBack)
  {
  sqlDataAdapter1.Fill(dataSet1);
  DropDownList1.DataSource = dataSet1;
  DropDownList1.DataTextField = "Title";
  DropDownList1.DataValueField = "Title_ID";
  DropDownList1.DataBind();
  }
}
```

VB.NET

```
Private Sub Page_Load(ByVal sender As System.Object,
➥ByVal e As System.EventArgs) Handles MyBase.Load
  If Not Page.IsPostBack Then
    SqlDataAdapter1.Fill(DataSet1)
    DropDownList1.DataSource = DataSet1
    DropDownList1.DataTextField = "Title"
    DropDownList1.DataValueField = "Title_ID"
    DropDownList1.DataBind()
  End If
End Sub
```

4. Right-click the SelectTitle.aspx page in the Solution Explorer window and select Build and Browse.

After you complete these steps, the DropDownList control will display a list of all the titles in the Titles database table (see Figure 10.5).

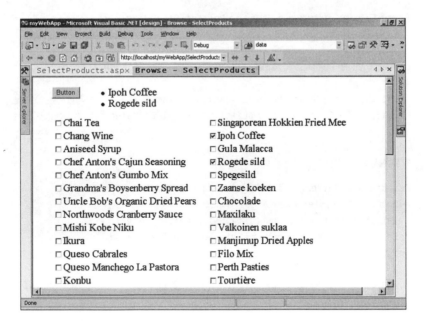

FIGURE 10.5   Binding the Titles table to a DropDownList control.

Notice that we assigned the value Title to the DataTextField property of the DropDownList control. The DataTextField property indicates the column from the data source that is displayed in the drop-down list.

We also assigned a value to the DataValueField property. Including this property is optional. The column assigned to the DataValueField is not displayed in the DropDownList control. However, you can retrieve the value of the DataValueField column when a user selects a list item in the DropDownList control.

You can use the SelectedItem property of the DropDownList control to detect the selected list item.

1. Switch to the Designer view of the SelectTitle.aspx page by selecting View, Designer.

2. Add a Button control to the page.

3. Add a Label control to the page and assign the value **lblTitle** to the control's ID property.

4. Add a second Label control to the page and assign the value **lblTitleID** to the control's ID property.

5. Double-click the Button control on the Designer surface. This will switch you to the Code Editor.

6. Enter the following code for the Button1_Click handler:

   C#

   ```csharp
   private void Button1_Click(object sender, System.EventArgs e)
   {
     lblTitle.Text = DropDownList1.SelectedItem.Text;
     lblTitleID.Text = DropDownList1.SelectedItem.Value;
   }
   ```

   VB.NET

   ```vbnet
   Private Sub Button1_Click(ByVal sender As System.Object,
   ➥ByVal e As System.EventArgs) Handles Button1.Click
     lblTitle.Text = DropDownList1.SelectedItem.Text
     lblTitleID.Text = DropDownList1.SelectedItem.Value
   End Sub
   ```

7. Right-click the SelectTitle.aspx in the Solution Explorer window and select Build and Browse.

After you complete these steps, you can display titles and title IDs in the Label controls by selecting a list item in the DropDownList control and clicking the Button control. Both the title and title ID are retrieved from the SelectedItem property.

Working with Multi-Select List Controls

Two of the list controls—the `ListBox` and `CheckBoxList` controls—enable you to select multiple list items at a time. You cannot use the `SelectedItem` property of these list controls to determine the currently selected items because the `SelectedItem` property only returns one list item.

NOTE

To create a `ListBox` control that enables you to select multiple list items, you need to assign the value `Multiple` to the `ListBox` control's `SelectionMode` property.

If you want to detect the selected items, you need to iterate through the contents of the Items collection of the list control. For example, suppose that you want to display a list of products from the Products database table in the Northwind database in a `CheckBoxList` control. Additionally, suppose that after a user selects one or more items from the check box list, you want the selected items to be displayed in a `Label` control (see Figure 10.6).

To create the necessary database objects, do the following:

1. Add a Web Form Page to your project named **SelectProducts.aspx**.

2. In the Server Explorer window, under the Data Connections tab, navigate to the Products database table under the Northwind data connection. (If you don't already have an existing data connection to the Northwind database, you'll need to create one.)

3. Drag and drop the Products database table from the Server Explorer window onto the Designer surface. This will add an `SqlConnection` and `SqlDataAdapter` object to your Web Form Page.

4. Add a DataSet to the page by dragging the `DataSet` object from under the Data tab on the Toolbox onto the Designer surface.

5. When the Add DataSet dialog box appears, select the Untyped Dataset option and click OK.

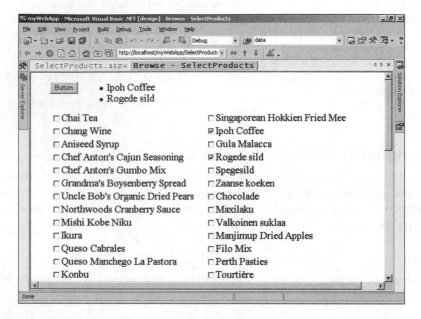

FIGURE 10.6   Working with the `CheckBoxList` control.

After you complete these steps, you'll have an `SqlDataAdapter` that can retrieve the Products database on your page. Furthermore, you will have a DataSet that can represent the contents of the Products database table.

Next, you'll need to add and populate the `CheckBoxList` control.

1. Add a `CheckBoxList` control to the page.

2. In the Properties window, select the `CheckBoxList1` control and assign the value **2** to the `CheckBoxList` control's `RepeatColumns` property. This will cause the `CheckBoxList` to be rendered in two columns.

3. Switch to the code-behind file for the SelectProducts.aspx page by selecting Code from the View menu.

4. Enter the following code for the `Page_Load` handler:

C#

```
private void Page_Load(object sender, System.EventArgs e)
{
  if (!Page.IsPostBack)
```

```
    {
    sqlDataAdapter1.Fill(dataSet1);
    CheckBoxList1.DataSource = dataSet1;
    CheckBoxList1.DataTextField = "ProductName";
    CheckBoxList1.DataBind();
    }
}
```

VB.NET

```
Private Sub Page_Load(ByVal sender As System.Object,
➥ByVal e As System.EventArgs) Handles MyBase.Load
  If Not Page.IsPostBack Then
    SqlDataAdapter1.Fill(DataSet1)
    CheckBoxList1.DataSource = DataSet1
    CheckBoxList1.DataTextField = "ProductName"
    CheckBoxList1.DataBind()
  End If
End Sub
```

5. Right-click the SelectProducts.aspx page in the Solution Explorer window and select Build and Browse.

When the SelectProducts.aspx page opens, the products from the Products database table will appear in a two-column check box list. Notice that you can check more than one item in the list.

Finally, we need to add the logic to our page to display the selected list items in the check box list in a Label control.

1. Add a Label control to the SelectProducts.aspx page.

2. Add a Button control to the page.

3. Double-click the Button control on the Designer surface. This will switch you to the Code Editor.

4. Enter the following code for the Button1_Click handler:

C#

```
private void Button1_Click(object sender, System.EventArgs e)
{
  Label1.Text = "";
  foreach (ListItem objListItem in CheckBoxList1.Items)
  {
```

```
    if (objListItem.Selected)
      Label1.Text += "<li>" + objListItem.Text;
  }
}
```

VB.NET

```
Private Sub Button1_Click(ByVal sender As System.Object,
➥ByVal e As System.EventArgs) Handles Button1.Click
  Dim objListItem As ListItem
  Label1.Text = ""
  For Each objListItem In CheckBoxList1.Items
    If objListItem.Selected Then
      Label1.Text &= "<li>" & objListItem.Text
    End If
  Next
End Sub
```

5. Right-click the SelectProducts.aspx page in the Solution Explorer window and select Build and Browse.

After the page opens, you can select multiple list items in the check box list and the selected items will appear in the Label control when you click the Button control.

Notice that each selected item is detected within the Button1_Click handler by iterating through the Items collection of the CheckBoxList control. Whenever the list item's selected property has the value True, the value of the Text property is added to the Label control.

You can follow a similar set of steps when retrieving multiple selected items from a ListBox control. Simply step through each of the items in the ListBox control and check whether the list item's selected property has the value True.

Advanced List Control Topics

In this section, you'll tackle three advanced topics that you'll face when working with the list controls. First, you learn how to programmatically add a default list item to a databound list control. Next, you learn how to display a default list item in a list control. Finally, you'll learn how to create interactions between multiple list controls.

Adding a Default List Item

When displaying a drop-down list of items, it is common to display the first list item with a message like "Please Select an Item." When binding a list control to database data, you'll need to add the first list item programmatically.

In this section, you'll learn how to create a DropDownList control that displays a list of authors. The first list item, which you will add programmatically, will display the message "Select an Author" (see Figure 10.7).

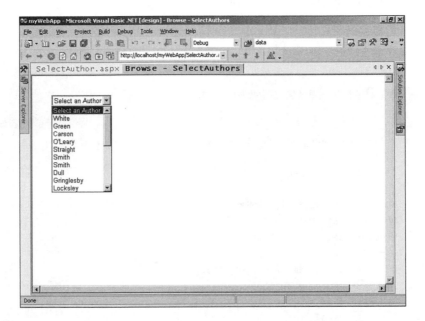

FIGURE 10.7   Adding a default item.

First, we need to create the page and add the necessary database objects.

1. Add a Web Form Page to your project named **SelectAuthor.aspx**.

2. In the Server Explorer window, under the Data Connections tab, navigate to the Authors database table located under the Pubs data connection. (If you don't already have an existing data connection to the Pubs database, you'll need to create one.)

3. Drag and drop the Authors database table from the Server Explorer window onto the Designer surface. This will add an SqlConnection and SqlDataAdapter object to your Web Form Page.

4. Add a DataSet to the page by dragging the `DataSet` object from under the Data tab on the Toolbox onto the Designer surface.

5. When the Add DataSet dialog box appears, select the Untyped Dataset option and click OK.

Next, you need to add the `DropDownList` control to the page and bind the control to the Authors DataSet. You'll also add a new list item that will be the first list item displayed by the `DropDownList` control.

1. Add a `DropDownList` control to the SelectAuthor.aspx page.

2. Switch to the code-behind file for the page by selecting Code from the View menu.

3. Enter the following code for the `Page_Load` handler:

   C#

   ```csharp
   private void Page_Load(object sender, System.EventArgs e)
   {
     if (!Page.IsPostBack)
     {
     sqlDataAdapter1.Fill(dataSet1);
     DropDownList1.DataSource = dataSet1;
     DropDownList1.DataTextField = "au_lname";
     DropDownList1.DataBind();
     DropDownList1.Items.Insert(0, "Select an Author");
     }
   }
   ```

   VB.NET

   ```vbnet
   Private Sub Page_Load(ByVal sender As System.Object,
   ➥ByVal e As System.EventArgs) Handles MyBase.Load
     If Not Page.IsPostBack Then
       SqlDataAdapter1.Fill(DataSet1)
       DropDownList1.DataSource = DataSet1
       DropDownList1.DataTextField = "au_lname"
       DropDownList1.DataBind()
       DropDownList1.Items.Insert(0, "Select an Author")
     End If
   End Sub
   ```

4. Right-click the SelectAuthor.aspx page in the Solution Explorer window and select Build and Browse.

When the page opens, notice that the first item displayed by the DropDownList control is "Select an Author." This list item was added programmatically to the DropDownList control's Items collection with the Insert() method. It appears at the top of the list because it was inserted at position 0.

Displaying a Default List Item

You might encounter the problem of selecting an initial default item when working with list controls. For example, you might want to display an alphabetical list of countries in a ListBox control. However, you might want to display U.S.A. as the default item, even if it appears toward the bottom of the list.

In this section, you'll learn how to display a default category when binding a ListBox control to the Categories database table. We'll take advantage of two methods of the ListItemCollection class named FindByText and FindByValue. The FindByText method enables you to find a matching list item by its Text property and the FindByValue enables you to find a matching list item by its Value property.

First, we need to create the necessary database objects:

1. Add a Web Form Page named **SelectCategory.aspx** to your project.

2. In the Server Explorer window, under the Data Connections tab, navigate to the Categories database table located under the Northwind data connection. (If you don't already have an existing data connection to the Northwind database, you'll need to create one.)

3. Drag and drop the Categories database table from the Server Explorer window onto the Designer surface. This will add an SqlConnection and SqlDataAdapter object to your Web Form Page.

4. Add a DataSet to the page by dragging the DataSet object from under the Data tab on the Toolbox onto the Designer surface.

5. When the Add DataSet dialog box appears, select the Untyped Dataset option and click OK.

Next, you'll need to add a ListBox control to the page. We'll display the category Seafood by default by taking advantage of the FindByText method:

1. Add a ListBox control to the page by dragging the ListBox control from under the Web Forms tab onto the Designer surface.

2. Switch to the code-behind file for the page by selecting View, Code.

3. Enter the following code for the Page_Load subroutine:

C#

```
private void Page_Load(object sender, System.EventArgs e)
{
  if (!Page.IsPostBack)
  {
  sqlDataAdapter1.Fill(dataSet1);
  ListBox1.DataSource = dataSet1;
  ListBox1.DataTextField = "CategoryName";
  ListBox1.DataBind();
  ListBox1.Items.FindByText("Seafood").Selected=true;
  }
}
```

VB.NET

```
Private Sub Page_Load(ByVal sender As System.Object,
➥ByVal e As System.EventArgs) Handles MyBase.Load
  If Not Page.IsPostBack Then
    SqlDataAdapter1.Fill(DataSet1)
    ListBox1.DataSource = DataSet1
    ListBox1.DataTextField = "CategoryName"
    ListBox1.DataBind()
    ListBox1.Items.FindByText("Seafood").Selected = True
  End If
End Sub
```

4. Right-click the SelectCategory.aspx page in the Solution Explorer window and
   select Build and Browse.

Notice that when the SelectCategory.aspx page first opens, the Seafood category is
selected by default in the list box. In the Page_Load handler, the FindByText method
finds the list item with the Text value Seafood and sets the Selected property of the
matching item to true. You can use the FindByValue method in an identical fashion
to match a list item with a particular Value property.

Creating Interactions Between List Controls

You can copy or move items from one list control to another. Creating these types of
interactions between list controls is useful when you want to enable users to select a
subset of items from a list control. For example, you might use one list control to
represent a set of products and another list control to represent a shopping cart.

In this section, we'll create a ListBox control that represents the products from the Products database table. We'll create a second ListBox control that represents a shopping cart (see Figure 10.8).

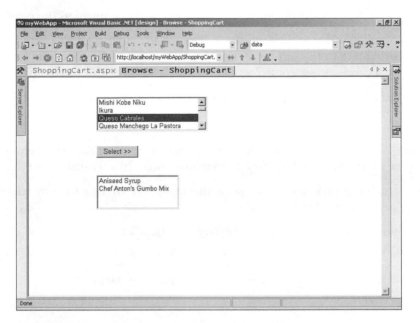

FIGURE 10.8   Copying items between list controls.

First, you need to create the necessary database objects:

1. Add a Web Form Page to your project named **ShoppingCart.aspx**.

2. In the Server Explorer window, under the Data Connections tab, navigate to the Products database table under the Northwind data connection. (If you don't already have an existing data connection to the Northwind database, you'll need to create one.)

3. Drag and drop the Products database table from the Server Explorer window onto the Designer surface. This will add an SqlConnection and SqlDataAdapter object to your Web Form Page.

4. Add a DataSet to the page by dragging the DataSet object from under the Data tab on the Toolbox onto the Designer surface.

5. When the Add DataSet dialog box appears, select the Untyped Dataset option and click OK.

After you complete these steps, you'll have an SqlDataAdapter that can retrieve the Products database on your page. Furthermore, you will have a DataSet that can represent the contents of the Products database table.

Next, you'll need to add the ListBox controls and Button control to the page.

1. Add two ListBox controls to the ShoppingCart.aspx page and assign the value **lstProducts** to the first ListBox control's ID property and the value **lstCart** to the second ListBox control's ID property.

2. Add a Button control to the page and assign the value **Select >>** to the Text property of the Button control.

Finally, you'll need to add the necessary application logic to the code-behind file to copy the items from the first list box to the second ListBox control:

1. Switch to the code-behind file for the ShoppingCart.aspx page by selecting Code from the View menu.

2. Enter the following code for the Page_Load handler:

C#

```csharp
private void Page_Load(object sender, System.EventArgs e)
{
  if (!Page.IsPostBack)
  {
  sqlDataAdapter1.Fill(dataSet1);
  lstProducts.DataSource = dataSet1;
  lstProducts.DataTextField = "ProductName";
  lstProducts.DataBind();
  }
}
```

VB.NET

```vbnet
Private Sub Page_Load(ByVal sender As System.Object,
➥ByVal e As System.EventArgs) Handles MyBase.Load
  If Not Page.IsPostBack Then
    SqlDataAdapter1.Fill(DataSet1)
    lstProducts.DataSource = DataSet1
    lstProducts.DataTextField = "ProductName"
    lstProducts.DataBind()
  End If
End Sub
```

3. Switch back to the Designer surface by selecting Designer from the View menu.

4. Double-click the Button control.

5. Enter the following code for the Button1_Click subroutine:

C#

```csharp
private void Button1_Click(object sender, System.EventArgs e)
{
  if (lstProducts.SelectedIndex != -1)
  {
    lstCart.Items.Add(lstProducts.SelectedItem.Text);
    lstProducts.Items.Remove(lstProducts.SelectedItem);
  }
}
```

VB.NET

```vbnet
Private Sub Button1_Click(ByVal sender As System.Object,
➥ByVal e As System.EventArgs) Handles Button1.Click
  If lstProducts.SelectedIndex <> -1 Then
    lstCart.Items.Add(lstProducts.SelectedItem.Text)
    lstProducts.Items.Remove(lstProducts.SelectedItem)
  End If
End Sub
```

6. Right-click the ShoppingCart.aspx page in the Solution Explorer window and select Build and Browse.

After the page opens, you can copy list items from one ListBox control to the next. Select a list item in the first list box and click the Button control and the list item will appear in the second ListBox control.

The list items are copied from one control to another in the Button1_Click handler. The selected list item from the first control is added to the Items collection of the second list control. Next, the item is removed from the previous list.

Summary

In this chapter, you learned how to work with the ASP.NET list controls. First, you learned the three methods of adding list items to a list control—declaratively, programmatically, and through databinding.

Next, you learned how to bind database data to a list control. You learned how to bind both a single option list control and a multi-option list control to the contents of a database table.

Finally, we tackled several advanced topics encountered when programming with the list controls. You learned how to add and display a default list item, and you also learned how to copy items from one list control to another.

11

Displaying Data with the Repeater Control

IN THIS CHAPTER

- Binding the Repeater Control to Database Data
- Using Templates with the Repeater Control
- Formatting the Output of a Databinding Expression
- Loading Templates from an External File
- Adding Child Controls to the Repeater Control

In this chapter, you learn how to use the first of the ASP.NET controls that was designed specifically for displaying data—the Repeater control. The Repeater control enables you to display a set of items from a data source with any type of formatting. For example, you can use a Repeater control to display a list of database records in a bulleted list, in an HTML table, or in a single paragraph.

In this chapter, you will learn

- How to display database records with the Repeater control

- How to format the items displayed by a Repeater control with templates

- How to load templates from an external file

- How to nest controls within a Repeater control

Binding the Repeater Control to Database Data

You can use a Repeater control to display a set of records retrieved from a database query. You can bind a Repeater control to either a DataSet or a DataReader (as well as other types of data such as collections and enumerations).

When you use the Repeater control, you are required to supply at least one template. The template contains the formatting information for each item in the data source.

For example, suppose that you need to display the contents of the Titles database table in a bulleted list (see Figure 11.1).

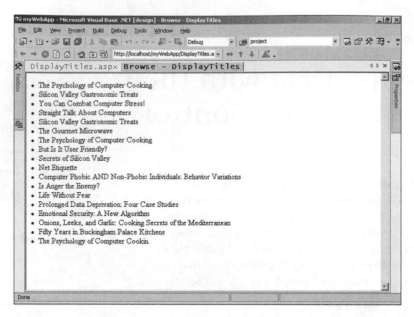

FIGURE 11.1   Displaying database records with the Repeater control.

First, you'll need to create the Web Form Page and the necessary database objects:

1. Add a Web Form Page to your project named **DisplayTitles.aspx**.

2. In the Server Explorer window, under the Data Connections tab, navigate to the Titles database table located under the Pubs data connection. (If you don't already have an existing data connection to the Pubs database, you'll need to create one.)

3. Drag and drop the Titles database table from the Server Explorer window onto the Designer surface. This will add an SqlConnection and SqlDataAdapter object to your Web Form Page.

4. Add a DataSet to the page by dragging the DataSet object from beneath the Data tab on the Toolbox onto the Designer surface.

5. When the Add DataSet dialog box appears, select the Untyped Dataset option and click OK.

Next, you'll need to add a Repeater control to the Web Form Page and bind the Repeater control to the Titles DataSet:

1. Add a Repeater control to the DisplayTitles.aspx page by dragging the Repeater control from under the Web Forms tab in the Toolbox onto the Designer surface.

2. Switch to the code-behind file for the DisplayTitles.aspx page by selecting Code from the View menu (or double-clicking the Designer surface).

3. Enter the following code for the Page_Load handler:

C#

```
private void Page_Load(object sender, System.EventArgs e)
{
  sqlDataAdapter1.Fill( dataSet1 );
  Repeater1.DataSource = dataSet1;
  Repeater1.DataBind();
}
```

VB.NET

```
Private Sub Page_Load(ByVal sender As System.Object,
➥ByVal e As System.EventArgs) Handles MyBase.Load
  SqlDataAdapter1.Fill(DataSet1)
  Repeater1.DataSource = DataSet1
  Repeater1.DataBind()
End Sub
```

TIP

Notice that you cannot precisely position a Repeater control on the Designer surface. A Repeater control always snaps to the top-left of a page, even when Grid Layout mode is enabled.

If you want to precisely position a Repeater control on a page, you need to add the Repeater control to another container control, such as an HTML Label, Flow Layout Panel, or Grid Layout Panel. You can drag and drop a Repeater control onto any of these other controls and precisely position these controls on a page.

If you were to build and browse the DisplayTitles.aspx page after completing these steps, you would get a blank page. Before you can use the Repeater control to format the items from a data source, you need to supply at least one template.

1. Switch to the Designer for the DisplayTitles.aspx page by selecting Designer from the View menu.

2. Switch to the HTML view of the page by clicking the HTML tab that appears at the bottom-left of the Designer window.

3. Find the <asp:Repeater> tag in the HTML source.

4. Enter the following `<ItemTemplate>` tag between the opening and closing `<asp:Repeater>` tags:

```
<asp:Repeater id="Repeater1" runat="server">
<ItemTemplate>
  <li>
  <%# DataBinder.Eval( Container, "DataItem.Title" )%>
  </li>
</ItemTemplate>
</asp:Repeater>
```

5. Right-click the DisplayTitles.aspx page in the Solution Explorer window and select Build and Browse.

When the DisplayTitles.aspx page opens, a bulleted list of all the book titles from the Titles database table is displayed.

The `<ItemTemplate>` tag tag>requires explanation. The `<ItemTemplate>` tag is used to format each item displayed by the Repeater control. You can place any HTML content between the opening and closing `<ItemTemplate>` tags that you want. In the case of the DisplayTitles.aspx page, you added an HTML `<li>` tag to display a bullet before each book title.

Notice the special expression that appears between the `<%#` and `%>` tags. This is an example of a databinding expression. A *databinding expression* is an expression that is evaluated when the `DataBind()` method is called.

The databinding expression in the DisplayTitles.aspx page is used to display each book title. The expression `DataBinder.Eval( Container, "DataItem.Title" )` displays the value of the Title column from the Repeater control's data source (the Titles database table). `Container` refers to the control that contains the databinding expression; in this case, the `RepeaterItem` control.

If you want, you can add multiple databinding expressions to a single template. For example, if you want to display the values of both the Title and Notes columns, you could use the following `<ItemTemplate>`:

```
<ItemTemplate>
  <li>
  <b><%# DataBinder.Eval( Container, "DataItem.Title" )%></b>
  - <%# DataBinder.Eval( Container, "DataItem.Notes" )%>
  </li>
</ItemTemplate>
```

In this case, the HTML <b> tag is used to display the value of the Title column in bold. The value of the Notes column is displayed after a single dash.

Using Templates with the Repeater Control

In the previous section, you learned how to use the <ItemTemplate> tags to format each item displayed by a Repeater control. The Repeater control actually supports several different templates:

- HeaderTemplate   Content contained in this template is displayed before any items from the data source.

- ItemTemplate   Content contained in this template is displayed for each item in the data source.

- AlternatingItemTemplate   Content contained in this template is displayed for alternating items in the data source.

- SeparatorTemplate   Content contained in this template is displayed between each item in the data source.

- FooterTemplate   Content contained in this template is displayed after any items from the data source.

For example, you can use the AlternatingItemTemplate to display every other item in a different color. The following Repeater control declaration displays alternating items in a green font:

```
<asp:Repeater id="Repeater1" runat="server">
  <ItemTemplate>
  <li>
    <%# DataBinder.Eval( Container, "DataItem.Title" )%>
  </li>
  </ItemTemplate>
  <AlternatingItemTemplate>
  <li>
  <font color="green">
    <%# DataBinder.Eval( Container, "DataItem.Title" )%>
  </font>
  </li>
  </AlternatingItemTemplate>
</asp:Repeater>
```

This Repeater control displays the first item with the ItemTemplate, the next item with the AlternatingItemTemplate, the next item with the ItemTemplate, and so on. The end result is that every other title is displayed in green.

The order in which you declare templates within a Repeater control does not matter. In this example, the ItemTemplate is declared before the AlternatingItemTemplate. However, the page would work the same way if the order of the declarations were reversed.

Formatting the Output of a Databinding Expression

If you want to display expressions, such as dates, times, or currency amounts in a template, you'll need some way to format the output of a databinding expression. There are two ways that you can format the output of a databinding expression. You can supply an additional argument within the DataBinder.Eval() method, or you can refer to a custom function.

The DataBinder.Eval() method accepts a third argument that represents a format specifier. There are format specifiers for dates, times, currencies, enumerations, and numeric values. For example, suppose that you want to format the Price column from the Titles database. To do this, you can use the following template:

```
<ItemTemplate>
<li>
<%# DataBinder.Eval( Container, "DataItem.Price", "{0:c}" )%>
</li>
</ItemTemplate>
```

In this template, the third argument passed to the DataBinder.Eval() method is the format specifier. The expression "{0:c}" formats the Price column as a currency amount (see Figure 11.2).

> **NOTE**
>
> For a list of valid format specifiers, see the .NET Framework SDK Documentation. Expand the entry .NET Framework SDK, Programming with the .NET Framework, Working with Base Types, Formatting Types.

You can also format the output of a databinding expression with a custom function. You can refer to any public method that you create within the code-behind file within a databinding expression. For example, the Price column in the Titles database table contains null values for a few of the rows. You might want to output the string "No Value" for those rows.

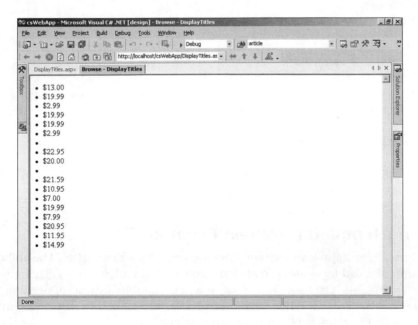

FIGURE 11.2   Formatting with the DataBinder.Eval() method.

The following template passes the value returned by the databinding expression to the FormatPrice() method:

```
<ItemTemplate>
  <li>
  <%# FormatPrice( DataBinder.Eval( Container, "DataItem.Price" ) )%>
  </li>
</ItemTemplate>
```

You can declare the FormatPrice() method in the code-behind file for the page as follows:

C#

```
public string FormatPrice( object Price )
{
if (Price == DBNull.Value)
    return "No Value";
else
    return String.Format( "{0:c}", Price );
}
```

VB.NET

```
Public Function FormatPrice(ByVal Price As Object)
  If IsDBNull(Price) Then
    Return "No Value"
  Else
    Return String.Format("{0:c}", Price)
  End If
End Function
```

When the Price column has a null value, the FormatPrice() method returns the string "No Value"; otherwise, it returns the formatted currency amount.

Loading Templates from an External File

You can dynamically load the templates used by a Repeater control. The ability to dynamically load templates is useful in a couple of situations. First, placing templates in an external file can make your code more manageable. Instead of needing to modify the main ASP.NET file whenever you want to make a change to a template, you can simply change the external template file.

You might also want to give the users of your application the option to view the same data using different templates. By selecting among different templates, a user can view the data formatted with different fonts and layouts.

In this section, we'll create a Web Form Page that enables a user to select a template to apply to a Repeater control from a drop-down list (see Figure 11.3).

First, we need to create the main Web Form Page:

1. Add a Web Form Page to your project named **DynamicTemplate.aspx**.

2. In the Server Explorer window, under the Data Connections tab, navigate to the Titles database table located under the Pubs data connection. (If you don't already have an existing data connection to the Pubs database, you'll need to create one.)

3. Drag and drop the Titles database table from the Server Explorer window onto the Designer surface. This will add an SqlConnection and SqlDataAdapter object to your Web Form Page.

4. Add a DataSet to the page by dragging the DataSet object from beneath the Data tab on the Toolbox onto the Designer surface.

5. When the Add DataSet dialog box appears, select the Untyped Dataset option and click OK.

6. Add a DropDownList control to the page and assign the value True to its AutoPostBack property.

7. Add a Repeater control to the page.

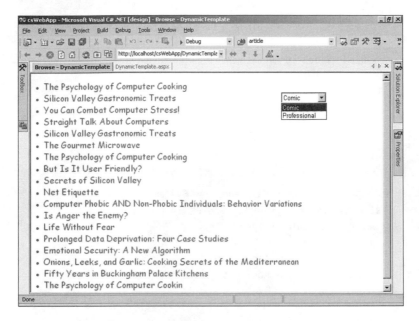

FIGURE 11.3   Dynamically loading templates.

Now you need to add the code to the DynamicTemplate.aspx page that dynamically loads the templates:

1. Switch to the code-behind file for the DynamicTemplate.aspx page by selecting View, Code.

2. Enter the following code for the Page_Load handler:

   C#

```csharp
private void Page_Load(object sender, System.EventArgs e)
{
    if (!Page.IsPostBack)
    {
        // Add DropDownList Options
        DropDownList1.Items.Add( "Comic" );
        DropDownList1.Items.Add( "Professional" );
    }
```

```
       // Display Selected Invoice
       if (DropDownList1.SelectedItem.Text == "Comic")
           Repeater1.ItemTemplate = LoadTemplate( "Comic.ascx" );
       else
           Repeater1.ItemTemplate = LoadTemplate( "Professional.ascx" );


       // Bind Titles to Repeater
       sqlDataAdapter1.Fill( dataSet1 );
       Repeater1.DataSource = dataSet1;
       Repeater1.DataBind();
   }
```

VB.NET

```
Private Sub Page_Load(ByVal sender As System.Object,
➥ByVal e As System.EventArgs) Handles MyBase.Load
  If Not Page.IsPostBack Then
    ' Add DropDownList Options
    DropDownList1.Items.Add("Comic")
    DropDownList1.Items.Add("Professional")
  End If


  ' Display Selected Invoice
  If DropDownList1.SelectedItem.Text = "Comic" Then
    Repeater1.ItemTemplate = LoadTemplate("Comic.ascx")
  Else
    Repeater1.ItemTemplate = LoadTemplate("Professional.ascx")
  End If


  ' Bind Titles to Repeater
  SqlDataAdapter1.Fill(DataSet1)
  Repeater1.DataSource = DataSet1
  Repeater1.DataBind()
End Sub
```

Next, you need to create the templates in the external files.

1. Add a file named Comic.ascx to your project. Select Project, Add New Item.
    Select Text File, name it **Comic.ascx** (*without the .txt extension*) and click Open.

2. Add the following code to the Comic.ascx file:

```
<font face="Comic Sans MS" size="4" color="green">
<li>
<%# DataBinder.Eval( Container, "DataItem.Title" )%>
</li>
</font>
```

3. Add a file named Professional.ascx to your project. Select Project, Add New Item. Select Text File, name it **Professional.ascx** (*without the .txt extension*) and click Open.

4. Add the following code to the Professional.ascx file:

```
<font face="Arial" size="3">
<li>
<%# DataBinder.Eval( Container, "DataItem.Title" )%>
</li>
</font>
```

Finally, you're ready to build the DynamicTemplate.aspx page and view it in the Web browser. Right-click the DynamicTemplate.aspx in the Solution Explorer window and select Build and Browse.

When the page opens, the titles from the Titles database table are formatted with the Comic template. If you select the Professional template from the drop-down list, the Professional.ascx file is loaded and used to format the titles.

You can also dynamically load the HeaderTemplate, FooterTemplate, AlternatingItemTemplate, and SeparatorTemplate using the same technique described in this section. The Repeater control has properties that correspond to each of these templates.

Adding Child Controls to the Repeater Control

You can add Web Form controls to the templates contained within a Repeater control. This is useful when you want to display lists of controls such as a list of TextBox controls, Image controls, or HyperLink controls.

The following ItemTemplate, for example, contains a TextBox control:

```
<asp:Repeater id="Repeater1" runat="server">
<ItemTemplate>
<p>
<asp:TextBox
  Text='<%# DataBinder.Eval( Container, "DataItem.ProductName" )%>'
```

```
  Runat="server" />
</ItemTemplate>
</asp:Repeater>
```

The TextBox control's Text property has a databinding expression for its value that represents the ProductName column from the Products database table. When the Repeater control is rendered, a list of TextBox controls containing product names is rendered (see Figure 11.4).

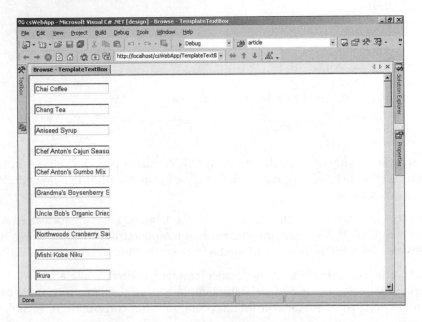

FIGURE 11.4   Adding a TextBox control to a Repeater.

Notice that single quotes (apostrophes) are used around the databinding expression instead of double quotes. When you are assigning a databinding expression to a property of a control inside a template, you must use single quotes.

You can place any control you want within a template. You can even add a Repeater control inside another Repeater control's template. This is useful when you want to display the contents of two database tables that have a master/detail relationship.

For example, imagine that you want to display the contents of both the Categories and Products tables. Suppose, furthermore, that you want to display all the products that match a category directly under each category.

First, you need to create the Web Form page and add the necessary database objects and controls:

1. Add a Web Form Page to your project named **NestedRepeater.aspx**.

2. In the Server Explorer window, under the Data Connections tab, navigate to the Categories database table located under the Northwind data connection. (If you don't already have an existing data connection to the Northwind database, you'll need to create one.)

3. Drag and drop the Categories database table from the Server Explorer window onto the Designer surface. This will add an SqlConnection and SqlDataAdapter object to your Web Form Page.

4. In the Server Explorer window, under the Data Connections tab, navigate to the Products database table located under the Northwind data connection.

5. Drag and drop the Products database table from the Server Explorer window onto the Designer surface. This will add a second SqlDataAdapter object to your Web Form Page.

6. Add a DataSet to the page by dragging the DataSet object from beneath the Data tab on the Toolbox onto the Designer surface.

7. When the Add DataSet dialog box appears, select the Untyped Dataset option and click OK.

8. Add a Repeater control to the NestedRepeater.aspx page.

Next, you need to add an ItemTemplate to the Repeater control that contains a second Repeater control that displays the matching products:

1. Switch to the HTML view of the NestedRepeater.aspx page by clicking the HTML tab that appears at the bottom-left of the Designer window.

2. Find the Repeater control in the HTML source of the page and place the following code between the opening and closing tags of the control:

```
<asp:Repeater id="Repeater1" runat="server">
<ItemTemplate>
<h2><%# DataBinder.Eval( Container, "DataItem.CategoryName" )%></h2>
  <asp:Repeater
    DataSource='<%# ShowProducts( DataBinder.Eval( Container,
➥"DataItem.CategoryID" ) )%>'
    Runat="server">
    <ItemTemplate>
    <li>
```

```
      <%# DataBinder.Eval( Container, "DataItem.ProductName" )%>
      </li>
      </ItemTemplate>
    </asp:Repeater>
  </ItemTemplate>
  </asp:Repeater>
```

Notice that the ItemTemplate for the main Repeater control contains a second Repeater control. The second Repeater control's DataSource property is assigned a databinding expression. The databinding expression takes advantage of the ShowProducts() method to retrieve the matching products.

Finally, we need to add the code to the page that retrieves the categories and products from the respective database tables:

C# Steps

1. Switch to the code-behind file for the DynamicTemplate.aspx page by selecting Code from the View menu.

2. Enter the following code for the Page_Load handler:

```
private void Page_Load(object sender, System.EventArgs e)
{
  sqlDataAdapter1.Fill(dataSet1);
  sqlDataAdapter2.Fill(dataSet1);
  Repeater1.DataSource = dataSet1;
  Repeater1.DataMember = "Categories";
  Repeater1.DataBind();
}
```

3. Add the ShowProducts() method to the code-behind file. Enter the following code below the Page_Load handler:

```
public DataView ShowProducts( object CategoryID )
{
string strFilter = "CategoryID=" + CategoryID;
DataView dvProducts = new DataView(
    dataSet1.Tables[ "Products" ],
    strFilter,
    "ProductName",
    DataViewRowState.CurrentRows );
return dvProducts;
}
```

4. Right-click the NestedRepeater.aspx page in the Solution Explorer window and select Build and Browse.

VB.NET Steps

1. Switch to the code-behind file for the NestedRepeater.aspx page by selecting Code from the View menu.

2. Enter the following code for the Page_Load subroutine:

```
Private Sub Page_Load(ByVal sender As System.Object,
➥ByVal e As System.EventArgs) Handles MyBase.Load
  SqlDataAdapter1.Fill(DataSet1)
  SqlDataAdapter2.Fill(DataSet1)
  Repeater1.DataSource = DataSet1
  Repeater1.DataMember = "Categories"
  Repeater1.DataBind()
End Sub
```

3. Add the ShowProducts() method to the code-behind file. Enter the following code below the Page_Load subroutine:

```
Public Function ShowProducts(ByVal CategoryID As Object) As DataView
  Dim strFilter As String
  Dim dvProducts As DataView

  strFilter = "CategoryID=" & CategoryID
  dvProducts = New DataView( _
    DataSet1.Tables("Products"), _
    strFilter, _
    "ProductName", _
    DataViewRowState.CurrentRows)
  Return dvProducts
End Function
```

4. Right-click the NestedRepeater.aspx page in the Solution Explorer window and select Build and Browse.

When the page opens, a list of categories and matching products is displayed (see Figure 11.5). Most of the work is taking place in the ShowProducts() method. This method takes the CategoryID and returns a filtered DataView that represents the rows from the Products table that match the CategoryID.

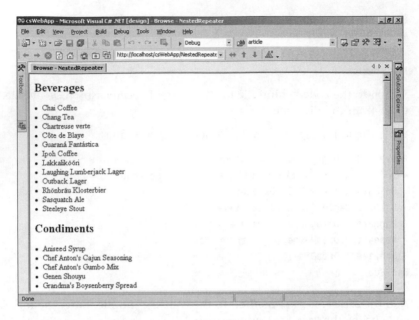

FIGURE 11.5   Using a nested Repeater control.

Summary

In this chapter, you learned how to use the Repeater control to format and display database data. First, you learned how to bind database data to the Repeater control. You learned how to use different types of templates with the Repeater control to control how the items displayed by the Repeater control are formatted.

Next, you learned how to dynamically load templates from an external file. You created a page that enables a user to pick a template to use with the Repeater control.

Finally, you learned how to nest controls within a Repeater control. You built a page that displays categories and matching records by nesting one Repeater control inside of another.

12

Displaying Data with the DataList Control

IN THIS CHAPTER

- Binding the DataList Control to Database Data

- Formatting the Appearance of a DataList

- Creating a Menu with a DataList

- Creating a Single-Page Master/Detail Form

In this chapter, you will learn how to use the DataList control to display and interact with database data. The DataList control is similar to the Repeater control. Like the Repeater control, the DataList control supports templates for formatting items from a data source.

However, the DataList control provides you with additional functionality. In this chapter, you'll learn:

- How to take advantage of auto formatting and style objects to format the content rendered by a DataList

- How to use a DataList to display data in multiple columns

- How to create interactive menus with a DataList

Binding the DataList Control to Database Data

The basic procedure for binding a DataList to database data is the same for the DataList control as for the Repeater control. You use the DataList control's DataSource property to indicate a data source and then you call the DataList control's DataBind() method to copy the items from the data source into the DataList control.

For example, suppose that you want to display the contents of the Authors database table with a DataList control. First, you'll need to create the necessary database objects:

1. Add a Web Form Page named **DisplayAuthors.aspx** to your project.

2. In the Server Explorer window, under the Data Connections tab, navigate to the Authors database table located under the Pubs data connection. (If you don't already have an existing data connection to the Pubs database, you'll need to create one.)

3. Drag and drop the Authors database table from the Server Explorer window onto the Designer surface. This will add an SqlConnection and SqlDataAdapter object to your Web Form Page.

4. Add a DataSet to the page by dragging the DataSet object from under the Data tab on the Toolbox onto the Designer surface.

5. When the Add DataSet dialog box appears, select the Untyped Dataset option and click OK.

Next, you need to add the DataList control to the page and bind the control to the Authors DataSet:

1. Add a DataList control to the page by dragging the DataList control from under the Web Forms tab in the Toolbox onto the Designer surface.

2. Switch to the code-behind file for the DisplayAuthors.aspx page by selecting Code from the View menu.

3. Enter the following code for the Page_Load handler:

C#

```
private void Page_Load(object sender, System.EventArgs e)
{
  sqlDataAdapter1.Fill( dataSet1 );
  DataList1.DataSource = dataSet1;
  DataList1.DataBind();
}
```

VB.NET

```
Private Sub Page_Load(ByVal sender As System.Object,
➥ByVal e As System.EventArgs) Handles MyBase.Load
  SqlDataAdapter1.Fill(DataSet1)
  DataList1.DataSource = DataSet1
  DataList1.DataBind()
End Sub
```

Finally, you need to add at least one template to the DataList control. You'll add an ItemTemplate to the control:

1. Switch back to the Designer by selecting Designer from the View menu.

2. Switch to HTML view by selecting the HTML tab on the bottom left of the window.

3. Enter the following ItemTemplate between the opening and closing <asp:DataList> tags:

```
<asp:DataList id="DataList1"
style="Z-INDEX: 101; LEFT: 80px; POSITION: absolute; TOP: 60px"
runat="server">
 <ItemTemplate>
   <%# DataBinder.Eval( Container, "DataItem.au_lname" ) %>
 </ItemTemplate>
</asp:DataList>
```

4. Right-click the DisplayAuthors.aspx page in the Solution Explorer window and select Build and Browse.

After you complete these steps, the page displayed in Figure 12.1 will appear. Notice that each item from the data source is displayed in a new row. The DataList has automatically rendered an HTML table creating a new table row for each item.

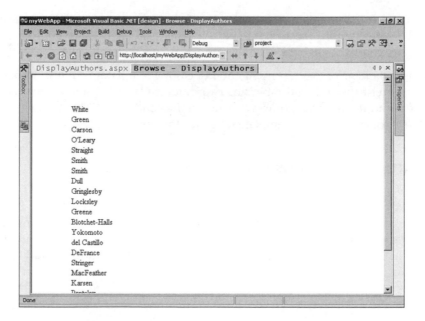

FIGURE 12.1   Displaying database records with the DataList control.

Using Templates with the DataList Control

The DataList control supports exactly the same templates at the Repeater control:

- HeaderTemplate   Content contained in this template is displayed before any items from the data source.

- ItemTemplate   Content contained in this template is displayed for each item in the data source.

- AlternatingItemTemplate   Content contained in this template is displayed for alternating items in the data source.

- SeparatorTemplate   Content contained in this template is displayed between each item in the data source.

- FooterTemplate   Content contained in this template is displayed after any items from the data source.

In the previous section, you used the ItemTemplate to format how each item from the data source is displayed. The ItemTemplate formats each table row rendered by the DataList control.

There are actually two ways that you can add templates to a DataList. In the previous section, we added the ItemTemplate by switching to the HTML view of the page and entering the template by hand. Alternatively, you can right-click the DataList control on the Designer surface and select the Edit Template option (see Figure 12.2).

When you edit a template with the Designer, you can enter the contents of the template directly into the DataList control. When you are finished editing a template, you right-click the DataList and select End Template Editing.

The disadvantage of this second method of editing templates is that it does not allow you to enter freestanding databinding expressions. Also, you cannot type HTML tags directly into the template. However, you can drag and drop HTML elements and ASP.NET controls onto the template from the Toolbox.

Formatting the Appearance of a DataList

Because a DataList control uses an HTML table to display its data (which results in the data being displayed in a structured manner), you are provided with several formatting options when working with a DataList control. In the following sections, you'll learn how to format the borders of a DataList control, use auto formatting with a DataList control, and display the data in a DataList control in multiple columns.

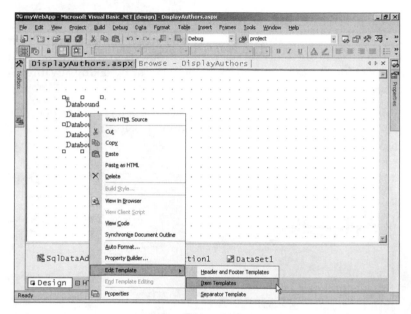

FIGURE 12.2   Editing templates with the Designer.

Formatting the Borders in a DataList Control

You can control the appearance of the borders rendered by a DataList control by modifying four of the DataList control's properties:

- GridLines   Indicates whether horizontal, vertical, or both horizontal and vertical lines appear between the cells rendered by a DataList control

- BorderColor   Indicates the color of the border lines around cells

- BorderStyle   Indicates the style of the outside border (for example, solid or dashed)

- BorderWidth   Indicates the pixel width of the outside border

You can modify these properties directly in the Properties window. Alternatively, you can open the Property Builder for the DataList by right-clicking the DataList, selecting Property Builder, and clicking the Borders tab.

Not all of these properties will render correctly in all browsers. Not surprisingly, all these properties work fine with recent versions of Microsoft Internet Explorer.

In the case of Netscape Navigator, however, you can only meaningfully assign the values Both or None to the GridLines property. Furthermore, the BorderStyle property is completely ignored.

Using Auto Formatting with the `DataList` Control

The `DataList` control supports `Style` objects for formatting the appearance of the control. You can edit the properties of the `Style` objects in the `DataList` control's Property sheet, or you can apply styles to the `DataList` by taking advantage of auto formatting.

To take advantage of auto formatting, right-click the `DataList` control on the Designer surface and select the Auto Format option. Selecting this option opens the dialog box shown in Figure 12.3.

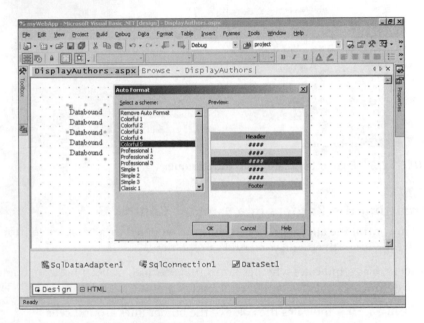

FIGURE 12.3   The Auto Format dialog box.

Notice that the Auto Format dialog box enables you to select among a variety of formatting schemes. For example, you can apply a Professional, Classic, or Colorful scheme to the `DataList` control.

If you don't like any of the pre-made style schemes, you can directly edit the `Style` objects associated with the `DataList` control. You can edit any of the following `Style` objects:

- `AlternatingItemStyle`   Formats alternating items
- `EditItemStyle`   Formats items selected for editing
- `FooterStyle`   Formats row that appears below all items

- HeaderStyle   Formats row that appears above all items
- ItemStyle   Formats each item
- SelectedItemStyle   Formats currently selected item
- SeparatorStyle   Formats content that appears between each item

For example, to format every other item displayed by the DataList control with a gray background—and create a banding effect—do the following:

1. Select the DataList control in the Properties window.

2. Expand the AlternatingItemStyle property.

3. Assign the value Gray to the BackColor property.

After you make these changes, the DataList will render the page in Figure 12.4.

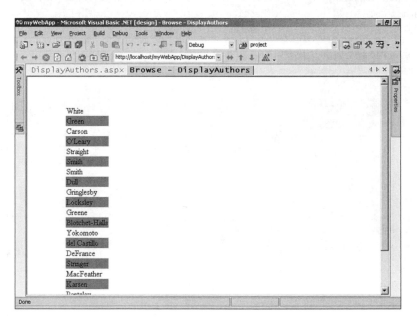

FIGURE 12.4   Using the DataList control's AlternatingItemStyle property.

Notice that the Style objects provide you with an alternative to using templates. If you want to display alternating items in a green font, you can create an AlternatingItemTemplate or you can edit the properties of the AlternatingItemStyle object.

WARNING

Style objects do not function exactly like templates. For example, if you use a
SelectedItemTemplate to format the currently selected item in a menu rendered with a
DataList, you need to rebind the DataList to its DataSource. If you use the
SelectedItemStyle object, on the other hand, you don't need to rebind. Because a template
might display a different databinding expression, you must always rebind to a datasource
when formatting items with a template.

Creating a Multicolumn DataList

You can use two of the properties of the DataList control, the RepeatColumns and
RepeatDirection properties, to render the items contained within a DataList in multiple columns. For example, creating multicolumn DataList controls is useful when
creating single row tab strips and navigation menus.

The RepeatColumns property specifies the number of columns to display with the
DataList control. The RepeatDirection property indicates whether items should be
repeated in a horizontal or vertical direction.

Perform the following steps to display a three-column list of products from the
Products database table (see Figure 12.5).

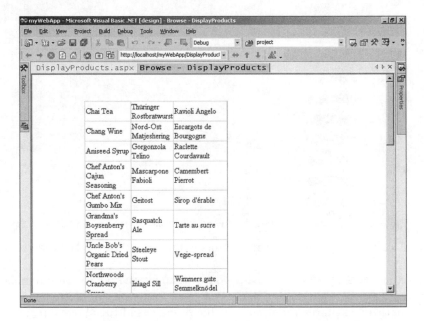

FIGURE 12.5 Rendering multiple columns with the DataList control.

First, you'll need to create a new Web Form Page and add the necessary database objects:

1. Add a Web Form Page named **DisplayProducts.aspx** to your project.

2. In the Server Explorer window, under the Data Connections tab, navigate to the Products database table located under the Northwind data connection. (If you don't already have an existing data connection to the Northwind database, you'll need to create one.)

3. Drag and drop the Products database table from the Server Explorer window onto the Designer surface. This will add an SqlConnection and SqlDataAdapter object to your Web Form Page.

4. Add a DataSet to the page by dragging the DataSet object from under the Data tab on the Toolbox onto the Designer surface.

5. When the Add DataSet dialog box appears, select the Untyped Dataset option and click OK.

Next, you'll need add the DataList control to the page and modify the control's RepeatColumns property:

1. Add a DataList control to the page.

2. In the Properties window, select the DataList control and assign the value **3** to the RepeatColumns property.

3. In the Properties window, assign the value **Both** to the GridLines property.

4. Click the HTML tab on the bottom of the window and enter the following ItemTemplate between the opening and closing <asp:DataList> tags:

```
<asp:DataList id="DataList1"
  style="Z-INDEX: 101; LEFT: 320px; POSITION: absolute; TOP: 140px"
  runat="server" RepeatColumns="3">
  <ItemTemplate>
    <%# DataBinder.Eval(Container, "DataItem.ProductName" )%>
  </ItemTemplate>
</asp:DataList>
```

Finally, you need to bind the DataList control to the Products DataSet:

1. Switch to the code-behind file for the DisplayProducts.aspx page by selecting Code from the View menu.

2. Enter the following code for the Page_Load subroutine:

C#

```csharp
private void Page_Load(object sender, System.EventArgs e)
{
  sqlDataAdapter1.Fill( dataSet1 );
  DataList1.DataSource = dataSet1;
  DataList1.DataBind();
}
```

VB.NET

```vbnet
Private Sub Page_Load(ByVal sender As System.Object,
➥ByVal e As System.EventArgs) Handles MyBase.Load
  SqlDataAdapter1.Fill(DataSet1)
  DataList1.DataSource = DataSet1
  DataList1.DataBind()
End Sub
```

3. Right-click the DisplayProducts.aspx page in Solution Explorer and select Build and Browse.

When the DisplayProducts.aspx page opens, the products are automatically displayed in three columns.

Creating a Menu with a DataList

You can use the DataList control to render an interactive menu of items. For example, you can use the DataList control to render a list of product category links. When a user clicks on a category link, you can display matching products.

To create an interactive menu of category links, we'll need to take advantage of a feature of the DataList control called *event-bubbling*. When a control supports event-bubbling, you can create a single event handler that executes whenever a control contained within the control raises an event.

To create our interactive menu of product category links, we'll need to add a LinkButton control to the DataList control's ItemTemplate. Each LinkButton will display a particular category link. However, clicking any category link will execute the same event handler. The Click event raised by clicking a category LinkButton will bubble up to be captured by the DataList control.

First, we'll need to create a new Web Form Page and add the necessary database objects:

1. Add a Web Form Page named DisplayMenu.aspx to your project.

2. In the Server Explorer window, under the Data Connections tab, navigate to the Categories database table located under the Northwind data connection. (If you don't already have an existing data connection to the Northwind database, you'll need to create one.)

3. Drag and drop the Categories database table from the Server Explorer window onto the Designer surface. This will add an `SqlConnection` and `SqlDataAdapter` object to your Web Form Page.

4. Add a DataSet to the page by dragging the `DataSet` object from under the Data tab on the Toolbox onto the Designer surface.

5. When the Add DataSet dialog box appears, select the Untyped Dataset option and click OK.

Next, we need to create the `DataList` control and add an `ItemTemplate` that contains a `LinkButton` control:

1. Add a `DataList` control to the page.

2. Right-click the `DataList` control and select ItemTemplates from the Edit Template menu.

3. Add a `LinkButton` control to the `DataList` control's `ItemTemplate` by dragging the `LinkButton` control onto the `ItemTemplate` on the Designer surface.

4. Select the `LinkButton` control in the Properties window and click the ellipsis that appears next to the `DataBindings` property.

5. In the DataBindings dialog box, select the radio button labeled Custom Binding Expression and enter the following expression in the text box:

   C#

   ```
   DataBinder.Eval(Container, "DataItem.CategoryName")
   ```

   VB.NET

   ```
   DataBinder.Eval(Container, "DataItem.CategoryName")
   ```

6. Click OK to close the DataBindings dialog box, right-click the `DataList` control, and select End Template Editing to stop editing the `ItemTemplate`.

Next, we need to bind the `DataList` control to the Categories DataSet:

1. Switch to the code-behind file for the DisplayMenu.aspx page by selecting Code from the View menu.

2. Enter the following code for the Page_Load handler:

   C#

   ```csharp
   private void Page_Load(object sender, System.EventArgs e)
   {
     if (!Page.IsPostBack)
     {
       sqlDataAdapter1.Fill(dataSet1);
       DataList1.DataSource=dataSet1;
       DataList1.DataBind();
     }
   }
   ```

   VB.NET

   ```vbnet
   Private Sub Page_Load(ByVal sender As System.Object,
   ➥ByVal e As System.EventArgs) Handles MyBase.Load
     If Not Page.IsPostBack Then
       SqlDataAdapter1.Fill(DataSet1)
       DataList1.DataSource = DataSet1
       DataList1.DataBind()
     End If
   End Sub
   ```

The next step is to highlight the selected item in the menu with a yellow background color:

1. Switch back to the Designer surface by selecting Designer from the View menu.

2. Select the DataList control in the Properties window.

3. Expand the SelectedItemStyle property.

4. Assign the value **Yellow** to the SelectedItemStyle BackColor property.

Finally, we need to add an event-handler that executes whenever you click a menu item.

C# Steps

1. In the Properties window, select the DataList control.

2. Click the Events icon at the top of the Properties window (the icon of the lightning bolt).

3. Double-click next to the `ItemCommand` event (this will switch you to the Code Editor).

4. Enter the following code for the `DataList_ItemCommand` handler:

```
private void DataList1_ItemCommand(object source,
➥System.Web.UI.WebControls.DataListCommandEventArgs e)
{
  DataList1.SelectedIndex = e.Item.ItemIndex;
}
```

5. Right-click the DisplayMenu.aspx page in Solution Explorer and select Build and Browse.

VB.NET Steps

1. Switch to the code-behind file for the DisplayMenu.aspx page by selecting View, Code.

2. In the Class Name drop-down list (at the top left of the Code Editor), select the `DataList1` control.

3. In the Method Name drop-down list (at the top right of the Code Editor), select the `ItemCommand` method.

4. Enter the following code for the `DataList1_ItemCommand` subroutine:

```
Private Sub DataList1_ItemCommand(ByVal source As Object,
➥ByVal e As System.Web.UI.WebControls.DataListCommandEventArgs) Handles
DataList1.ItemCommand
  DataList1.SelectedIndex = e.Item.ItemIndex
End Sub
```

5. Right-click the DisplayMenu.aspx page in Solution Explorer and select Build and Browse.

After the DisplayMenu.aspx page opens, you can click a particular category name and the selected category name will be highlighted with a yellow background color.

This sample contains several steps, so it deserves some explanation. Let's walk through the flow of events when you click a menu item:

1. Clicking a menu item raises a `LinkButton` control's `Click` event.

2. The `Click` event bubbles up to the `DataList` control, which raises the `DataList` control's `ItemCommand` event.

3. The ItemCommand event is handled by an event-handler named DataList1_ItemCommand.

4. The DataList1_ItemCommand handler assigns the index of the item clicked to the DataList control's SelectedIndex property.

5. The item that has the index of the SelectedIndex is rendered with the formatting properties of the SelectedItemStyle Style object.

6. The selected menu item is rendered with a yellow background color.

By taking advantage of event-bubbling, you can create a single event handler—the DataList1_ItemCommand—that executes whenever someone clicks a LinkButton. If the DataList control did not support event bubbling, you would need to capture the Click event of each and every LinkButton control individually.

Using the DataKeys Collection

In the previous section, you created an interactive menu of product categories with the DataList control. When a menu item is clicked, the index of the selected item is passed to the DataList1_ItemCommand handler.

Unfortunately, the index of the selected item in a menu doesn't usually do you any good. Typically, you don't want the index of the selected item. Instead, you need to know the primary key associated with the menu item.

For example, if you want to display a list of matching products when you click a category, you will need the primary key associated with the category to select the matching products. The Categories and Products tables are joined on a common CategoryID key.

There is an easy way around this problem. The DataList control supports a special collection of items named the DataKeys collection. You can automatically populate the DataKeys collection with values from the primary key column from the DataList control's data source.

To illustrate how the DataKeys collection works, you'll create a menu of authors' last names. When you select an author in the menu, the primary key associated with the author will be displayed in a Label control.

First, you need to create a new Web Form Page and the necessary database objects:

1. Add a Web Form Page named **AuthorMenu.aspx** to your project.

2. In the Server Explorer window, under the Data Connections tab, navigate to the Authors database table located under the Pubs data connection. (If you don't already have an existing data connection to the Pubs database, you'll need to create one.)

3. Drag and drop the Authors database table from the Server Explorer window onto the Designer surface. This will add an `SqlConnection` and `SqlDataAdapter` object to your Web Form Page.

4. Add a DataSet to the page by dragging the `DataSet` object from under the Data tab on the Toolbox onto the Designer surface.

5. When the Add DataSet dialog box appears, select the Untyped Dataset option and click OK.

Next, we need to create the `Label` and `DataList` controls and add an `ItemTemplate` to the DataList that contains a `LinkButton` control:

1. Add a `Label` control to the page.

2. Add a `DataList` control to the page.

3. Right-click the `DataList` control and select ItemTemplates from the Edit Template menu.

4. Add a `LinkButton` control to the `DataList` control's `ItemTemplate` by dragging the `LinkButton` control from under the Web Forms tab on the Toolbox onto the `ItemTemplate` on the Designer surface.

5. Select the `LinkButton` control in the Properties window and click the ellipsis that appears next to the `DataBindings` property.

6. In the DataBindings dialog box, select the Custom Binding Expression radio button and enter the following expression in the text box:

   C#

   ```
   DataBinder.Eval( Container, "DataItem.au_lname" )
   ```

   VB.NET

   ```
   DataBinder.Eval( Container, "DataItem.au_lname" )
   ```

7. Click OK to close the DataBindings dialog box, right-click the `DataList` control, and select End Template Editing to stop editing the `ItemTemplate`.

Next, you need to bind the `DataList` control to the Authors DataSet. This time, however, you'll assign a value to the `DataList` control's `DataKeyField` property before binding the `DataList`. The `DataKeyField` indicates the name of the primary key from the Authors table.

1. Switch to the code-behind file for the AuthorMenu.aspx page by selecting Code from the View menu.

2. Enter the following code for the Page_Load handler:

C#

```csharp
private void Page_Load(object sender, System.EventArgs e)
{
  if (!Page.IsPostBack)
  {
  sqlDataAdapter1.Fill(dataSet1);
  DataList1.DataSource = dataSet1;
  DataList1.DataKeyField = "au_id";
DataList1.DataBind();
  }
}
```

VB.NET

```vbnet
Private Sub Page_Load(ByVal sender As System.Object,
➥ByVal e As System.EventArgs) Handles MyBase.Load
  If Not Page.IsPostBack Then
    SqlDataAdapter1.Fill(DataSet1)
    DataList1.DataSource = DataSet1
    DataList1.DataKeyField = "au_id"
    DataList1.DataBind()
  End If
End Sub
```

The next step is to highlight the selected item in the menu. You'll highlight the selected menu item by changing its font to bold and italic:

1. Switch back to the Designer surface by selecting Designer from the View menu.

2. Select the DataList control in the Properties window.

3. Expand the SelectedItemStyle property.

4. Expand the SelectedItemStyle Font property.

5. Assign the value **True** to both the Bold and Italic properties.

Finally, we need to add a handler that executes whenever you click a menu item. This subroutine will assign the primary key of the selected item to the Label control.

C# Steps

1. In the Properties window, select the DataList control.

2. Click the Events icon at the top of the Properties window (the icon of the lightning bolt).

3. Double-click next to the ItemCommand event (this will switch you to the Code Editor).

4. Enter the following code for the DataList_ItemCommand handler:

```
private void DataList1_ItemCommand(object source,
➥System.Web.UI.WebControls.DataListCommandEventArgs e)
{
  DataList1.SelectedIndex = e.Item.ItemIndex;
  Label1.Text = (string)DataList1.DataKeys[ e.Item.ItemIndex ];
}
```

5. Right-click the AuthorMenu.aspx page in Solution Explorer and select Build and Browse.

VB.NET Steps

1. Switch to the code-behind file for the AuthorMenu.aspx page by selecting Code from the View menu.

2. In the Class Name drop-down list (at the top left of the code editor), select the DataList1 control.

3. In the Method Name drop-down list (at the top right of the code editor), select the ItemCommand method.

4. Enter the following code for the DataList1_ItemCommand subroutine:

```
Private Sub DataList1_ItemCommand(ByVal source As Object,
➥ByVal e As System.Web.UI.WebControls.DataListCommandEventArgs)
➥Handles DataList1.ItemCommand
  DataList1.SelectedIndex = e.Item.ItemIndex
  Label1.Text = DataList1.DataKeys( e.Item.ItemIndex )
End Sub
```

5. Right-click the AuthorMenu.aspx page in Solution Explorer and select Build and Browse.

After the AuthorMenu.aspx page opens, you can select an author by clicking a menu item. When you select an author, the primary key associated with the author appears in the Label control. In the case of the Authors database table, the primary key contains the author's Social Security number (see Figure 12.6).

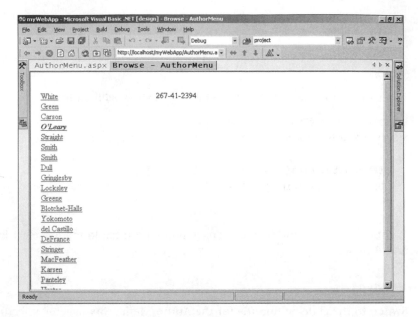

FIGURE 12.6   Using the DataKeys collection.

Creating a Single-Page Master/Detail Form

In this final section, you'll create a Web Form Page that uses both the DataList and Repeater controls. You'll create a single-page master/detail form that uses a DataList to display a menu of product categories and a Repeater control to display a list of matching products.

First, you need to create the new Web Form Page and the necessary database objects. You'll need to create one SqlDataAdapter for the Categories database table and a second SqlDataAdapter for the Products database table:

1. Add a Web Form Page named **MasterDetail.aspx** to your project.

2. In the Server Explorer window, under the Data Connections tab, expand the Tables folder located under the Northwind data connection. (If you don't already have an existing data connection to the Northwind database, you'll need to create one.)

3. Drag and drop the Categories database table from the Server Explorer window onto the Designer surface. This will add an SqlConnection and SqlDataAdapter object to your Web Form Page.

4. Drag and drop the Products database table from the Server Explorer window onto the Designer surface. This will add a second SqlDataAdapter object to your Web Form Page.

5. In the Properties window, select the second `SqlDataAdapter`.

6. Expand the `SelectCommand` property.

7. Assign the following select statement to the `CommandText` property:

```
SELECT
ProductID, ProductName, UnitPrice
FROM dbo.Products
Where CategoryID = @CategoryID
```

8. Add a DataSet to the page by dragging the `DataSet` object from under the Data tab on the Toolbox onto the Designer surface.

9. When the Add DataSet dialog box appears, select the Untyped Dataset option and click OK.

Next, you need to add a `DataList` control that displays the menu of product categories:

1. Add a `DataList` control to the page.

2. Right-click the `DataList` control and select ItemTemplates from the Edit Template menu.

3. Add a `LinkButton` control to the `DataList` control's `ItemTemplate` by dragging the `LinkButton` control from under the Web Forms tab on the Toolbox onto the `ItemTemplate` on the Designer surface.

4. Select the `LinkButton` control in the Properties window and click the ellipsis that appears next to the `DataBindings` property.

5. In the DataBindings dialog box, select Custom Binding Expression radio button and enter the following expression in the text box:

C#

```
DataBinder.Eval(Container, "DataItem.CategoryName")
```

VB.NET

```
DataBinder.Eval(Container, "DataItem.CategoryName")
```

6. Click OK to close the DataBindings dialog box, right-click the `DataList` control, and select End Template Editing to stop editing the `ItemTemplate`.

Next, you'll modify the `SelectedItemStyle` object so the selected menu item will appear with a yellow background:

1. In the Properties window, select the DataList control.

2. Expand the SelectedItemStyle property.

3. Assign the value **Yellow** to the SelectedItemStyle BackColor property.

Next, you must bind the DataList to the Categories DataSet:

1. Switch to the code-behind file for the MasterDetail.aspx page by selecting Code from the View menu.

2. Enter the following code for the Page_Load handler:

C#

```
private void Page_Load(object sender, System.EventArgs e)
{
  if (!Page.IsPostBack)
  {
  sqlDataAdapter1.Fill( dataSet1 );
  DataList1.DataSource = dataSet1;
  DataList1.DataKeyField = "CategoryID";
  DataList1.DataBind();
  }
}
```

VB.NET

```
Private Sub Page_Load(ByVal sender As System.Object,
➡ByVal e As System.EventArgs) Handles MyBase.Load
  If Not Page.IsPostBack Then
    SqlDataAdapter1.Fill(DataSet1)
    DataList1.DataSource = DataSet1
    DataList1.DataKeyField = "CategoryID"
    DataList1.DataBind()
  End If
End Sub
```

Next, you need to add a Repeater control to display the products. You'll display the name and price of each product:

1. Switch back to the Designer by selecting Designer from the View menu.

2. Add a Flow Layout Panel to the page by dragging the Flow Layout Panel from under the HTML tab in the Toolbox onto the Designer surface.

3. Add a Repeater control to the Flow Layout Panel by dragging the Repeater control from under the Web Forms tab in the Toolbox onto the Flow Layout Panel.

4. Switch to the HTML source for the page by clicking the HTML tab at the bottom of the Designer window.

5. Enter the following `ItemTemplate` between the opening and closing `<asp:Repeater>` tags:

```
<asp:Repeater id="Repeater1" runat="server">
  <ItemTemplate>
  <li>
  <%# DataBinder.Eval( Container, "DataItem.ProductName" ) %> -
  <%# DataBinder.Eval( Container, "DataItem.UnitPrice", "{0:c}" )%>
  </li>
  </ItemTemplate>
</asp:Repeater>
```

Finally, you need to retrieve the matching products when a product category is clicked in the `DataList` menu.

C# Steps

1. In the Properties window, select the `DataList` control.

2. Click the Events icon at the top of the Properties window (the icon of the lightning bolt).

3. Double-click next to the `ItemCommand` event (this will switch you to the code editor).

4. Enter the following code for the `DataList_ItemCommand` handler:

```
private void DataList1_ItemCommand(object source,
➥System.Web.UI.WebControls.DataListCommandEventArgs e)
{
  DataList1.SelectedIndex = e.Item.ItemIndex;
  int intPrimaryKey = (int)DataList1.DataKeys[e.Item.ItemIndex];
  sqlDataAdapter2.SelectCommand.Parameters["@CategoryID"].Value
➥ = intPrimaryKey;
  sqlDataAdapter2.Fill(dataSet1);
  Repeater1.DataSource = dataSet1;
  Repeater1.DataBind();
}
```

5. Right-click the MasterDetail.aspx page in Solution Explorer and select Build and Browse.

VB.NET Steps

1. Switch to the code-behind file for the MasterDetail.aspx page by selecting View, Code.

2. In the Class Name drop-down list (located at the top left of the code editor), select DataList1.

3. In the Method Name drop-down list (located at the top right of the code editor), select the ItemCommand method.

4. Enter the following code for the DataList1_ItemCommand:

```
Private Sub DataList1_ItemCommand(ByVal source As Object,
➥ByVal e As System.Web.UI.WebControls.DataListCommandEventArgs)
➥Handles DataList1.ItemCommand
  Dim intPrimaryKey As Integer

  DataList1.SelectedIndex = e.Item.ItemIndex
  intPrimaryKey = DataList1.DataKeys(e.Item.ItemIndex)
  SqlDataAdapter2.SelectCommand.Parameters("@CategoryID").Value
➥= intPrimaryKey
  SqlDataAdapter2.Fill(DataSet1)
  Repeater1.DataSource = DataSet1
  Repeater1.DataBind()
End Sub
```

5. Right-click the MasterDetail.aspx page in the Solution Explorer window and select Build and Browse.

When you finish these steps, the Designer surface should resemble Figure 12.7.

After you select Build and Browse and the MasterDetail.aspx page opens, you can click a category name and a list of matching products is displayed. The resulting page should resemble Figure 12.8.

Summary

In this chapter, you learned how to the DataList control to format and display database data. First, you learned how to use the DataList control to display database records in an HTML table. You learned how to apply advanced formatting to a DataList by taking advantage of auto formatting and Style objects. You also learned how to display the output of a DataList control in multiple columns.

Finally, you tackled an advanced Web Form Page that makes use of both the DataList and Repeater controls. You learned how to create a single page master/detail form that displays a menu of categories in a DataList control and a set of matching products in a Repeater control.

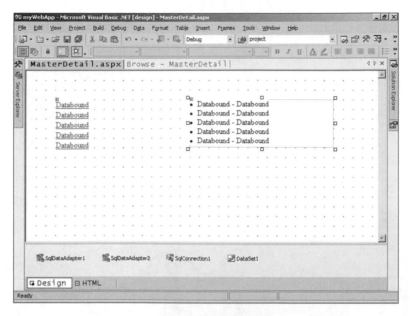

FIGURE 12.7 MasterDetail.aspx page in the Designer.

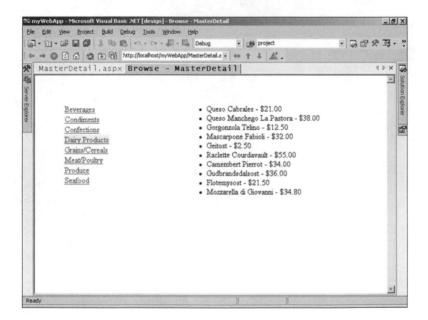

FIGURE 12.8 MasterDetail page in a Web browser.

13

Displaying Data with the DataGrid Control

IN THIS CHAPTER

- Automatically Displaying the Contents of a Database Table

- Customizing the Appearance of the DataGrid Control

- Sorting Data in a DataGrid

- Paging Through Records in a DataGrid

- Editing Database Records in a DataGrid

The DataGrid control is the most feature-rich control in the ASP.NET Framework. In this chapter, you'll learn how to use the DataGrid control to work with SQL Server database data. In particular, you'll learn:

- How to display data with the DataGrid control

- How to customize the appearance of the DataGrid control

- How to sort data with the DataGrid control

- How to page through data with the DataGrid control

- How to edit data with the DataGrid control

Automatically Displaying the Contents of a Database Table

Even though the DataGrid control is one of the most complicated controls in the ASP.NET Framework, it is also the easiest control to use for quickly displaying the contents of a database table. Unlike the Repeater or DataList control, the DataGrid control does not require you to create a template to display the contents of a database table.

For example, suppose that you need to quickly display the contents of the Northwind Products database table (see Figure 13.1).

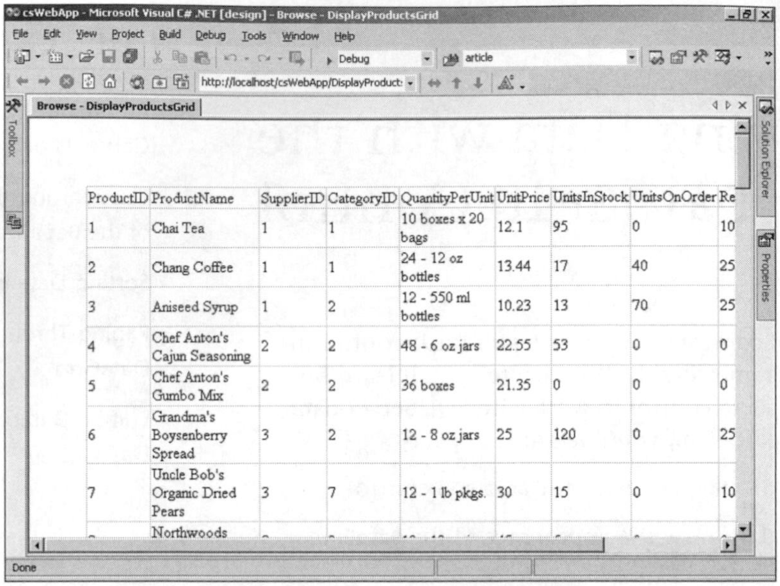

Figure 13.1   Displaying the Products table in a DataGrid.

First, you'll need to create the necessary database objects:

1. Add a Web Form Page named **DisplayProductsGrid.aspx** to your project.

2. Drag and drop the Products database table from under the Northwind data connection in the Server Explorer window onto the Designer surface.

3. Add an Untyped DataSet to the page.

Next, you need to add the DataGrid control to the page and bind the DataGrid to the Products DataSet:

1. Drag and drop the DataGrid control from under the Web Forms tab in the Toolbox onto the Designer surface.

2. Switch to the Code Editor by double-clicking the Designer surface.

3. Enter the following code for the Page_Load method:

C#

```csharp
private void Page_Load(object sender, System.EventArgs e)
{
```

```
    sqlDataAdapter1.Fill( dataSet1 );
    DataGrid1.DataSource = dataSet1;
    DataGrid1.DataBind();
}
```

VB.NET

```
Private Sub Page_Load(ByVal sender As System.Object,
➥ByVal e As System.EventArgs) Handles MyBase.Load
  SqlDataAdapter1.Fill(DataSet1)
  DataGrid1.DataSource = DataSet1
  DataGrid1.DataBind()
End Sub
```

4. Right-click the DisplayProductsGrid.aspx page in the Solution Explorer window
   and select Build and Browse.

When the DisplayProductsGrid.aspx page opens, all the columns and all the rows are
displayed from the Products database table.

TIP

If you prefer, you can display only certain columns from the Products table instead of all
columns. To do this, don't drag and drop the Products database table onto the Designer
surface. Instead, expand the Products table in the Server Explorer window, select one or more
columns while holding down the Ctrl key, and drag the selected columns onto the Designer
surface.

TIP

If you are using a DataGrid simply to display database data, it's a good idea to turn off View
State for the DataGrid (you're not using it and you are wasting bandwidth with View State
enabled). Disable View State for the DataGrid by assigning the value False to the DataGrid
control's EnableViewState property. To learn more about View State see Chapter 17,
"Maintaining Application State."

Customizing the Appearance of the DataGrid Control

One problem with the page that we created in the previous section is that it is not
very pretty. You wouldn't want to use it in a production application. The column

headings are named after the database table column names, and the content of the columns is not formatted. For example, the UnitPrice column is displayed as a decimal value (12.34) instead of a currency value ($12.34).

In this section, you'll learn how to format a DataGrid by taking advantage of auto formatting and by explicitly defining the columns in a DataGrid.

Applying Auto Formatting to a DataGrid

We can immediately improve the appearance of the DataGrid by taking advantage of auto formatting. Right-click the DataGrid and select Auto Format. The Auto Format dialog box will appear (see Figure 13.2). Notice that you can select among a variety of pre-made format schemes, such as Professional, Colorful, or Classic.

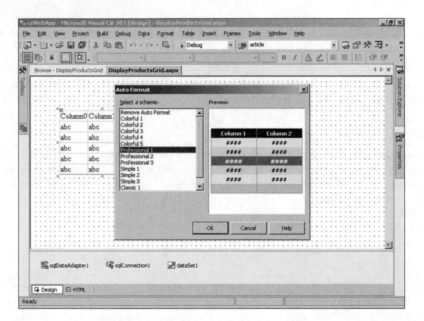

Figure 13.2   The Auto Format dialog box.

> **NOTE**
>
> Unfortunately, you cannot modify the list of format schemes displayed in the Auto Format dialog box. The list of format schemes is hard-coded into the System.Design.dll assembly within the AutoFormatDialog class.

If you don't like any of the pre-made format schemes, you can modify the appearance of a DataGrid directly by working with the Style objects associated with the

DataGrid control. The DataGrid control has the following Style objects that you can modify in the Properties window:

- **AlternatingItemStyle**   These formatting properties are applied to every other row displayed in the DataGrid.

- **EditItemStyle**   These formatting properties are applied to the row that is currently selected for editing.

- **FooterStyle**   These formatting properties are applied to the content of the DataGrid footer.

- **HeaderStyle**   These formatting properties are applied to the content of the DataGrid header.

- **ItemStyle**   These formatting properties are applied to every row displayed in the DataGrid.

- **PagerStyle**   These formatting properties are applied to the user interface for navigating through a DataGrid when paging is enabled.

- **SelectedItemStyle**   These formatting properties are applied to the row that is currently selected.

For example, if you want every other row displayed by a DataGrid to have a yellow background color, you can expand the AlternatingItemStyle property and modify the value of the BackColor property.

Specifying Columns in a DataGrid

By default, the DataGrid control will display all the columns from the database table to which it is bound. Typically, this isn't what you want because it provides you with little control over the formatting of each column.

You can control exactly which columns are displayed, and how the columns are formatted, by opening the Property Builder for a DataGrid. Right-click the DataGrid and select Property Builder, click the Columns tab, and you'll see the dialog box shown in Figure 13.3.

NOTE

It's a bad idea to retrieve columns in your SELECT statement that you don't plan to display. For example, if you retrieve all the columns from the Products table and only show the ProductName column in the DataGrid, you have pushed a lot of unnecessary data across the wire.

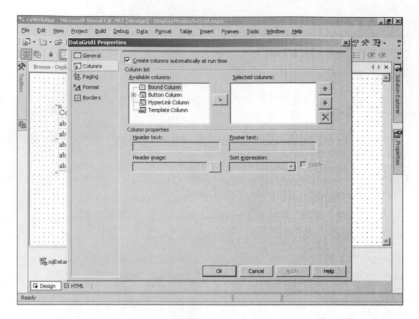

Figure 13.3   Property Builder Columns tab.

Notice that the Create Columns Automatically at Run Time check box is checked by default. The first thing that you should do, if you want to control the columns that appear in the DataGrid, is to uncheck this check box.

You can select columns to display by clicking Bound Column in the Available columns panel and clicking the arrow to move the Bound Column to the Selected columns panel. For each Bound Column, you can set the following properties:

- *Header text*—The text that appears at the top of the column

- *Header image*—An image that appears at the top of the column

- *Data Field*—The name of the database column to display in the column

- *Data formatting expression*—A format string used to format the values of this column

- *Footer text*—The text that appears at the bottom of the column

- *Sort expression*—Value passed to the SortCommand handler when sorting is enabled for the DataGrid

- *Read Only*—Indicates that the column should not be editable when the row is selected for editing

- *Visible*—Indicates whether the column is hidden or visible

For example, suppose that you want to modify the DisplayProductsGrid.aspx page that we created in the previous section so that it shows the ProductID, ProductName, and UnitPrice columns.

1. Right-click the DataGrid in the DisplayProductsGrid.aspx page, select Property Builder and click the Columns tab.

2. Uncheck the Create Columns Automatically at Run Time check box.

3. Add a Bound Column to the Selected columns panel with the following properties:

Property	Value
Header text	ID
Data Field	ProductID

4. Add a second Bound Column to the Selected columns panel with the following properties:

Property	Value
Header text	Name
Data Field	ProductName

5. Add a third Bound Column to the Selected columns panel with the following properties:

Property	Value
Header text	Price
Data Field	UnitPrice
Formatting expression	{0:c}

6. Click OK to close the DataGrid1 Properties dialog box.

7. Right-click the DisplayProductsGrid.aspx page in the Solution Explorer window and select Build and Browse.

After you complete these steps, the page shown in Figure 13.4 appears. Notice that the column headings are no longer the same as the database column names. Furthermore, the UnitPrice column is now formatted correctly.

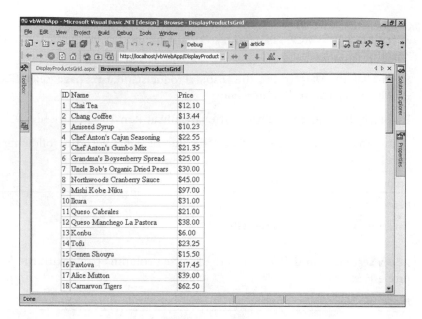

Figure 13.4   Specifying DataGrid columns.

NOTE

The Property Builder dialog box has a different appearance when you work with a Typed DataSet than when you work with an Untyped DataSet. When working with a Typed DataSet, the actual column names are displayed in the Available columns dialog box.

Displaying HyperLink Columns in a DataGrid

You can use a DataGrid to display a list of hyperlinks. This is useful when you want to create a two-page Master/Detail form. You can create the master page by using a DataGrid to show a list of links. Each link can pass the ID of a record to a detail page.

For example, suppose that you want to create a master and detail page that enables you to look up detailed information on different authors. First, you need to create the master page by using the DataGrid control. We'll start by creating the page and adding all the necessary database objects.

1. Add a Web Form Page to your project named **AuthorMaster.aspx**.

2. Drag and drop the Authors database table from the Server Explorer window onto the Designer surface.

3. Add an Untyped DataSet to the page.

Next, we need to add a DataGrid control to the page and configure it to display a list of links to the AuthorDetail.aspx page:

1. Add a DataGrid control to the page.

2. Right-click the DataGrid, select Property Builder, and click the Columns tab.

3. Uncheck the Create Columns Automatically at Run Time check box.

4. Add a HyperLink Column to the Selected columns panel with the following properties:

Property	Value
Header text	**Author**
Text field	**au_lname**
URL field	**au_id**
URL format string	**AuthorDetail.aspx?id={0}**

5. Double-click the Designer surface and enter the following code for the Page_Load method:

C#

```
private void Page_Load(object sender, System.EventArgs e)
{
  sqlDataAdapter1.Fill( dataSet1 );
  DataGrid1.DataSource = dataSet1;
  DataGrid1.DataBind();
}
```

VB.NET

```
Private Sub Page_Load(ByVal sender As System.Object,
➡ByVal e As System.EventArgs) Handles MyBase.Load
  SqlDataAdapter1.Fill(DataSet1)
  DataGrid1.DataSource = DataSet1
  DataGrid1.DataBind()
End Sub
```

6. Right-click the AuthorMaster.aspx page in the Solution Explorer window and select Build and Browse.

When the AuthorMaster.aspx page opens, the page should resemble the page in Figure 13.5. If you hover your mouse over the links, you can see that each link passes the author ID to the AuthorDetail.aspx page.

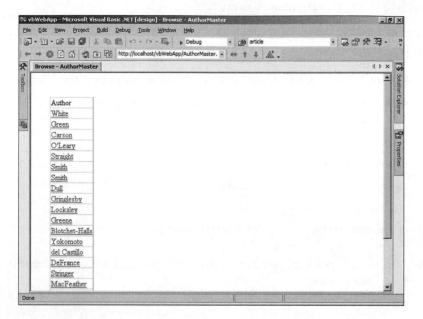

Figure 13.5   The AuthorMaster.aspx Page.

Next, we need to create the AuthorDetail.aspx page. On this page, we'll use a DataReader to represent the detail information for an author and display the information in Label controls. We'll start by creating the page and adding all the necessary database objects and controls:

1. Add a Web Form Page to your project named **AuthorDetail.aspx**.

2. In the Server Explorer window, drag the Pubs data connection from under the Data Connections tab onto the Designer surface.

3. Add an SqlCommand object to the page.

4. In the Properties window, select the sqlCommand1 object and assign the value **sqlConnection1** to its Connection property.

5. In the Properties window, select the sqlCommand1 object and assign the following value to the CommandText property (when the Regenerate Parameters dialog box appears, click Yes):

   ```
   Select * from Authors Where au_id=@authorID
   ```

6. Add three Web Forms Labels to the page. Provide the first Label with an ID of **lblFirstName**, the second Label with an ID of **lblLastName**, and the third Label with an ID of **lblPhone**.

Next, we need to add the application logic to the page that will grab the necessary author record from the Authors database table.

1. Double-click the Designer surface to switch to the Code Editor.

2. Enter the following code for the Page_Load handler:

C#

```
private void Page_Load(object sender, System.EventArgs e)
{
  System.Data.SqlClient.SqlDataReader dtrAuthor;

  string AuthorID = Request.QueryString[ "id" ];
  if (AuthorID == null)
    Response.Redirect( "AuthorMaster.aspx" );

  sqlCommand1.Parameters["@authorID"].Value=AuthorID;
  sqlConnection1.Open();
  dtrAuthor = sqlCommand1.ExecuteReader();
  if (dtrAuthor.Read())
  {
    lblFirstName.Text = (string)dtrAuthor["au_fname"];
    lblLastName.Text = (string)dtrAuthor["au_lname"];
    lblPhone.Text = (string)dtrAuthor["phone"];
  }
  sqlConnection1.Close();
}
```

VB.NET

```
Private Sub Page_Load(ByVal sender As System.Object,
➥ByVal e As System.EventArgs) Handles MyBase.Load
  Dim dtrAuthor As System.Data.SqlClient.SqlDataReader
  Dim AuthorID As String

  AuthorID = Request.QueryString("id")
  If IsNothing(AuthorID) Then
    Response.Redirect("AuthorMaster.aspx")
  End If

  SqlCommand1.Parameters("@authorID").Value = AuthorID
```

```
    SqlConnection1.Open()
    dtrAuthor = SqlCommand1.ExecuteReader()
    If dtrAuthor.Read() Then
      lblFirstName.Text = dtrAuthor("au_fname")
      lblLastName.Text = dtrAuthor("au_lname")
      lblPhone.Text = dtrAuthor("phone")
    End If
    SqlConnection1.Close()
  End Sub
```

3. Right-click the AuthorMaster.aspx page—*not the AuthorDetail.aspx page*—in the Solution Explorer window and select Build and Browse.

When you click a particular author's last name in the AuthorMaster.aspx page, the author's first name, last name, and phone number appears in the AuthorDetail.aspx page.

The Page_Load handler contains code that first checks whether an author ID has been passed to the page. If not, the user is automatically redirected to the AuthorMaster.aspx page. If an author ID can be retrieved, the author record is returned from the Authors database table and assigned to the Label controls.

Sorting Data in a DataGrid

You can use a DataGrid to sort records retrieved from a database table. When a DataGrid has sorting enabled, the DataGrid column headers appear as links. When you click a link, the rows in the DataGrid are sorted in order of that column.

For example, suppose that you want to display a DataGrid that enables you to sort the records in the Titles database table. First, you need to create the Web Form Page and add the necessary database objects:

1. Add a Web Form Page to your project named **SortGrid.aspx**.

2. Drag and drop the Titles database table from under the Pubs data connection in the Server Explorer window onto the Designer surface.

3. Add an Untyped DataSet to the page.

4. Add a DataView to the page.

Notice that we've added a DataView to the page. We need to add a DataView to create a sortable representation of the data in the DataSet.

Next, you need to add a `DataGrid` control to the page and enable sorting for the DataGrid:

1. Add a DataGrid to the page.

2. Right-click the DataGrid and select Property Builder. Check the Allow Sorting check box and click OK.

Next, you need to add the application logic to the page that retrieves the database data and binds the data to the DataGrid:

1. Switch to the Code Editor by double-clicking the Designer surface.

2. Enter the following code for the `Page_Load` handler:

   C#

   ```
   private void Page_Load(object sender, System.EventArgs e)
   {
     if (!Page.IsPostBack)
       BindGrid( "Title" );
   }
   ```

   VB.NET

   ```
   Private Sub Page_Load(ByVal sender As System.Object,
   ➥ByVal e As System.EventArgs) Handles MyBase.Load
     If Not Page.IsPostBack Then
       BindGrid("Title")
     End If
   End Sub
   ```

3. Enter the following `BindGrid()` method below the `Page_Load` handler:

   C#

   ```
   void BindGrid( string strSort )
   {
     sqlDataAdapter1.Fill( dataSet1 );
     dataView1 = dataSet1.Tables[0].DefaultView;
     dataView1.Sort = strSort;
     DataGrid1.DataSource = dataView1;
     DataGrid1.DataBind();
   }
   ```

VB.NET

```
Sub BindGrid(ByVal strSort As String)
  SqlDataAdapter1.Fill(DataSet1)
  DataView1 = DataSet1.Tables(0).DefaultView
  DataView1.Sort = strSort
  DataGrid1.DataSource = DataView1
  DataGrid1.DataBind()
End Sub
```

If you build and browse the page at this point, the DataGrid will appear with the data from the Titles database table. However, if you click a column heading, nothing happens. The data isn't sorted.

There's one last step you must perform to get the DataGrid to sort the data. The DataGrid control raises the SortCommand event whenever you click a column heading. You must add a handler for this event to the page.

C# Steps

1. Switch back to the Designer by selecting Designer from the View menu.

2. In the Properties window, select the DataGrid control and click the Events icon (the lightning bolt). Clicking the Events icon will display a list of all the events associated with the DataGrid.

3. Double-click next to the SortCommand event. This will switch you to the Code Editor and add a SortCommand event handler.

4. Enter the following code for the SortCommand handler:

    ```
    private void DataGrid1_SortCommand(object source,
    ➥System.Web.UI.WebControls.DataGridSortCommandEventArgs e)
    {
      BindGrid( e.SortExpression );
    }
    ```

5. Right-click the SortGrid.aspx page in the Solution Explorer window and select Build and Browse.

VB.NET Steps

1. In the Class Name drop-down list that appears at the top-left of the Code Editor, select the DataGrid1 control.

2. In the Method Name drop-down list that appears at the top-right of the Code Editor, select the SortCommand event. This will add a SortCommand event handler to the Code Editor.

3. Enter the following code for the SortCommand handler:

```
Private Sub DataGrid1_SortCommand(ByVal source As Object, ByVal
➥e As System.Web.UI.WebControls.DataGridSortCommandEventArgs)
➥Handles DataGrid1.SortCommand
  BindGrid(e.SortExpression)
End Sub
```

4. Right-click the SortGrid.aspx page in the Solution Explorer window and select Build and Browse.

After you complete these steps, the DataGrid will display the contents of the Titles table. If you click any of the column headings, that column will sort the rows displayed by the DataGrid.

Notice that you had to add the application logic yourself to the page to enable sorting. The contents of the DataGrid are sorted with the DataView object.

Using Caching with Sorting

One problem with the page that we created in the previous section is that it is not very efficient. Whenever you click a column to sort the DataGrid, all the data must be retrieved from the database again. Because accessing a database table is a slow operation, the page is not as efficient as it could be.

There's an easy way to fix this. You can cache the records retrieved from the database in the Web server's memory by taking advantage of the Cache object. Retrieving records from a database table is slow, but retrieving records from memory is lightning fast.

In the SortGrid.aspx page, make the following modifications to the BindGrid() method:

C#

```
void BindGrid( string strSort )
{
  dataSet1 = (DataSet)Cache[ "Titles" ];

  if (dataSet1 == null )
  {
    dataSet1 = new DataSet();
    sqlDataAdapter1.Fill( dataSet1 );
    Cache[ "Titles" ] = dataSet1;
  }
  dataView1 = dataSet1.Tables[0].DefaultView;
```

```
  dataView1.Sort = strSort;
  DataGrid1.DataSource = dataView1;
  DataGrid1.DataBind();
}
```

VB.NET

```
Sub BindGrid(ByVal strSort As String)
  DataSet1 = Cache("Titles")

  If DataSet1 Is Nothing Then
    DataSet1 = New DataSet()
    SqlDataAdapter1.Fill(DataSet1)
    Cache("Titles") = DataSet1
  End If
  DataView1 = DataSet1.Tables(0).DefaultView
  DataView1.Sort = strSort
  DataGrid1.DataSource = DataView1
  DataGrid1.DataBind()
End Sub
```

If you rebuild the page (by right-clicking the SortGrid.aspx page in the Solution Explorer window and selecting Build and Browse), the database will be accessed only once, when the page first opens. You can test this by temporarily stopping the Microsoft SQL Server service:

1. Open the Microsoft SQL Server Service Manager by going to Start, Programs, Microsoft SQL Server, Service Manager.

2. Click the Stop button.

Now that you've shut down Microsoft SQL Server, there's no possibility that the SortGrid.aspx page can retrieve data from the Titles database table. However, if you refresh the page in the browser, the DataGrid will continue to display the database records. The records have been cached in memory.

Performing Ascending and Descending Sorts

If you click a column heading twice in the SortGrid.aspx page, the rows in the DataGrid will not be sorted in a different order. Clicking a column heading always sorts in ascending order. In other words, our SortGrid.aspx page does not support ascending and descending sorts.

We can fix this by adding some memory to the page. The page needs to remember the last order in which the records were sorted and reverse the order.

To enable both ascending and descending sorts, make the following modifications to the SortCommand event handler:

C#

```csharp
private void DataGrid1_SortCommand(object source,
➥System.Web.UI.WebControls.DataGridSortCommandEventArgs e)
{
string strSort = (string)ViewState[ "Sort" ];
string strDirection = (string)ViewState[ "Direction" ];

if (strSort != e.SortExpression)
{
    strSort = e.SortExpression;
    strDirection = "asc";
}
else
{
    if (strDirection == "asc")
      strDirection = "desc";
    else
      strDirection = "asc";
}
ViewState[ "Sort" ] = strSort;
ViewState[ "Direction" ] = strDirection;

BindGrid( strSort + " " + strDirection );
}
```

VB.NET

```vbnet
Private Sub DataGrid1_SortCommand(ByVal source As Object,
➥ByVal e As System.Web.UI.WebControls.DataGridSortCommandEventArgs)
➥Handles DataGrid1.SortCommand
  Dim strSort As String
  Dim strDirection As String

  strSort = ViewState("Sort")
  strDirection = ViewState("Direction")

  If (strSort <> e.SortExpression) Then

    strSort = e.SortExpression
    strDirection = "asc"
  Else
```

```
    If (strDirection = "asc") Then
      strDirection = "desc"
    Else
      strDirection = "asc"
    End If
  End If
  ViewState("Sort") = strSort
  ViewState("Direction") = strDirection

  BindGrid(strSort + " " + strDirection)
End Sub
```

This code stores the previous sort order in the page's ViewState. If you click a column heading and it matches the column name stored in ViewState, the sort direction is reversed.

Paging Through Records in a DataGrid

If you have a large number of records that you need to display, it makes sense to divide the records into multiple logical pages (see Figure 13.6). The DataGrid control has built-in support for paging. You can navigate from page to page by using page numbers or by using next and previous links.

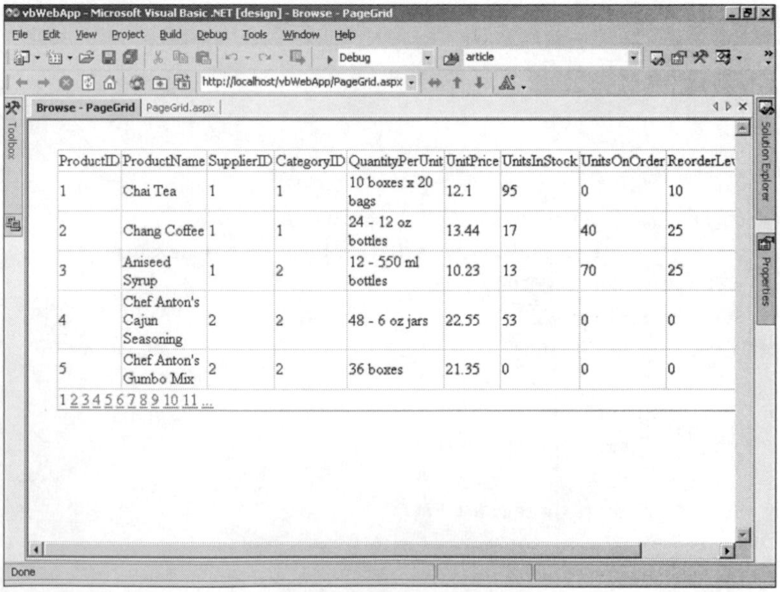

Figure 13.6   DataGrid with paging enabled.

For example, suppose that you want to display the contents of the Products database table by displaying five records per page. First, you need to create a new Web Form Page and add the necessary database objects:

1. Add a Web Form Page to your project named **PageGrid.aspx**.

2. Drag and drop the Products database table from the Server Explorer window onto the Designer surface.

3. Add an Untyped DataSet to the page.

Next, you need to add a DataGrid and enable paging for the DataGrid:

1. Add a DataGrid control to the page.

2. Right-click the DataGrid control and select Property Builder. Click the Paging tab (you should see the dialog box shown in Figure 13.7).

3. Select the Allow Paging check box.

4. Enter the value **5** for the Page Size property.

5. Change Mode to Page Numbers.

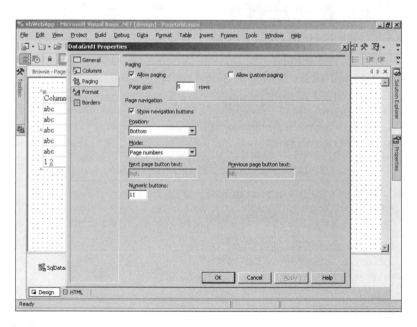

Figure 13.7   Property Builder paging tab.

Next, you need to add the application logic necessary to bind the DataGrid to the DataSet:

1. Double-click the Designer surface to switch to the Code Editor.

2. Enter the following code for the Page_Load handler:

C#

```
private void Page_Load(object sender, System.EventArgs e)
{
if (!Page.IsPostBack)
  BindGrid();
}
```

VB.NET

```
Private Sub Page_Load(ByVal sender As System.Object,
➥ByVal e As System.EventArgs)
➥Handles MyBase.Load
  If Not Page.IsPostBack Then
    BindGrid()
  End If
End Sub
```

3. Below the Page_Load handler, enter the following BindGrid() method:

C#

```
void BindGrid()
{
  sqlDataAdapter1.Fill( dataSet1 );
  DataGrid1.DataSource = dataSet1;
  DataGrid1.DataBind();
}
```

VB.NET

```
Sub BindGrid()
  SqlDataAdapter1.Fill(DataSet1)
  DataGrid1.DataSource = DataSet1
  DataGrid1.DataBind()
End Sub
```

If you build and browse the page at this point, you would see the records from the Products table displayed in the DataGrid. Furthermore, you would see a list of page numbers at the bottom of the DataGrid. If you click a page number, however, nothing would happen. The same set of records would be displayed.

Before paging will work in a DataGrid, you must add an event handler for the PageIndexChanged event. This event is raised whenever you click a page number:

C# Steps

1. Switch back to the Designer by selecting Designer from the View menu.

2. In the Properties window, select the DataGrid control.

3. Click the Events icon at the top of the Properties window (it looks like a lightning bolt).

4. Double-click next to the PageIndexChanged event. This will switch you back to the Code Editor.

5. Enter the following code for the PageIndexChanged handler:

```
private void DataGrid1_PageIndexChanged(object source,
➥System.Web.UI.WebControls.DataGridPageChangedEventArgs e)
{
  DataGrid1.CurrentPageIndex = e.NewPageIndex;
  BindGrid();
}
```

6. Right-click the PageGrid.aspx page in the Solution Explorer window and select Build and Browse.

VB.NET Steps

1. Select DataGrid1 in the Class Name drop-down list that appears at the top left of the Code Editor.

2. Select the PageIndexChanged event from the Method Name drop-down list that appears at the top right of the Code Editor.

3. Enter the following code for the PageIndexChanged subroutine:

```
Private Sub DataGrid1_PageIndexChanged(ByVal source As Object, ByVal
➥e As System.Web.UI.WebControls.DataGridPageChangedEventArgs)
➥Handles DataGrid1.PageIndexChanged
  DataGrid1.CurrentPageIndex = e.NewPageIndex
  BindGrid()
End Sub
```

4. Right-click the PageGrid.aspx page in the Solution Explorer window and select Build and Browse.

When the page opens, you can click the different page numbers that appear at the bottom of the DataGrid to navigate to different pages.

Customizing the Paging User Interface

You can customize the appearance of the navigation links for paging in two places. First, you can modify the appearance of the paging user interface by modifying the DataGridPagerStyle object exposed by the DataGrid control's PagerStyle property.

You can view all the formatting options made available by the DataGridPagerStyle object by selecting the DataGrid in the Properties window and expanding the PagerStyle property. For example, you can modify such properties as the background color, the font, the horizontal alignment, and the position of the paging user interface.

You can also modify the majority of these properties by taking advantage of the Property Builder. Right-click the DataGrid control on the Designer surface and select Property Builder. Select the Paging tab to view the list of properties that you can modify:

- *Allow Paging*—Enables or disables paging for the DataGrid. This property corresponds to the DataGrid control's AllowPaging property.

- *Page Size*—The number of records to display on a page. This property corresponds to the DataGrid control's PageSize property.

- *Show navigation buttons*—Hides or displays the paging user interface. This property corresponds to the DataGrid control's PagerStyle Visible property.

- *Position*—Indicates whether the paging user interface appears at the bottom, top, or both top and bottom of the DataGrid. This property corresponds to the DataGrid control's PagerStyle Position property.

- *Mode*—Indicates whether page numbers or next and previous links are displayed (you can't pick both). This property corresponds to the DataGrid control's PagerStyle Mode property.

- *Next page button text*—The text that appears for the previous page link. This property corresponds to the DataGrid control's PagerStyle NextPageText property.

- *Previous page button text*—The text that appears for the next page link. This property corresponds to the DataGrid control's PagerStyle PrevPageText property.

- *Numeric Buttons*—The number of page numbers to display before showing ellipsis points(useful when there are a lot of page numbers). This property corresponds to the DataGrid control's PagerStyle PageButtonCount property.

Using Caching with Paging

There's one big problem with our PageGrid.aspx page. Whenever you click a page number in the PageGrid.aspx page, the PageIndexChanged handler is executed. This handler retrieves all the records from the Products database table. It's important to realize that this handler doesn't only retrieve the records for the current page; it retrieves all records. If the Products database table contains three billion records, all three billion records would be retrieved just to show the five records for the currently selected page.

If you are working with a relatively small table, you might decide to live with this inefficiency. But, when it comes to large tables, the DataGrid control's built-in paging mechanism won't work.

For certain applications, you can get around this problem by taking advantage of the Cache object. You can cache all the records in the Web server's memory and avoid accessing the database whenever someone navigates to a new page. The following code modifies the BindGrid() method to take advantage of the Cache object:

C#

```csharp
void BindGrid()
{
  dataSet1 = (DataSet)Cache[ "Products" ];
  if (dataSet1 == null)
  {
    dataSet1 = new DataSet();
    sqlDataAdapter1.Fill( dataSet1 );
    Cache[ "Products" ] = dataSet1;
  }
  DataGrid1.DataSource = dataSet1;
  DataGrid1.DataBind();
}
```

VB.NET

```vbnet
Sub BindGrid()
  DataSet1 = Cache("Products")
  If DataSet1 Is Nothing Then
    DataSet1 = New DataSet()
    SqlDataAdapter1.Fill(DataSet1)
    Cache("Products") = DataSet1
  End If
  DataGrid1.DataSource = DataSet1
  DataGrid1.DataBind()
End Sub
```

This code will add the DataSet that represents the Products database table to the Cache the first time the page is accessed. Any time the page is accessed in the future, the database records will be retrieved from the server's memory instead of the database.

> **NOTE**
>
> Using the Cache object will not completely solve the problem. If you are working with a truly huge set of data, you might not want to cache the entire set of database records. In that case, you have no choice but to implement custom paging. The topic of custom paging is outside the scope of this book. To learn more about custom paging, see Chapter 11, "Using the DataList and DataGrid Controls," in *ASP.NET Unleashed*.

Editing Database Records in a DataGrid

In this section, you'll learn two ways of editing the database records displayed in a DataGrid.

First, you'll learn how to implement editing by using Bound Columns. This is the fastest method of implementing editing, but it has some significant limitations. Next, we'll take a look at how you can implement editing with Template Columns.

Editing with Bound Columns

Before walking through the steps necessary to enable editing with a DataGrid control, you need to be warned that you must write all the database logic to perform the editing yourself. Microsoft has provided you only with the user interface for editing. You must write the application logic to update the underlying database.

We'll write all the necessary code for updating a database table in this section. We'll create a DataGrid that enables us to update the Products database table.

Let's start by creating the page and adding the necessary database objects:

1. Add a Web Form Page to your project named **EditGrid.aspx**.

2. Drag and drop the Products database table from the Server Explorer window onto the Designer surface.

3. Add an Untyped DataSet to the page.

Next, we need to add a DataGrid control to the page and configure the DataGrid for editing:

1. Add a DataGrid control to the page.

2. Right-click the DataGrid, select Property Builder, and click the Columns tab.

3. Uncheck the Create Columns Automatically at Run Time check box.

4. In the Available columns panel, expand Button Column, and add the Edit, Update, Cancel Columns to the Selected columns panel.

5. Enter the following three bound columns:

Header Text	Data Field	Read Only
ID	**ProductID**	Checked
Name	**ProductName**	Unchecked
Price	**UnitPrice**	Unchecked

6. Click OK to close the Property Builder dialog box.

Next, we need to bind the DataGrid control to the DataSet that represents the Products database table:

1. Double-click the Designer surface to switch to the Code Editor.

2. Enter the following code for the Page_Load handler:

C#

```csharp
private void Page_Load(object sender, System.EventArgs e)
{
if (!Page.IsPostBack)
  BindGrid();
}
```

VB.NET

```vbnet
Private Sub Page_Load(ByVal sender As System.Object,
➥ByVal e As System.EventArgs) Handles MyBase.Load
  If Not Page.IsPostBack Then
    BindGrid()
  End If
End Sub
```

3. Enter the following BindGrid() method below the Page_Load handler:

C#

```csharp
void BindGrid()
{
```

```
        sqlDataAdapter1.Fill( dataSet1 );
        DataGrid1.DataSource = dataSet1;
        DataGrid1.DataKeyField = "ProductID";
        DataGrid1.DataBind();
    }
```

VB.NET

```
Sub BindGrid()
  SqlDataAdapter1.Fill(DataSet1)
  DataGrid1.DataSource = DataSet1
  DataGrid1.DataKeyField = "ProductID"
  DataGrid1.DataBind()
End Sub
```

If you build and browse the EditGrid.aspx page at this point, you would see the page in Figure 13.8. If you click the Edit link, however, nothing would happen. You must add a handler for the `EditCommand` event before the DataGrid will do anything.

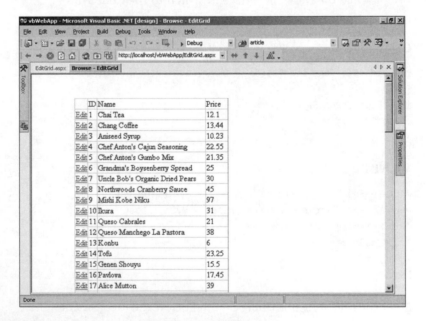

Figure 13.8   DataGrid with editing user interface.

C# Steps

1. Switch back to the Designer by selecting Designer from the View menu.

2. In the Properties window, select the DataGrid and click the Events icon at the top of the Properties window (the icon that looks like a lightning bolt).

3. Double-click the `EditCommand` event. This will switch you to the Code Editor.

4. Enter the following code for the `EditCommand` handler:

```
private void DataGrid1_EditCommand(object source,
➥System.Web.UI.WebControls.DataGridCommandEventArgs e)
{
  DataGrid1.EditItemIndex = e.Item.ItemIndex;
  BindGrid();
}
```

VB.NET Steps

1. In the Class Name drop-down list that appears at the top-left of the Code Editor, select `DataGrid1`.

2. In the Method Name drop-down list that appears at the top-right of the Code Editor, select the `EditCommand` event. This will add a new `EditCommand` handler to the Code Editor.

3. Enter the following code for the `EditCommand` handler:

```
Private Sub DataGrid1_EditCommand(ByVal source As Object,
➥ByVal e As System.Web.UI.WebControls.DataGridCommandEventArgs)
➥Handles DataGrid1.EditCommand
  DataGrid1.EditItemIndex = e.Item.ItemIndex
  BindGrid()
End Sub
```

The `EditCommand` event handler that we just added selects a row for editing and calls `BindGrid()` to display the updated `DataGrid` control. When you click the Edit link next to a row, any column that is not marked as read-only is automatically displayed as a single-line text box. Furthermore, the Edit link is replaced with an Update and Cancel link.

The next step is to create an event-handler for the `CancelCommand`—the event that is raised when you click the Cancel link.

C# Steps

1. Switch back to the Designer by selecting Designer from the View menu.

2. In the Properties window, select the DataGrid and click the Events icon (the lightning bolt) that appears at the top of the Properties window.

3. Double-click next to the CancelCommand event. This will switch you back to the Code Editor.

4. Enter the following code for the CancelCommand event:

```
private void DataGrid1_CancelCommand(object source,
➥System.Web.UI.WebControls.DataGridCommandEventArgs e)
{
  DataGrid1.EditItemIndex = -1;
  BindGrid();
}
```

VB.NET Steps

1. In the Class Name drop-down list, select the DataGrid control.

2. In the Method Name drop-down list, select the CancelCommand event. This will add a CancelCommand handler to the Code Editor.

3. Enter the following code for the CancelCommand handler:

```
Private Sub DataGrid1_CancelCommand(ByVal source As Object,
➥ByVal e As System.Web.UI.WebControls.DataGridCommandEventArgs)
➥Handles DataGrid1.CancelCommand
  DataGrid1.EditItemIndex = -1
  BindGrid()
End Sub
```

When you click the Cancel link, the value -1 is assigned to the EditItemIndex property. This value unselects all rows for editing.

Finally, we need to add the event handler for the UpdateCommand event. We'll use this handler to execute an SqlCommand to update the underlying database. Let's start by adding the SqlCommand object to the page:

1. Switch back to the Designer by selecting Designer from the View menu.

2. Add a SqlCommand object to the page.

3. In the Properties window, select the SqlCommand object.

4. In the Properties window, double-click next to Connection property to assign **sqlConnection1** as the value of the Connection property.

5. In the Properties window, enter the following code for the CommandText property:

```
UPDATE Products
SET ProductName = @ProductName, UnitPrice = @UnitPrice
WHERE (ProductID = @ProductID)
```

Now, we can execute the SqlCommand within the UpdateCommand handler:

C# Steps

1. In the Properties window, select the DataGrid and click the Events icon (the lightning bolt).

2. Double-click next to the UpdateCommand event. This will switch you back to the Code Editor.

3. Enter the following code for the UpdateCommand handler:

```
private void DataGrid1_UpdateCommand(object source,
➥System.Web.UI.WebControls.DataGridCommandEventArgs e)
{
  // Retrieve TextBox Controls from DataGrid
  TextBox txtProductName = (TextBox)e.Item.Cells[2].Controls[0];
  TextBox txtUnitPrice = (TextBox)e.Item.Cells[3].Controls[0];

  // Assign Parameters to SqlCommand
  sqlCommand1.Parameters["@ProductName"].Value= txtProductName.Text;
  sqlCommand1.Parameters["@UnitPrice"].Value = txtUnitPrice.Text;
  sqlCommand1.Parameters["@ProductID"].Value =
➥DataGrid1.DataKeys[ e.Item.ItemIndex ];

  // Execute SqlCommand
  sqlConnection1.Open();
  sqlCommand1.ExecuteNonQuery();

  // Deselect Row for Editing
  DataGrid1.EditItemIndex = -1;
  BindGrid();
  sqlConnection1.Close();
}
```

4. Right-click the EditGrid.aspx page in Solution Explorer and select Build and Browse.

VB.NET Steps

1. Double-click the Designer surface to switch back to the Code Editor.

2. Select DataGrid1 from the Class Name drop-down list that appears at the top left of the Code Editor.

3. Select the UpdateCommand event from the Method Name drop-down list that appears at the top right of the Code Editor. This will add an UpdateCommand event handler.

4. Enter the following code for the UpdateCommand handler:

```
Private Sub DataGrid1_UpdateCommand(ByVal source As Object,
➥ByVal e As System.Web.UI.WebControls.DataGridCommandEventArgs)
➥Handles DataGrid1.UpdateCommand
    ' Retrieve TextBox Controls from DataGrid
    Dim txtProductName As TextBox
    Dim txtUnitPrice As TextBox
    txtProductName = CType(e.Item.Cells(2).Controls(0), TextBox)
    txtUnitPrice = CType(e.Item.Cells(3).Controls(0), TextBox)

    ' Assign Parameters to SqlCommand
    SqlCommand1.Parameters("@ProductName").Value = txtProductName.Text
    SqlCommand1.Parameters("@UnitPrice").Value = txtUnitPrice.Text
    SqlCommand1.Parameters("@ProductID").Value =
➥DataGrid1.DataKeys(e.Item.ItemIndex)

    ' Execute SqlCommand
    SqlConnection1.Open()
    SqlCommand1.ExecuteNonQuery()

    ' Deselect Row for Editing
    DataGrid1.EditItemIndex = -1
    BindGrid()
    SqlConnection1.Close()
End Sub
```

5. Right-click the EditGrid.aspx page in the Solution Explorer window and select Build and Browse.

When the EditGrid.aspx page opens, you can click next to any row to edit it. You can change the contents of both the ProductName and UnitPrice columns in the underlying database table.

The UpdateCommand event handler requires some explanation. The first lines in the handler are used to retrieve the ProductName and UnitPrice TextBox controls from the DataGrid. The Cells collection represents the columns in the DataGrid, so passing the index 2 to the Cells collection returns the ProductName text box, and passing the index 3 returns the UnitPrice text box. The first two cells contain the Edit, Update, Cancel, and ProductID columns.

Next, the UpdateCommand handler initializes the parameters for the SqlCommand object and executes the Update command. Finally, the current row is deselected for editing by assigning the value -1 to the `DataGrid` control's `EditItemIndex` property, and the DataGrid is updated by calling `BindGrid()`.

Adding a Delete Button to the `DataGrid` Control

The `DataGrid` control that we created in the previous section enables you to update rows in the Products database table. However, it does not allow you to delete a row. In this section, we'll add an additional column to the DataGrid that contains a Delete link.

1. Right-click the `DataGrid` control on the Designer surface, select Property Builder, and click the Columns tab.

2. In the Available Columns panel, expand Button Columns, select the Delete column, and copy the Delete column over to the Selected columns panel.

3. Move the Delete column to the top of the list in the Selected columns panel by clicking the up arrow.

4. Click OK to close the Property Builder dialog box.

Next, you need to add a new `SqlCommand` object to the EditGrid.aspx page that represents an SQL `Delete` command.

1. Add a new `SqlCommand` object to the page.

2. In the Properties window, select the new `SqlCommand`.

3. Double-click next to the `SqlCommand`'s `Connection` property. This will assign the value `sqlConnection1` to the `Connection` property.

4. Enter the following SQL `Delete` command for the `CommandText` property:

```
DELETE FROM Products
WHERE (ProductID = @ProductID)
```

Finally, we need to add an event handler for the Delete link that will execute the `SqlCommand`.

C# Steps

1. In the Properties window, select the `DataGrid` control and click the Events icon (the lightning bolt).

2. Double-click next to the `DeleteCommand` event. This will switch you to the Code Editor.

3. Enter the following code for the `DeleteCommand` handler:

```
private void DataGrid1_DeleteCommand(object source,
➥System.Web.UI.WebControls.DataGridCommandEventArgs e)
{
  sqlCommand2.Parameters[ "@ProductID" ].Value
    = DataGrid1.DataKeys[ e.Item.ItemIndex ];
  sqlConnection1.Open();
  sqlCommand2.ExecuteNonQuery();
  BindGrid();
  sqlConnection1.Close();
}
```

4. Right-click the EditGrid.aspx page in the Solution Explorer window and select Build and Browse.

VB.NET Steps

1. Double-click the Designer surface to switch to the Code Editor.

2. From the Class Name drop-down list that appears at the top left of the Code Editor, select DataGrid1.

3. From the Method Name drop-down list that appears at the top right of the Code Editor, select DeleteCommand. This will add a DeleteCommand handler to the Code Editor.

4. Enter the following code for the DeleteCommand handler:

```
Private Sub DataGrid1_DeleteCommand(ByVal source As Object,
➥ByVal e As System.Web.UI.WebControls.DataGridCommandEventArgs)
➥Handles DataGrid1.DeleteCommand
  SqlCommand2.Parameters("@ProductID").Value =
➥DataGrid1.DataKeys(e.Item.ItemIndex)
  SqlConnection1.Open()
  SqlCommand2.ExecuteNonQuery()
  BindGrid()
  SqlConnection1.Close()
End Sub
```

5. Right-click the EditGrid.aspx page in the Solution Explorer and select Build and Browse.

After you complete these steps, you can delete any row displayed in the DataGrid control by clicking the Delete link. Clicking the Delete link causes the DeleteCommand handler to execute. This handler executes an SQL Delete command to delete the row from the underlying database table.

Using Smart Navigation with a DataGrid

When you click the Edit, Update, Cancel, or Delete link next to a row in the DataGrid control, the page containing the DataGrid is reloaded. Regardless of where you click in a DataGrid, the page reloads and you are brought back to the very top of the page.

This can be confusing. Fortunately, there is an easy fix for this problem. You can take advantage of something called smart navigation. Smart navigation automatically returns you to the same place in a DataGrid when the page containing the DataGrid is reloaded.

Perform the following steps to enable smart navigation for a page:

1. In the Properties window, select Document.

2. Assign the value **True** to the smartNavigation property.

You should be warned that smart navigation only works with Microsoft Internet Explorer 5.0 or later. It does not work with any version of the Netscape browser (it's ignored).

NOTE

Smart navigation is implemented with a JScript library that you can find in the following directory:

InetPub\wwwroot\aspnet_client\system_web\[version]

Editing with Template Columns

There are two significant limitations involved with using a DataGrid to edit database records when using bound columns. First, you cannot perform any validation. If you attempt to enter the value apple for the Price column, a big, fat error is generated when the page is rendered.

Second, you have no control over the appearance of the editing user interface. Columns selected for editing appear in a single-line TextBox control. You can't edit fields using other types of controls, such as RadioButtonList or DropDownList controls.

The solution to both of these problems is Template Columns. You can add validation controls to a Template Column. Furthermore, you can add any form controls, such as DropDownList and multi-line TextBox controls, to a Template Column that you want.

In this section, we'll create another page for editing the records in the Products database table. This time, however, we'll add a RequiredFieldValidator control to the ProductName column. We'll also enable users to select the category for a product from a DropDownList control (see Figure 13.9).

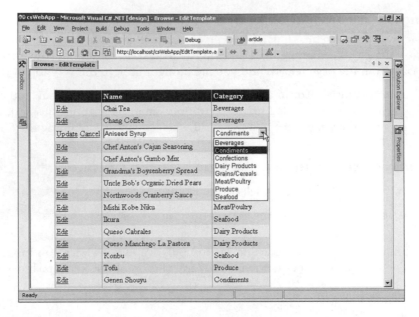

Figure 13.9   DataGrid with Template Columns.

First, let's create the Web Form Page and add the necessary database objects:

1. Add a Web Form Page to your project named **EditTemplate.aspx**.

2. Drag and drop the Products database table from the Server Explorer window onto the Designer surface.

3. Add an Untyped DataSet to the page.

4. Drag and drop the Categories database table from the Server Explorer window onto the Designer surface.

5. Add a second Untyped DataSet to the page.

After you complete these steps, you'll have two DataSets on the page—one DataSet represents the Products table, and one DataSet represents the Categories table.

Next, you need to add the DataGrid control to the page and configure its Template Columns:

1. Add a `DataGrid` control to the page.

2. Right-click the DataGrid, select Property Builder, and click the Columns tab.

3. Uncheck the Create Columns Automatically at Run Time check box.

4. Add an `Edit`, `Update`, `Cancel` column by expanding Button Column in the Available columns panel, selecting the `Edit`, `Update`, `Cancel` column, and moving it to the Selected columns panel.

5. Add the following two Template Columns to the Selected columns panel:

   Header text

   Name

   Category

6. Click OK to close the Property Builder dialog box.

7. Right-click the DataGrid and select Auto Format. Select the Professional 1 scheme and click OK.

Next, we need to add templates to the two Template Columns that we created in the DataGrid. For both the Name and Category columns, we need to create an `ItemTemplate` and `EditItemTemplate`.

1. Switch to HTML View by clicking the HTML tab at the bottom left of the Designer.

2. Find the DataGrid tag in the HTML source.

3. Inside the DataGrid tag, add the following code to the first `TemplateColumn`:

```
<asp:TemplateColumn HeaderText="Name">

<ItemTemplate>
  <%# DataBinder.Eval( Container, "DataItem.ProductName" ) %>
</ItemTemplate>

<EditItemTemplate>
  <asp:TextBox
    ID="txtProductName"
    Text='<%# DataBinder.Eval( Container, "DataItem.ProductName" ) %>'
    runat="server"/>
  <asp:RequiredFieldValidator
    ControlToValidate="txtProductName"
    Text="*"
    Runat="server"/>
</EditItemTemplate>

</asp:TemplateColumn>
```

4. Inside the DataGrid tag, add the following code to the second `TemplateColumn`:

```
<asp:TemplateColumn HeaderText="Category">

<ItemTemplate>
  <%# ShowCategory( DataBinder.Eval( Container,
➥"DataItem.CategoryID" ) )%>
</ItemTemplate>

<EditItemTemplate>
  <asp:DropDownList
    id="dropCategory"
    DataSource='<%# dataSet2 %>'
    SelectedIndex='<%# SelectCategory(  DataBinder.Eval( Container,
➥"DataItem.CategoryID" ) )%>'
    DataTextField='CategoryName'
    DataValueField='CategoryID'
    Runat="server" />
</EditItemTemplate>

</asp:TemplateColumn>
```

The first Template Column contains an `ItemTemplate` for displaying the value of the ProductName column and an `EditItemTemplate` for editing the value of the ProductName column. Notice that the `EditItemTemplate` contains a `RequiredFieldValidator` control. This control prevents a user from attempting to submit a blank value for ProductName.

The second Template Column contains an `ItemTemplate` for displaying the current category associated with the product. It also contains an `EditItemTemplate` that contains a drop-down list that displays a list of all the categories from the Categories database table so that a user can pick a new category when editing the row.

The `TemplateColumn` used for displaying the product category takes advantage of two methods. The `ItemTemplate` uses a `ShowCategory()` method to display the current category. The `EditItemTemplate` uses a `SelectCategory()` method to make the current category the default category in the `DropDownList` control.

We'll create those two methods by doing the following:

1. Switch to the Code Editor by double-clicking the Designer surface.

2. Type the following method (`ShowCategory()`) into the Code Editor:

C#

```csharp
public string ShowCategory(object CategoryID )
{
  if (CategoryID==DBNull.Value)
    return String.Empty;
  DataRow[] drows =
    dataSet2.Tables[0].Select("CategoryID=" + CategoryID);
  return (string)drows[0]["CategoryName"];
}
```

VB.NET

```vbnet
Function ShowCategory(ByVal CategoryID As Object) As String
  Dim drows() As DataRow

  If IsDBNull(CategoryID) Then
    Return String.Empty
  End If
  drows = DataSet2.Tables(0).Select("CategoryID=" & CategoryID)
  Return drows(0)("CategoryName")
End Function
```

3. Type the following method (SelectCategory()) into the Code Editor:

C#

```csharp
public int SelectCategory(object CategoryID )
{
  DataTable dtblCategories = dataSet2.Tables[0];
  for (int i = 0;i < dtblCategories.Rows.Count;i++)
    if ((int)dtblCategories.Rows[i]["CategoryID"] == (int)CategoryID )
      return i;
  return 0;
}
```

VB.NET

```vbnet
Function SelectCategory(ByVal CategoryID As Object) As Integer
  Dim i As Integer
  Dim dtblCategories = DataSet2.Tables(0)
  For i = 0 To dtblCategories.Rows.Count - 1
    If dtblCategories.Rows(i)("CategoryID") = CategoryID Then
      Return i
```

```
     End If
   Next
   Return 0
End Function
```

Next, we need to fill the two DataSets and bind the Products DataSet to the DataGrid:

1. Enter the following code for the Page_Load handler:

   C#

   ```
   private void Page_Load(object sender, System.EventArgs e)
   {
     if (!Page.IsPostBack)
       BindGrid();
   }
   ```

   VB.NET

   ```
   Private Sub Page_Load(ByVal sender As System.Object,
   ➥ByVal e As System.EventArgs)
   ➥Handles MyBase.Load
     If Not Page.IsPostBack Then
       BindGrid()
     End If
   End Sub
   ```

2. Enter the following BindGrid() method below the Page_Load handler:

   C#

   ```
   void BindGrid()
   {
     sqlDataAdapter1.Fill( dataSet1 );
     sqlDataAdapter2.Fill( dataSet2 );
     DataGrid1.DataSource = dataSet1;
     DataGrid1.DataKeyField = "ProductID";
     DataGrid1.DataBind();
   }
   ```

   VB.NET

   ```
   Sub BindGrid()
     SqlDataAdapter1.Fill(DataSet1)
   ```

```
    SqlDataAdapter2.Fill(DataSet2)
    DataGrid1.DataSource = DataSet1
    DataGrid1.DataKeyField = "ProductID"
    DataGrid1.DataBind()
End Sub
```

Now, we have to add the event handlers for the `EditCommand` and `CancelCommand` events.

C# Steps

1. Switch back to the Designer by selecting Designer from the View menu.

2. In the Properties window, select the `DataGrid` control and click the Events icon (the lightning bolt).

3. Double-click next to the `EditCommand` event. This will switch you back to the Code Editor.

4. Enter the following code for the `EditCommand` handler:

```
private void DataGrid1_EditCommand(object source,
➥System.Web.UI.WebControls.DataGridCommandEventArgs e)
{
  DataGrid1.EditItemIndex = e.Item.ItemIndex;
  BindGrid();
}
```

5. Switch back to the Designer by selecting Designer from the View menu.

6. In the Properties window, select the `DataGrid` control and click the Events icon.

7. Double-click next to the `CancelCommand` event. This will switch you back to the Code Editor.

8. Enter the following code for the `CancelCommand` handler:

```
private void DataGrid1_CancelCommand(object source,
➥System.Web.UI.WebControls.DataGridCommandEventArgs e)
{
  DataGrid1.EditItemIndex = -1;
  BindGrid();
}
```

VB.NET Steps

1. Select DataGrid1 from the Class Name drop-down list that appears at the top left of the Code Editor.

2. Select EditCommand from the Method Name drop-down list that appears at the top-right of the Code Editor. This will add an EditCommand handler to the Code Editor.

3. Enter the following code for the EditCommand handler:

```
Private Sub DataGrid1_EditCommand(ByVal source As Object,
➡ByVal e As System.Web.UI.WebControls.DataGridCommandEventArgs)
➡Handles DataGrid1.EditCommand
  DataGrid1.EditItemIndex = e.Item.ItemIndex
  BindGrid()
End Sub
```

4. Select DataGrid1 from the Class Name drop-down list that appears at the top-left of the Code Editor.

5. Select CancelCommand from the Method Name drop-down list that appears at the top-right of the Code Editor. This will add a CancelCommand handler to the Code Editor.

6. Enter the following code for the CancelCommand handler:

```
Private Sub DataGrid1_CancelCommand(ByVal source As Object,
➡ByVal e As System.Web.UI.WebControls.DataGridCommandEventArgs)
➡Handles DataGrid1.CancelCommand
  DataGrid1.EditItemIndex = -1
  BindGrid()
End Sub
```

The final step to get this DataGrid control to work is to add the logic for the UpdateCommand handler. First, we need to add an SqlCommand that represents the SQL Update command:

1. Switch back to the Designer by selecting Designer from the View menu.

2. Drag an SqlCommand object from under the Data tab in the Toolbox onto the Designer surface.

3. In the Properties window, select the SqlCommand object.

4. Double-click next to the Connection property. This will assign sqlConnection1 to the Connection property.

5. Enter the following SQL Update command for the CommandText property:

```
UPDATE  Products
SET ProductName = @ProductName, CategoryID = @CategoryID
WHERE (ProductID = @ProductID)
```

The final, final step is to create the UpdateCommand event handler. This event handler executes the SQL Update command represented by the SqlCommand object.

C# Steps

1. In the Properties window, select the DataGrid1 control and click the Events icon (the lightning bolt).

2. Double-click next to the UpdateCommand event. This will switch you to the Code Editor.

3. Enter the following code for the UpdateCommand handler:

```
private void DataGrid1_UpdateCommand(object source,
➥System.Web.UI.WebControls.DataGridCommandEventArgs e)
{
// Retrieve the Template TextBox Controls
TextBox txtProductName = (TextBox)e.Item.FindControl( "txtProductName" );
DropDownList dropCategory =
➥(DropDownList)e.Item.FindControl( "dropCategory" );

// Initialize SqlCommand Parameters
sqlCommand1.Parameters[ "@ProductName" ].Value = txtProductName.Text;
sqlCommand1.Parameters["@CategoryID" ].Value =
➥dropCategory.SelectedItem.Value;
sqlCommand1.Parameters["@ProductID"].Value =
➥DataGrid1.DataKeys[ e.Item.ItemIndex ];

// Execute SqlCommand
sqlConnection1.Open();
sqlCommand1.ExecuteNonQuery();

// Deselect Current Row for Editing
DataGrid1.EditItemIndex = -1;
BindGrid();
sqlConnection1.Close();
}
```

4. Right-click the EditTemplate.aspx page in the Solution Explorer window and select Build and Browse.

VB.NET Steps

1. Double-click the Designer surface to switch to the Code Editor.

2. Select DataGrid1 from the Class Name drop-down list located at the top-left of the Code Editor.

3. Select UpdateCommand from the Method Name drop-down list located at the top-right of the Code Editor. This will add the UpdateCommand event handler.

4. Enter the following code for the UpdateCommand handler:

```
Private Sub DataGrid1_UpdateCommand(ByVal source As Object,
➥ByVal e As System.Web.UI.WebControls.DataGridCommandEventArgs)
➥Handles DataGrid1.UpdateCommand
    ' Retrieve the Template TextBox Controls
    Dim txtProductName As TextBox
    Dim dropCategory As DropDownList
    txtProductName = CType(e.Item.FindControl("txtProductName"), TextBox)
    dropCategory = CType(e.Item.FindControl("dropCategory"), DropDownList)

    ' Initialize SqlCommand Parameters
    SqlCommand1.Parameters("@ProductName").Value = txtProductName.Text
    SqlCommand1.Parameters("@CategoryID").Value =
➥dropCategory.SelectedItem.Value
    SqlCommand1.Parameters("@ProductID").Value =
➥DataGrid1.DataKeys(e.Item.ItemIndex)

    ' Execute SqlCommand
    SqlConnection1.Open()
    SqlCommand1.ExecuteNonQuery()

    ' Deselect Current Row for Editing
    DataGrid1.EditItemIndex = -1
    BindGrid()
    SqlConnection1.Close()
End Sub
```

5. Right-click the EditTemplate.aspx page in the Solution Explorer window and select Build and Browse.

After you complete these steps, you'll be able to edit the records in the Products database table within the DataGrid control. Notice that if you attempt to update a product without entering a value for the Name text field, you are prevented from updating the record. A red asterisk appears next to the Name text box (see Figure 13.10).

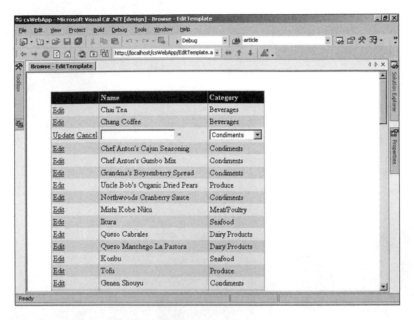

FIGURE 13.10   Required field in DataGrid.

Furthermore, notice that you can pick a product category from a drop-down list. The drop-down list displays all the product categories by retrieving them from the Categories database table.

Summary

In this chapter, you learned everything you need to know to take advantage of the DataGrid control in your applications. In the first section, you learned how to use the DataGrid control to automatically display the contents of a database table. You also learned how to create a two-page Master/Detail form with the DataGrid control by displaying records as links to a details page.

Next, you learned how to sort the data in a DataGrid control. You learned how to implement both simple sorting and ascending/descending sorting.

In the next section, you learned how to page through a database table displayed in a DataGrid. You learned how to enable paging and how to customize the appearance of the paging user interface.

Finally, you learned how to edit database data with the DataGrid control. You learned how to configure a DataGrid for editing by using both bound columns and template columns.

PART III

Working with ASP.NET Applications

IN THIS PART

14 Improving Application Performance with Caching

15 Configuring Your Application

16 Securing Your Application

17 Maintaining Application State

18 Handling Application-Wide Events

19 Deploying Your Application

14

Improving Application Performance with Caching

IN THIS CHAPTER

- Using Page Output Caching
- Using Partial Page Caching
- Using Data Caching

You can dramatically improve the performance of your ASP.NET application through caching. If you cache the content of a page in your Web server's memory, you can avoid regenerating the page content each and every time the page is requested.

In this chapter, you'll learn how to use the three caching mechanisms provided by the ASP.NET Framework. You'll learn

- How to use Page Output Caching to store the entire contents of a Web Form Page in memory
- How to use Partial Page Caching to store different regions of a Web Form Page in memory
- How to use Data Caching to cache an arbitrary object in memory

Using Page Output Caching

Page Output Caching enables you to store the entire contents of a page in your Web server's memory. Whatever content is rendered by the page is stored in the cache.

Visual Studio .NET has no direct support for Page Output Caching. You won't find a property for it in the Properties window. To enable Page Output Caching, you must add a directive to the HTML source of a page yourself.

We'll test Page Output Caching by creating a page that displays the current time in a `Label` control. If the page shows the same time when it is refreshed, we'll know that the content of the page is being cached in the Web server's memory.

Perform the following steps to create the TestCache.aspx page:

1. Add a Web Form Page to your project named **TestCache.aspx** to your project.

2. Add a Web Forms `Label` control to the page.

3. Double-click the Designer surface to switch to the Code Editor.

4. Enter the following code for the Page_Load handler:

   C#

   ```csharp
   private void Page_Load(object sender, System.EventArgs e)
   {
     Label1.Text = DateTime.Now.ToString( "T" );
   }
   ```

   VB.NET

   ```vbnet
   Private Sub Page_Load(ByVal sender As System.Object,
   ➡ByVal e As System.EventArgs)
   ➡Handles MyBase.Load
     Label1.Text = DateTime.Now.ToString("T")
   End Sub
   ```

5. Right-click the TestCache.aspx in the Solution Explorer window and select Build and Browse.

When the page opens, the current time is displayed. If you click the Refresh button, the time is updated. In other words, every time you click Refresh, the content of the page is regenerated.

To enable Page Output Caching, do the following:

1. Switch back to the Designer by selecting Designer from the View menu.

2. Switch to the HTML View of the page by clicking the HTML tab at the bottom-left of the Designer.

3. Enter the following directive at the very top of the page (see Figure 14.1):

   ```
   <%@ OutputCache Duration="15" VaryByParam="none" %>
   ```

4. Right-click the TestCache.aspx page in the Solution Explorer window and select Build and Browse.

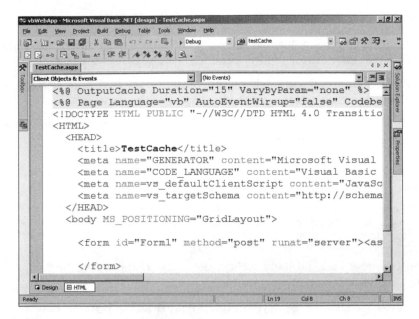

FIGURE 14.1 Adding the OutputCache directive.

This time, if you click Refresh after the page opens, the same time is displayed for 15 seconds. The OutputCache directive that we added causes the content of the TestCache.aspx page to be cached for 15 seconds.

Using the VaryByParam Attribute

There's a problem that you run into when taking advantage of Page Output Caching. What if you want a page to display different content depending on the value of a query string or form parameter passed to the page?

This is a common scenario. For example, if you are creating an online store, it is common to have a single page that acts as the product page. Depending on the value of a query string passed to the page, the page displays information on different products.

If you use the OutputCache directive discussed in the previous section, however, your page will not work as expected. The first product requested will be cached and future query string parameters will be ignored. So, the same product will be shown every time the page is requested.

Fortunately, there is an easy way around this problem. You can take advantage of the VaryByParam attribute to create different cached versions of a page. You can create a different cached version of a page whenever different query string or form parameters are passed to the page.

The `VaryByParam` attribute can take three types of values:

- `*`   Indicates that a different cached version of the page is generated whenever different query string or form parameters are passed to the page

- `none`   Indicates that a single cached version of the page is created, regardless of the query string or form parameters passed to the page

- `Param1;Param2;...`   A semicolon-delimited list of parameters used to create different cached versions of the page

NOTE

The `VaryByParam` attribute must be included when using the `OutputCache` directive, even when you don't care about caching different versions of the page.

To test the `VaryByParam` attribute, we'll create a page that displays the value of a query string parameter named ID.

1. Add a Web Form Page to your project named **TestVaryByParam.aspx**.

2. Click the HTML tab at the bottom of the Designer to switch to HTML View.

3. Enter the following directive at the very top of the page:

```
<%@ OutputCache Duration="60" VaryByParam="none" %>
```

4. Click the Design tab at the bottom of the Designer to switch to Design View.

5. Add a Web Forms `Label` control to the page.

6. Double-click the Designer surface to switch to the Code Editor.

7. Enter the following code for the `Page_Load` handler:

C#

```
private void Page_Load(object sender, System.EventArgs e)
{
  Label1.Text = Request.QueryString[ "id" ];
}
```

VB.NET

```
Private Sub Page_Load(ByVal sender As System.Object,
➥ByVal e As System.EventArgs)
➥Handles MyBase.Load
  Label1.Text = Request.QueryString("id")
End Sub
```

8. Build the current project by selecting Build *Project Name* from the Build menu.

After you build the project, launch Internet Explorer and enter the following path in your browser's address bar:

```
http://localhost/project name/TestVaryByParam.aspx?id=1
```

Next, request the same page but change the value of the ID query string parameter:

```
http://localhost/project name/TestVaryByParam.aspx?id=2
```

You should notice that the value 1 is still displayed by the Label control on the page. The first page that you requested is cached in memory for 60 seconds, so the page is not updated when you pass a different query string.

To create different cached versions of the TestVaryByParam.aspx page, do the following:

1. Open the TestVaryByParam.aspx page in the Designer by selecting Designer from the View menu.

2. Click the HTML tab at the bottom left of the Designer surface.

3. Modify the OutputCache directive so it looks like the following:

   ```
   <%@ OutputCache Duration="60" VaryByParam="*" %>
   ```

4. Build your current project by selecting *Build Project Name* from the Build menu.

After you complete these steps, refresh the browser. Now the page will correctly output the value of the ID query string. The content of the page is regenerated every time you pass a different query string or form parameter to the page.

It is important to understand that the content of the page is still being cached when you use the VaryByParam attribute. However, a different cached version of the page is generated whenever different query string or form parameters are passed to the page.

Using Controls in a Cached Page

If you place a Web Forms control in a cached page, the control will display the exact same content every time the page is requested. This creates problems when you want to provide a user with the ability to interact with the page.

For example, suppose that you want to display a list of product categories in a DropDownList control. If you cache the page, the same item will be selected in the DropDownList control every time a user requests the page. If a user selects a new item from the DropDownList control, the selection will be ignored.

You can get around this problem, once again, by taking advantage of the `VaryByParam` attribute. You can use the `VaryByParam` attribute not only with the names of form and query string parameters but also with the names of controls.

If you add a `DropDownList` control named `DropDownList1` to a cached page, you can use the following `OutputCache` directive to correctly vary the cached content of the page:

```
<%@ OutputCache Duration="50" VaryByParam="DropDownList1" %>
```

This `OutputCache` directive automatically generates different cached versions of the page depending on the selected item in the `DropDownList1` control.

NOTE

The `VaryByParam` attribute works with control names in a Web Form Page because adding a control to a page adds a form variable with the same name as the control.

Using the `VaryByHeader` **Attribute**

If you think about it, there's still a problem with the `OutputCache` directive. One of the most valuable features of Web Forms controls is that they will render different content depending on the browser being used to request the page. For example, a Web Form control will render Cascading Style Sheet attributes only when the control detects that a browser is capable of supporting these attributes.

However, if you cache the output of a page, the same content will be delivered to any browser that requests a page. For example, if the page is first requested by someone using an Internet Explorer 6.0 browser, everyone else will get the cached content generated for an Internet Explorer 6.0 browser.

One way around this problem is to use the `VaryByHeader` attribute. The `VaryByHeader` attribute enables you to generate different cached versions of a page depending on the value of a browser header. You can use this attribute with browser headers, such as the Accept-Language or the User-Agent header.

For example, suppose that you need to display both an English and German language version of a page. You can use the Accept-Language header to detect the preferred language of the user requesting the page:

C#

```csharp
switch (Request.Headers[ "Accept-Language" ])
{
  case "en-us":
    // Display English Content
    break;
```

```
  case "de":
    // Display German Content
    break;
}
```

VB.NET

```
Select Case Request.Headers("Accept-Language")
  Case "en-us"
    ' Display English Content
  Case "de"
    ' Display German Content
End Select
```

NOTE

You can change your preferred language when using Internet Explorer 6.0 by selecting Tools, Options. Under the General tab, click the Languages button.

If you want to cache both the English and German language version of the page, you can use the following OutputCache directive:

```
<%@ OutputCache Duration="60" VaryByParam="None" VaryByHeader="Accept-Language" %>
```

Another browser header that you can use with the VaryByHeader attribute is the User-Agent header. The User-Agent header indicates the type of browser being used to request the page. For example, my browser sends the following User-Agent header with each page request:

```
Mozilla/4.0 (compatible; MSIE 6.0; Windows NT 5.0; Q312461; .NET CLR 1.0.3705)
```

You might be tempted to use the User-Agent header with the OutputCache directive to cache different versions of a page, depending on the type of browser requesting the page. In general, this is not a good idea. The problem is that the User-Agent header is far too specific.

Notice that the User-Agent header not only contains the type of browser and the major version of the browser, it contains a number of other pieces of information. For example, my User-Agent header contains the platform, a quick fix number, and the version of the .NET Framework on my machine.

NOTE

Notice that the User-Agent header reports the version of the .NET Framework that you have installed on your machine (.NET CLR 1.0.3705). You can detect whether visitors to your Web site are running .NET from the header.

Because the information sent in the User-Agent header is likely to be different for the majority of users, you would not want to use this header with the `VaryByHeader` attribute. Instead, you should use the `VaryByCustom` attribute.

Using the `VaryByCustom` Attribute

The `VaryByCustom` attribute accepts the special value `browser`. When you assign this value to the `VaryByCustom` attribute, a different cached version of a page is generated depending on the type of browser and the major version of the browser.

For example, if a user requests a page from Internet Explorer 5.0, the page will be generated and cached. If another user requests a page from Internet Explorer 6.0, a new page will be generated and cached. But if a third user requests from Internet Explorer 5.5, a new page will *not* be generated—the first cached page will be served.

You can use the `VaryByCustom` attribute by adding the following directive to the HTML source of a page:

```
<%@ OutputCache Duration="60" VaryByParam="None" VaryByCustom="browser" %>
```

You might be wondering why this attribute is called the `VaryByCustom` attribute. The `VaryByCustom` attribute, in reality, enables you to generate different cached versions of a page depending on any custom criteria that you specify. When using the `VaryByCustom` attribute, you can add a method to the Global.asax file that contains your custom criteria.

> **NOTE**
>
> To learn more about the Global.asax file see Chapter 18, "Handling Application-Wide Events."

For example, suppose that you want to create different cached versions of a page depending on a user's SessionID (the unique string that identifies each user session).

1. Add a Web Form Page to your project named **VaryBySessionID.aspx** and click Open.

2. Add a `Label` control to the page by dragging the `Label` control from under the Web Forms tab in the Toolbox onto the Designer surface.

3. Click the HTML tab at the bottom of the Designer to switch to HTML View.

4. Add the following directive to the top of the page:

   ```
   <%@ OutputCache Duration="100" VaryByParam="none" VaryByCustom="SessionID" %>
   ```

5. Select View, Code to switch to the Code Editor.

6. Enter the following code for the Page_Load handler:

C#

```csharp
private void Page_Load(object sender, System.EventArgs e)
{
  Label1.Text = Session.SessionID;
}
```

VB.NET

```vbnet
Private Sub Page_Load(ByVal sender As System.Object,
➥ByVal e As System.EventArgs)
➥Handles MyBase.Load
  Label1.Text = Session.SessionID
End Sub
```

7. Right-click the Global.asax file in the Solution Explorer window and select View Code.

8. Enter the following GetVaryByCustomString() method under the Web Form Designer generated code region:

C#

```csharp
public override string GetVaryByCustomString(HttpContext context,
➥string arg)
{
if (arg == "SessionID" && Request.Cookies["ASP.NET_SessionId"] != null)
    return "SessionID=" + Request.Cookies["ASP.NET_SessionId"].Value;
  else
    return String.Empty;
}
```

VB.NET

```vbnet
Public Overrides Function GetVaryByCustomString(ByVal context
➥As HttpContext, ByVal arg As String) As String
  If arg = "SessionID" Then
    Return "SessionID=" & Request.Cookies("ASP.NET_SessionId").Value
  End If
End Function
```

9. In the Solution Explorer window, right-click the VaryBySessionID.aspx page and select Build and Browse.

Whenever a new user visits your Web site, the user will get different versions of all the pages. If the pages contain any custom user information, the information will appear correctly.

Of course, you can provide any criteria that you want within the GetVaryByCustomString() method. You can create different cached versions of pages depending on the time of day, a randomly generated number, or the weather in Columbus, Ohio.

TIP

You can detect different features of a user's browser with the HttpBrowserCapabilities class exposed by the Request.Browser property. For example, you can test whether a browser supports JavaScript by using Request.Browser.JavaScript. Any of these properties can be used in the GetVaryByCustomString() method.

Specifying the Cache Location

By default, when you use the OutputCache direction, the page is not only cached on the server. The page is actually cached in three possible locations—the server, any proxy servers, and the browser.

You can control exactly where a page is cached by taking advantage of the location attribute of the OutputCache directive. This attribute accepts any of the following values:

- Any   The default value—Cache the page on the browser, any proxy servers, and the server

- Client   Cache the page only on the Web browser

- Downstream   Cache the page on the Web browser or any proxy servers

- None   Don't cache the page

- Server   Cache the page only on the server

For example, the following OutputCache directive causes the page to be cached only on the Web server:

```
<%@ OutputCache Duration="100" VaryByParam="none" Location="Server" %>
```

Using Partial Page Caching

Suppose that your home page displays a random banner advertisement at the top of the page. Also suppose that you are displaying database records in the body of the page. It would be nice if you could cache this page so you can avoid hitting the database to retrieve the database records. However, if you cache this page, the same banner advertisement will be displayed to every user.

In situations when you want to cache only particular regions of a page, you need to take advantage of Partial Page Caching. Partial Page Caching enables you to cache the database records displayed in the body of the page without caching the banner advertisement.

Partial Page Caching is implemented with Web User Controls. You can use the same OutputCache directive (with some limitations discussed shortly) in a Web User Control as you can use within a Web Form Page.

NOTE

To learn more about Web User Controls see Chapter 5, "Creating Web User Controls."

To test out Partial Page Caching, let's create a page that contains a Web User Control with cached content. The Web User Control will display the current time.

1. Add a Web User Control to your project by selecting Add Web User Control from the Project menu. Name the new Web User Control **CachedControl.ascx** and click Open.

2. Click the HTML tab at the bottom left of the Designer surface to switch to HTML View.

3. Enter the following OutputCache directive at the top of the HTML page:

   ```
   <%@ OutputCache Duration="20" VaryByParam="none"%>
   ```

4. Click the Design tab at the bottom left of the Designer surface to switch back to Design View.

5. Drag a Label control from under the Web Forms tab in the Toolbox onto the Designer surface.

6. Double-click the Designer surface to switch to the Code Editor.

7. Enter the following code for the Page_Load handler:

   C#

   ```csharp
   private void Page_Load(object sender, System.EventArgs e)
   {
     Label1.Text = DateTime.Now.ToString( "T" );
   }
   ```

VB.NET

```
Private Sub Page_Load(ByVal sender As System.Object,
➥ByVal e As System.EventArgs)
➥Handles MyBase.Load
  Label1.Text = DateTime.Now.ToString("T")
End Sub
```

Next, we need to create a Web Form Page that contains the cached control. The Web Form Page itself will not be cached.

1. Add a Web Form Page to your project named **TestCachedControl.aspx**.

2. Add a Web Forms `Label` control to the page.

3. Add a Flow Layout Panel to the page by dragging the Flow Layout Panel from under the HTML tab in the Toolbox onto the Designer surface.

4. Add the `CachedControl.ascx` to the Flow Layout Panel by dragging `CachedControl.ascx` from the Solution Explorer window onto the Flow Layout Panel.

5. Double-click the Designer surface to switch to the Code Editor.

6. Enter the following code for the `Page_Load` handler:

   C#

   ```
   private void Page_Load(object sender, System.EventArgs e)
   {
     Label1.Text = DateTime.Now.ToString( "T" );
   }
   ```

   VB.NET

   ```
   Private Sub Page_Load(ByVal sender As System.Object,
   ➥ByVal e As System.EventArgs)
   ➥Handles MyBase.Load
     Label1.Text = DateTime.Now.ToString("T")
   End Sub
   ```

7. Right-click the TestCachedControl.aspx page in the Solution Explorer window and select Build and Browse.

When the TestCachedControl.aspx page opens, the current time is displayed in two places on the page. If you click the browser Refresh button, the page time updates, but the Web User Control time does not (for 20 seconds). The content of the Web User Control is cached.

Using Controls in a Cached Web User Control

Suppose that you want to place a control within a Web User Control. For example, you might want to add a DropDownList control to a Web User Control that enables a user to pick a product category or a DataList control that functions as a menu. However, if you cache the content of the Web User Control, the Web User Control will display the same content every time the page that contains the control is rendered. In other words, the state of the control contained within the Web User Control will be ignored.

When you use controls, such as DropDownList controls, in a cached Web User Control, you need to take advantage of an attribute of the OutputCache directive called the VaryByControl attribute. The VaryByControl attribute causes different versions of a Web User Control to be generated depending on the state of a control.

For example, if you add a DropDownList control named DropDownList1 to a Web User Control, you can cache different versions of the Web User Control depending on the state of the DropDownList1 control by using the following OutputCache directive:

```
<%@ OutputCache Duration="1000" VaryByControl="DropDownList1" %>
```

If you add this directive to a Web User Control, a new cached version of the Web User Control is generated whenever a user selects a new item from the drop-down list. If you have multiple controls inside the Web User Control, you can use a semicolon-delimited list to list more than one control with the VaryByControl attribute.

Using Properties in a Cached User Control

You cannot programmatically modify a property exposed by a cached Web User Control. You should never attempt to refer to a cached Web User Control within the Web Form Page that contains it.

For example, suppose that you have created a Web User Control named Menu.ascx that has a property named Color. Additionally, suppose that you decide to include the Web User Control in a Web Form Page named TestMenu.aspx. Adding the following Page_Load handler to the TestMenu.aspx page will generate an error:

C#

```
protected Menu Menu1;

private void Page_Load(object sender, System.EventArgs e)
{
  Menu1.Color = "blue";
}
```

VB.NET

```
Protected Menu1 As Menu

Private Sub Page_Load(ByVal sender As System.Object,
➥ByVal e As System.EventArgs) Handles MyBase.Load
  Menu1.Color = "blue"
End Sub
```

The page will work correctly the first time you request it. However, if you refresh the page, you'll receive a Null Reference exception. The error is generated because you are referring to the Menu1 Web User Control within the Page_Load handler.

On the other hand, there is nothing wrong with declaratively setting the value of a property. Within the HTML source of the TestMenu.aspx page, you can assign a value to the Color property as follows:

```
<uc1:Menu id="Menu1" runat="server" color="blue"></uc1:Menu>
```

Using Data Caching

You can add just about any object in the .NET Framework to the Cache, including DataSets, Hashtables, or custom classes. When an item is added to the cache, the item is stored in the Web server's memory. It remains in memory until it is automatically scavenged when memory becomes low.

> **NOTE**
>
> You can monitor the cache by using performance counters. When you install the .NET Framework, 10 performance counters are added for monitoring such things as the total number of entries in the cache.

The cache has application scope. That means that you can retrieve any item that you have added to the cache from any page that is located under the same virtual directory.

Behind the scenes, when you use either Page Output Caching or Partial Page Caching, the Cache object is used to store the generated content. In other words, the Cache object is the fundamental caching mechanism used by all other forms of caching in the ASP.NET Framework.

We've already discussed how you can use the Cache object to store a DataSet in memory in Chapter 8, "Overview of ADO.NET." In this section, you'll learn how to take advantage of some of the advanced features of the Cache object, such as file dependencies, expiration policies, and item priorities.

Adding and Removing Items from the Cache

You can insert a new item into the Cache by using the Insert method as follows:

C#

```
Cache.Insert( "someItem", someItem );
```

VB.NET

```
Cache.Insert( "someItem", someItem )
```

Or, and this does the very same thing, you can insert an item like the following:

C#

```
Cache[ "someItem" ] = someItem;
```

VB.NET

```
Cache( "someItem" ) = someItem
```

After you add an item to the Cache, the item can be retrieved from the Cache within any Web Form Page located within the same application. You retrieve an item from the Cache as follows:

C#

```
someItem = Cache[ "someItem" ];
```

VB.NET

```
someItem = Cache( "someItem" )
```

When items are retrieved from the Cache, the items are returned as instances of the Object class. When programming with C#, or using Option Strict with VB.NET, you'll need to cast the item returned from the Cache to the appropriate type as follows:

C#

```
someItem = (DataSet)Cache[ "someItem" ];
```

VB.NET

```
someItem = CType( Cache( "someItem" ), DataSet )
```

There are two warnings that you should always keep in mind when using the Cache object. First, and this is true even when you are programming with VB.NET, the Cache object is case sensitive. So, retrieving an item named SomeItem is very different from retrieving an item named someItem.

Second, you should always remember that an item that you have added to the Cache object is not guaranteed to be there when you later attempt to retrieve it. Items are automatically scavenged from the Cache. For this reason, you should always check whether an item exists before using it by comparing the item to either null or Nothing as in the following:

C#

```
if (Cache[ "someItem" ]!= null )
{
  // Use someItem
}
```

VB.NET

```
If Not Cache("someItem") Is Nothing Then
  ' Use someItem
```

```
End If
```

If you do want to explicitly remove an item from the Cache, you can use the `Remove()` method:

C#

```
Cache.Remove( "someItem" );
```

VB.NET

```
Cache.Remove( "someItem" )
```

For example, you might want to explicitly `Remove()` a DataSet from the Cache if you have just updated a record in the underlying database table.

Using File Dependencies

The `Cache` object supports something called a *file dependency*. After you add an item to the Cache with a file dependency, if the file is modified, the item is automatically dropped from the Cache. You can create a file dependency for a single file, a group of files, or even a directory.

For example, suppose that you want to create a drop-down list that displays a list of companies. Additionally, suppose that you want to store the list of companies in an XML file. You can cache the contents of the XML file in memory and create a file dependency. That way, if the contents of the XML file are modified, you can automatically reload the XML file into the Cache.

Let's try this example. First, we need to create the XML file.

1. Add a new XML file to your project by selecting Add New Item from the Project menu. Select XML File under Templates, name the new XML file **Companies.xml**, and click Open.

2. Enter the following list of companies in the XML Editor window (see Figure 14.2):

```
<?xml version="1.0" encoding="utf-8" ?>
<companies>
  <company>Amazon</company>
  <company>Microsoft</company>
  <company>Disney</company>
</companies>
```

3. Click Save to save the XML file.

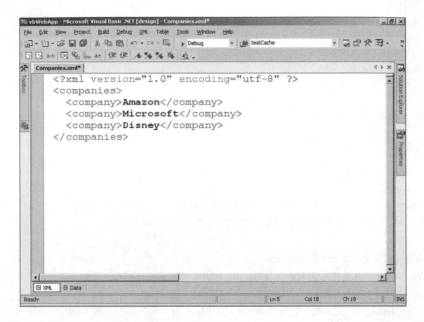

FIGURE 14.2   Using the XML Editor.

Next, we need to create a Web Form Page that displays the list of companies from the XML file in a `DropDownList` control. We'll cache the XML file with a file dependency on the XML file.

1. Add a Web Form Page to your project named **PickCompany.aspx**.

2. Add a `DropDownList` control to the page.

3. Add a `Label` control to the page.

4. Double-click the Designer surface to switch to the Code Editor.

5. Enter the following code for the `Page_Load` handler:

   C#

```csharp
private void Page_Load(object sender, System.EventArgs e)
{
  DataSet dstCompanies;

  dstCompanies = (DataSet)Cache["Companies"];
  if (dstCompanies == null)
  {
    Label1.Text = "Retrieving from file!";
    dstCompanies = new DataSet();
```

```
    dstCompanies.ReadXml(MapPath("Companies.xml"));
    Cache.Insert(
      "Companies",
      dstCompanies,
      new System.Web.Caching.CacheDependency(MapPath("Companies.xml")));
  }
  DropDownList1.DataSource = dstCompanies;
  DropDownList1.DataTextField = "company_text";
  DropDownList1.DataBind();
}
```

VB.NET

```
Private Sub Page_Load(ByVal sender As System.Object,
➥ByVal e As System.EventArgs) Handles MyBase.Load
  Dim dstCompanies As DataSet

  dstCompanies = Cache("Companies")
  If dstCompanies Is Nothing Then
    Label1.Text = "Retrieving from file!"
    dstCompanies = New DataSet()
    dstCompanies.ReadXml(MapPath("Companies.xml"))
    Cache.Insert( _
      "Companies", _
      dstCompanies, _
      New System.Web.Caching.CacheDependency(MapPath("Companies.xml")))
  End If
  DropDownList1.DataSource = dstCompanies
  DropDownList1.DataTextField = "company_text"
  DropDownList1.DataBind()
End Sub
```

6. Right-click the PickCompany.aspx page in the Solution Explorer window and select Build and Browse.

When the page first opens, the list of companies appears in the DropDownList control. The Label control displays the message Retrieving from File!. If you click Refresh, the message disappears because the XML file is now stored in the Cache.

The XML file will remain in the Cache unless the Companies.xml file is modified. You can test this by doing the following:

1. Double-click the Companies.xml file in the Solution Explorer window to open the file in the XML Editor.

2. Remove Disney from the list of companies in the XML file.

3. Save the XML file by clicking the Save button.

4. Refresh the PickCompany.aspx page.

When you refresh the PickCompany.aspx page, the changes you made to the XML file appear immediately. When you modified the XML file, the file was automatically dropped from the Cache and reloaded when you refreshed the page.

Using Expiration Policies

You can automatically dump items from the Cache at timed intervals by supplying either an absolute or sliding expiration policy for an item that you add to the Cache.

An absolute expiration policy is a date and time when you want an item to be automatically dropped. You can supply any date and time that you want. For example, if you are caching a list of banner advertisements, you might want to drop the banner advertisements from the Cache every hour to check for expired advertisements. You can do this by supplying an expiration time with the Insert() method as follows:

C#

```
Cache.Insert(
  "Ads",
  Ads,
  null,
  DateTime.Now.AddHours( 1 ),
  System.Web.Caching.Cache.NoSlidingExpiration );
```

VB.NET

```
Cache.Insert( _
  "Ads", _
  Ads, _
  Nothing, _
  DateTime.Now.AddHours(1), _
  System.Web.Caching.Cache.NoSlidingExpiration )
```

A sliding expiration policy works differently than an absolute expiration policy. A sliding expiration policy specifies an interval of time. As long as the item is requested within that interval, the item will remain in the Cache.

Sliding expiration policies are useful when you need to store a large number of items in the Cache. Using a sliding expiration policy, you can cache a large number of items and only the items that are most frequently accessed will remain in the Cache.

The following adds an item to the Cache with a sliding expiration policy of 10 minutes:

C#

```csharp
Cache.Insert(
  "someItem",
  someItem,
  null,
  System.Web.Caching.Cache.NoAbsoluteExpiration,
  TimeSpan.FromMinutes( 10 ));
```

VB.NET

```vbnet
Cache.Insert( _
  "someItem", _
  someItem, _
  Nothing, _
  System.Web.Caching.Cache.NoAbsoluteExpiration, _
  TimeSpan.FromMinutes(10) )
```

Be aware that you cannot add an item to the Cache with both an absolute expiration policy and sliding expiration policy. You must pick one or the other.

Setting Item Priorities

You can set different item priorities for items added to the Cache. When memory resources become low, items with lower priorities will be dropped before items with higher priorities.

The item priority is represented by values from the `CacheItemPriority` enumeration. The following lists the values from this enumeration in order of priority:

- `NotRemovable`   Should never be removed from the Cache
- `High`   Least likely to be removed from the Cache
- `AboveNormal`   Less likely to be removed from the Cache
- `Default`   Same as Normal
- `Normal`   Normal priority
- `BelowNormal`   More likely to be removed from the Cache
- `Low`   Most likely to be removed from the Cache

For example, you would use the following code to add an item to the Cache with `High` priority:

C#

```
Cache.Insert(
  "someItem",
  someItem,
  null,
  System.Web.Caching.Cache.NoAbsoluteExpiration,
  System.Web.Caching.Cache.NoSlidingExpiration,
  System.Web.Caching.CacheItemPriority.High,
  null);
```

VB.NET

```
Cache.Insert( _
  "Ads", _
  Ads, _
  Nothing, _
  System.Web.Caching.Cache.NoAbsoluteExpiration, _
  System.Web.Caching.Cache.NoSlidingExpiration, _
  System.Web.Caching.CacheItemPriority.High, _
  Nothing)
```

NOTE

The final parameter that you can pass to the Insert() method represents a callback function. You can supply a callback function that is automatically executed whenever an item is removed from the Cache.

Summary

In this chapter, you learned how to take advantage of the three caching mechanisms built into the ASP.NET Framework. In the first section, you learned how to use Page Output Caching to store the entire contents of a Web Form Page in memory. You also learned how to create different cached versions of the page, depending on the values of parameters passed to the page.

Next, you learned how to use Partial Page Caching to cache regions of a page. You learned how to implement Partial Page Caching with Web User Controls.

Finally, you learned how to use Data Caching to cache an arbitrary object in memory. You learned how to create file dependencies, expiration policies, and assign different item priorities for items added to the Cache.

15

Configuring Your Application

IN THIS CHAPTER

- Overview of the Machine.Config and Web.Config Files

- Configuration Sections

- Adding Custom Configuration Information

- Advanced Configuration Topics

In this chapter, you will learn how to configure your ASP.NET applications by taking advantage of the Machine.Config and Web.Config files. You can use these files to modify a variety of configuration settings, including security, compilation, and trace settings.

In this chapter, you will learn

- How to modify the different sections of the Machine.Config and Web.Config files

- How to store custom configuration information in the Machine.Config and Web.Config files

- How to perform advanced configuration tasks, such as locking configuration sections

Overview of the Machine.Config and Web.Config Files

One of the goals of the .NET Framework is to eliminate the need to use the Windows registry to store application configuration settings. This is good news because dependence on the Windows registry results in a number of problems:

- Storing configuration information in the Windows registry makes it difficult to move an application from one server to another. In particular, it makes it difficult to move an application from a development server to a production server because every registry setting must be moved from one server to the other.

- The Windows registry can become corrupted, causing your application to fail.

- You must use special utilities to edit the Windows registry, which makes it difficult to perform quick modifications.

The .NET Framework replaces the Windows registry with the Machine.Config and Web.Config files. These files are plain text files in XML format. You can edit them with any text editor, including Notepad.

The Machine.Config file contains configuration settings that apply to every .NET application on a server. It's the master configuration file. You can find this file at `\WINNT\Microsoft.NET\Framework\Version\CONFIG`.

Typically, you do not modify the Machine.Config file. Instead, you override configuration settings in the Machine.Config file within a lower-level Web.Config file. The Web.Config file doesn't contain any additional sections that are not included in the Machine.Config file.

You can place a Web.Config file in a number of different locations. The location of the Web.Config file determines the scope of its configuration settings:

- *wwwroot*—If you place a Web.Config file in the root directory of a Web site, it applies to all Web applications contained within the Web site.

- *virtual root*—If you place a Web.Config file in the root directory of a virtual directory, it applies to a particular ASP.NET application.

- *directory*—If you place a Web.Config file in a particular directory, it applies to all files in that directory and all files located in directories below that directory.

- *file*—You can apply settings in a Web.Config file to a single file (see the "Applying Configuration Settings to a Particular File" section later in this chapter).

The Machine.Config and Web.Config files work hierarchically. As you'll see in a moment, the Machine.Config file is huge. However, if you want to override a configuration setting in a Web.Config file, you don't need to copy the whole Machine.Config into the Web.Config file. You can copy only those settings that you want to override.

Configuration Sections

In this section, we'll examine each of the configuration sections in the Machine.Config file. This section will make more sense if you open the Machine.Config file in Notepad so you can take a look at it as you read about the different configuration sections. The Machine.Config file is located at `\WINNT\Microsoft.NET\Framework\Version\CONFIG`.

The first thing you should notice about the Machine.Config file is that it is an XML file. This has some inconvenient implications. In particular, it means that the Machine.Config file is case sensitive. Adding a <System.Web> tag is different from adding a <system.web> tag.

> **NOTE**
>
> In general, tag names in the Machine.Config file follow a naming convention called *camel casing*. When names are camel cased, the first letter of the first word in a name is lowercase, and the first letters of any remaining words in a name are uppercase. For example, requestEncoding instead of RequestEncoding.
>
> On the other hand, the values of attributes follow a convention called Pascal casing. The first letter of all words in the value of an attribute is uppercase. For example, SortByCategory instead of sortByCategory.

On the positive side, the fact that the Machine.Config file is an XML file makes it easy to edit. You can make any modifications to the Machine.Config or Web.Config directly within Notepad. As soon as you save the modified file, any changes that you make will immediately take effect.

> **TIP**
>
> You can buy user-friendly editors for modifying the Machine.Config and Web.Config files. For example, you can download an evaluation version of the Hunter Stone Web.Config Editor at http://hunterstone.com.

The <configSections> Section

The <configSections> section appears at the very top of the Machine.Config file. This section works almost like a table of contents. It contains a list of the configuration sections contained in the Machine.Config file and the .NET classes responsible for parsing them.

For example, the System.Diagnostics.DiagnosticsConfigurationHandler class parses the <system.diagnostics> section. You can add your own section handlers to this section if you want to store custom configuration information (see the "Creating a Custom Section Handler" section later in this chapter).

The <appSettings> Section

You can take advantage of the <appSettings> section to quickly add custom configuration information. For example, this is a good place to store the connection string for your database. You'll learn how to take advantage of this in the "Using the <appSettings> Section" discussion later in this chapter.

The `<system.diagnostics>` Section

You can add your own debug and trace listeners to this section (although tracing is handled differently in a Web Forms application). Debugging and tracing are discussed in detail in Chapter 6, "Debugging Your Web Form Pages."

The `<system.net>` Section

This section contains configuration settings for network connections. For example, this section specifies that the `HttpRequestCreator` module is responsible for handling all http requests from Internet hosts.

The `<system.net>` section also contains configuration information for the proxy server used when making requests. You might need to modify this section if you run into problems when accessing a Web service through a proxy server.

The `<system.web>` Section

The `<system.web>` section contains all of the configuration settings specific to ASP.NET applications. The bulk of the remaining configuration sections can be found inside the `<system.web>` section.

The `<trace>` Element

This element enables you to configure both page- and application-level tracing. Tracing is discussed in detail in Chapter 6.

The `<globalization>` Element

This element specifies the character encoding used when parsing requests, responses, and code files (such as .aspx and .ascx files). By default, UTF-8 (UCS Transformation Format, 8-bit form) encoding is used. If you do not specify an encoding, your server's Regional Options locale setting is used.

You might need to modify this section if you are working in a language with a different character set.

The `<httpRuntime>` Element

This element enables you to configure runtime settings, such as the number of threads to use when processing incoming requests and the number of requests that can be queued before new requests are rejected.

The `executionTimeout` attribute enables you to specify the maximum amount of time that a Web Form page is allowed to execute before timing out. (Its default value is 90 seconds.) You'll need to modify this value if you have a page that takes a very long time to execute.

The `maxRequestLength` specifies the maximum amount of data allowable in a form post operation. For security reasons, by default, no one can post more than four megabytes to your server in a form post. If you want users to upload files larger than four megabytes (such as big .jpg files), you'll need to increase this value.

The `<compilation>` Section

The `<compilation>` section enables you to configure different options relevant to compiling an application. The settings in this section apply only to the presentation page, not the application code in a code-behind file.

The `debug` attribute enables or disables debugging for the .aspx pages (presentation pages) of your application. When `debug="false"`, you cannot see the source code where the error occurred in the presentation page. You will need to set `debug="true"` to use the Visual Studio .NET debugger.

The `defaultLanguage` attribute sets the default language to use with presentation pages (for example, c# or vb). The default language for the .NET Framework is VB.NET. Again, this attribute does not affect code-behind files that you create in the Visual Studio .NET Code Editor.

The `explicit` and `strict` attributes only apply to VB.NET. When `explicit` is assigned the value `true`, you must declare all variables before using them. When `strict` is assigned the value `true`, lazy type conversion is not allowed. Again, these settings apply only to the presentation pages and not the code-behind files compiled by Visual Studio .NET.

Finally, the `<assemblies>` sub-element is used to list all the assemblies available in the presentation pages in your application. If you need to use an assembly that is not included in this list, such as System.Messaging, you'll need to add it.

Notice that the last entry is `<add assembly="*" />`. This statement automatically adds all assemblies located in the application root /bin directory or the `\WINNT\Microsoft.NET\Framework\Version` directory. This entry is used to automatically load any custom components or controls that you create.

The `<pages>` Element

This section contains configuration options that apply specifically to ASP.NET pages.

The `buffer` attribute enables or disables page buffering. When buffering is enabled, the complete content of a page is generated before being sent to the browser. When buffering is disabled, a page is sent to the browser as it is rendered. Generally, you want to leave buffering on because it results in better overall page performance.

The `enableSessionState` attribute turns on or off session state or enables you to make session state read-only. When you are not using session state, you should modify this attribute to improve the performance of your application.

The `enableViewState` attribute enables or disables view state. You can save some bandwidth by disabling view state. However, if you disable view state, many of the Web Forms Controls will no longer function correctly.

The `enableViewStateMac` attribute enables or disables a message authentication code that is used to verify content stored in view state. If you are worried about users modifying the contents of the hidden view state form field, you should leave this attribute with its default value of `true`.

The `smartNavigation` attribute enables Smart Navigation. When Smart Navigation is enabled, clicking a link in a page returns you to the same position when the page reloads. This feature only works with Internet Explorer 5.0 or later. For an example of Smart Navigation, see Chapter 13, "Displaying Data with the `DataGrid` Control."

The `autoEventWireup` attribute is `false` by default, and you should keep it that way when using Visual Studio .NET. If this attribute is set to `true`, methods declared with the proper name are automatically wired to the corresponding event. For example, a method named `Button1_Click` will automatically be wired to the `Click` event raised by the `Button1` control.

The `<customErrors>` Section

The `<customErrors>` sectioncontains configuration settings that control how errors are displayed.

The `mode` attribute determines whether custom error messages are displayed only for remote clients or the local machine. If you are debugging a remote server, you'll want to set the mode to the value `Off`. If you are debugging the local server, you'll want to set the mode to the value `RemoteOnly`.

The `defaultRedirect` attribute enables you to specify a page to which the user is automatically redirected to when an error occurs. This can be any page, including any Web Form or HTML page.

You can also list specific errors and redirect pages. For example, the following Web.Config file automatically redirects users to a page called Bad.htm when an .aspx page that does not exist is requested:

```
<configuration>
   <system.web>
      <customErrors defaultRedirect="genericerror.htm"
         mode="On">
         <error statusCode="404" redirect="Bad.htm"/>
      </customErrors>
   </system.web>
</configuration>
```

If you request a non-existent page named NotThere.aspx, you'll automatically be redirected to the Bad.htm page because requesting the NotThere.aspx page raises a "404 Not Found" status code from the server.

It's important to understand that the <customErrors> attribute only applies to pages mapped into the ASP.NET Framework. For example, if you request a normal HTML page, the <customErrors> section is ignored.

The <authentication> Section

The <authentication> section is used to configure Windows, Forms, and .NET Passport authentication. Forms authentication is discussed in detail in Chapter 16, "Securing Your Application."

The <identity> Element

The <identity> element is used to enable or disable impersonation. By default, all ASP.NET pages run under the security context of the ASPNET account. The ASPNET account is automatically added to your server when you install the .NET Framework.

This is a change from ASP Classic. ASP Classic uses per request impersonation. If you request an ASP Classic page, the page executes under the security context of the user making the request. For anonymous users, the page executes under the security context of the IUSR_MachineName account.

If you assign the value true to the impersonate attribute, ASP.NET pages will work in the same way as ASP Classic pages. They will use per-request impersonation.

There is a third option. Instead of using the ASPNET account or per-request impersonation, you can specify a specific account. If you supply a username and password, ASP.NET pages will run under the security context of the account associated with the username.

The <authorization> Section

The <authorization> section enables you to configure Windows, Forms, or .NET Passport authorization. Forms authentication is discussed in detail in Chapter 16.

The <machineKey> Element

The <machineKey> element is used with Forms authentication. It contains encryption options to use with the Forms authentication ticket. You'll need to modify this element when using Forms authentication in a Web Farm.

The `<securityPolicy>` Section

This section associates named security levels with security policy files. Security policy files contain rules for assigning permissions to code.

The `<sessionState>` Element

This element is used to configure ASP.NET session state. For example, you can use this element to enable out-of-process session state or enable cookieless sessions. Session state is explored in detail in Chapter 17, "Maintaining Application State."

The `<httpHandlers>` Section

An `httpHandler` is a .NET class that executes whenever you make a request for a page with a certain path. For example, a handler generates the Trace.axd page that displays application-level tracing information.

Another important handler that is listed in this section is the handler for .aspx pages—the `PageHandlerFactory` class. The `PageHandlerFactory` class is responsible for processing requests for .aspx pages.

If you want to map file extensions into the ASP.NET Framework, you need to modify the `<httpHandlers>` section. For example, if you want HTML pages to be processed as Web Form Pages, you need to associate the `PageHandlerFactory` with the .html extension by adding an entry that looks like the following:

```
<add verb="*" path="*.html" type="System.Web.UI.PageHandlerFactory"/>
```

You also must modify the application mappings in the Internet Service Manager to map .html pages into the ASP.NET Framework. To do this, perform the following steps:

1. Launch the Internet Services Manager by clicking the Start button and choosing Settings, Control Panel, Administrative Tools, Internet Services Manager.

2. Right-click Default Web Site and select Properties.

3. Select the Home Directory tab and click the Configuration button.

4. Select the App Mappings tab in the Configuration dialog box.

5. Click the Add button to open the Add/Edit Application Extension Mapping dialog box.

6. Enter the following path in the Executable text box:

```
C:\WINNT\Microsoft.NET\Framework\v1.0.3705\aspnet_isapi.dll
```

7. Enter the extension **.html** in the Extension dialog box.

8. Click OK to close the dialog box.

After you make these modifications, you can add ASP.NET code to an .html page in the same way as you can add code to an ASP.NET page.

WARNING

The order in which you add entries to the <httpHandlers> section matters. This section uses a first match algorithm, so if you want to override the default action associated with an .html file, place your new entry near the top.

The <httpModule> Section

An httpModule is a .NET class that participates in every page request. Examples of modules include the OutputCache module responsible for page output caching and the Session module responsible for session state. Modules also implement the different authentication models built into the ASP.NET Framework.

You can create your own modules and add them to this section. For example, you can create a logging module that logs every page that users request from your Web site into a database table. To learn how to create modules, see Chapter 18, "Handling Application-Wide Events."

The <processModel> Element

The <processModel> element has configuration settings relevant to the behavior of the ASP.NET process.

WARNING

Because the <processModel> configuration settings apply to the ASP.NET process, they do not take effect until you stop and restart the ASP.NET process. You can quickly stop and restart the ASP.NET process by executing the following command from a command prompt:

iisreset

The userName attribute identifies the Windows account under which ASP.NET executes. This attribute accepts one of two special values—Machine and System. By default, the ASP.NET process executes under the Machine account, which is equivalent to the ASPNET account. Alternatively, you can specify the System account, which corresponds to the local system account.

The `<processModel>` element has a number of attributes that enable you to automatically restart the ASP.NET process when problems are detected. If a problem is detected, a new process is launched. All existing requests are transferred from the old process to the new process. After the requests have been transferred, the old process is shut down. If everything works right, someone requesting pages from the Web site should never notice that one process has been replaced by another.

> **NOTE**
>
> If the ASP.NET process shuts down, you lose any information stored in in-process session state and the cache. You can prevent a shutdown from clearing session state by using out-of-process session state. For more information, see Chapter 17.

For example, the `timeout` attribute enables you to specify an amount of time that the ASP.NET process is allowed to execute before being shut down and replaced. Oddly enough, you can actually make your Web application more stable by shutting it down periodically to start with a clean slate. For example, shutting the process down once a day will clear away any corrupted memory.

The `memoryLimit` attribute enables you to specify a percentage of system memory. If the ASP.NET process eats more than the specified memory limit, it is automatically shut down and replaced. This attribute is useful when you want to contain memory leaks.

The `<webControls>` Element

This element contains the path to the client-side JavaScript libraries used by Web Controls. For example, the JavaScript libraries used by the Web Forms Validation controls can be found at this location.

The `<clientTarget>` Section

This section defines several standard aliases for different types of browsers. For example, an uplevel browser is defined as Microsoft Internet Explorer 4.0. These aliases are used by Web Forms controls to enable the controls to render different content for different browsers.

The `<browserCaps>` Section

The `<browserCaps>` section is large. It contains a list of different browsers and their capabilities. The different browsers are identified by their user-agent header.

You can access the information contained in the `<browserCaps>` section by using the `HttpBrowserCapabilities` class. For example, the following code detects whether a browser supports Java applets:

C#

```
if (Request.Browser.JavaApplets)
{
  // Browser supports Java Applets
}
```

VB.NET

```
If Request.Browser.JavaApplets Then
  ' The browser supports Java Applets
End If
```

The HttpBrowserCapabilities class is exposed by the Browser property. The class uses the user-agent header to perform a lookup of the features that the browser supports from the Machine.Config file.

The <webServices> Section

This section contains configuration settings specific to XML Web services. For example, the <wsdlHelpGenerator> element specifies the location of the Web service Help Page that appears automatically when you enter the path to a Web service in a Web browser (the path to an .asmx file).

Adding Custom Configuration Information

You can place your own application configuration information in the Machine.Config or Web.Config file. Placing the information in a configuration file is useful when you want to make configuration information, such as database connection strings, available to all pages in an application.

There are two ways that you can add your custom configuration information. You can add key and value pairs to the <appSettings> section, or you can create your own section handler. Both methods are discussed in the following sections.

Using the <appSettings> Section

If you want to quickly add a single string to the Web.Config file that can be read by Web Form Pages in your application, you can take advantage of the <appSettings> section. You can add any key and value pair that you want to the <appSettings> section.

You can read the value of particular keys from the <appSettings> section in a Web Form Page by taking advantage of the ConfigurationSettings class. This class returns a collection of all the key and value pairs from the <appSettings> section.

The <appSettings> section is most commonly used to store database connection strings. In this section, you'll learn how to add a database connection string to a Web.Config file and read it from pages in your application.

First, you need to create a Web.Config file with the database connection string:

1. Double-click the Web.Config file in the Solution Explorer window.

2. Add the following <appSettings> section immediately below the opening <configuration> tag in the Web.Config file:

```
<appSettings>
  <add key="dsn"
    value="Server=localhost;UID=sa;PWD=secret;database=pubs" />
</appSettings>
```

You'll need to enter the appropriate login and password for your database. Substitute your login for the UID parameter and your password for PWD parameter. Also, remember that the Web.Config file is case sensitive (even in the case of VB.NET).

3. Click Save.

Next, we'll create a page that displays the records from the Titles database table in a DataGrid control. We'll read the database connection string from the Web.Config file that we just created.

1. Create a new Web Form Page named **TestAppSettings.aspx** and click Open.

2. In the Server Explorer window, expand the Data Connection to the Pubs database table. If a Data Connection to the Pubs database does not exist, you'll need to create one.

3. Drag the Titles database table from the Server Explorer window onto the Designer surface. This will add an SqlConnection and an SqlDataAdapter to the page.

4. Drag a DataSet from beneath the Data tab in the Toolbox onto the Designer surface. This will open the Add Dataset dialog box.

5. In the Add Dataset dialog box, select Untyped Dataset and click OK.

6. Drag a DataGrid from beneath the Web Forms tab in the Toolbox onto the Designer surface.

7. Double-click the Designer surface. This will switch you to the Code Editor.

8. Enter the following code for the Page_Load handler:

C#

```csharp
private void Page_Load(object sender, System.EventArgs e)
{
sqlConnection1.ConnectionString =
    System.Configuration.ConfigurationSettings.AppSettings[ "dsn" ];
sqlDataAdapter1.Fill( dataSet1 );
DataGrid1.DataSource = dataSet1;
DataGrid1.DataBind();
}
```

VB.NET

```vbnet
Private Sub Page_Load(ByVal sender As System.Object,
➥ByVal e As System.EventArgs) Handles MyBase.Load
  SqlConnection1.ConnectionString =
➥ConfigurationSettings.AppSettings("dsn")
  SqlDataAdapter1.Fill(DataSet1)
  DataGrid1.DataSource = DataSet1
  DataGrid1.DataBind()
End Sub
```

9. Right-click the TestAppSettings.aspx page in the Solution Explorer and select Build and Browse.

After you complete these steps, the TestAppSettings.aspx page displays all the records from the Titles database table in a DataGrid control. The connection to the Pubs database is made using the connection string read from the Web.Config file.

Creating a Custom Section Handler

You can add your own configuration sections to the Machine.Config or Web.Config files. This is useful when you want to group several configuration settings into a common section. For example, you might want to create one configuration section that contains all the database connection strings that you use in your application.

Before you can create your own configuration section, however, you must create your own section handler. The section handler is used to parse your custom configuration section.

There are a number of ways that you can create your own section handler. Here, we will simply derive a new class from the NameValueSectionHandler class already included in the .NET Framework. Perform the following steps to create a new section handler named mySectionHandler:

C# Steps

1. Add a new class to your project by selecting Project, Add Class. Name the new class **mySectionHandler.cs** and click Open.

2. Enter the following code for the mySectionHandler.cs class:

```
namespace ProjectName
{
  public class mySectionHandler:
    System.Configuration.NameValueSectionHandler
  {
  }
}
```

Replace the placeholder *ProjectName* with the name of your current project in Visual Studio .NET.

VB.NET Steps

1. Add a new class to your project by selecting Project, Add Class. Name the new class **mySectionHandler.vb** and click Open.

2. Enter the following code for the mySectionHandler.vb class:

```
Public Class mySectionHandler
    Inherits System.Configuration.NameValueSectionHandler
End Class
```

Next, we need to add our custom configuration section to the Web.Config file.

1. Double-click the Web.Config file in the Solution Explorer window.

2. Enter the following sections immediately below the opening <configuration> tag:

```
<configSections>
  <section name="mySection"
    type="ProjectName.mySectionHandler, ProjectName" />
</configSections>

<mySection>
  <add key="FirstKey" value="Value of first key" />
  <add key="SecondKey" value="Value of second key" />
</mySection>
```

Replace the placeholder *ProjectName* with the name of your project in Visual Studio .NET.

Finally, to test our new section handler, we'll create a Web Form Page that reads the value of FirstKey and displays it in a Label control.

1. Add a new Web Form Page named **TestSectionHandler.aspx** and click Open.

2. Drag a Label control from under the Web Forms tab in the Toolbox onto the Designer surface.

3. Double-click the Designer surface to switch to the Code Editor.

4. Enter the following code for the Page_Load handler:

   C#

   ```csharp
   private void Page_Load(object sender, System.EventArgs e)
   {
     System.Collections.Specialized.NameValueCollection config =
       (System.Collections.Specialized.NameValueCollection)
       System.Configuration.ConfigurationSettings.GetConfig( "mySection" );
     Label1.Text = config[ "FirstKey" ];
   }
   ```

   VB.NET

   ```vbnet
   Private Sub Page_Load(ByVal sender As System.Object,
   ➥ByVal e As System.EventArgs) Handles MyBase.Load
     Dim config As System.Collections.Specialized.NameValueCollection
     config = ConfigurationSettings.GetConfig("mySection")
     Label1.Text = config("FirstKey")
   End Sub
   ```

5. Right-click the TestSectionHandler.aspx page and select Build and Browse.

When the page opens, the value assigned to FirstKey in the Web.Config file is displayed in the Label control. The value is retrieved with the help of the GetConfig() method of the ConfigurationSettings class.

> **NOTE**
>
> You might be wondering why we needed to derive a new class from the existing NameValueSectionHandler class—especially since we didn't provide any implementation code for the new class. Why not use the NameValueSectionHandler class directly in the Web.Config file?

The problem is that you cannot refer to a class in the System namespace within a Web.Config file without performing some extra work (you must supply the strong name for the class). You can, however, refer to any class contained in your application. By deriving a new class from the `NameValueSectionHandler` class, we've snuck the `NameValueSectionHandler` into our application.

TIP

You can add an attribute, named `allowDefinition`, to the declaration of your section handler that determines where your section can be used. This attribute can accept one of the following three values—`Everywhere`, `MachineOnly`, or `MachineToApplication`. For example, if you declare your section handler as follows:

```
<section name="mySection"
  type="myApp.mySectionHandler, myApp"
  allowDefinition="MachineOnly"/>
```

Then you can add `mySection` only to a Machine.Config file and not a lower-level Web.Config file.

Advanced Configuration Topics

In this section, we'll discuss two advanced configuration topics. First, you'll learn how you can apply configuration settings in the Web.Config file to a particular file. You'll also learn how to lock down configuration settings so a developer of a particular Web application cannot change them.

Applying Configuration Settings to a Particular File

You can apply configuration settings to a particular location by taking advantage of the `<location>` tag. The `<location>` tag enables you to apply configuration settings to a particular file or directory.

For example, suppose that you want to password protect only one file in your application. You can do this by creating the following Web.Config file in the root directory of your application:

```
<configuration>
 <system.web>
  <authentication mode="Windows"/>
 </system.web>
 <location path="secret.aspx">
  <system.web>
  <authorization>
```

```
        <deny users="*" />
      </authorization>
      </system.web>
   </location>
</configuration>
```

Notice that there are two `<system.web>` sections in this Web.Config file. The first `<system.web>` section applies to all files in the current directory and all subdirectories. It enables Windows authentication for the application.

The second `<system.web>` section appears within a `<location>` tag. The `<location>` tag restricts the scope of the `<system.web>` section to a file named Secret.aspx. Secret.aspx is password protected so that users can never open it.

You can use the `<location>` tag with any section that is declared with the `allowLocation="true"` attribute in the `<configSections>` section of the Machine.Config or Web.Config file. The `allowLocation` attribute is `true` by default.

> **NOTE**
>
> Authentication and authorization are discussed in detail in Chapter 16.

Locking Configuration Settings

You might want to lock down certain settings in the Web.Config file so that they cannot be overridden by a particular application. You can lock configuration settings by taking advantage of the `<location>` tag and the `allowOverride` attribute.

For example, you normally do not want people uploading an ASP.NET application to a production Web server that has debugging enabled. When debugging is enabled for an application, sensitive information, such as database connection strings, could be revealed to the world when runtime errors are encountered. Furthermore, the performance of an application suffers while in debug mode.

You can prevent any ASP.NET application in a Web site from executing in debug mode by adding the following Web.Config file to the wwwroot directory of the Web site:

```
<configuration>
<location allowOverride="false">
  <system.web>
    <compilation debug="false" />
  </system.web>
</location>
</configuration>
```

Any application that attempts to override this debug setting in a Web.Config file will generate a configuration error. The value of the debug setting has been locked down.

You can also use the `allowOverride` attribute in combination with the `path` attribute to lock settings for a particular application or a particular folder in an application. For example, if both the development and production Web application are located on the same server, you can use the following Web.Config file to disable debugging only for the production server:

```
<configuration>
<location path="ProductionApp" allowOverride="false">
  <system.web>
    <compilation debug="false" />
  </system.web>
</location>
<location path="DevelopmentApp">
  <system.web>
    <compilation debug="true" />
  </system.web>
</location>
</configuration>
```

Summary

In this chapter, you learned how to configure your ASP.NET applications using the Machine.Config and Web.Config configuration files.

First, you were provided with an overview of the different sections of the Machine.Config file. You learned the purpose of each of the major sections and elements of the file.

Next, you learned two methods of adding custom configuration information to the Web.Config file. You learned how to take advantage of the `<appSettings>` section to quickly add confiiguration information. You also learned how to create your own section handler that can be used with a custom configuration section.

Finally, we examined two advanced configuration topics. You learned how to use the `<location>` tag to apply configuration settings to a particular file or directory. You also learned how to use the `allowOverride` attribute to lock configuration settings.

16

Securing Your Application

IN THIS CHAPTER

- Overview of Forms Authentication

- Enabling Forms Authentication

- Storing Usernames and Passwords in the Web.Config File

- Storing Usernames and Passwords in a Database Table

- Implementing Custom Roles with Form Authentication

Most Web applications include password-protected areas. For example, if you are building an online store, you'll need to force users to register before they buy a product. Or, if you are creating an employee directory, you might want to password protect the page for adding new employees so that only administrators of the application can access the page.

In this chapter, you will learn how to password protect pages in your Web application by taking advantage of Forms Authentication. In particular, you will learn

- How to configure authentication and authorization for Forms Authentication

- How to create a simple login page that enables registered users to log in to your Web application

- How to authenticate users against a data store

- How to implement a role-based security system that enables you to group users into different roles

Overview of Forms Authentication

The .NET Framework includes three built-in methods of authenticating users—Windows Authentication, Forms Authentication, and .NET Passport Authentication. All three authentication methods follow a similar model. In other words, if you understand how to configure one, you can configure the other two.

Windows Authentication uses Windows accounts and groups. Microsoft .NET Passport Authentication uses

Microsoft Passport user accounts (the same user accounts that are used by such Microsoft services as HotMail and MSN).

In this chapter, we'll concentrate on Forms Authentication because this is the type of authentication that you are most likely to set up for a Web application. Forms Authentication, unlike the other two authentication models, enables you to store usernames and passwords in a custom data store, such as a database table or XML file.

Authentication and Authorization

Before diving into the topic of Forms Authentication, you need to understand how Microsoft distinguishes between the following two terms:

- *Authentication*—The process of identifying a user
- *Authorization*—The process of determining the resources a user is allowed to access

Forms Authentication handles authentication by creating a browser cookie that identifies a user. It handles authorization by enabling you to create a configuration file that lists the resources a user is allowed to access.

When you configure Forms Authentication, you need to create two Web.Config files (or a single Web.Config file with two sections). You need to create a Web.Config file that indicates the type of authentication you want to perform, and a Web.Config file that authorizes access to different users or roles.

A minimal authentication Web.Config file looks as follows:

```
<configuration>
<system.web>
  <authentication mode="Forms" />
</system.web>
</configuration>
```

This file simply enables Forms Authentication for an application as opposed to Windows or Passport Authentication. The default authentication method, as specified in the Machine.Config file, is Windows Authentication. This configuration file overrides the default setting.

The <authentication> section must be placed in the root Web.Config file for an application. You can enable only one method of authentication for an application. For example, one application cannot use both Forms Authentication and Passport Authentication.

An authentication Web.Config file doesn't do anything interesting by itself. To password protect pages, you need to add another Web.Config file that contains an <authorization> section. A minimal authorization Web.Config file looks like the following:

```
<configuration>
<system.web>
  <authorization>
    <deny users="?" />
  </authorization>
  </system.web>
</configuration>
```

This Web.Config file prevents anonymous (unauthenticated) users from accessing any pages in the current directory or any subdirectory. If an anonymous user attempts to access a page, the user is automatically redirected to a page named Login.aspx.

TIP

By default, unauthorized users are redirected to the application root Login.aspx page. You can supply an alternative path for the Login page by modifying the loginUrl attribute in the authentication Web.Config file as follows:

```
<configuration>
<system.web>
  <authentication mode="Forms">
    <forms loginUrl="mylogin.aspx" />
  </authentication>
  </system.web>
  </configuration>
```

WARNING

Forms Authentication only applies to resources mapped into the .NET Framework. By default, it does not apply to HTML, classic ASP, or image files. To apply Forms Authentication to these files, you need to map the proper file extensions to the ASP.NET Framework in the Internet Services Manager.

For example, to protect GIF files, you need to map the .gif file extension to the aspnet_isapi.dll extension under the App Mappings tab. Be aware that mapping new extensions into the ASP.NET Framework has performance implications.

The `<authentication>` section accepts two different elements: `<deny>` and `<allow>`. The `<deny>` element can be used to deny access to a list of users or roles. The `<allow>` element enables access.

You can specify users or roles by name. You can also use two special symbols: ? and *. The question mark (?) represents all anonymous users. The asterisk (*) represents all users, regardless of whether they are authenticated.

Consider, for example, the following Web.Config file:

```
<configuration>
<system.web>
  <authorization>
    <allow users="Jane" />
    <deny users="*" />
  </authorization>
  </system.web>
</configuration>
```

This authorization Web.Config file denies access to all the pages in a directory to all users except Jane. The `<authorization>` section uses a first match algorithm. The order of the `<allow>` and `<deny>` elements here is important. If you reversed the order, all users, including Jane, would be denied access.

You can add multiple authorization Web.Config files to a single application. For example, you can prevent anonymous users from accessing pages in certain folders and not others. You can also password protect an entire application by adding an `<authorization>` section to the root Web.Config file.

You should keep in mind that the Web.Config file works by inheritance. Unless you override an authentication section in a lower-level Web.Config file, authentication settings will apply to all the files in a folder and all of its subfolders.

Enabling Forms Authentication

In this section, we'll walk through each of the steps required to enable Forms Authentication. We'll password-protect all the pages in a directory named SecretFiles so that only users who log in can view the pages.

The first step is to enable Forms Authentication by modifying the Web.Config file located in the root directory of your application.

1. Double-click the root Web.Config file in the Solution Explorer window.

2. Delete all the contents of the Web.Config file (don't let this make you nervous!).

3. Enter the following configuration settings:

```
<configuration>
<system.web>
  <authentication mode="Forms" />
</system.web>
</configuration>
```

4. Click the Save button to save the modified Web.Config file.

This Web.Config file enables Forms Authentication for your entire application. Making these modifications does not password protect any pages. However, it is a necessary step before you can password protect a page.

Next, we need to create the Web Form Page that we want to password protect.

1. Add a new folder to your application named **SecretFiles** by right-clicking your application name in the Solution Explorer Window and selecting Add, New Folder.

2. Add a new Web Form Page to the SecretFiles folder by right-clicking SecretFiles in the Solution Explorer window and selecting Add, Add Web Form. Provide the name **Secret.aspx** for the new Web Form Page and click Open.

3. Drag a Flow Layout Panel control from under the HTML tab in the Toolbox onto the Secret.aspx page.

4. Enter the text **This Content is Secret!** in the Flow Layout Panel.

Finally, to password protect the files in the SecretFiles folder, we must add a second Web.Config file to the SecretFiles folder. This second Web.Config file contains an <authentication> section that prevents anonymous users from accessing the folder.

1. Right-click the SecretFiles folder in the Solution Explorer window and select Add, Add New Item. When the Add New Item dialog box appears, select Web Configuration File in the Templates panel and click Open.

2. Delete all the contents of the new Web.Config file.

3. Enter the following configuration settings into the Web.Config file:

```
<configuration>
<system.web>
  <authorization>
    <deny users="?" />
  </authorization>
  </system.web>
</configuration>
```

4. Click Save.

After you complete this last set of steps, all of the files in the SecretFiles folder are password protected. If you right-click the Secret.aspx page in the Solution Explorer window and select Build and Browse, you'll receive a "404 File Not Found Error" (see Figure 16.1). You have been automatically redirected to a page named Login.aspx that doesn't exist. We'll create the Login.aspx page in the next section.

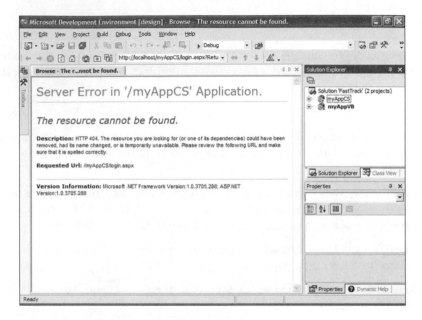

FIGURE 16.1   Accessing a password-protected page.

Creating a Simple Login Page

If a user attempts to access a password protected page, he or she is automatically redirected to a page named Login.aspx. In this section, you'll learn how to create a simple forms authentication Login.aspx page (see Figure 16.2).

Our login page will allow a user to log in only when the user enters the username Administrator and the password Secret. Perform the following steps to add the necessary controls to the Login.aspx page:

1. Add a new Web Form Page to the root folder of your project named **Login.aspx**.

2. Drag a Label control from the Web Forms tab in the Toolbox onto the Designer surface. Clear the Text property of the Label control.

FIGURE 16.2   A simple login page.

3. Drag a `TextBox` control from the Web Forms tab onto the Designer surface and assign the following values to its properties:

Property	Value
ID	txtUsername

4. Drag a second **TextBox** control from the Web Forms tab in the Toolbox onto the Designer surface and assign the following values to its properties:

Property	Value
ID	txtPassword
TextMode	Password

5. Drag two HTML labels from the HTML tab onto the Designer surface. Enter the text **Username** for the first label and the text **Password** for the second label. Position the labels next to the **TextBox** controls.

6. Drag a `Button` control from the Web Forms tab onto the Designer surface.

Next, we need to add the application logic to the page that authenticates the username and password that the user enters into the form.

1. Double-click the Button control. This will switch you to the Code Editor and create a Button1_Click handler.

2. Enter the following code for the Button1_Click handler:

   C#

```
private void Button1_Click(object sender, System.EventArgs e)
{
  if (txtUsername.Text == "Administrator" && txtPassword.Text == "Secret")
    System.Web.Security.FormsAuthentication.RedirectFromLoginPage(
➥txtUsername.Text, false );
  else
    Label1.Text = "Invalid Username/Password";
}
```

   VB.NET

```
Private Sub Button1_Click(ByVal sender As System.Object,
➥ByVal e As System.EventArgs) Handles Button1.Click
  If txtUsername.Text = "Administrator" And
➥txtPassword.Text = "Secret" Then
    System.Web.Security.FormsAuthentication.RedirectFromLoginPage(
➥txtUsername.Text, False)
  Else
    Label1.Text = "Invalid Username/Password"
  End If
End Sub
```

3. Right-click the Secret.aspx page (not the Login.aspx page) in the Solution Explorer window and select Build and Browse.

When you complete the last step, the Secret.aspx page will not appear. Instead, you'll be automatically redirected to the Login.aspx page. If you enter Administrator and Secret, you will be automatically redirected back to the Secret.aspx page (the user-name and password are case sensitive).

The Button1_Click handler first checks whether the txtUsername and txtPassword TextBox controls contain the values Administrator and Secret. If the values match, the RedirectFromLoginPage() method is called.

The RedirectFromLoginPage() method does two things. First, it issues an Authentication Ticket to the user's browser. The Authentication Ticket is an encrypted cookie that identifies the user. It also automatically redirects the user back to the original page that the user requested by secretly calling the Response.Redirect() method.

The RedirectFromLoginPage() method accepts two parameters. The first parameter represents a username. The username can be any string, including an email address. The second parameter indicates whether a persistent cookie should be created. When the second parameter has the value true, the user does not have to log in the next time the user visits the Web site. The Authentication cookie is saved persistently on the user's browser.

NOTE

The RedirectFromLoginPage() method redirects the user to the original page the user requested. There is a special situation, however, when the user requests the Login.aspx page directly. In that situation, there is no page to which the user can be redirected, so the user is redirected to the Default.aspx page.

Retrieving the Username

After a user has logged in, you can retrieve the user's username by using the User.Identity.Name property (a property of the Page class). This is useful when you want to customize pages for particular users.

For example, you can display the username on the Secret.aspx page by doing the following:

1. Double-click the Secret.aspx page in the Solution Explorer window.

2. Drag a Label control from under the Web Forms tab onto the Designer surface.

3. Double-click the Designer surface to switch to the Code Editor.

4. Enter the following code for the Page_Load handler:

   C#

   ```csharp
   private void Page_Load(object sender, System.EventArgs e)
   {
     Label1.Text = User.Identity.Name;
   }
   ```

   VB.NET

   ```vbnet
   Private Sub Page_Load(ByVal sender As System.Object,
   ➥ByVal e As System.EventArgs) Handles MyBase.Load
     Label1.Text = User.Identity.Name
   End Sub
   ```

5. Right-click the Secret.aspx in the Solution Explorer window and select Build and Browse.

When the Secret.aspx page opens, the username of the current user is displayed in the Label control.

Creating a Sign Out Link

You can add a Sign Out link to the pages in your application by taking advantage of the FormsAuthentication.SignOut() method. This method removes the Authentication Ticket cookie from the user's browser.

Perform the following steps to create add a Sign Out link to the Secret.aspx page:

1. Double-click the Secret.aspx page in the Solution Explorer window.

2. Drag a LinkButton control from under the Web Forms tab on the Toolbox onto the Designer surface.

3. In the Properties window, assign the value **Sign Out** to the LinkButton control's Text property.

4. Double-click the LinkButton control on the Designer surface. This will switch you to the Code Editor and add a LinkButton1_Click handler.

5. Enter the following code for the LinkButton1_Click handler:

   C#

   ```
   private void LinkButton1_Click(object sender, System.EventArgs e)
   {
   System.Web.Security.FormsAuthentication.SignOut();
   Response.Redirect( "../Login.aspx?ReturnUrl=" +
   ➥Server.UrlEncode( Request.Path ) );
   }
   ```

   VB.NET

   ```
   Private Sub LinkButton1_Click(ByVal sender As System.Object,
   ➥ByVal e As System.EventArgs) Handles LinkButton1.Click
     System.Web.Security.FormsAuthentication.SignOut()
     Response.Redirect("..\Login.aspx?ReturnUrl=" &
   ➥Server.UrlEncode(Request.Path))
   End Sub
   ```

6. Right-click the Secret.aspx page in the Solution Explorer window and select Build and Browse.

When the Secret.aspx page opens, a Sign Out link appears. If you click the Sign Out link, you are redirected to the Login.aspx page. Furthermore, if you attempt to go directly back to the Secret.aspx page after signing out, you are redirected to the Login.aspx page.

The second line of code in the `LinkButton1_Click` handler performs the redirection. Notice that a query string parameter named `ReturnUrl` is passed back to the Login.aspx page. The `FormsAuthentication.RedirectFromLoginPage()` method uses this query string parameter when redirecting a user who has successfully logged in.

Storing Usernames and Passwords in the Web.Config File

In the Login.aspx page that we built in the previous section, we checked whether the user entered the username Administrator and the password Secret. Our application isn't particularly useful because only one person can ever log in. In this section, you'll learn how you can store a list of usernames and passwords in the Web.Config file.

Storing usernames and passwords in the Web.Config file is valuable when you need to maintain a limited number of usernames and passwords. For example, if your Web application contains a private section for administrators of the application, you can password protect the section and store a list of valid administrators in the Web.Config file.

Perform the following steps to modify the pages that we created in the previous section:

1. Double-click the application root Web.Config file in the Solution Explorer window and enter the following configuration settings:

```
<configuration>
<system.web>
  <authentication mode="Forms">
    <forms>
      <credentials passwordFormat="Clear">
      <user name="Bob" password="Secret" />
      <user name="Jane" password="Secret" />
      <user name="Fred" password="Secret" />
      </credentials>
    </forms>
  </authentication>
</system.web>
</configuration>
```

2. Right-click the Login.aspx page in the Solution Explorer window and select Code from the View menu. Modify the `Button1_Click` handler as follows:

C#

```
private void Button1_Click(object sender, System.EventArgs e)
{
if (System.Web.Security.FormsAuthentication.Authenticate(
➥txtUsername.Text, txtPassword.Text) )
  System.Web.Security.FormsAuthentication.RedirectFromLoginPage(
➥txtUsername.Text, false );
else
  Label1.Text = "Invalid Username/Password";
}
```

VB.NET

```
Private Sub Button1_Click(ByVal sender As System.Object,
➥ByVal e As System.EventArgs) Handles Button1.Click
  If System.Web.Security.FormsAuthentication.Authenticate(
➥txtUsername.Text, txtPassword.Text) Then
    System.Web.Security.FormsAuthentication.RedirectFromLoginPage(
➥txtUsername.Text, False)
  Else
    Label1.Text = "Invalid Username/Password"
  End If
End Sub
```

3. Right-click the Secret.aspx page in the Solution Explorer window and select Build and Browse.

After you complete these steps, you can view the Secret.aspx page only if you enter one of the username and password combinations contained in the application Web.Config file. We modified the Login.aspx page to use the Authenticate() method to check usernames and passwords. The Authenticate() method simply performs a match against usernames and passwords in the Web.Config file.

> **NOTE**
>
> Note the attribute named passwordFormat included in the <credentials> tag of the Web.Config file. This attribute enables you to store the hash value of a password instead of the password itself in the Web.Config file. If you have multiple people administering a Web server and you don't want everyone's passwords in plain view, it is a good idea to hide the passwords by hashing them.
>
> You can assign the value MD5 or SHA1 to this attribute to use one of these hashing algorithms. If you need to generate hash values for the passwords, you can take advantage of a utility function of the FormsAuthentication class—one of the longest named methods in the .NET Framework—named HashPasswordForStoringInConfigFile().

Storing Usernames and Passwords in a Database Table

If you need to maintain a large number of usernames and passwords, storing them in the Web.Config file quickly becomes unmanageable. A better choice is to store user credentials in a database table.

In this section, we'll configure our application to use Forms Authentication with a database table. We will start over from scratch by creating the necessary database objects, a registration page, and a new login page.

Let's start by creating the database objects. Perform the following steps to create the database table that will contain the usernames and passwords:

1. In the Server Explorer window, expand the Data Connection to the Northwind database.

2. Right-click Tables and select New Table.

3. Enter the following table columns:

Column Name	Data Type	Length	Allow Nulls
User_ID	int	4	False
User_Username	Varchar	20	False
User_Password	Varchar	20	False

4. Mark the User_ID column as an identity column by assigning the value **True** to its Identity property (look in the Property sheet at the bottom of the Table Editor).

5. Click Save to save the table and name the new table **UserList**.

Next, we need to create a stored procedure that verifies username and passwords against the UserList table. We'll name our stored procedure CheckPassword. It will return one of three possible values:

0—Username and password are valid

1—Password is invalid

2—Username is invalid

Do the following to create the stored procedure:

1. Right-click the Stored Procedures folder under the Northwind Data Connection and select New Stored Procedure.

2. Enter the following code for the new stored procedure:

```
CREATE PROCEDURE dbo.CheckPassword
(
  @username Varchar(20),
  @password Varchar(20)
)
AS
/*
Check for valid Username and Password
*/
If Exists
(
Select User_ID From UserList
Where User_Username = @Username
And User_Password = @Password
)
Return 0

/*
Check for valid Username
*/

If Exists
(
Select User_ID From UserList
Where User_Username = @Username
)
Return 1

/*
Username doesn't exist
*/
Return 2
```

3. Click Save to save the CheckPassword stored procedure.

Next, we need to create the Web Form Page that we want to password protect.

1. Add a new folder named Confidential by right-clicking your project name in the Solution Explorer Window and selecting Add, New Folder.

2. Add a new Web Form Page to the Confidential folder by right-clicking it in the Solution Explorer window and selecting Add, Add Web Form. Provide the name **TopSecret.aspx** for the new Web Form Page and click Open.

3. Drag a Flow Layout Panel from the HTML tab in the Toolbox onto the TopSecret.aspx page.

4. Enter the text **Ultra Security Clearance Required!** in the Flow Layout Panel.

Next, we need to add the necessary Web.Config files to enable Forms Authentication and to password protect the Confidential folder.

1. Modify the application root Web.Config file as follows:

```
<configuration>
<system.web>
  <authentication mode="Forms" />
</system.web>
</configuration>
```

2. Add a new Web.Config file to the Confidential folder by right-clicking it in Solution Explorer, selecting Add, Add New Item, Web Configuration File, and clicking Open.

3. Enter the following configuration settings for the new Web.Config file:

```
<configuration>
<system.web>
  <authorization>
    <deny users="?" />
  </authorization>
</system.web>
</configuration>
```

Finally, we need to create the Login.aspx page. (If a Login.aspx page already exists in your project, you can modify it.)

1. Add a new Web Form Page to your project by right-clicking the name of your project in the Solution Explorer window and selecting Add, Add Web Form. Provide the name **Login.aspx** for the new Web Form Page and click Open.

2. Drag a Label control from the Web Forms tab in the Toolbox onto the Designer surface. Clear the Text property of the Label control.

3. Drag a TextBox control from the Web Forms tab in the Toolbox onto the Designer surface and assign the following values to its properties:

Property	Value
ID	txtUsername

4. Drag a second `TextBox` control from the Web Forms tab in the Toolbox onto the Designer surface and assign the following values to its properties:

Property	Value
ID	txtPassword
TextMode	Password

5. Drag two HTML labels from the HTML tab in the Toolbox onto the Designer surface. Enter the text **Username** for the first label and the text **Password** for the second label. Position the labels next to the `TextBox` controls.

6. Drag a `Button` control from the Web Forms tab onto the Designer surface.

Next, you need to add the `CheckPassword` stored procedure to the Login.aspx page and create the `Button_Click` handler that calls the stored procedure:

1. Drag the `CheckPassword` stored procedure from the Stored Procedures folder under the Data Connections folder in the Server Explorer window onto the Designer surface.

2. Double-click the `Button` control. This will switch you to the Code Editor and add a `Button_Click` handler.

3. Enter the following code for the `Button1_Click` handler:

C#

```
private void Button1_Click(object sender, System.EventArgs e)
{
    int intResult = 0;
    sqlCommand1.Parameters[ "@username" ].Value = txtUsername.Text;
    sqlCommand1.Parameters[ "@password" ].Value = txtPassword.Text;
    sqlConnection1.Open();
    sqlCommand1.ExecuteNonQuery();
    intResult = (int)sqlCommand1.Parameters[ "@RETURN_VALUE" ].Value;
    sqlConnection1.Close();

    switch (intResult)
    {
    case 0:
        System.Web.Security.FormsAuthentication.RedirectFromLoginPage(
            txtUsername.Text, false );
        break;
    case 1:
        Label1.Text = "Invalid Password";
```

```
    break;
  case 2:
    Label1.Text = "Invalid Username";
    break;
  }
}
```

VB.NET

```
Private Sub Button1_Click(ByVal sender As System.Object,
➥ByVal e As System.EventArgs) Handles Button1.Click
  Dim intResult As Integer

  SqlCommand1.Parameters("@Username").Value = txtUsername.Text
  SqlCommand1.Parameters("@Password").Value = txtPassword.Text
  SqlConnection1.Open()
  SqlCommand1.ExecuteNonQuery()
  intResult = SqlCommand1.Parameters("@RETURN_VALUE").Value
  SqlConnection1.Close()

  Select Case intResult
  Case 0
    System.Web.Security.FormsAuthentication.RedirectFromLoginPage(
➥txtUsername.Text, False)
  Case 1
    Label1.Text = "Invalid Password"
  Case 2
    Label1.Text = "Invalid Username"
  End Select
End Sub
```

4. Right-click the TopSecret.aspx page (not the Login.aspx page) in the Solution Explorer window and select Build and Browse.

The Login.aspx page calls the CheckPassword stored procedure to verify the username and password entered into the form. If the username and password combination is valid, the user is redirected to the original page requested; otherwise, an appropriate error message is displayed in a Label control.

You can test the Login.aspx page by entering one or more usernames and passwords into the UserList table. Double-click the UserList table in the Server Explorer window and enter the usernames and passwords directly into the grid. Alternatively, you can add the Register.aspx page to your project as discussed in the next section to your project.

Adding a Registration Page

One of the primary advantages of using Forms Authentication with a database table is that it makes it easy to create a registration form. To enable users to register at your Web site, they only need to complete a form that adds their usernames and passwords to the appropriate database table.

In this section, we'll extend the database application that we created in the previous section with a registration form (see Figure 16.3).

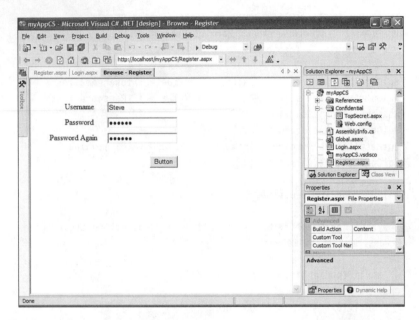

FIGURE 16.3   The registration form.

First, we need to create the stored procedure that adds a new user to the UserList table.

1. Right-click the Stored Procedures folder under the Northwind Data Connection in the Server Explorer window and select New Stored Procedure.

2. Enter the following code for the new stored procedure:

```
CREATE PROCEDURE dbo.AddUser
(
  @Username Varchar( 20 ),
  @Password Varchar( 20 )
)
AS
```

```
If Exists
(
  Select User_ID From UserList
  Where User_Username = @Username
)
Return 1

Insert UserList
(
  User_Username,
  User_Password
)
Values
(
  @Username,
  @Password
)
```

3. Click Save.

Next, we need to add a link to the Login.aspx page to the Register.aspx page.

1. Open the Login.aspx page by double-clicking the page in the Solution Explorer window.

2. Add a HyperLink control to the page by dragging the control from under the Web Forms tab in the Toolbox onto the Designer surface.

3. Assign the value **New users click here to register!** to the HyperLink control's Text property.

4. Double-click the Designer surface to switch to the Code Editor.

5. Enter the following Page_Load handler:

C#

```csharp
private void Page_Load(object sender, System.EventArgs e)
{
if (!Page.IsPostBack)
  HyperLink1.NavigateUrl =
    String.Format(
      "Register.aspx?ReturnURL={0}",
      Server.UrlEncode( Request.QueryString[ "ReturnURL" ] ) );
}
```

VB.NET

```
Private Sub Page_Load(ByVal sender As System.Object,
➥ByVal e As System.EventArgs) Handles MyBase.Load
  If Not Page.IsPostBack Then
    HyperLink1.NavigateUrl = String.Format("Register.aspx?ReturnURL={0}",
➥ Server.UrlEncode(Request.QueryString("ReturnURL")))
  End If
End Sub
```

Perform the following steps to create the Register.aspx page and add the necessary controls to the page:

1. Add a new Web Form Page to your project named **Register.aspx**.

2. Add a TextBox control to the Web Form Page and assign the following values to its properties:

Property	Value
ID	txtUsername

3. Add a second TextBox control to the Web Form Page and assign the following values to its properties:

Property	Value
ID	txtPassword
TextMode	Password

4. Add a third TextBox control to the Web Form Page and assign the following values to its properties:

Property	Value
ID	txtPassword2
TextMode	Password

5. Add three HTML Label elements to the Web Form Page. Enter the text **Username**, **Password**, and **Password Again** into the labels and position them appropriately on the page.

6. Add a RequiredFieldValidator control to the page. Assign the following values to the control's properties:

Property	Value
ControlToValidate	txtUsername
Text	Required!

7. Add a second `RequiredFieldValidator` control to the page. Assign the following values to the control's properties:

Property	Value
ControlToValidate	txtPassword
Text	Required!

8. Add a `CompareValidator` control to the page. Assign the following values to the control's properties:

Property	Value
ControlToValidate	txtPassword
ControlToCompare	txtPassword2
Text	Passwords must match!

9. Add a `Label` control to the Designer surface.

10. Add a `Button` control to the Designer surface.

Next, you need to add the application logic to the page that adds the new username and password to the database table.

1. Drag the `AddUser` stored procedure from the Server Explorer window onto the Register.aspx page.

2. Double-click the `Button` control. This will switch you to the Code Editor and add a `Button1_Click` handler.

3. Enter the following code for the `Button1_Click` handler:

C#

```csharp
private void Button1_Click(object sender, System.EventArgs e)
{
  int intResult = 0;

  sqlCommand1.Parameters[ "@Username" ].Value = txtUsername.Text;
  sqlCommand1.Parameters[ "@Password" ].Value = txtPassword.Text;
  sqlConnection1.Open();
  sqlCommand1.ExecuteNonQuery();
  intResult = (int)sqlCommand1.Parameters[ "@RETURN_VALUE" ].Value;
  sqlConnection1.Close();

  if (intResult == 0)
    System.Web.Security.FormsAuthentication.RedirectFromLoginPage(
```

```
      txtUsername.Text, false );
  else
    Label1.Text = "Username already taken!";
}
```

VB.NET

```
Private Sub Button1_Click(ByVal sender As System.Object,
➥ByVal e As System.EventArgs) Handles Button1.Click
  Dim intResult As Integer

  SqlCommand1.Parameters("@Username").Value = txtUsername.Text
  SqlCommand1.Parameters("@Password").Value = txtPassword.Text
  SqlConnection1.Open()
  SqlCommand1.ExecuteNonQuery()
  intResult = SqlCommand1.Parameters("@RETURN_VALUE").Value
  SqlConnection1.Close()

  If intResult = 0 Then
    System.Web.Security.FormsAuthentication.RedirectFromLoginPage(
➥txtUsername.Text, False)
  Else
    Label1.Text = "Username already taken!"
  End If
End Sub
```

4. Right-click the TopSecret.aspx page in the Solution Explorer window and select Build and Browse.

When you build and browse the TopSecret.aspx page, you'll be redirected to the Login.aspx page. If you click the New Users Click Here to Register! link, the Register.aspx page opens.

The Register.aspx page prevents you from entering a username that already exists in the UserList table. If you enter a new username and password, the username and password will be added to the database, and you will be automatically redirected to the TopSecret.aspx page.

Implementing Custom Roles with Forms Authentication

Custom roles enable you to apply security settings to groups of users. For example, instead of explicitly denying access to a page to Jane and Bob, you can add Jane and Bob to a custom role named Guests and deny access to all members of that role.

You can create custom roles when configuring Forms Authentication such as Administrators, Supervisors, and Moderators roles. The roles do not need to correspond to Windows groups. You can make up any set of roles that you want.

After you create the custom roles, you can refer to them in the Web.Config file to control access to pages in a folder. For example, you can specify that only Administrators have the right to access the pages in a particular folder.

In this section, we'll modify the application that we created in the previous section to associate different roles with different users.

First, we need to add an additional column to the UserList database table that we'll use to represent the roles associated with a user:

1. Right-click the UserList table in the Server Explorer window and select Design Table.

2. Add a new column named **User_Roles**. Assign the data type **varchar** and the length **500** to the column.

3. Click the Save UserList button to save the changes to the UserList table.

Next, we need to create a new stored procedure to retrieve the roles for a user:

1. Under the Northwind Data Connection, right-click Stored Procedures and select New Stored Procedure.

2. Enter the following code for the stored procedure:

```
CREATE PROCEDURE dbo.GetRoles
(
  @Username Varchar(20)
)
AS
SELECT User_Roles
FROM UserList
WHERE User_Username = @Username
```

3. Save the new stored procedure by clicking the Save button.

Next, we need to modify the Global.asax file to associate the proper roles with a user.

1. Open the Global.asax file by double-clicking it in the Solution Explorer window.

2. Drag the GetRoles stored procedure from the Server Explorer window onto the Designer surface. This will add a new SqlConnection and a SqlCommand object to the page.

3. Double-click the Designer surface to switch to the Code Editor and enter the
   following code for the Application_AuthenticateRequest() method:

C#

```csharp
protected void Application_AuthenticateRequest(Object sender, EventArgs e)
{
  HttpContext Context = HttpContext.Current;
  string[] arrUserRoles = null;

  // Only assign roles if user is authenticated
  if (!Request.IsAuthenticated)
    return;

  // Get the roles for the user from the database
  sqlCommand1.Parameters[ "@Username" ].Value = User.Identity.Name;
  sqlConnection1.Open();
  arrUserRoles = ((string)sqlCommand1.ExecuteScalar()).Split(',');
  sqlConnection1.Close();

  // Assign the roles to the user
  Context.User =
    new System.Security.Principal.GenericPrincipal(Context.User.Identity,
➥arrUserRoles);
}
```

VB.NET

```vbnet
Sub Application_AuthenticateRequest(ByVal sender As Object,
➥ByVal e As EventArgs)
  Dim arrUserRoles As String()

  ' Only assign roles if user is authenticated
  If Not Request.IsAuthenticated Then Return


  ' Get the roles for the user from the database
  SqlCommand1.Parameters("@Username").Value = User.Identity.Name
  SqlConnection1.Open()
  arrUserRoles = SqlCommand1.ExecuteScalar().Split(",")
  SqlConnection1.Close()
```

```
   ' Assign the roles to the user
    HttpContext.Current.User =
➥New System.Security.Principal.GenericPrincipal(
➥Context.User.Identity, arrUserRoles)
   End Sub
```

Finally, we need to modify the authorization Web.Config file to allow only users in the Administrators role access to pages. Modify the Web.Config file in the Confidential folder as follows:

```
<configuration>
<system.web>
  <authorization>
     <allow roles="Administrators" />
   <deny users="*" />
  </authorization>
</system.web>
</configuration>
```

This Web.Config file allows members of the Administrators role access to pages but denies access to everyone else.

You can test the custom roles by assigning a comma-delimited list of roles to the User_Roles column in the UserList table. For example, if you assign the string Administrators,Operators to the User_Roles column, that user will be associated with both the Administrators and Operators roles.

Summary

In this chapter, you learned how to password protect pages in your application by taking advantage of Forms Authentication. You learned how to configure both authentication and authorization for Forms Authentication by using the Web.Config file.

You discovered how to store usernames and passwords in two places—the Web.Config file and a database table. Finally, you tackled an advanced feature of Forms Authentication; You created an application that makes use of custom user roles.

17

Maintaining Application State

IN THIS CHAPTER

• Using View State

• Using Session State

• Using Application State

Variables within a Web Form Page do not retain their values between requests. Requesting a Web Form Page is similar to starting and stopping an application. After the page is finished being processed, you must start all over again with a blank slate.

If you need to maintain the value of a variable across multiple page requests, you need to do something special. In this chapter, you learn about three methods of maintaining the state of variables. You will learn

- How to use View State to retain the state of variables for a particular page

- How to use Session State to retain the state of variables for a particular user

- How to use Application State to retain the state of variables for a particular application

Using View State

View State enables you to preserve the state of a page when posting the page back to itself. It's important to understand that View State does not work when posting from one page to another. You can only take advantage of View State when performing postbacks.

Let's create a simple page that illustrates how View State works. We'll preserve the state of a Label control.

1. Create a Web Form Page named **ShowViewState.aspx**.

2. Add Web Form TextBox, Button, and Label controls to the page. Clear the text in the Label control.

3. Double-click the Button control to switch to the Code Editor and add a Button1_Click event handler.

4. Enter the following code for the Button1_Click handler:

C#

```csharp
private void Button1_Click(object sender, System.EventArgs e)
{
    Label1.Text += "<li>" + TextBox1.Text;
}
```

VB.NET

```vbnet
Private Sub Button1_Click(ByVal sender As System.Object,
➥ByVal e As System.EventArgs) Handles Button1.Click
    Label1.Text &= "<li>" & TextBox1.Text
End Sub
```

5. Right-click ShowViewState.aspx in the Solution Explorer window and select Build and Browse.

After the page opens, enter some text in the text box and click the button. You should notice that every time you submit new text, the text is appended to the list of items displayed by the Label (see Figure 17.1). The previous text added to the label is preserved between page requests through View State.

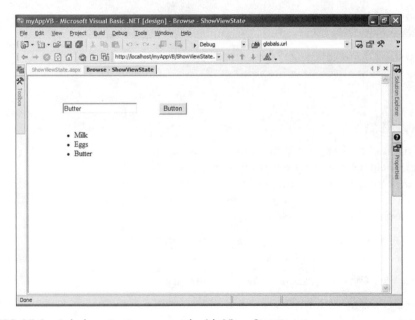

FIGURE 17.1   Label contents preserved with View State.

Every Web Form control automatically preserves the values of all of its properties through View State. For example, if you select an item in a list box and post the page containing the ListBox control back to the server multiple times, the same list item will continue to be selected. The value of a List control's SelectedItem property is automatically retained through View State.

View State also applies to the items displayed in a DataGrid. You only need to load data from a database into a DataGrid once. If you post the page containing the DataGrid back to itself, the DataGrid will not lose its data. A DataGrid automatically retains the values of all of its rows in View State.

How View State Really Works

View State works by taking advantage of a hidden form field that is automatically added to every Web Form Page. You can see this hidden form field if you select View Source when displaying a Web Form Page in a browser. For example, the View State hidden form field looks like the following when I click View Source for the ShowViewState.aspx page:

```
<input type="hidden" name="__VIEWSTATE"
value="dDwxNTg0NTEzNzMyO3Q802w8aTwxPjs+O2w8dDw7bDxpPDE+Oz47bDx0PHA
8cDxsPFRleHQ7PjtsPExhYmVsXDxsaVw+aGVsbG9cPGxpXD5taWxrOz4+Oz470z47P
j47Pj47PgIWH/qU4XKz/lwgBle3ON0unW/h" />
```

Immediately before a page is rendered, the values of the properties of all controls in a page are converted into a string. When the page is rendered, this string is assigned to the hidden __VIEWSTATE form field. When the page is posted back to the server, the string is parsed and all the values are reassigned to the properties of the controls in the page.

> **NOTE**
>
> If you want to know the messy details, View State is saved right after the PreRender event and before the Render method is called. View State is loaded right after the Init event and before the Load event. You can modify the way in which View State is saved and loaded by overriding a control's SaveViewState and LoadViewState methods.

Disabling View State

View State can be both a blessing and a curse. View State enables you to magically retain the state of all the controls on a page. However, the hidden VIEWSTATE form field can become very large, which can slow down the rendering of a page.

You don't always need to take advantage of View State. If you don't need to preserve the state of controls across post backs, you don't need to use View State.

For example, suppose that you have a Web Form Page that displays all the products in the Products database table in a DataGrid. The information about all the products is automatically stuffed into View State. If you are simply viewing the data in the DataGrid, you don't really need to do this. You only need to preserve the state of a DataGrid when performing such operations as sorting, editing, or paging a DataGrid. If you are only viewing the data, the View State consumed by the DataGrid is a waste of bandwidth.

You can disable View State for any control by assigning the value False to its EnableViewState property. You should always disable View State for controls such as the Repeater, DataList, and DataGrid controls when you are simply displaying data.

You also can disable View State for all the controls in a page by using the DOCU-MENT EnableViewState property. To disable View State for a page, select DOCUMENT in the Properties window and assign the value False to the EnableViewState property.

Finally, you can disable View State for an entire application (or particular directory or file in an application) within the Web.Config file. Add the following tag to the System.Web section of the Web.Config file:

```
<pages enableViewState="false" />
```

NOTE

The enableViewState attribute in the Web.Config file overrides the enableViewState property for a page. So, disabling View State in the Web.Config file prevents any page from using View State in an application.

You can display the amount of View State that each control in a page is consuming by enabling tracing for a page. In the Properties window, select DOCUMENT and assign the value True to the Trace property. If you build and browse the page, you'll see the amount of View State associated with each control in the Control Tree section appended at the bottom of the page (see Figure 17.2).

NOTE

You'll notice that if you disable View State for a page, the Page control will still consume a little bit of View State. If you want to entirely disable View State, you need to remove the server-side <form> tag from the HTML source of the page.

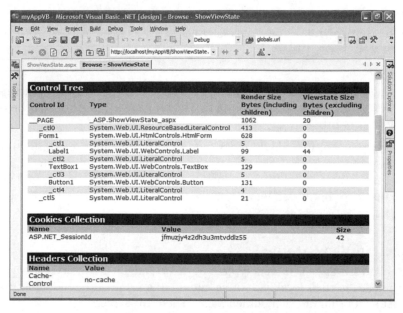

FIGURE 17.2 Viewing View State statistics.

Adding Custom Information to View State

You can add your own data to View State by taking advantage of the ViewState collection. Any data that you add to the ViewState collection will be stuffed into the __VIEWSTATE hidden form field and will be preserved across postbacks.

For example, the following statement adds the string "Hello World" to the ViewState collection:

C#

```
ViewState[ "myItem" ] = "Hello World";
```

VB.NET

```
ViewState("myItem") = "Hello World"
```

After an item has been added to the ViewState collection, you can retrieve the item by passing the name of the item to the collection:

C#

```
Response.Write( ViewState[ "myItem" ] );
```

VB.NET

```
Response.Write(ViewState("myItem"))
```

> **WARNING**
>
> The ViewState collection is case sensitive, so adding an item named myItem is different from adding an item named MyItem.

You can add almost any object to the ViewState collection, including strings, integers, ArrayLists, Hashtables, and even DataSets. The only requirement is that the object must be serializable.

However, remember that anything you add to View State must be stuffed into the __VIEWSTATE hidden form field. Consequently, adding a DataSet to View State can significantly impact the rendering time for a page. In general, you should stick to objects that have optimized View State serializers—strings, integers, Booleans, arrays, ArrayLists, and Hashtables.

Protecting View State

By default, View State is not encrypted. In theory, anyone requesting a page can copy the page to their local hard drive, modify the value of the hidden __VIEWSTATE form field, and submit the modified page back to the server.

For example, if you are storing a shopping cart in View State, someone could modify the price of all the products in the shopping cart and submit the modified page. A great way for users to give themselves massive discounts!

You can protect the integrity of View State by adding a Message Authentication Code (MAC) to the hidden __VIEWSTATE form field. After the View State MAC is enabled, an exception is thrown if someone tampers with the View State.

You can enable the View State MAC for a particular Web Form Page by selecting DOCUMENT in the Properties window and assigning the value True to the EnableViewStateMAC property. You can enable the View State MAC for an application or directory by adding the following tag to the System.Web section of the Web.Config file:

```
<pages enableViewStateMac="true" />
```

The View State MAC is disabled by default. Enabling the View State MAC adds some extra work to the processing of the page, so it has an impact on performance. If you don't need it, don't enable it.

Enabling the View State MAC does not result in the View State being encrypted. If you want to encrypt the contents of View State, you need to enable the View State MAC and perform an additional step. You need to add the following tag to the System.Web section of the Web.Config file:

```
<machineKey validation="3DES" />
```

This tag causes all View State to be encrypted using the Triple Data Encryption Standard. Again, this has an impact on performance, so don't enable it unless you need it.

Using Session State

Session State enables you to preserve the values of variables across page requests for a particular user. Session State is typically used for storing shopping carts, user preferences, or user security information, such as usernames and passwords.

Items added to Session State are preserved for the duration of a user's visit to a Web site. The server detects that the user has left when the user does not request a page for more than 20 minutes. At that point, all of the user's Session State information is automatically destroyed.

NOTE

You can change the default timeout period for Session State from 20 minutes to another value. You can modify the timeout period in code by setting the `Timeout` property of the `Session` object to a value in minutes. You can also modify the timeout period in the Web.Config file by modifying the value of the `timeout` attribute of the `<sessionState>` tag.

Items that you add to Session State are stored in the Web Server's memory. You can add almost any type of object to Session State, including strings, integers, `ArrayLists`, `Hashtables`, `DataSets`, and `DataTables`. The only requirement is that the object be serializable.

To illustrate how Session State works, we'll create two Web Form Pages. In the first page we'll add an item to Session State, and on the next page we'll retrieve and display the value of that item. These pages will illustrate how Session State preserves information when a user navigates from page to page.

To create the first page, do the following:

1. Create a new Web Form Page named **Session1.aspx**.

2. Add a `HyperLink` control to the page and set the following properties:

Property	Value
Text	**Click Here**
NavigateUrl	**Session2.aspx**

3. Switch to the Code Editor by selecting Code from the View menu.

4. Enter the following code for the `Page_Load` handler:

C#

```csharp
private void Page_Load(object sender, System.EventArgs e)
{
  Session[ "myItem" ] = "Hello!";
}
```

VB.NET

```vb
Private Sub Page_Load(ByVal sender As System.Object,
➥ByVal e As System.EventArgs) Handles MyBase.Load
  Session("myItem") = "Hello!"
End Sub
```

The Session1.aspx page adds a single item named myItem to Session State.

Now, let's create a second page that retrieves that item and displays it:

1. Create a Web Form Page named **Session2.aspx**.

2. Add a Label control to the page.

3. Switch to the Code Editor by selecting Code from the View menu.

4. Enter the following code for the Page_Load handler:

   C#

   ```csharp
   private void Page_Load(object sender, System.EventArgs e)
   {
     Label1.Text = (string)Session[ "myItem" ];
   }
   ```

   VB.NET

   ```vb
   Private Sub Page_Load(ByVal sender As System.Object,
   ➥ByVal e As System.EventArgs) Handles MyBase.Load
     Label1.Text = Session("myItem")
   End Sub
   ```

5. Right-click the Session1.aspx page in the Solution Explorer window and select Build and Browse.

When the Session1.aspx page opens, you'll see a link to the Session2.aspx page (see Figure 17.3). If you click the link, the Session2.aspx page will display the value of the Session State item named myItem (see Figure 17.4). After an item has been added to Session State, the item is available on any other Web Form Page that the user visits.

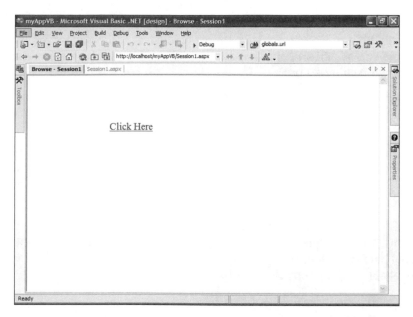

FIGURE 17.3   The Session1.aspx page.

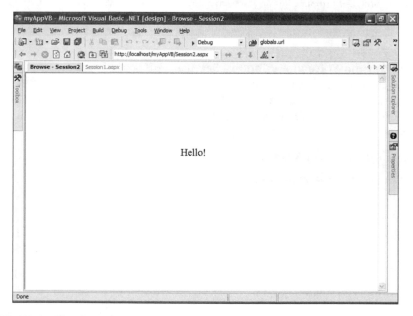

FIGURE 17.4   The Session2.aspx page.

Configuring Out-of-Process Session State

By default, Session State is stored in the same process as the Web server. In other words, when you add an item to Session State, it's added to the same memory being used by the Web server process. This has several bad consequences.

If the Web server process is stopped or becomes corrupted, all Session State information is lost. For example, if you are storing shopping carts in Session State and your Web server crashes, all the shopping carts will disappear.

Furthermore, because in-process Session State is stored on a particular Web server, you can't load balance requests across multiple servers. In other words, if you use in-process Session State, you can't create a Web farm. This restriction limits the scalability of your Web application.

ASP.NET supports two out-of-process forms of Session State that get around these two problems. You can store Session State in either an external Windows Service or an external database table. Enabling out-of-process Session State makes Session State more reliable and more scalable.

NOTE

You might be wondering why Session State is not configured to be out-of-process by default. The reason is performance. Storing Session State in an external Windows Service or database table is slower than in-process Session State.

Storing Session State in a Windows Service

You can store Session State in an external Windows Service running on the same machine as the Web server or on a different machine on your network. There are two configuration steps that you must complete to store Session State in a Windows NT Service:

1. Start the ASP.NET State Service

2. Modify the Web.Config file

The ASP.NET State Service is automatically installed on your machine when you install Visual Studio .NET. By default, it is not running. Do the following to start the State Service:

1. Go to Start, open the Control Panel, select Administrative Tools, and launch the Services applet.

2. Find the ASP.NET State Service applet and click Start. On a production Web site, you'll need to modify the service to startup automatically.

Next, you need to modify the Web.Config file to configure Session State to use the ASP.NET State Service. In the application root Web.Config file, find the <sessionState> tag and modify it as follows:

```
<sessionState
  mode="StateServer"
  stateConnectionString="tcpip=127.0.0.1:42424"
  stateNetworkTimeout="10" />
```

This setting causes Session State to use the ASP.NET State Service instead of in-process Session State. Furthermore, it specifies that the State Service can be found on the local machine at port 42424. You can specify an IP address or hostname of another server on your network here. Finally, a connection timeout value of 10 seconds is supplied.

You can test whether the State Service is running by opening the Session1.aspx page that we created in the first part of this section. After the page opens in your browser, open a command prompt and execute the following command:

iisreset

This command will stop and start the Web service. Next, click the link to go to the Session2.aspx page. You should notice that the item added to Session State is not lost. The text Hello! appears in the Label control, even though you stopped and started the Web service.

Storing Session State in a SQL Server Database
The most reliable, and slowest, method of storing Session State is to use a SQL Server database. When you store Session State in an external database, the state information is kept in a temporary database table.

> **NOTE**
> You can store Session State information only with a Microsoft SQL Server database (version 7.0 or later). It doesn't work with Oracle or Microsoft Access.

Configuring SQL Server Session State requires completing the following two steps:

1. Run the SQL State Installation script to create the necessary database objects.
2. Modify the Web.Config file.

The SQL State Installation script is automatically installed on your computer when you install Visual Studio .NET. You can execute this script by doing the following:

1. Launch Query Analyzer by going to Start, Programs, Microsoft SQL Server.

2. Select Open from the File menu and browse to the following file:

   `\Winnt\Microsoft.NET\Framework\`*`Version`*`\InstallSqlState.sql`

3. Execute the SQL script by clicking Execute Query (the green VCR run button).

The SQL State Installation script adds a new database to SQL Server named ASPState. The script adds several stored procedures for managing Session State to this database.

The actual Session State information is stored in two database tables in the TempDB database named AspStateTempApplications and AspStateTempSessions. The AspStateTempApplications table contains a list of all the ASP.NET Web Applications that are using the database to store Session State. The AspStateTempSessions includes a row that corresponds to each user's Session State information.

Before you can use SQL State, you need to modify the application root Web.Config file. Find the `<sessionState>` tag and modify it as follows:

```
<sessionState
  mode="SQLServer"
  sqlConnectionString="data source=127.0.0.1;user id=sa;password=secret" />
```

The important attribute here is the `sqlConnectionString` attribute. You'll need to enter the correct password for your database.

You can test SQL Server Session State by opening the Session1.aspx page that we created at the beginning of this section. After you open the page, a new row will be added to the AspStateTempSessions table. You can view the row by executing the following command from Query Analyzer:

```
SELECT * FROM tempDB..AspStateTempSessions
```

There is one row per user in the AspStateTempSessions table. When you add objects to Session State, the objects are serialized and stored in either the SessionItemShort or SessionItemLong column. For example, after opening the Session1.aspx page, the text Hello! is stored in the SessionItemShort column. If a user's Session State information becomes too long, the state information is stored in the SessionItemLong column instead of the SessionItemShort column.

Enabling Cookieless Sessions

By default, Session State relies on browser cookies. When you first request a Web Form Page from an ASP.NET Web Application, the server automatically adds a cookie to your browser called the `ASP.NET_SessionID` cookie. The server uses that cookie to identify you when you request a new page.

Session State depends on this cookie to associate the right Session State information with the right user. If cookies are disabled on a browser, Session State will fail. The Web server will assume that you are a new user each and every time that you request a new page.

When you are creating a public Web application, it's dangerous to rely on cookies. For a variety of reasons, cookies don't always work. This means that Session State will not always work.

Fortunately, there is a way around this problem. Session State supports something called Cookieless Sessions. As the name implies, you can use Cookieless Sessions to maintain Session State without relying on browser cookies.

You can enable Cookieless Sessions by modifying a single attribute in the Web.Config file. Find the `<sessionState>` tag in the application root Web.Config file and modify it as follows:

```
<sessionState
  cookieless="true" />
```

Cookieless Sessions are compatible with both in-process and out-of-process Session State, so you can use Cookieless Sessions regardless of whether you are storing state information in process or in a database table.

You can test Cookieless Sessions by opening the Session1.aspx page that we created at the beginning of this section. When the page opens, you should notice that the contents of the address bar look a little strange. The address bar should look something like the following:

```
http://localhost/myApp/(rtobxqzq5cjkswbtmpgj0x45)/Session1.aspx
```

The string of characters between the parentheses is the current Session ID. When you click the link in the Session1.aspx page, this Session ID is passed to the Session2.aspx page in the URL. The Web server can identify you without using cookies as you move from page to page by extracting this Session ID.

You should be aware that Cookieless Sessions do not work in exactly the same way as normal Session State. Normally, when you open multiple instances of a browser when visiting a Web site, all browser instances share the same Session State. On the other hand, if you open multiple browser instances when using Cookieless Sessions, the Session State information will not be shared.

Cookieless Sessions also force you to design your pages in a particular way. If you want to take advantage of Cookieless Sessions, you need to make all the links in your pages use relative URLs. If you add an absolute URL, the Session ID information will be lost.

> **TIP**
>
> You can use the `Response.AppPathModifier()` method to automatically build a URL that contains the Session ID. For example, this method is useful when you need to build an absolute URL to link to a secure Web Form Page (using `https://`).

Using Application State

There's one last form of state that's left to be discussed in this chapter—Application State. Whereas View State is scoped to a particular page and Session State is scoped to a particular user, Application State is scoped to an entire application. In other words, any items that you add to Application State are available within any page and by any user within an application.

In the ASP.NET world, an application is defined by a virtual directory. All the Web Form Pages located under the same virtual directory live in the same application. That means that if you add an item to Application State, that item is available within any other page beneath the virtual directory.

Application State is similar to the `Cache` object (for more information on the `Cache` object, see Chapter 14, "Improving Application Performance with Caching"). You can use either object to store data in memory. In most situations, you should use the `Cache` object instead of Application State for the following reasons:

- Items are automatically dumped from the `Cache` when memory resources become low. Items are never automatically removed from Application State. If you add too much data to Application State, the entire application is restarted.

- The `Cache` object automatically handles synchronizing access to items stored in the `Cache`. When using Application State, you must manually lock and unlock items to prevent conflicts.

- The `Cache` object supports advanced functionality, such as expiration policies and file dependencies that are not supported by Application State.

Again, whenever you are tempted to use Application State, consider using the `Cache` object instead. Application State is mainly a holdover from ASP Classic.

With these warnings in mind, let's look at a simple example of using Application State. We'll create a page that automatically keeps track of the number of times that it has been requested.

1. Create a Web Form Page named **TrackAccess.aspx**.

2. Add a `Label` control to the page.

3. Switch to the Code Editor by selecting Code from the View menu.

4. Enter the following code for the Page_Load handler:

   C#

```csharp
private void Page_Load(object sender, System.EventArgs e)
{
  Application.Lock();
  if (Application[ "AccessCount" ] == null)
    Application[ "AccessCount" ] = 1;
  else
    Application[ "AccessCount" ] = (int)Application[ "AccessCount" ] + 1;
  Application.UnLock();
  Label1.Text = Application[ "AccessCount" ].ToString();
}
```

   VB.NET

```vbnet
Private Sub Page_Load(ByVal sender As System.Object,
➥ByVal e As System.EventArgs) Handles MyBase.Load
  Application.Lock()
  Application("AccessCount") += 1
  Application.UnLock()
  Label1.Text = Application("AccessCount")
End Sub
```

5. Right-click the TrackAccess.aspx page in the Solution Explorer window and select Build and Browse.

When the page opens, click the browser Refresh button a couple times. Each time the page is requested, the value of the AccessCount variable is incremented by one (see Figure 17.5). The value of this variable is stored in Application State between page requests.

Unlike View State or Session State, items in Application State can be accessed by multiple users at a time. Consequently, you must take special precautions when accessing items from Application State.

Notice the use of the Lock() method in the TrackAccess.aspx page. The Lock() method prevents read and write access by other sessions while AccessCount is being updated. You can't lock an item in Application State selectively. You must lock all items in Application State to lock a single item.

After Lock() is called, every other session must wait until UnLock() is called to access any item from Application State. For this reason, you should call UnLock() as quickly as possible in your code. If you forget to call UnLock(), this method is automatically called after the page has been processed.

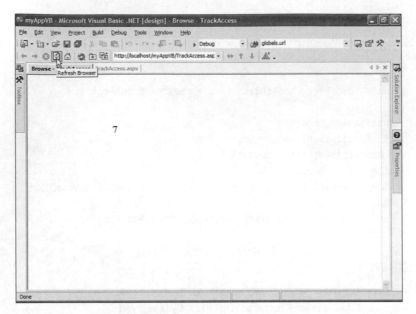

FIGURE 17.5   The TrackAccess.aspx page.

Summary

In this chapter, you learned three methods of maintaining state in your application. In the first section, you learned how to use View State to preserve the state of controls and variables when posting back to the same page.

Next, you learned how to use Session State to maintain state during the lifetime of a user session. You learned how to store Session State in the Web server process, in a Windows NT Service, and in an external database.

Finally, we briefly examined the topic of Application State. You learned how to use Application State to store information that can be accessed within any page and by any user of an application.

18

Handling Application-Wide Events

IN THIS CHAPTER

• Using the Global.asax File

• Using Custom HttpModules

An ASP.NET application raises certain events at the application level. For example, an application event is raised whenever a new user requests a page, whenever an application shuts down, and whenever an unhandled exception occurs.

This chapter discusses two methods of handling application-wide events. You learn how to implement application event-handlers both by using the Global.asax file and by using custom HttpModules. In particular, in this chapter you will learn

- How to automatically track errors in your application with the Global.asax file

- How to rewrite requests for one page into requests for another page in the Global.asax file

- How to implement a custom file cache with the Global.asax file

- How to create a cookieless authentication module

- How to log the performance of an application with a custom HttpModule

Using the Global.asax File

When you create a new ASP.NET Web application with Visual Studio .NET, a Global.asax file is automatically added to your project. Every ASP.NET Web application can have one, and only one, Global.asax file. This file must be located in the root directory of the application.

If you open the Global.asax file from the Solution Explorer window, you are presented with the file in Design view (see Figure 18.1). In Design view, you can add components, such as database components, by dragging the components from the Toolbox. If you double-click the Designer surface, you are switched to the Code Editor. Within the Code Editor, you can modify the existing list of event handlers or add new event handlers.

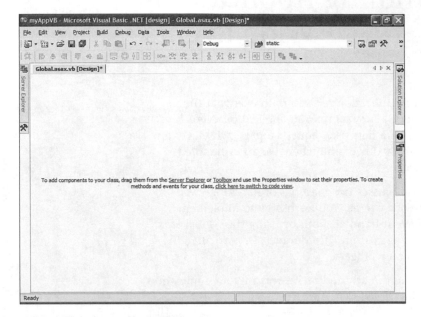

FIGURE 18.1   Global.asax file in Design view.

By default, the Global.asax file contains the following event handlers:

- `Application_Start`   Raised when an application starts (for example, after rebooting the Web server or modifying the Global.asax file).

- `Session_Start`   Raised when a new user requests the first page.

- `Application_BeginRequest`   Raised whenever any page is requested.

- `Application_AuthenticateRequest`   Raised after a user has been identified. Use this method to implement custom roles with Forms authentication (see Chapter 16, "Securing Your Application").

- `Application_Error`   Raised when any unhandled exception occurs in the application.

- `Session_End`   Raised when a user session ends (by default, 20 minutes after a user has made the last page request).

- `Application_End`   Raised when an application is stopped.

There are additional event handlers that you can add to the Global.asax file. You can add handlers for any events raised by the `HttpApplication` class. You also can use the Global.asax file to handle events raised by any custom HttpModules contained in your application.

Handling Application-Wide Errors

One of the most useful events that you can handle in the Global.asax file is the `Error` event. This event is raised whenever any unhandled exception is raised in an application. In other words, this event is raised whenever there is any error in a page or component that is not handled otherwise.

You can use the `Application_Error` method to record unhandled errors so that you can monitor the health of your Web application. For example, you can automatically email errors to yourself or record errors to a file.

To automatically email yourself errors, use the following `Application_Error` handler:

C#

```csharp
protected void Application_Error(Object sender, EventArgs e)
{
  Exception objError;
  string strSubject, strMessage;

  // Create the Error Message
  objError = Server.GetLastError().GetBaseException();
  strSubject = "Error in page " + Request.Path;
  strMessage = "Error Message: " + objError.Message
    + Environment.NewLine
    + "Stack Trace:"
    + Environment.NewLine
    + objError.StackTrace;
```

```
// Send the Error Mail
System.Web.Mail.SmtpMail.SmtpServer = "yourDomain.com";
System.Web.Mail.SmtpMail.Send("error@yourDomain.com",
➥"admin@yourDomain.com", strSubject, strMessage);
}
```

VB.NET

```
Sub Application_Error(ByVal sender As Object, ByVal e As EventArgs)
  Dim objError As Exception
  Dim strSubject, strMessage As String

  ' Create the Error Message
  objError = Server.GetLastError().GetBaseException()
  strSubject = "Error in page " & Request.Path
  strMessage = "Error Message: " & objError.Message & vbNewLine
  strMessage &= "Stack Trace: " & vbNewLine
  strMessage &= objError.StackTrace

  ' Send the Error Mail
  System.Web.Mail.SmtpMail.SmtpServer = "yourDomain.com"
  System.Web.Mail.SmtpMail.Send("error@yourDomain.com",
➥"admin@yourDomain.com", strSubject, strMessage)
End Sub
```

This `Application_Error` handler retrieves the last error with the help of the `Server.GetLastError()` method. Notice that the `GetBaseException()` method is used to retrieve the original exception that raised the current error.

The error message is created with the help of two properties of the `Exception` class—the `Message` and `StackTrace` properties. The `Message` property returns a human-readable description of the error, and the `StackTrace` property returns the list of statements that occurred immediately before the error.

You'll need to change any reference to *yourDomain.com* in the previous code to the name of your domain. Also, you'll want to change the email *admin@yourDomain.com* to your email address.

The `Application_Error` method is executed whenever there is an unhandled exception. This includes requests for non-existent pages and runtime errors. You can test the `Application_Error` method by performing the following steps:

1. Add a new Web Form Page to your project named **CauseError.aspx**.

2. Switch to the Code Editor by double-clicking the Designer surface.

3. Enter the following code in the Page_Load handler:

C#

```csharp
private void Page_Load(object sender, System.EventArgs e)
{
  int zero = 0;
  Response.Write( 9/zero );
}
```

VB.NET

```vbnet
Private Sub Page_Load(ByVal sender As System.Object,
➥ByVal e As System.EventArgs) Handles MyBase.Load
  Dim Ka

  Ka.Boom()
End Sub
```

4. Right-click the CauseError.aspx page in the Solution Explorer and select Build and Browse.

When the CauseError.aspx page opens, you'll receive a runtime error. The Application_Error method will email you the error message and stack trace for the error.

Rewriting Page Requests

The Application_BeginRequest method executes at the start of each and every page request. One way to take advantage of this method is by creating a page filter. When someone requests a certain page, you can cause another page to be automatically loaded.

The Application_BeginRequest method is particularly valuable when used in conjunction with the Context.RewritePath method. The Context.RewritePath method rewrites one page request into another page request.

For example, one problem that you'll encounter when maintaining a Web application is the problem of handling changes to the structure of your site. If you remove or rearrange the pages in an application and there are links to the original pages, users will encounter Page Not Found errors.

If you need to remove existing pages from an application, you can use the Application_BeginRequest and Context.RewritePath methods to rewrite requests for old pages to new pages. In other words, you can use the Application_BeginRequest and Context.RewritePath methods to hide changes to your application from the rest of the world.

1. Open the Global.asax file from the Solution Explorer window and switch to the Code Editor.

2. Enter the following code for the Application_BeginRequest method:

   C#

   ```csharp
   protected void Application_BeginRequest(Object sender, EventArgs e)
   {
     switch (Request.Path.ToLower())
     {
       case "/myapp/products.aspx":
         Context.RewritePath( "/myapp/default.aspx" );
         break;
       case "/myapp/services.aspx":
         Context.RewritePath( "/myapp/default.aspx" );
         break;
     }
   }
   ```

   VB.NET

   ```vbnet
   Sub Application_BeginRequest(ByVal sender As Object, ByVal e As EventArgs)
     Select Case Request.Path.ToLower()
       Case "/myapp/products.aspx"
         Context.RewritePath("/myapp/default.aspx")
       Case "/myapp/services.aspx"
         Context.RewritePath("/myapp/default.aspx")
     End Select
   End Sub
   ```

3. Select Build Solution from the Build menu.

After you complete these steps, any requests for the /myApp/Products.aspx or /myApp/Services.aspx pages will be automatically rewritten as requests for the Default.aspx page.

TIP

When you use Context.RewritePath to rewrite the page path, you can use Request.RawUrl to get the original page path.

Detecting the Start and End of a User Session

The Session State module exposes two events that you can handle in the Global.asax file with the Session_Start and Session_End methods. The Session_Start method executes when a new user makes a page request. The Session_End method executes when a user has not made a page request for more than 20 minutes.

For example, you can use the Session_Start and Session_End methods to load and save a shopping cart for a user. In the Session_Start method, you can load the shopping cart from the database into Session State. In the Session_End method, you can save the shopping cart from Session State back to the database.

Another way in which you can use the Session_Start and Session_End methods is for tracking the number of users currently using an application.

1. Open the Global.asax file from the Solution Explorer window and switch to the Code Editor.

2. Enter the following code for the Session_Start method:

   C#

   ```csharp
   protected void Session_Start(Object sender, EventArgs e)
   {
     Application.Lock();
     Application[ "numUsers" ] = (int)Application[ "numUsers" ] + 1;
     Application.UnLock();
   }
   ```

   VB.NET

   ```vbnet
   Sub Session_Start(ByVal sender As Object, ByVal e As EventArgs)
     Application.Lock()
     Application("numUsers") += 1
     Application.UnLock()
   End Sub
   ```

3. Enter the following code for the Session_End method:

   C#

   ```csharp
   protected void Session_End(Object sender, EventArgs e)
   {
     Application.Lock();
     Application[ "numUsers" ] = (int)Application[ "numUsers" ] - 1;
     Application.UnLock();
   }
   ```

VB.NET

```
Sub Session_End(ByVal sender As Object, ByVal e As EventArgs)
  Application.Lock()
  Application("numUsers") -= 1
  Application.UnLock()
End Sub
```

4. Enter the following code for the Application_Start method:

C#

```
protected void Application_Start(Object sender, EventArgs e)
{
  Application[ "numUsers" ] = 0;
}
```

VB.NET

```
Sub Application_Start(ByVal sender As Object, ByVal e As EventArgs)
  Application("numUsers") = 0
End Sub
```

Next, we need to create a page that displays the number of active sessions:

1. Add a new Web Form Page to your project named **TrackSessions.aspx**.

2. Add a Web Form Label to the page.

3. Switch to the Code Editor by double-clicking the Designer surface.

4. Enter the following code for the Page_Load handler:

C#

```
private void Page_Load(object sender, System.EventArgs e)
{
  Label1.Text = "There are " + Application[ "numUsers" ]
    + " active sessions";
}
```

VB.NET

```
Private Sub Page_Load(ByVal sender As System.Object,
➥ByVal e As System.EventArgs) Handles MyBase.Load
```

```
    Label1.Text = "There are "
    Label1.Text &= Application("numUsers")
    Label1.Text &= " active sessions"
End Sub
```

5. Right-click the TrackSessions.aspx page in the Solution Explorer window and select Build and Browse.

When the TrackSessions.aspx page opens, it will display the number of active sessions (see Figure 18.2). When new users request a page from the application, the session count increases. Twenty minutes after a user leaves the application, the session count will decrease.

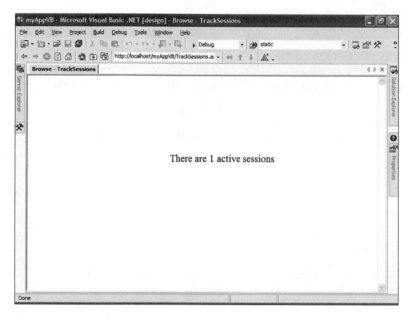

FIGURE 18.2 The TrackSessions.aspx page.

NOTE

You can't test the TrackSessions.aspx page by opening multiple instances of Internet Explorer on the same computer because all instances share the same session. If you open both Internet Explorer and Netscape, however, the TrackSessions.aspx should display two sessions because cookies are not shared across different types of browsers.

Implementing Custom Caching

There are two methods that you can add to the Global.asax file—
`Application_ResolveRequestCache` and `Application_UpdateRequestCache`—that you can
handle to implement custom page caching. For example, suppose that you want to
cache every dynamic Web Form Page in an application to the hard drive. The first
time anyone requests a particular Web Form Page, the generated output of the page
is saved to a static file.

1. Open the Global.asax file from the Solution Explorer window and switch to the
   Code Editor.

2. Enter the following code for the `Application_ResolveRequestCache` handler:

C#

```csharp
protected void Application_ResolveRequestCache(Object sender, EventArgs e)
{
  // Build path to static file
  string strCachedPage =
    System.IO.Path.GetFileNameWithoutExtension( Request.Path ) + ".cache";

  // Only execute request when cached page not found
  if (System.IO.File.Exists( Server.MapPath( strCachedPage) ))
  {
    Response.WriteFile( strCachedPage );
    this.CompleteRequest();
  }
}
```

VB.NET

```vbnet
Sub Application_ResolveRequestCache(ByVal sender As Object,
➥ByVal e As EventArgs)
  ' Build path to static file
  Dim strCachedPage As String = _
    System.IO.Path.GetFileNameWithoutExtension(Request.Path) & ".cache"

  ' Only execute request when cached page not found
  If System.IO.File.Exists(Server.MapPath(strCachedPage)) Then
    Response.WriteFile(strCachedPage)
    Me.CompleteRequest()
  End If
End Sub
```

3. Enter the following code for the `Application_UpdateRequestCache` handler:

C#

```csharp
protected void Application_UpdateRequestCache(Object sender, EventArgs e)
{
  // Build path to static file
  string strCachedPage =
    System.IO.Path.GetFileNameWithoutExtension( Request.Path ) + ".cache";

  // Save page output to hard drive
  System.IO.StreamWriter objWriter;
  objWriter = System.IO.File.CreateText( Server.MapPath( strCachedPage) );
  Server.Execute(Request.Path, objWriter);
  objWriter.Close();
}
```

VB.NET

```vbnet
Sub Application_UpdateRequestCache(ByVal sender As Object,
➡ByVal e As EventArgs)
  ' Build path to static file
  Dim strCachedPage As String = _
    System.IO.Path.GetFileNameWithoutExtension(Request.Path) & ".cache"

  ' Save page output to hard drive
  Dim objWriter As System.IO.StreamWriter
  objWriter = System.IO.File.CreateText(Server.MapPath(strCachedPage))
  Server.Execute(Request.Path, objWriter)
  objWriter.Close()
End Sub
```

4. Select Build Solution from the Build menu.

The `Application_ResolveRequestCache` method checks for a cached version of the page being requested on the hard drive. If the file exists, the method sends the contents of the static file to the output stream and prevents the original page that was requested from being processed.

For example, if you request a page named Products.aspx, the method looks for a file named Products.cache. If the file is found, the contents of this file are sent to the browser and the Products.aspx page is never processed.

The `Application_UpdateRequestCache` method uses the `Server.Execute` method to capture the rendered contents of the requested page and save it to the hard drive. The `Application_UpdateRequestCache` method is executed for each page in an application only once—the first time a page is requested by any user.

> **WARNING**
>
> Unfortunately, there is no method in the framework for reading the response output stream. This means that we have to use a trick—the `Server.Execute` method—to get the rendered content of a page.
>
> An unfortunate implication of this trick is that a page is executed twice when it is cached. The page must be executed a second time by the `Server.Execute` method to get the rendered content. Although this is bad, keep in mind that it only happens with the very first page request and never happens again.

There is one additional set of steps you must perform to get the custom caching to work. You must provide the ASPNET account with Write permissions on the folder that contains the pages being cached:

1. Right-click the folder containing the pages that you want to cache and select Properties.

2. Select the Security Tab.

3. Grant Write permissions to either the ASPNET or Guest account.

After you enable the custom file caching, every page in your application is dynamically generated only once. Thereafter, the output of the page is read directly from the hard drive. If you want to regenerate the content of a page, you need to delete the cached file on the hard drive that corresponds to it. For example, to regenerate the Products.aspx page, you would need to delete Products.cache.

Using Custom HttpModules

An HttpModule is a .NET class that participates in each and every page request. You can implement the same type of functionality in an HttpModule as you can implement in the Global.asax file. Like the Global.asax file, an HttpModule can be used to handle application-wide events. However, unlike the Global.asax, an HttpModule must be explicitly compiled and registered in the Web.Config file before it can be used.

Behind the scenes, ASP.NET Session State, caching, and authentication are all implemented as HttpModules. If you don't like the way that Microsoft implemented any particular one of these HttpModules, you can simply replace Microsoft's HttpModule with one of your own.

You can create your own custom HttpModule by implementing the `IHttpModule` interface. The `IHttpModule` interface has the following two methods:

- `Init`   Used to initialize any resources and to wire-up any event handlers needed by the HttpModule

- `Dispose`   Used to release any resources used the HttpModule

In the following sections, we'll create two modules—an authentication module and a performance logging module.

Creating the Cookieless Authentication Modules

All three of the built-in authentication systems included in the .NET Framework are implemented with modules. In this section, we'll create our own authentication module.

One problem with using the Forms authentication module included with the .NET Framework is that it assumes that users have cookies enabled on their browsers. Many organizations, especially government organizations, do not allow employees to have cookies enabled on their browsers for security reasons.

In this section, we'll create a cookieless authentication module. Instead of using a cookie to identify a user, the module uses an authentication key passed in either a form or query string variable.

Because we don't want usernames and passwords exposed in the browser address bar, we'll use a hash algorithm to hide them. The authentication key is calculated by hashing a user's combined username and password.

Additionally, we will store usernames and passwords in an XML file. We'll cache the XML file in the authentication module for better performance. We'll also create a file dependency on the XML file so that changes to the file will be immediately reflected in the module.

Let's start by creating the cookieless authentication module itself:

C# Steps

1. Add a new class to your project named **CookielessAuthenticationModule.cs**.

2. Add the following code to the class:

```
using System;
using System.Web;
using System.Security.Principal;
```

```
namespace myApp
{
  public class CookielessAuthenticationModule : IHttpModule
  {
    public void Init(HttpApplication application)
    {
    application.AuthenticateRequest += new

➥EventHandler( AuthenticateRequest );
    }

    public void Dispose() {}

    private void AuthenticateRequest(Object sender, EventArgs e)
    {
      string authKey;
      HttpContext context = ((HttpApplication)sender).Context;

      // Calculate Login Url
      string urlLogin = context.Request.ApplicationPath
➥+ "/CookielessLogin.aspx";
      urlLogin += "?ReturnUrl=" +
➥context.Server.UrlEncode( context.Request.RawUrl );
      if (context.Request.Path.ToLower().IndexOf( "cookielesslogin.aspx")
➥ != -1)
      return;

      // Check for authKey
      if (context.Request[ "authKey" ] == null)
        context.Response.Redirect( urlLogin );
      authKey = context.Request[ "authKey" ];

      // Validate authKey
      if (!CookielessAuthentication.ValidateKey( authKey ))
        context.Response.Redirect( urlLogin );

      // Create the User
      string username = CookielessAuthentication.GetUsername( authKey );
      GenericIdentity userIdentity = new
➥GenericIdentity( username, "cookieless" );
      context.User = new GenericPrincipal(userIdentity, null);
    }
```

```
    }
  }
```

VB.NET Steps

1. Add a new class to your project named **CookielessAuthenticationModule.vb**.

2. Add the following code to the class:

```vbnet
Imports System.Security.Principal

Public Class CookielessAuthenticationModule
  Implements IHttpModule

  Public Sub Init(ByVal application As HttpApplication)
➥Implements IHttpModule.Init
    AddHandler application.AuthenticateRequest,
➥AddressOf AuthenticateRequest
  End Sub

  Public Sub Dispose() Implements IHttpModule.Dispose
  End Sub

  Private Sub AuthenticateRequest(ByVal sender As Object,
➥ByVal e As EventArgs)
    Dim authKey As String
    Dim context As HttpContext
    Dim urlLogin As String
    Dim username As String
    Dim userIdentity As GenericIdentity

    context = sender.Context

    ' Calculate Login Url
    urlLogin = context.Request.ApplicationPath + "/CookielessLogin.aspx"
    urlLogin += "?ReturnUrl=" +
➥context.Server.UrlEncode(context.Request.RawUrl)
    If context.Request.Path.ToLower().IndexOf("cookielesslogin.aspx")
➥<> -1 Then
      Return
    End If
```

```
      ' Check for authKey
      If context.Request("authKey") = Nothing Then
        context.Response.Redirect(urlLogin)
      End If
      authKey = context.Request("authKey")

      ' Validate authKey
      If Not CookielessAuthentication.ValidateKey(authKey) Then
        context.Response.Redirect(urlLogin)
      End If

      ' Create the User
      username = CookielessAuthentication.GetUsername(authKey)
      userIdentity = New GenericIdentity(username, "cookieless")
      context.User = New GenericPrincipal(userIdentity, Nothing)
    End Sub

  End Class
```

The CookielessAuthentication module contains the two methods required by the IHttpModule interface—Init and Dispose. The Init method is used to wire the AuthenticateRequest method to the application AuthenticateRequest event. The Dispose method is added but contains no content because we have no resources to clean up after the module exits.

All the work happens in the AuthenticateRequest method. This method attempts to retrieve the authentication key from a query string or form variable. If the authentication key cannot be retrieved, the user is redirected to the CookielessLogin.aspx page.

The AuthenticateRequest method calls a method named ValidateKey to check whether the authentication key is valid. The ValidateKey method is one method of the CookielessAuthentication utility class.

To create the CookielessAuthentication utility class, do the following:

C# Steps

1. Add a new class to your project named **CookielessAuthentication.cs**.

2. Add the following code to the CookielessAuthentication class:

```
using System;
using System.Data;
using System.Web;
```

```csharp
using System.Security.Principal;
using System.Web.Caching;
using System.Web.Security;

namespace myApp
{
  public class CookielessAuthentication
  {

  public static DataTable AuthKeys
  {
  get
    {
    HttpContext context = HttpContext.Current;
    DataSet dstKeys = (DataSet)context.Cache[ "Users" ];
    if (dstKeys == null)
    {
      dstKeys = new DataSet();
      dstKeys.ReadXml( context.Server.MapPath( "Users.xml" ) );
      CalculateKeys( dstKeys );
      context.Cache.Insert( "Users", dstKeys,
        new CacheDependency( context.Server.MapPath( "Users.xml" )));
    }
    return dstKeys.Tables[0];
    }
  }

  private static DataSet CalculateKeys(DataSet dstKeys)
  {
    dstKeys.Tables[0].Columns.Add("AuthKey");
    foreach(DataRow drow in dstKeys.Tables[0].Rows)
    drow[ "AuthKey" ] = HashKey( (string)drow[ "name" ],
      (string)drow[ "password" ]);
    return dstKeys;
  }

  private static string HashKey(string Username, string Password)
  {
    return FormsAuthentication.HashPasswordForStoringInConfigFile(
      Username + Password, "md5" );
  }
```

```csharp
public static bool ValidateKey(string Key)
{
  string strMatch = "AuthKey='" + Key + "'";
  DataRow[] arrMatches = AuthKeys.Select( strMatch );
  if (arrMatches.Length == 0 )
    return false;
  return true;
}

public static string GetUsername(string Key)
{
  string strMatch = "AuthKey='" + Key + "'";
  DataRow[] arrMatches = AuthKeys.Select( strMatch );
  if (arrMatches.Length == 0 )
    return String.Empty;
  return (string)arrMatches[0]["name"];
}

public static bool Authenticate(string Username, string Password)
{
  string strMatch = String.Format("name='{0}' AND password='{1}'",
    Username, Password);
  DataRow[] arrMatches = AuthKeys.Select( strMatch );
  if (arrMatches.Length == 0 )
    return false;

  // Create the User
  GenericIdentity userIdentity = new GenericIdentity( Username,
    "cookieless" );
  HttpContext.Current.User = new GenericPrincipal(userIdentity, null);

  return true;
}

public static void RedirectFromLoginPage()
{
  HttpContext context = HttpContext.Current;
  string urlReturn = context.Request[ "ReturnUrl" ];
  if (urlReturn == null)
    urlReturn = context.Request.ApplicationPath + "/default.aspx";
    urlReturn = AddAuthKey( urlReturn );
    context.Response.Redirect( urlReturn );
```

```csharp
}

public static string AddAuthKey(string Url)
{
  if (Url.IndexOf( "?" ) == -1)
    return String.Format( "{0}?authKey={1}", Url, GetAuthKey() );
  else
    return String.Format( "{0}&authKey={1}", Url, GetAuthKey() );
}

public static string GetAuthKey()
{
  HttpContext context = HttpContext.Current;
  string username = context.User.Identity.Name;
  string strMatch = "name='" + username + "'";
  DataRow[] arrMatches = AuthKeys.Select( strMatch );
  if (arrMatches.Length == 0 )
    return String.Empty;
  return (string)arrMatches[0]["AuthKey"];
}


}
}
```

VB.NET Steps

1. Add a new class to your project named **CookielessAuthentication.vb**.

2. Add the following code to the CookielessAuthentication class:

```vbnet
Imports System.Security.Principal
Imports System.Web.Caching
Imports System.Web.Security

Public Class CookielessAuthentication
    Public Shared ReadOnly Property AuthKeys() As DataTable

        Get
            Dim context As HttpContext
            Dim dstKeys As DataSet
            context = HttpContext.Current
            dstKeys = context.Cache("Users")
            If dstKeys Is Nothing Then
```

```
                    dstKeys = New DataSet()
                    dstKeys.ReadXml(context.Server.MapPath("Users.xml"))
                    CalculateKeys(dstKeys)
                    context.Cache.Insert("Users", dstKeys, _
        New CacheDependency(context.Server.MapPath("Users.xml")))
                End If
                Return dstKeys.Tables(0)
            End Get
        End Property


        Private Shared Function CalculateKeys(ByVal dstKeys As DataSet)
    ➥As DataSet
            Dim drow As DataRow

            dstKeys.Tables(0).Columns.Add("AuthKey")
            For Each drow In dstKeys.Tables(0).Rows
                drow("AuthKey") = HashKey(drow("name"), drow("password"))
            Next
            Return dstKeys
        End Function


        Private Shared Function HashKey(ByVal Username As String,
    ➥ByVal Password As String) As String
            Return FormsAuthentication.HashPasswordForStoringInConfigFile(
    ➥Username + Password, "md5")
        End Function


        Public Shared Function ValidateKey(ByVal Key As String) As Boolean
            Dim strMatch As String
            Dim arrMatches() As DataRow
            strMatch = "AuthKey='" + Key + "'"
            arrMatches = AuthKeys.Select(strMatch)
            If arrMatches.Length = 0 Then
                Return False
            Else
                Return True
            End If
        End Function


        Public Shared Function GetUsername(ByVal Key As String) As String
            Dim strMatch As String
```

```vb
        Dim arrMatches() As DataRow

        strMatch = "AuthKey='" + Key + "'"
        arrMatches = AuthKeys.Select(strMatch)
        If arrMatches.Length = 0 Then
            Return String.Empty
        Else
            Return arrMatches(0)("name")
        End If
    End Function


    Public Shared Function Authenticate(ByVal Username As String,
➥ByVal Password As String) As Boolean
        Dim strMatch As String
        Dim arrMatches() As DataRow
        Dim userIdentity As GenericIdentity

        strMatch = String.Format("name='{0}' AND password='{1}'",
➥Username, Password)
        arrMatches = AuthKeys.Select(strMatch)
        If arrMatches.Length = 0 Then
            Return False
        End If

        ' Create the User
        userIdentity = New GenericIdentity(Username, "cookieless")
        HttpContext.Current.User = New GenericPrincipal(
➥userIdentity, Nothing)
        Return True
    End Function

    Public Shared Sub RedirectFromLoginPage()
        Dim context As HttpContext
        Dim urlReturn As String

        context = HttpContext.Current
        urlReturn = context.Request("ReturnUrl")
        If urlReturn = Nothing Then
            urlReturn = context.Request.ApplicationPath + "/default.aspx"
        End If
        urlReturn = AddAuthKey(urlReturn)
        context.Response.Redirect(urlReturn)
```

```
    End Sub

    Public Shared Function AddAuthKey(ByVal Url As String) As String
            If Url.IndexOf("?") = -1 Then
            Return String.Format("{0}?authKey={1}", Url, GetAuthKey())
        Else
            Return String.Format("{0}&authKey={1}", Url, GetAuthKey())
        End If
    End Function

    Public Shared Function GetAuthKey() As String
        Dim context As HttpContext
        Dim username As String
        Dim strMatch As String
        Dim arrMatches() As DataRow

        context = HttpContext.Current
        username = context.User.Identity.Name
        strMatch = "name='" + username + "'"
        arrMatches = AuthKeys.Select(strMatch)
        If arrMatches.Length = 0 Then
            Return String.Empty
        End If
        Return arrMatches(0)("AuthKey")
    End Function

End Class
```

Next, we need to create the XML file that will contain the usernames and passwords:

1. Add a new XML file to your project named **Users.xml**.

2. Enter the following two usernames and passwords:

```
<?xml version="1.0" encoding="utf-8" ?>
<users>
  <user name="Steve" password="secret" />
  <user name="Bob" password="secret" />
</users>
```

Next, you need to create the CookielessLogin.aspx page. This is the page to which a user is redirected when a valid authentication key cannot be retrieved.

1. Add a new Web Form Page to your project named **CookielessLogin.aspx**.

2. Add two TextBox controls and a Button control to the page. Assign the ID txtUsername to the first text box and the ID txtPassword to the second text box.

3. Double-click the Button control to switch to the Code Editor and enter the following code for the Button1_Click method:

   C#

```
private void Button1_Click(object sender, System.EventArgs e)
{
  if (CookielessAuthentication.Authenticate(txtUsername.Text,
➥txtPassword.Text))
    CookielessAuthentication.RedirectFromLoginPage();
}
```

   VB.NET

```
Private Sub Button1_Click(ByVal sender As System.Object,
➥ByVal e As System.EventArgs) Handles Button1.Click
  If CookielessAuthentication.Authenticate(txtUsername.Text,
➥txtPassword.Text) Then
    CookielessAuthentication.RedirectFromLoginPage()
  End If
End Sub
```

4. Build the project by selecting Build *Project Name* from the Build menu.

Finally, you need to register the cookieless authentication module in the Web.Config file:

1. Open the Web.Config file from the Solution Explorer window.

2. Erase the existing content from the Web.Config file (don't let this make you nervous) and enter the following code:

```
<configuration>
  <system.web>
    <httpModules>
        <add name="CookielessAuthenticationModule"
          type="myApp.CookielessAuthenticationModule,myApp" />
    </httpModules>
  </system.web>
</configuration>
```

After you complete these steps, if you attempt to open any page in the same project in a browser, you'll be automatically redirected to the CookielessLogin.aspx page. If you enter a username and password combination from the Users.xml file, you'll be redirected back to the original page with an authentication key appended as a query string.

After you've implemented the cookieless authentication module, you must be careful to pass the authentication key in every link. If you don't pass the authentication key, the user will be redirected back to the CookielessLogin.aspx page. You can automatically append the authentication key to any URL by taking advantage of the AddAuthKey method of the CookielessAuthentication class.

Creating the Performance Logging Module

You can use the performance logging HttpModule to identify especially slow executing pages in a Web application. The module tracks the average execution time of every page by storing this information the cache. If you want to view the execution times of all the pages in your application, you can open the ShowPerformance.aspx page to read the cached data.

Let's start by creating the HttpModule itself.

C# Steps

1. Add a new class to your project named **PerformanceModule.cs**.

2. Enter the following code for the PerformanceModule.cs class:

```
using System;
using System.Web;
using System.Collections;

namespace myApp
{
  public class PerformanceModule : IHttpModule
  {
    public void Init(HttpApplication application)
    {
      // Initialize Page Speeds Hashtable
      application.Context.Cache[ "PageSpeeds" ] = new Hashtable();

      // Wireup EndRequest Event Handler
      application.EndRequest += new EventHandler( EndRequest );
    }
```

```
public void Dispose(){}

void EndRequest(Object sender, EventArgs e)
{
  // Calculate Page Execution Time
  HttpContext context = ((HttpApplication)sender).Context;
  TimeSpan timeDiff = DateTime.Now - context.Timestamp;

  // Retrieve Hashtable of Page Speeds from Cache
  string cacheKey = context.Request.Path.ToLower();
  Hashtable colPageSpeeds = (Hashtable)context.Cache[ "PageSpeeds" ];
  PageSpeed objPageSpeed  = (PageSpeed)colPageSpeeds[cacheKey];
  if (objPageSpeed == null)
    objPageSpeed = new PageSpeed( cacheKey );

  // Update Page Execution Time
  objPageSpeed.Update( timeDiff.Ticks );

  // Save Changes to Cache
  ((Hashtable)context.Cache[ "PageSpeeds" ])[cacheKey] = objPageSpeed;
}

  }
}
```

VB.NET Steps

1. Add a new class to your project named **PerformanceModule.vb**.

2. Enter the following code for the PerformanceModule.vb class:

```
Public Class PerformanceModule
  Implements IHttpModule

  Public Sub Init(ByVal application As HttpApplication)
➡Implements IHttpModule.Init

    ' Initialize Page Speeds Hashtable
    application.Context.Cache("PageSpeeds") = New Hashtable()

    ' Wireup EndRequest Event Handler
    AddHandler application.EndRequest, AddressOf EndRequest
  End Sub
```

```
        Public Sub Dispose() Implements IHttpModule.Dispose
        End Sub

        Sub EndRequest(ByVal sender As Object, ByVal e As EventArgs)
          Dim context As HttpContext
          Dim timeDiff As TimeSpan
          Dim cacheKey As String
          Dim colPageSpeeds As Hashtable
          Dim objPageSpeed As PageSpeed

          ' Calculate Page Execution Time
          context = sender.Context
          timeDiff = DateTime.Now.Subtract(context.Timestamp)

          ' Retrieve Hashtable of Page Speeds from Cache
          cacheKey = context.Request.Path.ToLower()
          colPageSpeeds = context.Cache("PageSpeeds")
          objPageSpeed = colPageSpeeds(cacheKey)
          If objPageSpeed Is Nothing Then
            objPageSpeed = New PageSpeed(cacheKey)
          End If

          ' Update Page Execution Time
          objPageSpeed.Update(timeDiff.Ticks)

          ' Save Changes to Cache
          context.Cache("PageSpeeds")(cacheKey) = objPageSpeed
        End Sub

    End Class
```

The performance module tracks the execution speed of every page requested in an application. In the Init method, a hashtable is created in the cache that contains the performance data. Additionally, the EndRequest method is wired to the application EndRequest event.

The execution speed of the page is calculated within the EndRequest method. The HttpContext.TimeStamp property is used to retrieve the time when the page started executing. The DateTime.Now property is used to retrieve the current time. This information is stored in a class named PageSpeed.

NOTE

The `DateTime.Now` property is only accurate to 10 milliseconds. This means that the module discussed in this section is only valuable when tracking the performance of relatively slow running pages (pages that require more than 10 milliseconds to execute).

If you need more accurate performance statistics, you should take advantage of performance counters from your code. See the following two knowledge base articles available at the Microsoft.com Web site: Q306978 and Q306979.

Next, we need to create the `PageSpeed` class. The `PageSpeed` class represents the performance information for an individual page.

C# Steps

1. Add a new class to your project named **PageSpeed.cs**.

2. Add the following code to the PageSpeed.cs page:

```csharp
using System;

namespace myApp
{
  public class PageSpeed
  {
    string _path;
    int _numberOfRequests = 0;
    long _executionTimeSum = 0;
    long _executionTimeLast = 0;

    public PageSpeed(string path )
    {
      _path = path;
    }

    public void Update(long executionTime)
    {
      _numberOfRequests ++;
      _executionTimeSum += executionTime;
      _executionTimeLast = executionTime;
    }

    public string Path
    {
      get { return _path; }
```

```csharp
    }

    public int NumberOfRequests
    {
      get { return _numberOfRequests; }
    }

    public string ExecutionTimeAverage
    {
      get
      {
      long lngMilliseconds =
      (_executionTimeSum/_numberOfRequests)/TimeSpan.TicksPerMillisecond;
      return String.Format( "{0} milliseconds", lngMilliseconds );
      }
    }

    public string ExecutionTimeLast
    {
      get
      {
        long lngMilliseconds =
          _executionTimeLast/TimeSpan.TicksPerMillisecond;
        return String.Format( "{0} milliseconds", lngMilliseconds );
      }
    }

  }
}
```

VB.NET Steps

1. Add a new class to your project named **PageSpeed.vb**.

2. Add the following code to the PageSpeed.vb page:

```vbnet
Public Class PageSpeed
  Private _path As String
  Private _numberOfRequests As Integer = 0
  Private _executionTimeSum As Long = 0
  Private _executionTimeLast As Long = 0

  Public Sub New(ByVal path As String)
```

```
    _path = path
  End Sub

  Public Sub Update(ByVal executionTime As Long)
    _numberOfRequests += 1
    _executionTimeSum += executionTime
    _executionTimeLast = executionTime
  End Sub

  Public ReadOnly Property Path() As String
    Get
      Return _path
    End Get
  End Property

  Public ReadOnly Property NumberOfRequests() As Integer
    Get
      Return _numberOfRequests
    End Get
  End Property

  Public ReadOnly Property ExecutionTimeAverage() As String
    Get
      Dim lngMilliseconds As Long
      lngMilliseconds = (_executionTimeSum / _numberOfRequests)
➥  / TimeSpan.TicksPerMillisecond
      Return String.Format("{0} milliseconds", lngMilliseconds)
    End Get
  End Property

  Public ReadOnly Property ExecutionTimeLast() As String
    Get
      Dim lngMilliseconds As Long
      lngMilliseconds = _executionTimeLast / TimeSpan.TicksPerMillisecond
      Return String.Format("{0} milliseconds", lngMilliseconds)
    End Get
  End Property

End Class
```

The PageSpeed class has one important method named Update. When Update is called, the PageSpeed class updates the average execution time for the page that the class represents.

Next, we need to create a page that displays the performance data:

1. Create a new Web Form Page named **ShowPerformance.aspx**.

2. Add a DataGrid to the page.

3. Double-click the Designer surface to switch to the Code Editor.

4. Enter the following code for the Page_Load method:

C#

```csharp
private void Page_Load(object sender, System.EventArgs e)
{
  Hashtable colPageSpeeds = (Hashtable)Cache["PageSpeeds"];

  DataGrid1.DataSource = colPageSpeeds.Values;
  DataGrid1.DataBind();
}
```

VB.NET

```vbnet
Private Sub Page_Load(ByVal sender As System.Object,
➥ByVal e As System.EventArgs) Handles MyBase.Load
  Dim colPageSpeeds As Hashtable
  colPageSpeeds = Cache("PageSpeeds")

  DataGrid1.DataSource = colPageSpeeds.Values
  DataGrid1.DataBind()
End Sub
```

Finally, we need to register the performance module in the Web.Config file:

1. Open the Web.Config file from the Solution Explorer window.

2. Erase all the current contents of the Web.Config file (don't let this make you nervous) and enter the following code:

```xml
<configuration>
  <system.web>
    <httpModules>
      <add name="PerformanceModule"
        type="myApp.PerformanceModule,myApp" />
    </httpModules>
  </system.web>
</configuration>
```

After you complete these steps, build and browse the ShowPerformance.aspx page. If you press Refresh a couple times, you should see the ShowPerformance.aspx page with its average execution time displayed in the DataGrid. If you open any other page, the new page should appear with performance statistics in the DataGrid as well (see Figure 18.3).

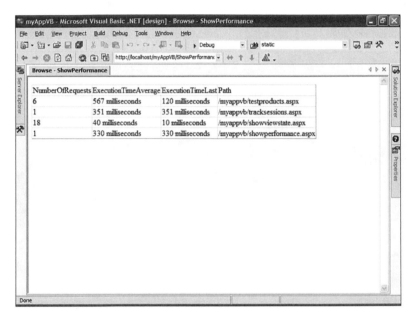

FIGURE 18.3 The ShowPerformance.aspx page.

Summary

In this chapter, you've learned how to handle application events by taking advantage of both the Global.asax file and custom HttpModules. In the first section, you learned how to handle several application-wide events by adding `Application_BeginRequest`, `Application_Error`, `Application_ResolveRequestCache`, and `Session_Start` methods to the Global.asax file.

Next, we tackled the more advanced topic of custom HttpModules. We created two modules—a cookieless authentication module and a performance logging module.

19

Deploying Your Application

IN THIS CHAPTER

• Web Application Deployment Overview

• Creating Web Setup Projects

So you've finished your Web application and are ready to release the application onto the world. This chapter is about how you do this.

In this chapter, you will learn

- Three methods of deploying an ASP.NET Web application

- About important, last-minute checks you should perform before deployment

- How to use Web Setup Projects to distribute your Web application project

Web Application Deployment Overview

There are three main methods of copying an ASP.NET Web application from a development server onto a production Web site:

- Use XCopy deployment

- Use the Visual Studio .NET Copy Project command

- Use a Web Setup Project

XCopy deployment refers to the process of simply copying files from one server to another using the DOS XCopy command or using the Windows Explorer to copy one folder from one location to another. In other words, you can deploy an ASP.NET application simply by copying all the files from your project directory to a production Web site.

For example, if your Visual Studio .NET project is named myApp in the Solution Explorer window, you can drag the \InetPub\wwwroot\myApp folder from your development computer to the \InetPub\wwwroot folder on the "live" Web site (or FTP the folder in the case of a remote server being hosted by an ISP).

The fact that you can deploy an application in such a simple manner is amazing, especially if you have come from a background of developed Web applications in ASP Classic. Unlike ASP Classic, ASP.NET does not depend on the computer registry, so you can deploy an ASP.NET application without worrying about registering components on the production Web server.

However, there are drawbacks to XCopy deployment. The most important drawback is that simply copying your project from one server to another will also copy your source code from the development server to the production Web site. You should avoid placing your source code (the .cs or .vb files in your project) onto a "live" Web server.

> **NOTE**
>
> In theory, you should be safe placing the source code for your project on a production Web server because access to source code files is blocked in the Machine.Config file. Source code files are mapped in the <httpHandlers> section to the ForbiddenHandler, which displays an access denied message. However, it is best in this kind of situation to err on the side of caution and not place your source code files on a production machine.

A better alternative to using XCopy deployment is to use the Visual Studio .NET Copy Project command. This command enables you to copy only those files needed to run your application without including the source code files.

There is a button for the Copy Project command at the top of the Solution Explorer window. You can also access the Copy Project command from beneath the Project menu.

The Copy Project command provides you with three options for copying a project. You can choose to copy only the files needed to run the application, all project files, or all files in the source project directory (see Figure 19.1). You should select the first choice when deploying an application onto a production Web server because the first choice does not copy the source code files.

Notice that the Copy Project command supports copying a project using either FrontPage extensions or a File Share. Most companies disable FrontPage extensions on a production Web server for security reasons (FrontPage extensions are just one more point of entry for a potential hacker). Consequently, you'll want to use File Share access unless you are copying the project to a remote host over the Internet.

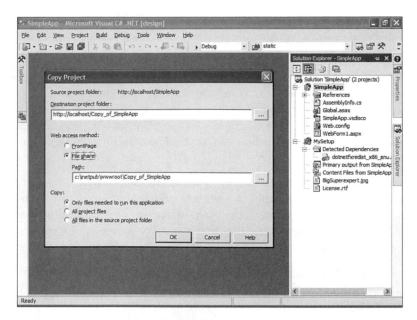

FIGURE 19.1 The Copy Project dialog box.

There is one last method that you can use for deploying your application. You can create something called a Web Setup Project. A Web Setup Project enables you to create a Microsoft Installer package for a project. This is useful when you need to distribute your project and want the installer to perform all the necessary setup tasks. For example, the installer automatically creates a new virtual directory for the project on the target computer and sets whatever permissions for the virtual directory that you specify. We'll look at Web Setup Projects in detail later in this chapter in the "Creating Web Setup Projects" section.

Things You Should Check Before Deployment

Before you deploy an application, you should complete the following checklist:

- *Did you remember to build your application in Release mode?*—Executing a Web application in debug mode carries a severe performance penalty. Before deploying your application, make sure that your project has been built within Visual Studio .NET in Release mode. Also, check that the debug attribute in the <compilation> section of the Web.Config file is set to false. See Chapter 6, "Debugging Your Web Form Pages," for more information.

- *Did you disable page and application tracing?*—You should make sure that tracing is disabled for your application for security reasons. Make sure that you have disabled both page and application tracing. Disable remote page tracing on a server by setting the localOnly attribute to true in the <trace> section of the Web.Config or Machine.Config file. You should also disable application tracing by setting the enabled attribute to false. See Chapter 6 for more information.

- *Did you enable custom errors?*—Displaying error messages can be a serious security risk because sensitive information, such as database passwords, can be exposed. Therefore, if you have disabled custom errors, you should re-enable custom errors in the Web.Config or Machine.Config file. Assign the value On or RemoteOnly to the mode attribute of the <customErrors> tag. See Chapter 6 for more information.

- *Did you disable the .vsdisco handler?*—Make sure that dynamic discovery is disabled for your application. Remove the reference to the .vsdisco handler in the <httpHandlers> section in the Web.Config or Machine.Config file. See the final section of Chapter 21, "Building XML Web Services," for more information.

- *Are you using sa to login to SQL Server?*—Don't use an account that has SQL administrator privileges for database-driven Web Form Pages on a production server. In particular, don't use the sa account. Either use SQL Server Integrated Security (the ASPNET account) or use SQL Server Mixed Security with an account that has restricted permissions.

- *Have you applied all the latest security patches?*—Make sure that you have applied all the latest security patches to both Windows and Internet Information Server (IIS). There have been several serious security holes in IIS. Check http://www.microsoft.com/technet/security for the latest security updates. You can use the IIS 5.0 Hotfix Checking Tool to automatically check for any necessary security updates for IIS.

TIP

You can lock down settings in the Machine.Config file in your production Web server to prevent applications from being deployed with settings that present a security risk. To learn more, see Chapter 15, "Configuring Your Application."

Creating Web Setup Projects

If you need to distribute a finished ASP.NET Web application to a client and you want the application to configure itself automatically on the client's Web server, you should consider creating a Web Setup Project. You can use a Web Setup Project to create an installer for your ASP.NET Web application that automatically creates a virtual directory and installs all the necessary files for your application.

Suppose that you have an existing ASP.NET Web application named MyWebApp open in Visual Studio .NET. Perform the following steps to create a Web Setup Project:

1. Right-click the name of the Solution in the Solution Explorer window and select New Project from the Add menu. Select the Setup and Deployment folder under Project Types and select Setup Wizard under Templates. Name your Web Setup Project **MySetup** and click OK.

2. The first page of the Web Setup Wizard will appear (see Figure 19.2). Click Next to start the wizard.

3. In the Choose a project type page, select Create a Setup for a Web Application and click Next.

4. In the Choose project outputs to include page, check Primary Output from MyWebApp and Content Files from myWebApp and click Next.

5. The Choose Files to Include page enables you to add additional files. Don't add any additional files to your Web Setup Project and click Next.

6. In the Create Project page, click Finish.

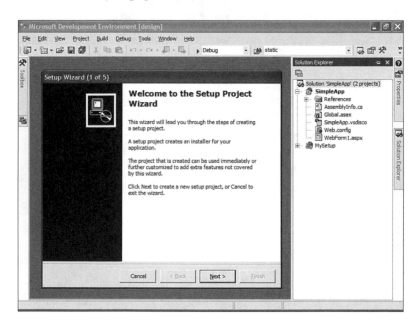

FIGURE 19.2   The Web Setup Wizard.

After you complete these steps, a new project named MySetup will appear in the Solution Explorer window. The final step is to build the Web Setup Project. Right-click MySetup and select Build.

WARNING

There is a bug in the current version of Visual Studio .NET that causes error messages to be displayed when you build a Web Setup Project that contains multiple folders with the same name. You can ignore these error messages; the Web Setup Project will build successfully.

The finished installer is named MySetup.msi. You can find this file in the following folder:

```
\My Documents\Visual Studio Projects\MyWebApp\MySetup\Debug\MySetup.msi
```

You can distribute the MySetup.msi file to your clients. When the MySetup.msi file is executed, you get the standard Windows installer (see Figure 19.3). The installer creates a virtual directory and installs the content files and assemblies from the MyWebApp project.

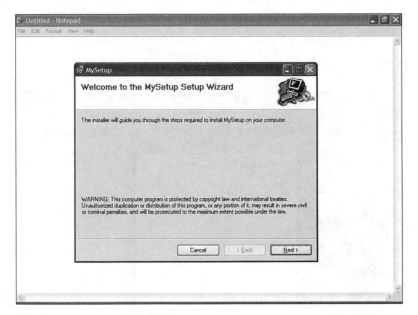

FIGURE 19.3   Executing the installer.

If you want to remove an ASP.NET Web application that was added to a server with the installer, you can remove the application from the Add/Remove Programs applet in the Windows Control Panel.

NOTE

You might have noticed that building the MySetup project not only creates a MySetup.msi file, it also creates a Setup.exe file. You only need to distribute the MySetup.msi file. The

> Setup.exe file simply calls the MySetup.msi. Microsoft included the Setup.exe file because so many people are used to executing a program named Setup.exe when installing an application.

If you want to quickly test the installer on the same computer as Visual Studio .NET, you can right-click MySetup in the Solution Explorer window and select Install. You can uninstall the application by right-clicking and choosing UnInstall.

Modifying Properties of a Web Setup Project

If you select the MySetup project in the Solution Explorer window and open the Properties window, you'll see several useful properties that you can set. For example, you can supply a product name, the URL for a support Web site, and an icon for the Web application that appears in the Add/Remove Programs applet.

The value of the Product Name property is used both in the title bar and the description text during the installation process. The support URL appears in the Add/Remove Programs applet.

You can also modify the properties of the virtual directory that the installer creates when installing a Web application. To view the virtual directory properties, right-click the MySetup project in Solution Explorer and select View, File System. After you select this option, you should see the screen in Figure 19.4.

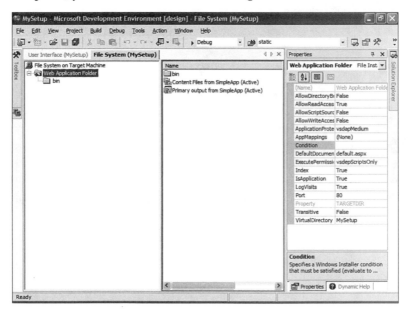

FIGURE 19.4 The File System Editor.

The File System Editor provides you with a representation of the file system where your application will be installed. If you select the Web Application Folder and open the Properties window, you'll see a list of virtual directory properties that you can modify. For example, you can change the name of the virtual directory by modifying the VirtualDirectory property.

Modifying the User Interface of the Web Setup Project

You can modify the appearance of the dialog boxes that a user views when executing the installer by right-clicking MySetup in Solution Explorer and selecting View, User Interface. You will see the User Interface Editor in Figure 19.5.

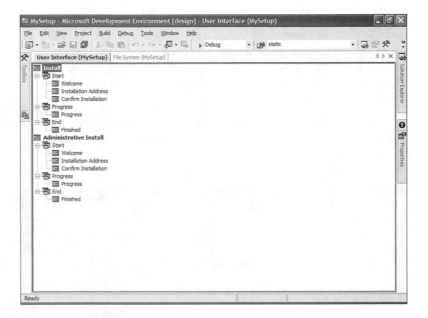

FIGURE 19.5   The User Interface Editor.

If you select any of the dialog boxes, you can modify the dialog's properties in the Properties window. For example, you can modify the banner image that appears at the top of each dialog box by performing the following steps:

1. Right-click MySetup in Solution Explorer and select File System from the View menu.

2. In the File System Editor, right-click Web Application Folder and select File from the Add menu.

3. Browse to a .bmp or .jpg image on your hard drive and click Open.

4. Right-click MySetup in Solution Explorer and select User Interface from the View menu.

5. In the User Interface Editor, select the Welcome dialog box.

6. Assign the .bmp or .jpg image that you added previously to the BannerBitMap property.

7. Right-click the MySetup project and select Build.

After you complete these steps, the image you selected will appear in the Welcome dialog box when a user executes the installer (see Figure 19.6).

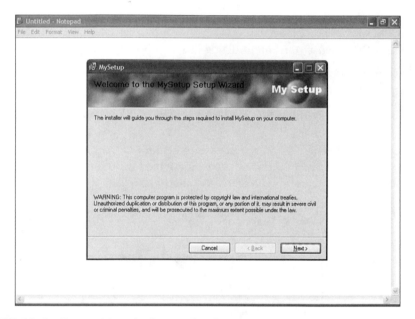

FIGURE 19.6   Customizing the banner image.

TIP

The recommended size for the banner image is 500×70 pixels.

You can also use the User Interface Editor to create additional dialog boxes, such as splash screens or license agreement dialog boxes. For example, perform the following steps to add a license agreement:

1. Right-click MySetup in Solution Explorer and select File System from the View menu.

2. In the File System Editor, right-click Web Application Folder and select File from the Add menu.

3. Browse to an .rtf file on your hard drive that contains the text of the license agreement and click Open (you can create the .rtf file with WordPad).

4. Right-click MySetup in Solution Explorer and select User Interface from the View menu.

5. In the User Interface Editor, right-click the Start node and select Add Dialog. Select the License Agreement dialog and click OK.

6. You can rearrange the order of the dialog boxes in the User Interface Editor by dragging one dialog box above or beneath another. Move the License Agreement dialog box above the Installation Address dialog box.

7. Select the License Agreement dialog box and open the Properties window.

8. Assign the license agreement file that you added previously to the LicenseFile property.

9. Right-click MySetup in the Solution Explorer window and select Build.

After you complete these steps, the license agreement will appear when the installer executes (see Figure 19.7). If the user does not agree to the terms of the license, the only choice left to the user is canceling installation.

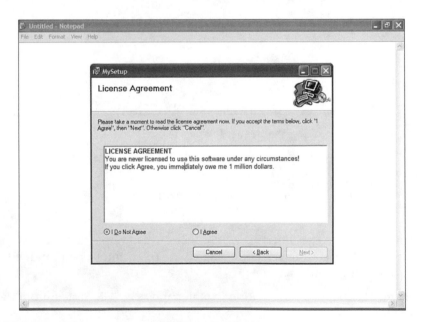

FIGURE 19.7   Adding a License Agreement dialog.

Summary

In this chapter, you learned how to deploy an ASP.NET Web application. In the first section, you were provided with an overview of the different methods for deploying a project. You were also provided with a deployment checklist that you should consult before deploying a Web application onto a production server.

Next, we looked at Web Setup Projects in detail. You learned how to create an installer for a Web application. You also learned how to customize the appearance of the installer dialog boxes.

PART IV

Components, Web Services, and Custom Controls

IN THIS PART

20 Building Business Components

21 Building XML Web Services

22 Creating Custom Web Form Controls

20

Building Business Components

IN THIS CHAPTER

- Why Use Components?

- Components Versus Classes

- Creating a Simple Component

- Creating a Database Component

- Creating Multi-Tiered Applications

- Creating a Library of Components

- Accessing the Current HttpContext in a Component

In this chapter, you'll learn how to create custom components with C# and Visual Basic .NET. Components enable you to reuse the same application logic—the same code—across multiple pages. You can place any type of application logic in a component that you want. For example, you can place all of your database access logic in a component, you can expose an XML Web service from a component, or you can implement custom business logic in a component.

In this chapter, you will learn

- The advantages of using components in your Web applications

- How to create simple components

- How to retrieve database data in a component

- How to package components in reusable class libraries

- How to access intrinsic ASP.NET objects in components such as the Cache, Trace, and Session objects

Why Use Components?

Before we get started building components, we should pause for a moment and consider whether building components is really necessary. Why bother? What advantages do we get by separating our application into components?

One important advantage of using components is that they enable you to reuse the same application logic across multiple pages. For example, if you need to execute a complicated function to perform a tax calculation on multiple pages, you can place the function in a single component and call the very same function from multiple pages.

TIP

Even if you just think that you *might* want to use the same logic elsewhere, it's a good idea to package the logic into a separate component. You don't want to waste time extracting code from existing applications when, all of a sudden, you discover that you need to reuse the code.

Another important advantage of using components is that they enable you to isolate changes that might occur in one part of an application from other parts of an application. In other words, components can make your applications less brittle.

For example, suppose that you build an application that displays sales data. Furthermore, suppose that when you created the application, you stored all the data in an Oracle database. One fine day, a decision is made to transfer all the data from the Oracle database to an SQL Server database.

If you coded all of your database access functions directly into your Web Form Pages, you would need to go back and alter all of the pages. If, on the other hand, you separated the data access functions into a set of data access components, you could modify the components without touching a single Web Form Page or any other part of your application's business logic.

Finally, placing your application logic into separate components makes it easier for multiple developers to work on a project at the same time. If you divide an application into multiple components, each developer can focus on implementing a particular part of an application without worrying about stumbling over the work of other developers.

For simple applications, you might never need to use components. However, as your applications grow more complicated, dividing your applications into components can make your life significantly easier.

TIP

Creating components also makes it easier to build scaffolding during development, for example, quickly putting together a component that returns a sample value allows you to build around it before it's implemented.

Components Versus Classes

Visual Studio .NET enables you to add two types of entities related to classes to your projects. You can add a C# or Visual Basic .NET component to your project by selecting Add Component from the Project menu, or you can add a C# or Visual Basic .NET class to your project by selecting Add Class from the Project menu.

The only difference between components and classes is that components support the Visual Studio .NET designer interface better than classes. Because components provide you with more flexibility, we'll build our custom components in this chapter by using components.

Adding a class to your project adds a file with the skeleton for a class declaration. The file automatically contains the following code:

C#

```
using System;

namespace myApp
{
  /// <summary>
  /// Summary description for Class1.
  /// </summary>
  public class Class1
  {
    public Class1()
    {
      //
      // TODO: Add constructor logic here
      //
    }
  }
}
```

VB.NET

```
Public Class Class1

End Class
```

A component is similar to a class. When you add a new component to a project, the file for the component automatically contains the following code:

C#

```csharp
using System;
using System.ComponentModel;
using System.Collections;
using System.Diagnostics;

namespace myApp
{
  /// <summary>
  /// Summary description for Component.
  /// </summary>
  public class Component : System.ComponentModel.Component
  {
    /// <summary>
    /// Required designer variable.
    /// </summary>
    private System.ComponentModel.Container components = null;

    public Component(System.ComponentModel.IContainer container)
    {
      /// <summary>
      /// Required for Windows.Forms Class Composition Designer support
      /// </summary>
      container.Add(this);
      InitializeComponent();


      //
      // TODO: Add any constructor code after InitializeComponent call
      //
    }

    public Component()
    {
      /// <summary>
      /// Required for Windows.Forms Class Composition Designer support
      /// </summary>
      InitializeComponent();


      //
      // TODO: Add any constructor code after InitializeComponent call
      //
    }
```

```
    }
}
```

VB.NET

```
Public Class Component1
    Inherits System.ComponentModel.Component

End Class
```

You'll notice that the declaration for a component includes some extra code. A component, unlike a class, derives from the `System.ComponentModel.Component` class. It also contains a Component Designer generated code region.

The extra code contained in a component declaration enables you to build components by using the Visual Studio .NET Designer interface. You can drag and drop other components from the Toolbox or Server Explorer window onto your component. For example, if you want to add a database connection to your component, you can drag and drop the connection from the Toolbox (see Figure 20.1).

You can also add a component to the Toolbox, but you can't add a class to the Toolbox. If you want to create a component that you want to easily use in multiple pages, you'll need to create a component rather than a class.

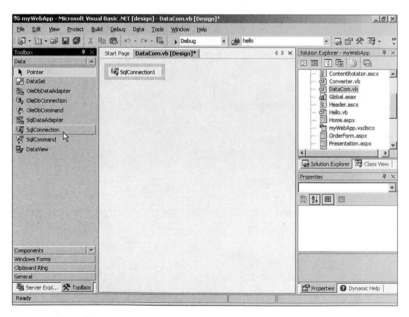

FIGURE 20.1   Using the Designer interface with a component.

Creating a Simple Component

Let's start by creating a simple component that converts inches to millimeters and millimeters to inches. This component will have two methods, `ConvertToMillimeters()` and `ConvertToInches()`, respectively.

NOTE

When you create a component in VB.NET, any public functions or subroutines that you declare in the component are exposed as methods. Consequently, to create your component to convert inches and millimeters, you need to create a component that contains two public functions. In C#, you can just create the methods directly.

To do so, perform the following steps:

C# Steps

1. Select Add Component from the Project menu. Name the component **Converter.cs** and click Open.

2. Select Code from the View menu.

3. Add the following code to the body of the component (do not remove the section labeled `Component Designer generated code`):

```
public decimal ConvertToMillimeters(Decimal Inches)
{
  return Inches * 25.4m;
}

public decimal ConvertToInches(Decimal Millimeters)
{
  return Millimeters * 0.03937m;
}
```

VB.NET Steps

1. Select Add Component from the Project menu. Name the component **Converter.vb** and click Open.

2. Select Code from the View menu.

3. Add the following code to the body of the component (do not remove the section labeled `Component Designer generated code`):

```
Function ConvertToMillimeters(ByVal Inches As Decimal) As Decimal
    Return Inches * 25.4
End Function

Function ConvertToInches(ByVal Millimeters As Decimal) As Decimal
    Return Millimeters * 0.03937
End Function
```

Next, we want to test our component in a Web Form Page. We'll create a page that contains a form for converting millimeters to inches.

1. Add a new Web Form Page to your project named **TestConverter.aspx**.

2. Add Label, TextBox, and Button controls to the TestConverter.aspx page.

3. Double-click the Button control (this will switch you to the Code Editor).

4. Enter the following code for the Button1_Click handler:

   C#

   ```csharp
   private void Button1_Click(object sender, System.EventArgs e)
   {
     Converter objConverter = new Converter();
     Label1.Text = objConverter.ConvertToInches(
   ➥Decimal.Parse(TextBox1.Text)).ToString();
   }
   ```

   VB.NET

   ```vbnet
   Private Sub Button1_Click(ByVal sender As System.Object,
   ➥ByVal e As System.EventArgs) Handles Button1.Click
     Dim objConverter As Converter

     objConverter = New Converter()
     Label1.Text = objConverter.ConvertToInches(TextBox1.Text)
   End Sub
   ```

5. Right-click the TestConverter.aspx page in the Solution Explorer window and select Build and Browse.

After you create the Web Form Page to test the component, you should be able to enter a value in millimeters into the text box, click the Button control, and the value converted to inches should be displayed in the Label control (see Figure 20.2).

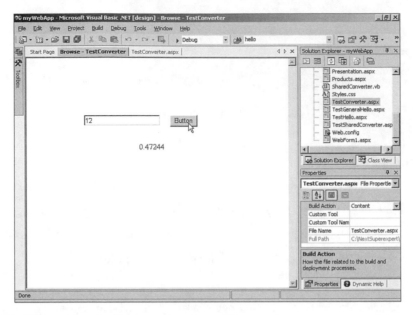

FIGURE 20.2   Using the Designer interface with a component.

Notice that we need to explicitly declare and create an instance of the component in the Button1_Click subroutine. After we create an instance of the component, we can simply call the component's ConvertToInches() method to convert the contents of the TextBox control to inches.

You should also notice that IntelliSense works with our new component. When you type the name of an instance of a component followed by a period (for example, **objConverter.**), a list of all the available methods of the component is displayed in a list box.

Creating Components with Static/Shared Methods

In the previous section, we created a component for converting inches and millimeters. Before we could use the component in the Web Form Page, however, we were required to explicitly declare and instantiate an instance of the component.

There's an easier way to use a component in your applications. Instead of declaring *instance methods*, you can declare *static methods* (called shared methods in VB.NET). You don't have to instantiate a component before you call its static methods.

Let's create a simple component with static methods for converting ounces to grams and grams to ounces.

C# Steps:

1. Create a new component for your project named **StaticConverter.cs**.

2. Switch to the Code Editor by selecting Code from the View menu.

3. Add the following code to the body of the component (do not remove the section labeled `Component Designer generated code`):

```
public static decimal ConvertToOunces(decimal grams)
{
  return grams * 0.0353m;
}

public static decimal ConvertToGrams(decimal ounces)
{
  return ounces * 28.35m;
}
```

VB.NET Steps

1. Create a new component for your project named **SharedConverter.vb**.

2. Switch to the Code Editor by selecting Code from the View menu.

3. Add the following code to the body of the component (do not remove the section labeled `Component Designer generated code`):

```
Shared Function ConvertToOunces(ByVal grams As Decimal) As Decimal
  Return grams * 0.0353
End Function

Shared Function ConvertToGrams(ByVal ounces As Decimal) As Decimal
  Return ounces * 28.35
End Function
```

Notice that both the `ConvertToOunces()` and `ConvertToGrams()` methods are declared as static (shared) methods. The method declarations include the keyword `Static` or `Shared`. Because of the way these methods are declared, we can access the methods from a Web Form Page without creating an instance of the component.

Next, we need to create a Web Form Page to test our component.

C# Steps

1. Create a new Web Form Page named **TestStaticConverter.aspx**.

2. Add `Label`, `TextBox`, and `Button` controls to the page.

3. Double-click the `Button` control (this will switch you to the Code Editor).

4. Enter the following code for the `Button1_Click` subroutine:

```
private void Button1_Click(object sender, System.EventArgs e)
{
  Label1.Text =
    StaticConverter.ConvertToGrams(Decimal.Parse(TextBox1.Text)).ToString();
}
```

5. Right-click the TestStaticConverter.aspx page in the Solution Explorer window and select Build and Browse.

VB.NET Steps

1. Create a new Web Form Page named **TestSharedConverter.aspx**.

2. Add `Label`, `TextBox`, and `Button` controls to the page.

3. Double-click the `Button` control (this will switch you to the Code Editor)

4. Enter the following code for the `Button1_Click` subroutine:

```
Private Sub Button1_Click(ByVal sender As System.Object,
➥ByVal e As System.EventArgs) Handles Button1.Click
  Label1.Text = SharedConverter.ConvertToGrams(TextBox1.Text)
End Sub
```

5. Right-click the TestSharedConverter.aspx page in the Solution Explorer window and select Build and Browse.

You'll notice that we did not explicitly declare the `StaticConverter` or `SharedConverter` component in the Web Form Page. Because the `ConvertToGrams()` method is a static method, we can call the method directly.

After reading this section, you might conclude that it makes sense to create every method as a static (shared) method. However, this type of method has an important limitation—you cannot refer to an instance method or property from a static (shared) method. Consequently, if your component needs to maintain state by using an instance property, you cannot take advantage of static (shared) methods.

Adding Properties to a Component

As you've seen in previous sections, any public function or public subroutine declared in a component is exposed as a method of the component. So far, we've discussed how you can add methods to a component, but we have not discussed properties.

You can add properties to a component in two ways—by declaring a public variable or by using property accessor functions. Because using property accessor functions is the preferred method, we'll use that method here.

We'll create a component with a single property and a single method. The property, named `Language`, will accept a string that represents a language such as French or Indonesian. The `SayHello()` method will return the string `Hello` in the language specified.

C# Steps

1. Create a new component for your project named **Hello.cs**.

2. Switch to the Code Editor by selecting Code from the View menu.

3. Add the following code to the body of the component (do not remove the section labeled `Component Designer generated code`):

```csharp
string _language;

public string Language
{
  get
  {
    return _language;
  }
  set
  {
    _language = value;
  }
}

public string SayHello()
{
  switch ( _language.ToLower() )
  {
    default:
      return "Hello";
    case "spanish":
      return "Hola";
    case "french":
      return "Bonjour";
    case "indonesian":
      return "Selamat";
  }
}
```

VB.NET Steps

1. Create a new component for your project named **Hello.vb**.

2. Switch to the Code Editor by selecting Code from the View menu.

3. Add the following code to the body of the component (do not remove the section labeled Component Designer generated code):

```
Dim _language As String

Public Property Language() As String
  Get
    Return _language
  End Get
  Set(ByVal Value As String)
    _language = Value
  End Set
End Property

Function SayHello() As String
  Select Case _language.ToLower
    Case "english"
      Return "Hello"
    Case "spanish"
      Return "Hola"
    Case "french"
      Return "Bonjour"
    Case "indonesian"
      Return "Selamat"
    End Select
End Function
```

The property is declared in this component by using property accessor functions. The Language property contains a Get() method and a Set() method. When you assign a value to the Language property, the Set() method is called. When you read a value from the Language property, the Get() method is called.

Notice that we use a private variable, named _language, with the Language property. Internal to our component, we use the _language property instead of the Language property.

To test our component, we need to create a new Web Form Page:

1. Create a new Web Form Page named **TestHello.aspx**.

2. Add Label, TextBox, and Button controls to the TestHello.aspx page.

3. Double-click the Button control (this will switch you to the Code Editor).

4. Enter the following code for the Button1_Click handler:

   C#

   ```
   private void Button1_Click(object sender, System.EventArgs e)
   {
     Hello objHello = new Hello();
     objHello.Language = TextBox1.Text;
     Label1.Text = objHello.SayHello();
   }
   ```

   VB.NET

   ```
   Private Sub Button1_Click(ByVal sender As System.Object,
   ➥ByVal e As System.EventArgs) Handles Button1.Click
     Dim objHello As Hello

     objHello = New Hello()
     objHello.Language = TextBox1.Text
     Label1.Text = objHello.SayHello()
   End Sub
   ```

5. Right-click the TestHello.aspx page in the Solution Explorer window and select Build and Browse.

If you enter the text **French** into the text box and click the button, the text Bonjour should appear in the Label control (see Figure 20.3).

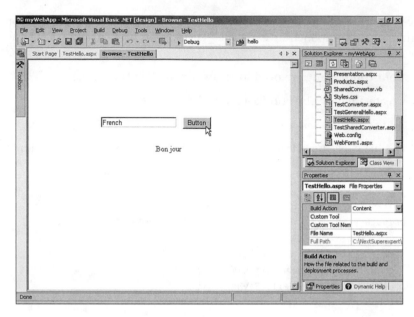

FIGURE 20.3   Adding properties to a component.

Creating a Database Component

Because you can take full advantage of the Visual Designer when building a component, you easily add all of your database logic to a component. In this section, we'll
create a simple database component that retrieves all the records from the Products
database table.

C# Steps

1. Create a component named **Products.cs**.

2. Drag the Products database table from under the Northwind data connection
   onto the Designer surface. Doing this will add both an SqlConnection and
   SqlDataAdapter to the component.

3. Add an Untyped DataSet to the component.

4. Switch to the Code Editor by selecting Code from the View menu.

5. Enter the following method in the body of the component:

```
public DataSet GetProducts()
{
  sqlDataAdapter1.Fill(dataSet1);
```

```
  return dataSet1;
}
```

6. Add the following two statements to the top of the component:

```
using System.Data;
using System.Data.SqlClient;
```

VB.NET Steps

1. Create a component named **Products.vb**.

2. Drag the Products database table from under the Northwind data connection onto the Designer surface. Doing this will add both an `SqlConnection` and `SqlDataAdapter` to the component.

3. Add an Untyped DataSet to the component.

4. Switch to the Code Editor by selecting Code from the View menu.

5. Enter the following function in the body of the component:

```
Function GetProducts() As DataSet
  SqlDataAdapter1.Fill(DataSet1)
  Return DataSet1
End Function
```

That was easy, wasn't it? We only need two statements to return a DataSet.

Next, we'll create a test page that grabs the data from the Products component and displays the data in a DataGrid.

1. Create a new page named **TestProducts.aspx**.

2. Add a DataGrid to the page.

3. Switch to the Code Editor by selecting Code from the View menu.

4. Enter the following code for the Page_Load handler:

C#

```
private void Page_Load(object sender, System.EventArgs e)
{
  Products objProducts = new Products();
  DataGrid1.DataSource = objProducts.GetProducts();
  DataGrid1.DataBind();
}
```

VB.NET

```
Private Sub Page_Load(ByVal sender As System.Object,
➥ByVal e As System.EventArgs) Handles MyBase.Load
  Dim objProducts As New Products()

  DataGrid1.DataSource = objProducts.GetProducts()
  DataGrid1.DataBind()
End Sub
```

5. Right-click the TestProducts.aspx page in the Solution Explorer window and select Build and Browse.

Notice that the TestProducts.aspx page does not include any database components such as a DataSet or SqlConnection. All the database components are hidden away in the Products component.

Using DataReaders with Components

In the previous section, we created a database component that returned database records with a DataSet. However, you should be aware that retrieving records with a DataAdapter and DataSet is significantly slower, in almost all situations, than retrieving the same records with a DataReader. In this section, we'll take a look at how we can modify our database component to use a DataReader instead of a DataSet.

> **NOTE**
>
> Using a DataReader can be two to three times faster than using a DataSet (depending on the number of rows being requested from the database). To learn more about the speed differences between a DataReader and a DataSet, see the "Performance Comparison: Data Access Techniques" article posted at the msdn.microsoft.com Web site at
> `http://msdn.microsoft.com/library/en-us/dnbda/html/bdadotnetarch031.asp`.

C# Steps

1. Create a new component named **ProductsDR.cs**.

2. Drag the Data Connection to the Northwind database from the Server Explorer window onto the Designer surface.

3. Add an `SqlCommand` object to the page.

4. In the Properties window, double-click next to the `Connection` property to assign the Northwind database connection to the `SqlCommand` object.

5. Assign the following SQL SELECT command to the SqlCommand object's CommandText property:

```
SELECT * FROM Products
```

6. Switch to the Code Editor by selecting Code from the View menu.

7. Enter the following method in the body of the component:

```
public SqlDataReader GetProducts()
{
  sqlConnection1.Open();
  return sqlCommand1.ExecuteReader(CommandBehavior.CloseConnection);
}
```

8. Add the following two statements to the top of the component:

```
using System.Data;
using System.Data.SqlClient;
```

VB.NET Steps

1. Create a new component named **ProductsDR.vb**.

2. Drag the Data Connection to the Northwind database from the Server Explorer window onto the Designer surface.

3. Add an SqlCommand object to the page.

4. In the Properties window, double-click next to the Connection property to assign the Northwind database connection to the SqlCommand object.

5. Assign the following SQL SELECT command to the SqlCommand object's CommandText property:

```
SELECT * FROM Products
```

6. Switch to the Code Editor by selecting Code from the View menu.

7. Enter the following method in the body of the component:

```
Public Function GetProducts() As SqlDataReader
  SqlConnection1.Open()
  Return SqlCommand1.ExecuteReader(CommandBehavior.CloseConnection)
End Function
```

8. Add the following statement to the top of the component:

```
Imports System.Data.SqlClient
```

We can bind the data returned from the ProductsDR component to a DataGrid in exactly the same way as we bound the data returned by the Products component in the previous section. However, the data is retrieved much faster with a DataReader than a DataSet.

Notice that when we call the ExecuteReader() method, we pass the special parameter CommandBehavior.CloseConnection. This parameter causes the database connection being used by the DataReader to close automatically after all the records are retrieved by the DataReader. If we did not include this parameter, the database connection would never be explicitly closed.

Creating Multi-Tiered Applications

As an application grows more complex, you'll need to divide it into multiple tiers. The traditional method of doing this is to use the three-tiered application model. According to this model, an application should be divided into the following tiers:

- *Presentation Tier*—Contains the user interface for the application

- *Business Tier*—Contains the business rules for the application

- *Data Tier*—Contains the data access components for the application

In an ASP.NET application, you use Web Form Pages for the presentation tier. The business and data tiers are typically implemented with business components.

In this section, we'll create a simple three-tiered application by creating separate components for the business and data tiers. We'll create a simple order entry application.

We'll work our way up the tiers starting from the data tier. For the data tier, we'll create a component that writes orders to the file system. To create the data component, do the following:

C# Steps

1. Create a new component named **DataCom.cs**.

2. Switch to the Code Editor by selecting Code from the View menu.

3. Add the following code to the body of the component (do not remove the section labeled Component Designer generated code):

```
public static void SaveOrder(string OrderID, decimal OrderAmount)
{
   System.IO.TextWriter objWriter;

   objWriter = System.IO.File.AppendText("c:\\Orders.txt");
```

```
    objWriter.WriteLine("OrderID: " + OrderID);
    objWriter.WriteLine("OrderAmount:" + OrderAmount.ToString());

    objWriter.Close();
}
```

VB.NET Steps

1. Create a new component named **DataCom.vb**.

2. Switch to the Code Editor by selecting Code from the View menu.

3. Add the following code to the body of the component (do not remove the section labeled Component Designer generated code):

```
Public Shared Sub SaveOrder(ByVal OrderID As String,
➥ByVal OrderAmount As Decimal)
  Dim objWriter As System.IO.TextWriter

  objWriter = System.IO.File.AppendText("c:\Orders.txt")
  With objWriter
    .WriteLine("OrderID: " & OrderID)
    .WriteLine("OrderAmount:" & OrderAmount)
  End With
  objWriter.Close()
End Sub
```

The DataCom component has a single method, named SaveOrder, that saves an order ID and order amount to a file named Orders.txt located at the root of the C: drive.

Next, we'll create the business tier by creating a single business component. The business component will implement the business rule that you cannot enter an order for an amount less than $1.00 or an order greater than $500.00.

C# Steps

1. Create a new component for your project named **BizCom.cs**.

2. Switch to the Code Editor by selecting Code from the View menu.

3. Add the following code to the body of the component (do not remove the section labeled Component Designer generated code):

```
public static bool AddOrder(string OrderID,decimal OrderAmount)
{
  if (OrderAmount > 1 && OrderAmount < 500)
  {
```

```
      DataCom.SaveOrder(OrderID, OrderAmount);
      return true;
   }
   else
      return false;
}
```

VB.NET Steps

1. Create a new component for your project named **BizCom.vb**.

2. Switch to the Code Editor by selecting Code from the View menu.

3. Add the following code to the body of the component (do not remove the section labeled `Component Designer generated code`):

```
Public Shared Function AddOrder(ByVal OrderID As String,
➥ByVal OrderAmount As Decimal) As Boolean
   If OrderAmount > 1 And OrderAmount < 500 Then
      DataCom.SaveOrder(OrderID, OrderAmount)
      Return True
   Else
      Return False
   End If
End Function
```

The `BizCom` class checks whether the `OrderAmount` is greater than 1 and less than 500. If the order passes the check, the BizCom component calls the DataCom component to save the order.

Finally, we need to create the presentation tier. We'll create the presentation tier by creating a Web Form Page named Presentation.aspx:

1. Add a new Web Form Page to your project named **Presentation.aspx**.

2. Add an HTML Label with the text `Order ID`.

3. Add a `TextBox` control.

4. Add a second HTML Label with the text `Order Amount`.

5. Add a second `TextBox` control.

6. Add a Web Forms `Label` control.

7. Add a Web Forms `Button` control.

8. Add a `Button1_Click` handler by double-clicking the `Button` control (this will switch you to the Code Editor).

9. Enter the following code for the `Button1_Click` handler:

C#

```csharp
private void Button1_Click(object sender, System.EventArgs e)
{
  if (BizCom.AddOrder(TextBox1.Text, Decimal.Parse(TextBox2.Text)) )
  {
    Label1.Text = "Order Added!";
    TextBox1.Text = "";
    TextBox2.Text = "";
  }
  else
    Label1.Text = "Could Not Add Order!";
}
```

VB.NET

```vbnet
Private Sub Button1_Click(ByVal sender As System.Object,
➥ByVal e As System.EventArgs) Handles Button1.Click
  If BizCom.AddOrder(TextBox1.Text, TextBox2.Text) Then
    Label1.Text = "Order Added!"
    TextBox1.Text = ""
    TextBox2.Text = ""
  Else
    Label1.Text = "Could Not Add Order!"
  End If
End Sub
```

10. Right-click the Presentation.aspx page in the Solution Explorer window and select Build and Browse.

If you enter a value between 1 and 500 into the Order Amount text box, and submit the form, a new order is added to the Order.txt file. If you do not enter a valid order amount, the error message "Could Not Add Order!" is displayed (see Figure 20.4).

NOTE

You must supply the ASPNET account with permissions to write to the hard drive to write to the Orders.txt file:

1. Right-click the C: drive.

2. Select the Security Tab.

3. Grant Write permissions to either the ASPNET or Guest account.

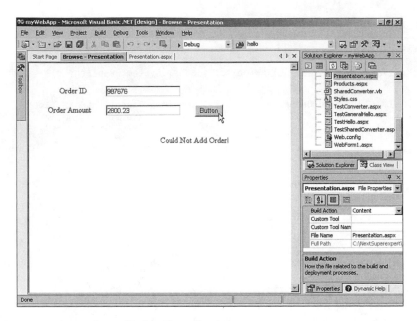

FIGURE 20.4   A simple multi-tiered application.

Creating a Library of Components

To get the most out of using components, you'll want to reuse the same components in multiple projects. In other words, you'll want to develop a standard library of components that you can use in your projects.

When you add a component (or a class) to your project, the component is compiled into the same assembly as the rest of your project. For example, if you are working on a project named myWebApp, the component is compiled into the myWebApp.dll assembly when you compile the project.

> **NOTE**
>
> An assembly is the actual file (or files) on your hard drive that contains the application logic for your project. When you compile a project by selecting Build and Browse, the project is compiled into an assembly.

If you want to use the same component in multiple projects, you'll need to compile the component into an independent assembly. You can create a component that is independent from any particular Web Application project by creating a Class Library project. A single class library can contain multiple components.

To do so, perform the following steps:

C# Steps

1. Open the File menu, and select New, Project.

2. Select the Visual C# Projects folder and select the Class Library template. Name the project `MyLibrary` and click OK.

3. Delete the Class1.cs file from the MyLibrary project by right-clicking the Class1.cs file in the Solution Explorer window and selecting Delete.

4. Add a new component to the MyLibrary project named `GeneralHello.cs`.

5. Enter the following code for the GeneralHello component (do not modify the section labeled `Component Designer generated code`):

```
public string SayHello()
{
  return "Hello!";
}
```

6. Compile the component by selecting Build MyLibrary from the Build menu.

VB.NET Steps

1. Open the File menu, and select New, Project.

2. Select the Visual Basic Projects folder and select the Class Library template (see Figure 20.5). Name the project `MyLibrary` and click OK.

3. Delete the Class1.vb file from the MyLibrary project by right-clicking the Class1.vb file in the Solution Explorer window and selecting Delete.

4. Add a new component to the MyLibrary project named `GeneralHello.vb`.

5. Enter the following code for the GeneralHello component (do not modify the section labeled `Component Designer generated code`):

```
Public Function SayHello() As String
  Return "Hello!"
End Function
```

6. Compile the component by selecting Build MyLibrary from the Build menu.

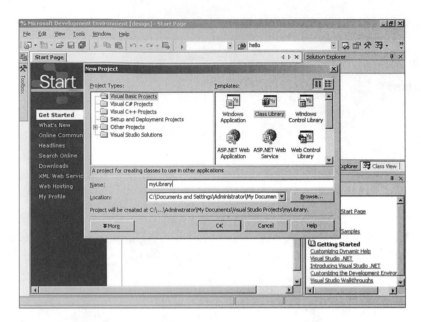

FIGURE 20.5   Creating a Class Library project.

After completing these steps, you'll have a new component named GeneralHello. The component has one method—SayHello()—that simply returns the string Hello!.

The component is stored in an assembly on your hard drive named MyLibrary.dll. If you want to use the GeneralHello component in another project, you need to add a reference to this assembly to the project:

1. Create a new ASP.NET Web Application project named **MyProject** by selecting New Project from the File menu.

2. Add a reference to the GeneralHello assembly by selecting Add Reference from the Project menu. Select the Projects tab and click the Browse button. Browse to the MyLibrary.dll assembly and click Open (see Figure 20.6). The MyLibrary.dll assembly will be located at the following path:

   ```
   \My Documents\Visual Studio Projects\MyLibrary\bin\Debug
   ```

3. Add a new Web Form Page to the project named TestGeneralHello.aspx.

4. Add a Label control to the TestGeneralHello.aspx page.

5. Switch to the Code Editor by selecting Code from the View menu.

6. Enter the following code for the Page_Load handler:

C#

```
private void Page_Load(object sender, System.EventArgs e)
{
  Label1.Text = MyLibrary.GeneralHello.SayHello();
}
```

VB.NET

```
Private Sub Page_Load(ByVal sender As System.Object,
➥ByVal e As System.EventArgs) Handles MyBase.Load
  Label1.Text = myLibrary.GeneralHello.SayHello
End Sub
```

7. Right-click the TestGeneralHello.aspx page and select Build and Browse.

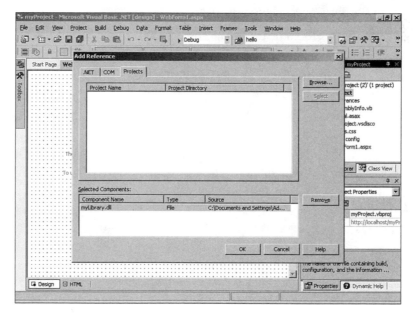

FIGURE 20.6   Adding a reference to an assembly.

The TestGeneralHello.aspx page uses the GeneralHello component to display the text Hello! in a Label control. You can use the GeneralHello component in the TestGeneralHello.aspx page even though the component is not defined in the same project. Because you added a reference to the GeneralHello.dll assembly, the component is available to the project.

This means that if you want to use a class library developed by a friend, your friend would simply need to email you the assembly. All the information about the class library is contained in the assembly.

> **NOTE**
>
> Any references that you add to a project appear under the References folder in the Solution Explorer window.

Adding Components to the Toolbox

If you create a genuinely useful set of components that you plan to use with multiple projects, you'll want to add the components to the Toolbox. Do the following to add the components in the MyLibrary project to the Toolbox:

1. Open the TestGeneralHello.aspx page.

2. Right-click the Toolbox and select Add Tab. Enter the name **MyLibrary** for the new tab.

3. Right-click beneath your new tab on the Toolbox and select Customize Toolbox.

4. In the Customize Toolbox dialog box, select the .NET Framework Components tab.

5. Click Browse and navigate to the MyLibrary.dll file on your hard drive. It should be in the following directory:

    ```
    \My Documents\Visual Studio Projects\MyLibrary\bin\Debug
    ```

6. Click OK.

After you complete these steps, the GeneralHello component will appear in the Toolbox beneath the MyLibrary tab. If you want to use the GeneralHello component in a page, you can simply drag and drop the component from the Toolbox onto the page. After the component has been added to the page, it will appear in the component bar at the bottom of the Designer window (see Figure 20.7).

When you drag a component onto a page, code for declaring and initializing the component is automatically added to the code-behind class for the page. For example, if you add the GeneralHello component to a page, the following two statements are added:

C#

```
protected MyLibrary.GeneralHello generalHello1;
this.generalHello1 = new MyLibrary.GeneralHello(this.components);
```

VB.NET

```
Protected WithEvents GeneralHello1 As MyLibrary.GeneralHello
Me.GeneralHello1 = New MyLibrary.GeneralHello(Me.components)
```

The declaration statement is added to the top of the code-behind file for the page and the initialization statement is added to the Web Form Designer generated code region.

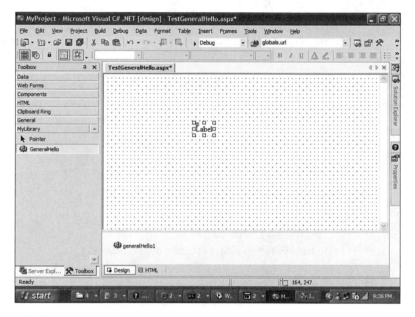

FIGURE 20.7   Custom component added to the Toolbox.

Accessing the Current HttpContext in a Component

Within a Web Form Page, you have access to all the information about the current request. You have direct access to objects such as the Request, Response, Session, User, Trace, and Cache objects. Within a component, on the other hand, you must do a little work before you access these objects.

Before you can access the intrinsic ASP.NET objects, you must first retrieve a reference to the current HttpContext. The `HttpContext` object has properties that expose all the standard ASP.NET intrinsic objects.

For example, suppose that you want to create a database component that caches database data in the server's memory. Instead of accessing the database with each database query, the component will check the cache first. To create this component, you'll need some way of referring to the `Cache` object. You can get to the `Cache` object by getting a reference to the current HttpContext.

Perform the following steps to create the CachedData component:

C# Steps

1. Create a new component named **CachedData.cs**.

2. Drag the Products table from under the Northwind Data Connection onto the Designer surface. This will add both an `SqlConnection` and `SqlDataAdapter` to the component.

3. Add an Untyped DataSet to the component.

4. Switch to the Code Editor by selecting Code from the View menu.

5. Enter the following method:

```
public DataSet GetResults(string CommandText)
{
  // Get reference to current HttpContext
  HttpContext Context = HttpContext.Current;

  // Try to retrieve data from Cache
  dataSet1 = (DataSet)Context.Cache[CommandText.ToLower()];

  // If can't, get from database
  if (dataSet1 == null)
  {
    Context.Trace.Warn("Retrieving data from DB");
    dataSet1 = new DataSet();
    sqlDataAdapter1.SelectCommand.CommandText = CommandText;
    sqlDataAdapter1.Fill(dataSet1);
    Context.Cache[CommandText.ToLower()] = dataSet1;
  }
  else
    Context.Trace.Warn("Retrieving data from memory");
```

```
   // In either case, return the DataSet
   return dataSet1;
}
```

6. Add the following statements to the top of the component:

```
using System.Web;
using System.Data;
using System.Data.SqlClient;
```

VB.NET Steps

1. Create a new component named **CachedData.vb**.

2. Drag the Products table from under the Northwind Data Connection onto the Designer surface. This will add both an `SqlConnection` and `SqlDataAdapter` to the component.

3. Add an Untyped DataSet to the component.

4. Switch to the Code Editor by selecting Code from the View menu.

5. Enter the following method:

```
Function GetResults(ByVal CommandText As String) As DataSet
  ' Get reference to current HttpContext
  Dim Context As HttpContext = HttpContext.Current

  ' Try to retrieve data from Cache
  DataSet1 = Context.Cache(CommandText.ToLower())

  ' If can't, get from database
  If (DataSet1 Is Nothing) Then
    Context.Trace.Warn("Retrieving data from DB")
    DataSet1 = New DataSet()
    SqlDataAdapter1.SelectCommand.CommandText = CommandText
    SqlDataAdapter1.Fill(DataSet1)
    Context.Cache(CommandText.ToLower()) = DataSet1
  Else
    Context.Trace.Warn("Retrieving data from memory")
  End If

  ' In either case, return the DataSet
  Return DataSet1
End Function
```

The first line in the GetResults() method returns a reference to the current HttpContext. Notice that after the reference is retrieved, both the Cache and Trace objects can be used.

The CachedData component first attempts to retrieve a DataSet representing the results of an SQL query from the cache. If the results are not present in the cache, the component retrieves the results from the database and adds the results to the cache. In either case, the results are returned.

You can test the component by building the following page:

1. Add a page to your project named **TestCachedData.aspx**.

2. Select Document in the Properties window and assign the value FlowLayout to the pageLayout property and the value True to the Trace property.

3. Add a TextBox, Web Forms Button, Web Forms Label control, and DataGrid to the page.

4. Double-click the Button control to add a Button1_Click handler and switch to the Code Editor.

5. Enter the following code for the Button1_Click handler:

   C#

```csharp
private void Button1_Click(object sender, System.EventArgs e)
{
  CachedData objCachedData = new CachedData();
  DataGrid1.DataSource = objCachedData.GetResults(TextBox1.Text);
  DataGrid1.DataBind();
}
```

   VB.NET

```vbnet
Private Sub Button1_Click(ByVal sender As System.Object,
➥ByVal e As System.EventArgs) Handles Button1.Click
  Dim objCachedData As New CachedData()
  DataGrid1.DataSource = objCachedData.GetResults(TextBox1.Text)
  DataGrid1.DataBind()
End Sub
```

6. Right-click TestCachedData.aspx in the Solution Explorer window and select Build and Browse.

When the page opens, you can type any SELECT statement into the text box and click the button to see the results in the DataGrid (see Figure 20.8). For example

```
SELECT * FROM Categories
```

When you execute the SELECT statement for the first time, the results are retrieved from the database. Subsequently, the results are retrieved from the cache. You can verify this by looking at the Trace Information section.

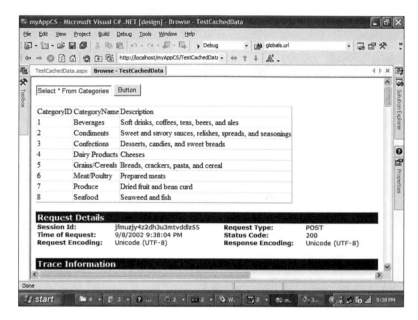

FIGURE 20.8   Testing the CachedData component.

Summary

In this chapter, you learned how to create both C# and VB.NET business components. First, you learned how to create simple business components by adding methods and properties to a component. You also learned how to create a simple business component that retrieves database data.

Next, we looked at how you can use components to divide an application into multiple tiers. We created a simple multi-tier application by creating components for the business and data tiers.

We then examined how you can package a library of components in a separate assembly. You learned how to create a separate Class Library project and refer to the class library in an ASP.NET Web Application project. You also learned how you can add components to the Toolbox.

Finally, we discussed the importance of the HttpContext object. You learned how to use the HttpContext object to refer to ASP.NET intrinsics, such as the Cache and Trace objects within a component.

21

Building XML Web Services

IN THIS CHAPTER

- What Is a Web Service?
- Creating a Simple ASP.NET Web Service
- Exposing Database Data Through a Web Service
- Exposing a Custom Object Through a Web Service
- Advanced Web Service Topics

In this chapter, you are introduced to XML Web services in the ASP.NET Framework. You will learn how to create and consume Web services that expose simple data, database data, and custom objects.

In this chapter, you will learn

- How to create a Web service that returns a random fortune

- How to create a Web service that exposes the contents of the Products database table

- How to create an Invoice Web service that exposes instances of a custom class

- How to improve the performance of a Web service by caching Web service data

- How to take advantage of dynamic discovery when building Web services

What Is a Web Service?

The primary function of a Web service is to enable application-to-application communication. You can use a Web service to transmit a variety of different types of data across a network, including documents, DataSets, custom objects, and binary data. The network can be a local network or it can be the Internet.

In this chapter, we'll focus on using Web services to transmit information from one Web server to another. However, Web services can also be used to transmit information from a Web server to a desktop application or from one desktop application to another desktop application.

The following are some examples of how Web services can be used:

- *Product Catalog Web Service*—Your company creates a set of products that are sold through several partner Web sites. Different partners sell different subsets of your catalog of products. You want to enable your partners to automatically keep their Web sites updated with your latest product information.

  If you expose the product catalog through a Web service, your partners can automatically query the Web service to show the latest product information on their Web pages.

- *Credit Card Authorization Web Service*—You need to authorize credit cards in real-time to authorize purchases at your Web site. In that case, you could use a credit card authentication Web service. The Web service would enable you to send a purchase amount, credit card number, and credit card expiration date, and you receive an authentication code.

- *Driving Directions Web Service*—You want to supply customers with driving directions to your business at your Web site. You want customers to be able to enter their home address and get detailed driving directions to your place of business. In that case, you can take advantage of a Web service that returns driving directions. Microsoft already has a Web service like this called MapPoint .NET (see msdn.microsoft.com).

- *Security Web Service*—You want to maintain a single database of usernames and passwords used for logging into any of the Web applications maintained by your business. In that case, you can create a Web service that validates usernames and passwords. This Web service can be used by different applications, even when the applications are hosted at different locations.

One thing that you need to keep in mind while reading this chapter is that Web services are still a very new technology. At this date in time, there are not a lot of useful Web services out there. However, it is expected that eventually there will be a huge market in business-to-business and business-to-consumer Web services.

TIP

Visit uddi.microsoft.com or www.xmethods.com for a directory of existing Web services.

It's also important to understand that XML Web services are not a Microsoft technology. If they were, the technology would fail. Web services are supported by several Web application technologies including Java, Cold Fusion, and Delphi.

One of the big promises of Web services is that they will enable communication between different applications running on different platforms. Most large organizations use a variety of technologies (.NET and Java, for example). Web services have the promise of enabling applications written on different platforms to seamlessly communicate.

Web services work by sending XML using the HTTP protocol. This is important because it means that a Web service will work in all the same situations as a Web page. In other words, if you can access a Web page from a Web server, you can access a Web service. Web services do not have the same firewall issues as other remote invocation technologies.

ASP.NET Web Services

An ASP.NET Web service is Microsoft's implementation of Web services in the .NET Framework. An ASP.NET Web service is a .NET class that has certain methods and properties that can be accessed across a network.

You create an ASP.NET Web service by marking certain methods and properties of a class with the WebMethod attribute. That's all you have to do. After you have marked a method as a Web method, the method can be invoked over the network. If the Web server is on the Internet, the method can be invoked from anywhere in the known universe.

For example, suppose that you want to create a Fortune Web service. This Web service will randomly return your fortune. You can implement this Web service with the following class:

C#

```csharp
using System;
using System.Web.Services;

namespace myApp
{
  public class FortuneService
  {

    [WebMethod]
    public string GetFortune()
    {
      Random objRand = new Random();
      switch (objRand.Next(3))
      {
        case 0:
          return "Things look bad!";
      case 1:
```

```
    return "Things look good!";
  default:
    return "Stay home and hide!";
    }
  }


 }
}
```

VB.NET

```
Imports System.Web.Services

Public Class FortuneService
    Inherits System.Web.Services.WebService

    <WebMethod()> Public Function GetFortune() As String
        Dim objRand As New Random()
        Select Case objRand.Next(3)
            Case 0
                Return "Things look bad!"
            Case 1
                Return "Things look good!"
            Case Else
                Return "Stay home and hide!"
        End Select
    End Function

End Class
```

Notice that all that you need to do to implement the Fortune Service is to create a
.NET class. This class has one method exposed as a Web method—GetFortune(). All
the rest of the work of getting Web services to function is taken care of behind the
scenes by the .NET Framework.

Creating a Simple ASP.NET Web Service

In this section, we'll build a simple Web service and test the service from the
browser. We'll create a Math Service that adds two numbers together.

You should think of creating a Web service in the same way as you would think of creating a class in a class library. Although you can add a Web service directly to an existing ASP.NET Web application, you'll typically need to package the Web service in a separate project so that you can reuse the same Web service in multiple projects. Consequently, the first step in creating the Math Service is to add a new ASP.NET Web Service project to our solution:

1. Select New from the File menu and select Project.

2. In the New Project dialog, select ASP.NET Web Service. In the location text box, name the new project **myServices** and click OK.

Next, we need to create the actual Web service:

1. Right-click the myServices project in the Solution Explorer window and select Add, Add Web Service.

2. Enter the name **MathService** for the new Web service and click Open.

3. Double-click the Designer surface to switch to the Code Editor and enter the following method in the body of the class declaration:

C#

```
[WebMethod]
public int AddNumbers(int val1, int val2)
{
  return val1 + val2;
}
```

VB.NET

```
<WebMethod()> Function AddNumbers(ByVal val1 As Integer,
➥ByVal val2 As Integer) As Integer
  Return val1 + val2
End Function
```

4. Right-click the MathService.asmx service in the Solution Explorer window and select Build and Browse.

When the MathService.asmx Web service opens in the browser, you'll get something called the Web Service Help Page (see Figure 21.1). The ASP.NET Framework automatically generates the Web Service Help Page. It lists all the Web methods available in a Web service.

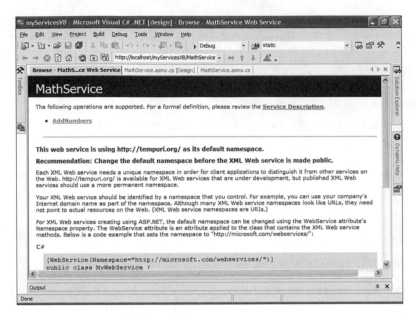

FIGURE 21.1 The Web Service Help Page.

TIP

You can customize the appearance of the Web Service Help Page by modifying the DefaultWsdlHelpGenerator.aspx file that you can find in the `\WINNT\Microsoft.NET\Framework\`*Framework Version*`\CONFIG` directory.

You can test any of the Web methods listed in the Web Service Help page. For example, if you click the AddNumbers link, you can test the Web method. You should get a form that enables you to enter two numbers. If you click the Invoke button, you'll get the XML file in Figure 21.2.

There's one other thing that you should notice about the Web Service Help page. If you return to the main page, you should notice a link labeled Service Description. If you click this link, the Web Services Description Language (WSDL) file is opened (see Figure 21.3).

The WSDL file is an XML file that contains the public interface for the Web service. For example, it lists all the Web methods of the Web service, the data types of all its parameters, and the Web method return types. You'll need to use the WSDL file when communicating with the Web service. For now, you should notice that you always get the WSDL file for an ASP.NET Web service by entering the URL followed by ?WSDL as in the following:

```
http://localhost/myApp/MathService.asmx?WSDL
```

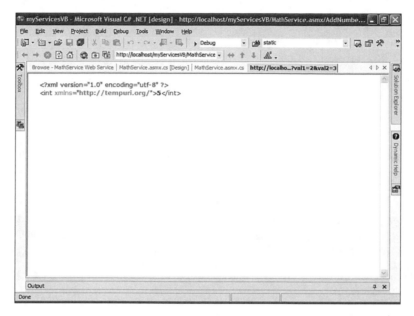

FIGURE 21.2   The XML file returned by invoking AddNumbers.

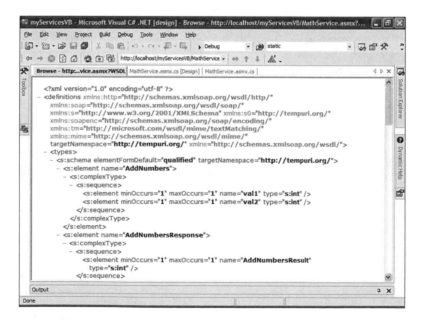

FIGURE 21.3   The Web Services Description Language file.

Invoking a Web Service from a Web Form Page

As you saw in the previous section, creating a Web service is very easy. Just create a class and decorate certain methods and properties with the WebMethod attribute.

In this section, you'll learn how to invoke a Web service. Visual Studio .NET also makes this process very easy. The development environment takes care of all the messy details of generating the necessary code to communicate with the Web service across the network for you.

When reading this section, it helps to pretend that we are trying to communicate with a Web service in Australia (if you happen to live in Australia, think of New Jersey). Suppose that you want to invoke the Math Service from a Web Form Page to add two numbers together. To do this, the only information that you need from the Australian Web service is the WSDL file. Remember that you can always retrieve the WSDL file for an ASP.NET Web service by appending the query string ?WSDL to the URL for the Web service.

Let's go ahead and do this in Visual Studio .NET:

1. Create a new ASP.NET Web Application project named TestMyServices by right-clicking the name of your Solution in the Solution Explorer window and selecting Add, Add New Project.

2. Right-click the References folder in the Solution Explorer window and select Add Web Reference. Doing this will open the Add Web Reference dialog box (see Figure 21.4).

3. Enter the following URL in the address bar:

   http://localhost/myServices/MathService.asmx?WSDL

4. Click the Add Reference Button.

When you complete these steps, Visual Studio .NET will automatically retrieve the WSDL file from the Math Service and generate something called a *Web service proxy class*. The Web service proxy class acts as a local representation of the remote Web service class.

After you retrieve the WSDL file, you should see a new folder named Web References in the Solution Explorer window. There should be a Web reference named localhost in this folder. This Web reference contains the proxy class for the Math Service.

You can view the contents of the proxy class itself by selecting Show All Files from the Project menu, expanding localhost in the Solution Explorer window, and expanding the Reference.map file. Hiding behind the Reference.map file, you'll discover a file named Reference.cs or Reference.vb. This is the Web service proxy class. Double-click it to view its contents.

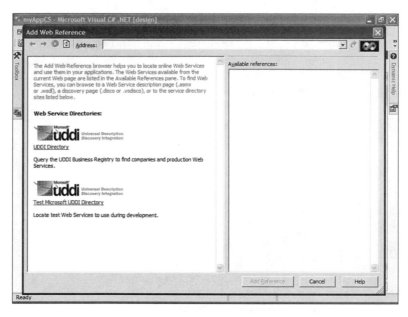

FIGURE 21.4   The Add Web Reference dialog box.

The Math Service proxy class has the following three methods:

- `AddNumbers`   Call this method to synchronously invoke the `AddNumbers` method on the remote Web service.

- `BeginAddNumbers`   Call this method to asynchronously invoke the `AddNumbers` method onWeb services the remote Web service.

- `EndAddNumbers`   This method is called when a response is returned from calling the `BeginAddNumbers` method.

The easiest method of invoking the remote `AddNumbers` method of the Math Service is by simply calling the `AddNumbers` method of the proxy class. You'll use the other two methods only when you need to interact with a Web service asynchronously (asynchronous Web services are not discussed in this book).

Let's go ahead and add the proxy class to a Web Form Page:

1. Add a new Web Form Page to the TestMyServices project named **testMathService.aspx**.

2. Add two `TextBox` controls and a `Button` and Web Forms `Label` control to the TestMathService.aspx page.

3. Double-click the `Button` control to switch to the Code Editor.

4. Enter the following code for the `Button1_Click` handler:

C#

```
private void Button1_Click(object sender, System.EventArgs e)
{
  localhost.MathService objService = new localhost.MathService();
  Label1.Text = objService.AddNumbers
    (
      Int32.Parse(TextBox1.Text),
      Int32.Parse(TextBox2.Text)
    ).ToString();
}
```

VB.NET

```
Private Sub Button1_Click(ByVal sender As System.Object,
➡ByVal e As System.EventArgs) Handles Button1.Click
  Dim objService As New localhost.MathService()

  Label1.Text = objService.AddNumbers(TextBox1.Text, TextBox2.Text)
End Sub
```

5. Right-click the TestMathService.aspx page and select Build and Browse.

If you enter numeric values into the two `TextBox` controls and click the button, the values are passed to the remote Web service. The response from the Web service is displayed in the `Label` control.

Web Services and Namespaces

When you create a Web service, you should supply it with a unique namespace. That way, if two companies create a Web service with the same name (for example, two Web services named MathService.asmx), there is still a way to distinguish between them.

You can supply any string for a namespace. However, it is a good idea to use the URL for your company as the namespace because you know that this URL will be unique.

You add a namespace to a Web service class by using the `WebService` attribute before the class declaration as in the following:

C#

```csharp
[WebService(Namespace="http://yourDomain.com/webservices/")]
public class MathService
{
  ...
}
```

VB.NET

```vbnet
<WebService(Namespace:="http://yourDomain.com/webservices/")>
➥Public Class MathServicea
  ...
End Class
```

Exposing Database Data Through a Web Service

You'll remember from our discussion of DataSets in Chapter 8, "Overview of ADO.NET," that you can seamlessly convert a DataSet to and from XML. Because a DataSet can be easily converted into XML, this means that you can pass a DataSet both to and from a Web service.

WARNING

You cannot use DataReaders with a Web service. A DataReader, unlike a DataSet, requires an open database connection. A DataReader, therefore, cannot be persisted to a static XML representation.

In this section, we'll create a Product Web service that exposes the contents of the Products database table. We'll create the Web service so that it accepts a parameter that represents the product category. That way, people can query the Product Web service for different subsets of products.

First, we need to create the Products Web service itself:

1. Add a new Web service to the myServices project named `ProductService.asmx`.

2. Drag the Products database table from beneath the Northwind database in the Server Explorer window onto the Designer surface. This will add an `SqlConnection` and `SqlDataAdapter` to the Designer.

3. Add an Untyped DataSet to the Designer by dragging the DataSet from the Toolbox.

4. Select the SqlDataAdapter in the Properties window, expand the `SelectCommand` property and assign the following SQL `SELECT` statement to the `CommandText` property:

```
SELECT Products.* FROM Products
INNER JOIN Categories
ON Products.CategoryID = Categories.CategoryID
WHERE (Categories.CategoryName = @CategoryName)
```

5. Double-click the Designer surface to switch to the Code Editor.

6. Enter the following `GetProducts()` method in the body of the class:

C#

```
[WebMethod]
public DataSet GetProducts(string Category)
{
  sqlDataAdapter1.SelectCommand.Parameters[ "@CategoryName" ].Value
➥= Category;
  sqlDataAdapter1.Fill( dataSet1);
  return dataSet1;
}
```

VB.NET

```
<WebMethod()> Function GetProducts(ByVal Category As String) As DataSet
  SqlDataAdapter1.SelectCommand.Parameters("@CategoryName").Value
➥= Category
  SqlDataAdapter1.Fill(DataSet1)
  Return DataSet1
End Function
```

7. Right-click the ProductService.asmx file in the Solution Explorer window and select Build and Browse.

After the Web Service Help Page opens, you can test the Product Web service by clicking the `GetProducts()` link. For example, you can enter the category Seafood when invoking the Web service to retrieve all the seafood products. Invoking the Web service returns an XML file that represents the DataSet returned by the Web service (see Figure 21.5).

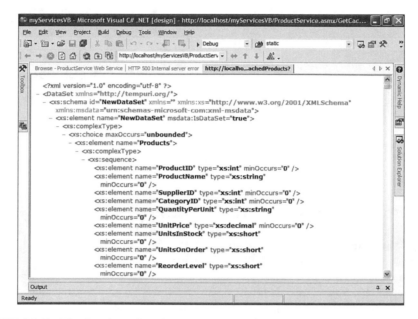

FIGURE 21.5   The Products DataSet as XML.

Next, we need to create a Web Form Page to test the Product service. First, we need to add the Web reference:

1. Right-click the References folder in the TestMyServices project and select Add Web Reference.

2. Enter the following URL in the address bar:

   ```
   http://localhost/myServices/ProductService.asmx?WSDL
   ```

3. Click Add Reference.

Now, we are finally ready to create the Web Form Page. We'll create a page that displays the DataSet returned from the Product service in a DataGrid:

1. Add a new Web Form Page to the TestMyServices project named **TestProductService.aspx**.

2. Add TextBox, Button, and DataGrid controls to the page.

3. Double-click the Button control and enter the following code for the Button1_Click handler:

C#

```csharp
private void Button1_Click(object sender, System.EventArgs e)
{
  localhost1.ProductService objService = new localhost1.ProductService();
  DataGrid1.DataSource = objService.GetProducts(TextBox1.Text);
  DataGrid1.DataBind();
}
```

VB.NET

```vbnet
Private Sub Button1_Click(ByVal sender As System.Object,
  ➥ByVal e As System.EventArgs) Handles Button1.Click
  Dim objService As New localhost1.ProductService()

  DataGrid1.DataSource = objService.GetProducts(TextBox1.Text)
  DataGrid1.DataBind()
End Sub
```

4. Right-click the TestProductService.aspx page in the Solution Explorer window
   and select Build and Browse.

NOTE

The Web service proxy class is declared in the TestMyServices page using
`localhost1`.ProductService. The `localhost1` prefix refers to the namespace. If this is the
first Web reference that you have added to the TestMyServices project, the correct namespace
would be `localhost`. If this is the second Web reference, the correct namespace would be
`localhost1`, and so on.

After the TestProductService.aspx page opens, you can enter different categories of
products (for example, Seafood, Beverages, or Produce) in the text box and click the
button to display matching products in the DataGrid (see Figure 21.6).

Exposing a Custom Object Through a Web Service

You can expose custom objects through a Web service. This is useful when you need
to represent structured information, such as invoices, job descriptions, resumes, and
product orders with a Web service.

In this section, we'll create a simple Invoice Web service that exposes instances of a
custom Invoice class. This Web service could be used, for example, to pass invoices
between different offices in a company.

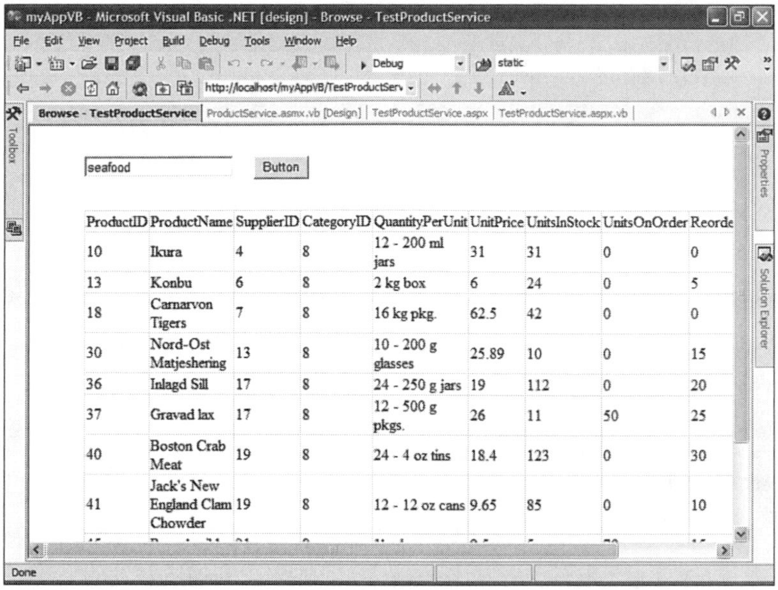

FIGURE 21.6   The TestProductService.aspx page.

Let's start by creating the Invoice class itself:

C# Steps

1. Add a new class to the myServices project named **Invoice.cs**.

2. Enter the following code for the Invoice.cs class:

```
using System;

namespace myServices
{
  public class Invoice
  {
    public DateTime Date;
    public Decimal Amount;
    public string Description;
  }
}
```

VB.NET Steps

1. Add a new class to the myServices project named **Invoice.vb**.

2. Enter the following code for the Invoice.vb class:

```
Public Class Invoice
    Public [Date] As DateTime
    Public Amount As Decimal
    Public Description As String
End Class
```

Our Invoice class has three properties—Date, Amount, and Description.

The next step is to expose an instance of this class through a Web service:

1. Add a new Web service named **InvoiceService.asmx** to the myServices project.

2. Double-click the Designer to switch to the Code Editor and enter the following Web method:

    C#

    ```
    [WebMethod]
    public Invoice GetInvoice()
    {
      Invoice objInvoice = new Invoice();

      objInvoice.Date = DateTime.Now;
      objInvoice.Amount = 1322.34m;
      objInvoice.Description = "Dell Laptop";

      return objInvoice;
    }
    ```

    VB.NET

    ```
    <WebMethod()> Function GetInvoice() As Invoice
      Dim objInvoice As New Invoice()

      objInvoice.Date = DateTime.Now
      objInvoice.Amount = 1322.34
      objInvoice.Description = "Dell Laptop"

      Return objInvoice
    End Function
    ```

3. Right-click the InvoiceService.asmx file in the Solution Explorer window and select Build and Browse.

If you test the Invoice service by clicking the GetInvoice link in the Web Services Help Page, an XML representation of the `Invoice` class is returned.

The final step is to invoke the Invoice service from a Web Form Page. Perform the following steps to add a Web reference to the Invoice service:

1. Right-click the References folder in the TestMyServices project and select Add Web Reference.

2. Enter the following URL in the address bar:

```
http://localhost/myServices/InvoiceService.asmx?WSDL
```

Perform the following steps to create a Web Form Page that displays the properties of an invoice:

1. Add a new Web Form Page to the TestMyServices project named **TestInvoiceService.aspx**.

2. Add a `Label` control to the TestInvoiceService.aspx page.

3. Double-click the Designer surface to switch to the Code Editor.

4. Enter the following code for the `Page_Load` handler:

C#

```csharp
private void Page_Load(object sender, System.EventArgs e)
{
  localhost2.Invoice objInvoice;
  localhost2.InvoiceService objService = new localhost2.InvoiceService();

  objInvoice = objService.GetInvoice();
  Label1.Text = "<li> Invoice Date: ";
  Label1.Text += objInvoice.Date.ToString("D");
  Label1.Text += "<li> Invoice Amount: ";
  Label1.Text += objInvoice.Amount.ToString( "c" );
  Label1.Text += "<li> Invoice Description: ";
  Label1.Text += objInvoice.Description;
}
```

VB.NET

```vbnet
Private Sub Page_Load(ByVal sender As System.Object,
➥ByVal e As System.EventArgs) Handles MyBase.Load
  Dim objInvoice As localhost2.Invoice
  Dim objService As New localhost2.InvoiceService()
```

```
   objInvoice = objService.GetInvoice()
   Label1.Text = "<li> Invoice Date: "
   Label1.Text &= objInvoice.Date.ToString("D")
   Label1.Text &= "<li> Invoice Amount: "
   Label1.Text &= objInvoice.Amount.ToString("c")
   Label1.Text &= "<li> Invoice Description: "
   Label1.Text &= objInvoice.Description
End Sub
```

5. Right-click the TestInvoiceService.aspx page in the Solution Explorer window and select Build and Browse.

After you complete these steps, the invoice passed by the Invoice service is displayed in the Label control (see Figure 21.7).

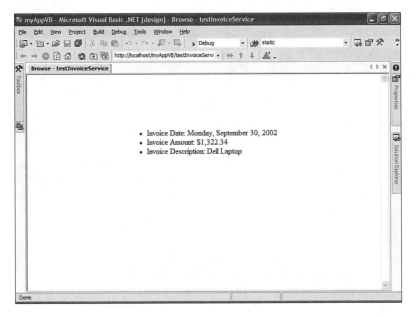

FIGURE 21.7   The custom Invoice object displayed in a Label control.

You should notice that we never declared the Invoice class in the TestMyServices project. The definition of the Invoice class is included in the WSDL file for the Invoice service.

Advanced Web Service Topics

In this section, we'll tackle three advanced Web service topics. First, you'll learn how to gracefully handle errors when calling a Web method. Next, you'll learn how to take advantage of caching when working with a Web service. Finally, you'll learn how to use dynamic discovery to add a single Web reference that represents multiple Web services.

Handling Errors When Calling Web Methods

You might be wondering about what happens when you attempt to call a Web method from a Web service and the Web service is unavailable. In that case, by default, your Web Form Page will wait 90 seconds for the Web method to timeout and then the Web Form Page will display a "This operation has timed out" error message.

90 seconds is a long time to keep a user waiting for a response. You can change the timeout period for a Web service proxy by modifying the value of the Timeout property as follows:

C#

```csharp
localhost1.HelloService objService = new localhost1.HelloService();

objService.Timeout = 10000;

try
{
  Label1.Text = objService.SayHello();
}
catch
{
  Label1.Text = "Web service unavailable!";
}
```

VB.NET

```vbnet
Private Sub Page_Load(ByVal sender As System.Object,
➡ByVal e As System.EventArgs) Handles MyBase.Load
  Dim objService As New superexpert.HelloService()

  objService.Timeout = 10000
```

```
  Try
    Label1.Text = objService.SayHello()
  Catch
    Label1.Text = "Web service unavailable!"
  End Try
End Sub
```

The Timeout property accepts a value in milliseconds. In this code, the Web service proxy class is set to timeout after 10 seconds (10,000 milliseconds).

Caching the Output of Web Methods

Most likely, if you are using a Web service to publish a catalog of products, your list will not change very often. In that case, you should take advantage of caching to reduce the load on your Web server.

There are two ways that you can cache the data returned by a Web method. You can use the WebMethod attribute to enable caching for a particular Web method. Alternatively, you can use the Cache object.

The WebMethod attribute has a property called CacheDuration. You can use the CacheDuration property to cache the output generated by a WebMethod for a certain number of seconds. The following is an example of how this property can be used with a Web method that returns the current time:

C#

```
[WebMethod(CacheDuration=30)]
public string GetTime()
{
  return DateTime.Now.ToString( "T" );
}
```

VB.NET

```
<WebMethod(CacheDuration:=30)> Function GetTime() As String
  Return DateTime.Now.ToString("T")
End Function
```

The GetTime() Web method in this case will cache its output for 30 seconds.

As an alternative to using the CacheDuration property, you can use the Cache object. (To learn more about the Cache object see Chapter 14, "Improving Application Performance with Caching.") The advantage of using the Cache object is it can be used to cache the same data across multiple Web methods.

The following shows how you can use the Cache object in a Web method:

C#

```csharp
[WebMethod]
public DataSet GetCachedProducts()
{
  DataSet dstProducts =
    (DataSet)Context.Cache[ "Products" ];
  if (dstProducts == null)
  {
    dstProducts = new DataSet();
    sqlDataAdapter1.Fill( dstProducts );
    Context.Cache[ "Products" ] = dstProducts;
  }
  return dstProducts;
}
```

VB.NET

```vbnet
<WebMethod()> Function GetCachedProducts() As DataSet
  Dim dstProducts As DataSet

  dstProducts = Context.Cache("Products")
  If dstProducts Is Nothing Then
    dstProducts = New DataSet()
    SqlDataAdapter1.Fill(dstProducts)
    Context.Cache("Products") = dstProducts
  End If
  Return dstProducts
End Function
```

The GetCachedProducts Web method caches the products database table in memory so that the database is not hit each and every time the Web method is called. Notice that you must refer to the Cache object within a Web method by using Context.Cache.

Using Dynamic Discovery

When you add a reference to a standard class library to a project, you only need to add a single reference. You don't need to add a reference for each and every class contained in the library.

When adding a reference to a Web service, on the other hand, we've had to add a separate reference for each Web service. This is true even though all the Web services are collected together in the same project.

We've been adding references to Web services by referring to the WSDL file for a Web service. There's an alternative. Instead of adding a reference to a WSDL file, you can add a reference to a .vsdisco file.

Whenever you create a new project in Visual Studio .NET, a .vsdisco file is automatically added to your project. The .vsdisco file is the dynamic discovery file. When you request a project's dynamic discovery file, the ASP.NET Framework automatically searches for all the Web services contained in the project and displays them. If you enter the path to a project .vsdisco file when adding a Web reference, you get a proxy class that represents all the Web services in a project.

For security reasons, dynamic discovery is disabled by default. You can enable dynamic discovery by editing the Machine.Config file located in the \WINNIT\Microsoft.NET\Framework*Framework Version*\Config folder.

Open the Machine.Config file in Notepad, find the `<httpHandlers>` section, and remove the comments around the .vsdisco handler.

If you don't want to modify the Machine.Config file (or you don't have access to this file), you can also enable dynamic discovery for a ASP.NET Web Service project by adding the following section to the `<system.web>` section of the project root Web.Config file:

```
<httpHandlers>
  <add verb="*" path="*.vsdisco"
    type="System.Web.Services.Discovery.DiscoveryRequestHandler,
➥System.Web.Services, Version=1.0.3300.0, Culture=neutral,
➥PublicKeyToken=b03f5f7f11d50a3a" validate="false"/>
</httpHandlers>
```

> **WARNING**
>
> Dynamic discovery will not work unless you provide the Web services in a project with a proper namespace by supplying a value for the WebService attribute's Namespace property. See the earlier section in this chapter, "Web Services and Namespaces."

After you complete these steps to enable dynamic discovery, you can replace all the individual Web references that you previously added with a single Web reference. Right-click the References folder and select Add Web Reference. In the address bar of the Add Web Reference dialog box, enter the path to the dynamic discovery file:

```
http://localhost/myServices/myServices.vsdisco
```

After you click Add Reference, you'll have a single reference for all the Web services in the myServices project.

For example, to invoke the AddNumbers() method of the Math Service from a Web Form Page, you would use code like the following:

C#

```
localhost.MathServiceSoap objService =
    new localhost.MathServiceSoap();
Label1.Text = objService.AddNumbers(1,2).ToString();
```

VB.NET

```
Dim objService As New localhost.MathServiceSoap()
Label1.Text = objService.AddNumbers(1, 2)
```

Notice that you refer to the Math Service as MathServiceSoap instead of MathService. The expression Soap is automatically appended to the name of each of the Web service proxy classes when the Web reference is generated.

Summary

In this chapter, you learned how to build Web services in the ASP.NET Framework. In the first section, you were given a quick overview of Web services. You learned that, within the ASP.NET Framework, a Web service is nothing more than a class that has certain methods and properties marked with the WebMethod attribute.

Next, we walked through the steps necessary for creating several Web services. We created a Web service that exposes database data. We also created a Web service that exposes a custom object.

Finally, we examined some advanced issues that you'll encounter when building Web services. We discussed how you can control the timeout value for a Web service, how you can improve the performance of a Web service through caching, and how you can create one Web reference that represents many Web services.

Creating Custom Web Form Controls

IN THIS CHAPTER

- Custom Web Form Controls Versus Web User Controls
- Overview of Custom Web Form Controls
- Creating a Simple Non-Composite Control
- Creating a Simple Composite Control
- Adding Designer Support to a Custom Web Form Control

In this chapter, you will learn how to extend the ASP.NET Framework with your own custom Web Form controls. You learn how to create the same type of controls that Microsoft developed for the ASP.NET Framework, like the TextBox and DataGrid controls.

By the end of this chapter, you'll understand how to

- Create non-composite Web Form controls that render any content that you please

- Create composite controls built from combining existing Web Form controls

- Add Designer support to your controls so that they will work well in a development environment, such as Visual Studio .NET

Custom Web Form Controls Versus Web User Controls

The ASP.NET Framework supports two methods of creating custom controls. You can create either Web User Controls or custom Web Form controls. In this section, we'll examine the question of when it's more appropriate to create one type of control rather than another.

We discussed Web User Controls in Chapter 5, "Creating Web User Controls." The primary advantage of Web User Controls is that you create a Web User Control in exactly the same way as you create a normal Web Form Page. You create a Web User Control simply by dragging and dropping controls from the Toolbox.

On the other hand, creating a custom Web Form control takes a little more work. You can't use the Visual Studio

.NET Designer when building a custom Web Form control. Instead, you must programmatically specify the content or add each control that you want to display.

The primary disadvantage of Web User Controls is that they do not provide good Designer support. When you add a Web User Control to a Web Form Page, you get a gray blob on the Designer surface that represents the control (see Figure 22.1). You must take the additional step of building and browsing the page before you can see what the page will actually look like. Furthermore, because you cannot add a Web User Control to the Toolbox, you cannot easily reuse the same Web User Control in multiple projects.

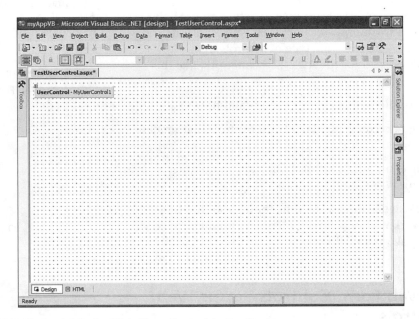

FIGURE 22.1   Adding a Web User Control to the Designer.

Custom Web Form controls, on the other hand, offer excellent Designer support. You can add a custom Web Form control to the Toolbox. Furthermore, when you drag a custom Web Form control onto a page, it appears in the same way it will appear when it is displayed in a browser.

The one area in which Web User Controls and custom Web Form controls do not differ is performance. Although the two types of controls are compiled in different ways, they are both compiled. A custom Web Form control must be manually compiled before being used. A Web User Control is dynamically compiled when the page that contains it is first requested. So, at the end of the day, there are no performance differences.

Overview of Custom Web Form Controls

When building custom Web Form controls, there are two basic questions that you must answer:

- What control should I derive from?

- Should I create a non-composite or composite control?

Let's start with the first question. When you create a new Web Form control, you must derive the new control from an existing control in the ASP.NET Framework. Typically, you derive a new control from either the Control (System.Web.UI.Control) class or the WebControl (System.Web.UI.WebControls.WebControl) class.

> **NOTE**
>
> You can create a custom Web control that derives from any existing control in the ASP.NET Framework. For example, you might want to derive a new control from the Label or DataGrid class when you want to automatically get all the functionality of the existing control.

All controls in the ASP.NET Framework, including both HTML and Web controls, ultimately derive from the Control class. Almost all of the controls in the System.Web.UI.WebControls namespace, such as the TextBox and DataGrid controls, derive from the WebControl class.

The difference between deriving from the Control and WebControl classes is support for formatting. You'll need to derive your control from the WebControl class when you want to take advantage of all the common formatting properties of Web controls. For example, if you derive from the WebControl class, you automatically get support for specifying different fonts and background colors.

To make this discussion more concrete, consider the difference between two existing controls in the ASP.NET Framework—the Label control and the Literal control. Because the Label control derives from the base WebControl class, the Label control includes properties such as the AccessKey, BackColor, and Font properties. Because the Literal control derives from the base Control class and not the base WebControl class, the Literal control does not support these properties.

In most cases, you'll derive a new custom control from the WebControl class to take advantage of these additional formatting properties. In the next section, you'll be provided with examples of controls that derive both from the base Control and the base WebControl classes.

Another decision that you must make before building a new control is whether it makes more sense to create a non-composite or composite control. When you create a non-composite control, you are responsible for specifying all the content that the control renders. When you create a composite control, you build the control out of existing controls.

A good example of a composite control is an Address Form control. You can create a new Address Form composite control by combining existing TextBox and Validation controls. In that case, you can take advantage of all the existing functionality of these controls.

On the other hand, you'll want to create a non-composite control when you need more control over what your control renders. For example, a Color Picker control that enables you to pick a color from a table of colors would be a good example of a non-composite control. We'll build both types of controls in the following sections.

Creating a Simple Non-Composite Control

A Web Form Page is really nothing more than a collection of controls. More accurately, because some controls contain other controls, a Web Form Page is a control tree.

TIP

You can view a Web Form Page's control tree by enabling Tracing for a page. To learn more about tracing, see Chapter 6, "Debugging Your Web Form Pages."

When you request a Web Form Page, the page calls the RenderControl() method of each of its child controls. The RenderControl() method checks the Visible property of the control. If Visible has the value True, the RenderControl() method calls the control's Render() method.

Consequently, if you want to control the content rendered by a control, you can override the control's Render() method. For example, Listing 22.1 contains the code for a simple control that displays Hello World!.

LISTING 22.1.CS   HelloWorld.cs

```
using System;
using System.Web.UI;

namespace myControls
{
  public class HelloWorld : System.Web.UI.Control
```

LISTING 22.1.CS   Continued

```csharp
  {
    override protected void Render(HtmlTextWriter writer)
    {
      writer.Write( "Hello World!" );
    }
  }
}
```

LISTING 22.1.VB   HelloWorld.vb

```vb
Imports System.Web.UI

Public Class HelloWorld
    Inherits System.Web.UI.Control

    Protected Overrides Sub Render(ByVal writer As HtmlTextWriter)
        writer.Write("Hello World!")
    End Sub
End Class
```

Notice that the HelloWorld control in Listing 22.1 derives from the System.Web.UI.Control class. Furthermore, the HelloWorld class overrides the Render() method and writes the value Hello World!.

The control in Listing 22.1 derives from the base Control class. This means that it does not automatically support formatting properties such as the Font and BackColor properties. If you need support for these formatting properties, you need to make two changes. You need to derive from the base WebControl class and you need to override the RenderContents() method instead of the Render() method.

The WebControl class Render() method does three things. First, the method creates an opening HTML tag; next it calls the RenderContents() method; and finally it creates the closing HTML tag. By overriding the RenderContents() method, you can place content in between the opening and closing tags created automatically by the Render() method.

The opening and closing HTML tags that are automatically created by the WebControl class Render() method add the necessary attributes to support formatting. If you override the Render() method instead of the RenderContents() method, all the automatic formatting is lost.

The control in Listing 22.2 contains the code for a simple control that derives from the base WebControl class.

LISTING 22.2.CS   HelloWorldWebControl.cs

```
using System;
using System.Web.UI;

namespace myControls
{
  public class HelloWorldWebControl : System.Web.UI.WebControls.WebControl
  {
    override protected void RenderContents(HtmlTextWriter writer)
    {
      writer.Write( "Hello World!" );
    }
  }
}
```

LISTING 22.2.VB   HelloWorldWebControl.vb

```
Imports System.Web.UI

Public Class HelloWorldWebControl
  Inherits System.Web.UI.WebControls.WebControl

  Protected Overrides Sub RenderContents(ByVal writer As HtmlTextWriter)
    writer.Write("Hello World!")
  End Sub

End Class
```

When developing controls to work in the Visual Studio .NET environment, you should normally stick with controls that derive from WebControl rather than Control. Controls that derive from the base WebControl class provide better Designer support. For example, you can absolutely position a control that derives from WebControl on the Designer surface.

Using the HtmlTextWriter Class

In the previous section, we created a simple non-composite control named the HelloWorldWebControl that displays the text Hello World!. We created the control by overriding the RenderContents() method. You might have noticed that we did not use the Response.Write() method to output the text. Instead, we used something called the HtmlTextWriter() class.

WARNING

You should never use the Response.Write() method inside a custom Web control. If you use the Response.Write() method to output a string of text, the text can appear either before or after all the page content. In other words, using Response.Write() ignores the page's control tree.

The HtmlTextWriter class has several methods that make it easier to output HTML formatted content:

- AddAttribute   Adds an HTML attribute to the tag being rendered
- AddStyleAttribute   Adds a style attribute to the tag being rendered
- RenderBeginTag   Renders an opening HTML tag
- RenderEndTag   Renders a closing HTML tag that corresponds to the last opening HTML tag
- Write   Writes arbitrary content
- WriteLine   Writes arbitrary content followed by a line terminator

For example, suppose that you need to output the text Hello World! using a green font. You could output this text using the following call to the Write method of the HtmlTextWriter class:

C#

```
writer.Write( "<font color=\"green\">Hello World!</font>" );
```

VB.NET

```
writer.Write("<font color=""green"">Hello World!</font>")
```

However, this method of writing HTML content is messy and hard to read. Instead, you can take advantage of the methods of the HtmlTextWriter class to output the text like the following:

C#

```
writer.AddAttribute( "color", "green" );
writer.RenderBeginTag( "font" );
```

```
writer.Write( "Hello World!" );
writer.RenderEndTag();
```

VB.NET

```
writer.AddAttribute("color", "green")
writer.RenderBeginTag("font")
writer.Write("Hello World!")
writer.RenderEndTag()
```

This code is easier to read. Furthermore, when you use the methods of the
HtmlTextWriter class, the rendered content is automatically indented. For example, if
you render an HTML table with the HtmlTextWriter class, the table cells are correctly
indented.

When calling the RenderBeginTag and AddAttribute methods in the previous code, we
passed a string that represents the attribute or tag to the method. Instead of passing
a string, you can pass a value from either the HtmlTextWriterTag or
HtmlTextWriterAttribute enumerations.

The HtmlTextWriterTag enumeration contains common HTML tags and the
HtmlTextWriterAttribute enumeration contains common HTML attributes. There is
also an HtmlTextWriterStyle enumeration that contains common style attributes that
can be used with the AddStyleAttribute method.

When you use the enumerations with the HtmlTextWriter methods, the
HtmlTextWriter will render different content for downlevel browsers than uplevel
browsers. Consider the following code:

```
writer.AddStyleAttribute( HtmlTextWriterStyle.BackgroundColor, "Yellow" );
writer.RenderBeginTag( HtmlTextWriterTag.Div);
writer.Write( "Hello World!" );
writer.RenderEndTag();
```

This code displays the text Hello World! within a <div> tag with a yellow background. When the HtmlTextWriter class renders this content to an uplevel browser, it
renders the following content:

```
<div style="background-color:Yellow;">
    Hello World!
</div>
```

However, when this content is rendered to a downlevel browser, the following
content is rendered:

```
<table cellpadding="0" cellspacing="0" border="0" width="100%"
bgcolor="Yellow"><tr><td>
    Hello World!
</td></tr></table>
```

Notice that the <div> tag has been automatically downgraded to a <table> tag, and the background-color attribute has been downgraded to a bgcolor attribute. When possible, you should use the enumerations so that your controls will render correctly in both uplevel and downlevel browsers.

Creating a Non-Composite Content Rotator Control

In this section, we'll tackle a more realistic sample of a non-composite control. We'll walk through each step of creating a Content Rotator control. Our Content Rotator control will randomly display one entry from an XML file named Content.xml.

Perform the following steps to create a new project for the Content Rotator control:

1. Open the New Project dialog box by selecting New from the File menu, and pointing to Project.

2. Select Web Control Library under Templates.

3. Select Close Solution under Location.

4. Name the new project **myControls** and click OK.

Next, we need to create the Content Rotator control:

C# Steps

1. Add references to the System.Data and System.XML assemblies to the myControls project by right-clicking the References folder and selecting Add Reference.

2. Add a new class named ContentRotator.cs to the myControls project by selecting Add Class from the Project menu.

3. Enter the following code for the ContentRotator.cs class:

```
using System;
using System.Data;
using System.Web;
using System.Web.UI;
using System.Web.UI.WebControls;

namespace myControls
{
    /// <summary>
    /// Summary description for ContentRotator.
```

```csharp
/// </summary>
public class ContentRotator : WebControl
{
  protected override void RenderContents(HtmlTextWriter writer)
  {
    // Don't retrieve content in Designer
    if (HttpContext.Current != null)
    {
      // Get path to content file
      string contentFile =
        HttpContext.Current.Server.MapPath( "Content.xml" );

      // Load content into dataset
      DataSet dstContent = new DataSet();
      dstContent.ReadXml( contentFile );

      // Get random entry
      Random objRan = new Random();
      DataTable dtblContent = dstContent.Tables[0];
      int intRan = objRan.Next( dtblContent.Rows.Count);

      // Render the results
      writer.Write( (string)dtblContent.Rows[intRan]["item_Text"]);
    }
    else
    {
      writer.Write( "Random Content" );
    }
  }
}
```

4. Build the myControls project by select Build myControls from the Build menu.

VB.NET Steps

1. Add a new class named **ContentRotator.vb** to the myControls project by select-ing Add Class from the Project menu.

2. Enter the following code for the ContentRotator.vb class:

```vbnet
Imports System
Imports System.Data
```

```
Imports System.Web
Imports System.Web.UI
Imports System.Web.UI.WebControls

Public Class ContentRotator
  Inherits WebControl

  Protected Overrides Sub RenderContents(ByVal writer As HtmlTextWriter)
    Dim contentFile As String
    Dim dstContent As DataSet
    Dim dtblContent As DataTable
    Dim intRan As Integer

    ' Don't retrieve content in Designer
    If Not HttpContext.Current Is Nothing Then

      ' Get path to content file
      contentFile = HttpContext.Current.Server.MapPath("Content.xml")

      ' Load content into dataset
      dstContent = New DataSet()
      dstContent.ReadXml(contentFile)

      ' Get random entry
      Dim objRan As New Random()
      dtblContent = dstContent.Tables(0)
      intRan = objRan.Next(dtblContent.Rows.Count)

      ' Render the results
      writer.Write(dtblContent.Rows(intRan)("item_Text"))
    Else
      writer.Write("Random Content")
    End If
  End Sub
End Class
```

3. Build the myControls project by select Build myControls from the Build menu.

Next, we need to create a separate project for testing our control:

1. Open the New Project dialog box by selecting New from the File menu, and pointing to Project.

2. Select ASP.NET Web Application under Templates.

3. Select Add to Solution under Location.

4. Name the new project **TestControls** and click OK.

Next, we need to add the `Content Rotator` control to the Toolbox:

1. Add a new Web Form Page to your project named **TestContentRotator.aspx**.

2. Right-click the Toolbox under the General tab and select Customize Toolbox.

3. Select the tab labeled .NET Framework Components.

4. Click the Browse button and browse to the following file:

   ```
   My Documents\Visual Studio Projects\myControls\myControls\bin\
   ➥Debug\myControls.dll
   ```

5. Click OK.

After you complete these steps, the `Content Rotator` control should appear under the General tab. Before we can test the control, we need to add a Content.xml file to the TestControls project.

1. Open the Add New Item dialog box by right-clicking the TestControls project in the Solution Explorer window and selecting Add, Add New Item. Select XML File under Templates, name the file **Content.xml** and click Open.

2. Enter the following content for the Content.xml file:

   ```
   <?xml version="1.0" encoding="utf-8" ?>
   <content>
   <item>Aliens attack!</item>
   <item>Life discovered on Mars!</item>
   <item>Moon explodes!</item>
   </content>
   ```

3. Save the changes to the Content.xml file by clicking the Save Content.xml button.

The final step is to add the control to a page and test it:

1. Drag the `Content Rotator` control onto the TestContentRotator.aspx page.

2. Right-click the TestContentRotator.aspx file in the Solution Explorer window and select Build and Browse.

Every time you click the Refresh button on your browser, a new entry from the Content.xml file will be randomly selected and displayed in the TestControl.aspx page.

There's one special thing that you should notice about the code for the Content Rotator control. The following conditional is used to check whether the Content Rotator is being displayed at design time (on the Designer surface) or at run time (when the TestControl.aspx page is executing):

C#

```
if (HttpContext.Current != null)
{
    ...
}
```

VB.NET

```
If Not HttpContext.Current Is Nothing Then
...
End If
```

When there is no HttpContext, the control is not actually being displayed in a browser. Therefore, you can use this check to skip actions that you don't want performed when manipulating the control in the Designer.

> **NOTE**
> We should really implement caching for our Content Rotator control so that we can cache the Content.xml file in memory. The best way to implement the caching would be to create a file dependency on the Content.xml file. To learn more about creating file dependencies, see Chapter 14, "Improving Application Performance with Caching."

Creating a Simple Composite Control

A composite control enables you to reuse existing controls in a new control. For example, you can create a new Address Form composite control by combining together exiting TextBox and Validation controls.

When we created our non-composite control in the previous section, we overrode the RenderContents() method. When you create a composite control, on the other hand, you typically override the CreateChildControls() method.

Every control in the ASP.NET Framework has a Controls collection. The Controls collection contains all of a control's child controls. For example, the Controls collection of an Address Form control would include TextBox and Validation controls.

The `CreateChildControls()` method is responsible for creating all the controls contained in the `Controls` collection. When you override this method, you add each of a control's child controls using logic that looks like the following:

C#

```
protected override void CreateChildControls()
{
  // Add Street TextBox
  TextBox txtStreet = new TextBox();
  txtStreet.ID = "txtStreet";
  Controls.Add( txtStreet );
}
```

VB.NET

```
Protected Overrides Sub CreateChildControls()
  ' Add Street TextBox
  Dim txtStreet As New TextBox()
  txtStreet.ID = "txtStreet"
  Controls.Add(txtStreet)
End Sub
```

This code adds a `TextBox` to the `Controls` collection. You can add any control you need—including `Repeater`, `DropDownLists`, and `DataGrid` controls—by tossing it into the `Controls` collection.

There is an important method that works with the `CreateChildControls` method called the `EnsureChildControls()` method. The `EnsureChildControls()` method calls the `CreateChildControls()` method. However, it is guaranteed to call the `CreateChildControls()` method only once. You can safely call the `EnsureChildControls` method over and over again without worrying about the `Controls` collection being re-created.

You need to call the `EnsureChildControls()` method within your control before accessing any child controls. For example, suppose that the `Address Form` control has a property named `Street` that returns the current value of the txtStreet text box:

C#

```
public string Street
{
  get
  {
    EnsureChildControls();
    return txtStreet.Text;
```

```
  }
}
```

VB.NET

```
Public ReadOnly Property Street() As String
  Get
    EnsureChildControls()
    Return txtStreet.Text
  End Get
End Property
```

If you neglect to include `EnsureChildControls()` in the `Street` property, you would receive a Null Reference Exception. You would receive a Null Reference Exception because the child `txtStreet` text box would not have been created yet.

The `CreateChildControls()` method is unique in that you don't know exactly when it will be called. It could be called whenever someone happens to read a property of your control. If the `CreateChildControls()` method is not called before a control's `PreRender()` method is called, the `CreateChildControls()` method is called automatically at that point.

Using the `INamingContainer` Interface

When implementing a composite control, you should always implement the `INamingContainer` interface. This interface is a marker interface. This means that it doesn't actually have any methods that you must override.

> **NOTE**
>
> The `INamingContainer` interface is in the `System.Web.UI` namespace, so you'll need to import this namespace when implementing the interface.

You can implement the `INamingContainer` interface when declaring a control like the following:

C#

```
public class AddressForm : WebControl, INamingContainer
{
  ...
}
```

VB.NET

```
Public Class AddressForm
    Inherits WebControl
```

```
    Implements INamingContainer
  ...
End Class
```

The INamingContainer interface creates a new namespace for your control. You need to implement this interface when developing composite controls to prevent ID naming collisions.

For example, if you don't implement this interface in the case of the AddressForm control, the values of any TextBox controls contained within AddressForm control will not be retained across postbacks. The framework would not be able to assign the values to the TextBox controls because it would not be able to resolve the IDs of the TextBox controls.

Using Render with Composite Controls

When you create a composite control, you override the CreateChildControls() method. You use the CreateChildControls() method to specify all the child controls of the composite control.

However, typically, you'll also want to override the Render() method of a composite control. You'll use the Render() method to lay out the controls that you create in the CreateChildControls() method.

For example, when creating an AddressForm control, you'll normally want to lay out the TextBox and Validation controls within an HTML table. That way, all the controls are not bunched together haphazardly on the page.

Listing 22.3 illustrates how you use both the CreateChildControls() and the Render() method for the AddressForm control.

LISTING 22.3.CS   Partial AddressForm.cs
```
private TextBox txtStreet;
private TextBox txtCity;

protected override void CreateChildControls()
{
  // Clear child controls
  Controls.Clear();

  // Add Street TextBox
  txtStreet = new TextBox();
  txtStreet.ID = "txtStreet";
  Controls.Add( txtStreet );
```

LISTING 22.3.CS   Continued

```csharp
  // Add City TextBox
  txtCity = new TextBox();
  txtCity.ID = "txtState";
  Controls.Add( txtCity );
}

protected override void Render(HtmlTextWriter writer)
{
  // Add WebControl Formatting
  AddAttributesToRender(writer);

  // Open table
  writer.AddAttribute(HtmlTextWriterAttribute.Border, "1");
  writer.AddAttribute(HtmlTextWriterAttribute.Cellpadding, "4");
  writer.RenderBeginTag( HtmlTextWriterTag.Table);

  // Create first row
  writer.RenderBeginTag( HtmlTextWriterTag.Tr);
  writer.RenderBeginTag( HtmlTextWriterTag.Td);
  writer.Write( "Street:" );
  writer.RenderEndTag();
  writer.RenderBeginTag( HtmlTextWriterTag.Td);
  txtStreet.RenderControl(writer);
  writer.RenderEndTag();
  writer.RenderEndTag();

  // Create second row
  writer.RenderBeginTag( HtmlTextWriterTag.Tr);
  writer.RenderBeginTag( HtmlTextWriterTag.Td);
  writer.Write( "City:" );
  writer.RenderEndTag();
  writer.RenderBeginTag( HtmlTextWriterTag.Td);
  txtCity.RenderControl(writer);
  writer.RenderEndTag();
  writer.RenderEndTag();

  // Close table
  writer.RenderEndTag();
}
```

LISTING 22.3.VB   Partial AddressForm.vb

```vb
Dim txtStreet As TextBox
Dim txtCity As TextBox


Protected Overrides Sub CreateChildControls()
  ' Clear child controls
  Controls.Clear()

  ' Add Street TextBox
      txtStreet = New TextBox()
      txtStreet.ID = "txtStreet"
      Controls.Add(txtStreet)

      ' Add City TextBox
      txtCity = New TextBox()
      txtCity.ID = "txtState"
      Controls.Add(txtCity)
    End Sub

    Protected Overrides Sub Render(ByVal writer As HtmlTextWriter)

      ' Add WebControl Formatting
      AddAttributesToRender(writer)

      ' Open table
      writer.AddAttribute(HtmlTextWriterAttribute.Border, "1")
      writer.AddAttribute(HtmlTextWriterAttribute.Cellpadding, "4")
      writer.RenderBeginTag(HtmlTextWriterTag.Table)

      ' Create first row
      writer.RenderBeginTag(HtmlTextWriterTag.Tr)
      writer.RenderBeginTag(HtmlTextWriterTag.Td)
      writer.Write("Street:")
      writer.RenderEndTag()
      writer.RenderBeginTag(HtmlTextWriterTag.Td)
      txtStreet.RenderControl(writer)
      writer.RenderEndTag()
      writer.RenderEndTag()

      ' Create second row
      writer.RenderBeginTag(HtmlTextWriterTag.Tr)
```

LISTING 22.3.VB   Continued

```
        writer.RenderBeginTag(HtmlTextWriterTag.Td)
        writer.Write("City:")
        writer.RenderEndTag()
        writer.RenderBeginTag(HtmlTextWriterTag.Td)
        txtCity.RenderControl(writer)
        writer.RenderEndTag()
        writer.RenderEndTag()

        ' Close table
        writer.RenderEndTag()
    End Sub
```

Notice that the `txtStreet` and `txtCity` TextBox controls are created in the `CreateChildControls()` method. However, they are actually rendered within the `Render()` method by calling `txtStreet.RenderControl(writer)` and `txtCity.RenderControl(writer)`.

You don't need to include a `Render()` method in a composite control. If you leave it out, each of the controls created in the `CreateChildControls()` method will be automatically rendered. However, the `Render()` method provides you with access to the `HtmlTextWriter` class that makes it easier to layout the controls contained in a composite control.

Composite Controls and Designer Support

When you create a non-composite control and add the control to the Visual Studio .NET Designer, you see exactly what will be displayed by the control when the control is displayed in a Web Form Page. In other words, whatever is rendered by a non-composite control at design time is exactly the same as whatever is rendered by the control at runtime.

By default, this is not true in the case of a composite control. You have to perform some additional work to get a composite control to look the same at design time as it does at runtime. I'm giving you this warning now so that you are not surprised when the composite control that we create in the next section does not appear correctly in the Designer.

The extra work involves creating something called a `ControlDesigner`. You can use a `ControlDesigner` with both composite and non-composite controls to specify how a control will appear at design time. We'll discuss the `ControlDesigner` designer class later in this chapter in the "Using the `ControlDesigner` Class" section.

Creating a Composite Address Form Control

We've discussed pieces of the AddressForm control. In this section, we are going to put everything together and build the AddressForm composite control from start to finish (see Figure 22.2).

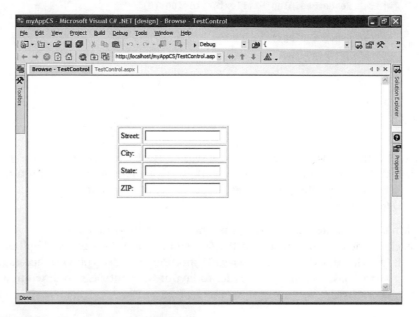

FIGURE 22.2   The AddressForm control.

Let's start by creating a new Control Library project:

1. Open the New Project dialog box by selecting New from the File menu and pointing to Project.

2. Select Web Control Library under Templates.

3. Select Close Solution under Location.

4. Name the new project **myCompositeControls** and click OK.

Next, we need to create the AddressForm control:

C# Steps

1. Add a new class named **AddressForm.cs** to the myCompositeControls project by selecting Add Class from the Project menu.

2. Enter the following code for the AddressForm.cs class:

```csharp
using System;
using System.Web.UI;
using System.Web.UI.WebControls;

namespace myCompositeControls
{
    public class AddressForm : WebControl, INamingContainer
    {
        private TextBox txtStreet;
        private TextBox txtCity;
        private TextBox txtState;
        private TextBox txtZip;
        private RequiredFieldValidator valStreet;
        private RequiredFieldValidator valCity;
        private RequiredFieldValidator valState;
        private RequiredFieldValidator valZip;

        public string Street
        {
            get
            {
                EnsureChildControls();
                return txtStreet.Text;
            }
        }

        public string City
        {
            get
            {
                EnsureChildControls();
                return txtCity.Text;
            }
        }
        public string State
        {
            get
            {
                EnsureChildControls();
                return txtState.Text;
            }
        }
```

```csharp
public string Zip
{
    get
    {
        EnsureChildControls();
        return txtZip.Text;
    }
}

public override ControlCollection Controls
{
    get
    {
        EnsureChildControls();
        return base.Controls;
    }
}

protected override void CreateChildControls()
{
    // Clear child controls
    Controls.Clear();

    // Add Street TextBox
    txtStreet = new TextBox();
    txtStreet.ID = "txtStreet";
    Controls.Add( txtStreet );

    // Add Street Validation
    valStreet = new RequiredFieldValidator();
    valStreet.ControlToValidate = "txtStreet";
    valStreet.Text = "*";
    Controls.Add( valStreet );

    // Add City TextBox
    txtCity = new TextBox();
    txtCity.ID = "txtCity";
    Controls.Add( txtCity );

    // Add City Validation
    valCity = new RequiredFieldValidator();
    valCity.ControlToValidate = "txtCity";
```

```csharp
        valCity.Text = "*";
        Controls.Add( valCity );

        // Add State TextBox
        txtState = new TextBox();
        txtState.ID = "txtState";
        Controls.Add( txtState );

        // Add State Validation
        valState = new RequiredFieldValidator();
        valState.ControlToValidate = "txtState";
        valState.Text = "*";
        Controls.Add( valState );

        // Add Zip TextBox
        txtZip = new TextBox();
        txtZip.ID = "txtZip";
        Controls.Add( txtZip );

        // Add State Validation
        valZip = new RequiredFieldValidator();
        valZip.ControlToValidate = "txtZip";
        valZip.Text = "*";
        Controls.Add( valZip );
    }

    protected override void Render(HtmlTextWriter writer)
    {
        // Add WebControl Formatting
        AddAttributesToRender(writer);

        // Open table
        writer.AddAttribute(HtmlTextWriterAttribute.Border, "1");
        writer.AddAttribute(HtmlTextWriterAttribute.Cellpadding,
➥"4");

        writer.RenderBeginTag( HtmlTextWriterTag.Table);

        // Create first row
        writer.RenderBeginTag( HtmlTextWriterTag.Tr);
        writer.RenderBeginTag( HtmlTextWriterTag.Td);
        writer.Write( "Street:" );
        writer.RenderEndTag();
```

```
writer.RenderBeginTag( HtmlTextWriterTag.Td);
txtStreet.RenderControl(writer);
valStreet.RenderControl(writer);
writer.RenderEndTag();
writer.RenderEndTag();

// Create second row
writer.RenderBeginTag( HtmlTextWriterTag.Tr);
writer.RenderBeginTag( HtmlTextWriterTag.Td);
writer.Write( "City:" );
writer.RenderEndTag();
writer.RenderBeginTag( HtmlTextWriterTag.Td);
txtCity.RenderControl(writer);
valCity.RenderControl(writer);
writer.RenderEndTag();
writer.RenderEndTag();

// Create third row
writer.RenderBeginTag( HtmlTextWriterTag.Tr);
writer.RenderBeginTag( HtmlTextWriterTag.Td);
writer.Write( "State:" );
writer.RenderEndTag();
writer.RenderBeginTag( HtmlTextWriterTag.Td);
txtState.RenderControl(writer);
valState.RenderControl(writer);
writer.RenderEndTag();
writer.RenderEndTag();

// Create fourth row
writer.RenderBeginTag( HtmlTextWriterTag.Tr);
writer.RenderBeginTag( HtmlTextWriterTag.Td);
writer.Write( "ZIP:" );
writer.RenderEndTag();
writer.RenderBeginTag( HtmlTextWriterTag.Td);
txtZip.RenderControl(writer);
valZip.RenderControl(writer);
writer.RenderEndTag();
writer.RenderEndTag();

// Close table
writer.RenderEndTag();
}
```

```
        }
    }
```

3. Build the myCompositeControls project by selecting Build
   myCompositeControls from the Build menu.

VB.NET Steps

1. Add a new class named **AddressForm.vb** to the myCompositeControls project by
   selecting Add Class from the Project menu.

2. Enter the following code for the AddressForm.vb class:

```vbnet
Imports System
Imports System.Web.UI
Imports System.Web.UI.WebControls


Public Class AddressForm
    Inherits WebControl
    Implements INamingContainer

    Private txtStreet As TextBox
    Private txtCity As TextBox
    Private txtState As TextBox
    Private txtZip As TextBox
    Private valStreet As RequiredFieldValidator
    Private valCity As RequiredFieldValidator
    Private valState As RequiredFieldValidator
    Private valZip As RequiredFieldValidator

    Public ReadOnly Property Street() As String
        Get
            EnsureChildControls()
            Return txtStreet.Text
        End Get
    End Property


    Public ReadOnly Property City() As String

        Get
```

```
        EnsureChildControls()
        Return txtCity.Text
    End Get
End Property


Public ReadOnly Property State() As String

    Get

        EnsureChildControls()
        Return txtState.Text
    End Get
End Property


Public ReadOnly Property Zip() As String
    Get

        EnsureChildControls()
        Return txtZip.Text
    End Get
End Property


Public Overrides ReadOnly Property Controls() As ControlCollection
    Get
        EnsureChildControls()
        Return MyBase.Controls
    End Get
End Property


Protected Overrides Sub CreateChildControls()
    ' Clear child controls
    Controls.Clear()

    ' Add Street TextBox
    txtStreet = New TextBox()
    txtStreet.ID = "txtStreet"
    Controls.Add(txtStreet)

    ' Add Street Validation
    valStreet = New RequiredFieldValidator()
    valStreet.ControlToValidate = "txtStreet"
```

```vbnet
        valStreet.Text = "*"
        Controls.Add(valStreet)

        ' Add City TextBox
        txtCity = New TextBox()
        txtCity.ID = "txtCity"
        Controls.Add(txtCity)

        ' Add City Validation
        valCity = New RequiredFieldValidator()
        valCity.ControlToValidate = "txtCity"
        valCity.Text = "*"
        Controls.Add(valCity)

        ' Add State TextBox
        txtState = New TextBox()
        txtState.ID = "txtState"
        Controls.Add(txtState)

        ' Add State Validation
        valState = New RequiredFieldValidator()
        valState.ControlToValidate = "txtState"
        valState.Text = "*"
        Controls.Add(valState)

        ' Add Zip TextBox
        txtZip = New TextBox()
        txtZip.ID = "txtZip"
        Controls.Add(txtZip)

        ' Add State Validation
        valZip = New RequiredFieldValidator()
        valZip.ControlToValidate = "txtZip"
        valZip.Text = "*"
        Controls.Add(valZip)
    End Sub

    Protected Overrides Sub Render(ByVal writer As HtmlTextWriter)
        ' Add WebControl Formatting
        AddAttributesToRender(writer)

        ' Open table
```

```
writer.AddAttribute(HtmlTextWriterAttribute.Border, "1")
writer.AddAttribute(HtmlTextWriterAttribute.Cellpadding, "4")
writer.RenderBeginTag(HtmlTextWriterTag.Table)

' Create first row
writer.RenderBeginTag(HtmlTextWriterTag.Tr)
writer.RenderBeginTag(HtmlTextWriterTag.Td)
writer.Write("Street:")
writer.RenderEndTag()
writer.RenderBeginTag(HtmlTextWriterTag.Td)
txtStreet.RenderControl(writer)
valStreet.RenderControl(writer)
writer.RenderEndTag()
writer.RenderEndTag()

' Create second row
writer.RenderBeginTag(HtmlTextWriterTag.Tr)
writer.RenderBeginTag(HtmlTextWriterTag.Td)
writer.Write("City:")
writer.RenderEndTag()
writer.RenderBeginTag(HtmlTextWriterTag.Td)
txtCity.RenderControl(writer)
valCity.RenderControl(writer)
writer.RenderEndTag()
writer.RenderEndTag()

' Create third row
writer.RenderBeginTag(HtmlTextWriterTag.Tr)
writer.RenderBeginTag(HtmlTextWriterTag.Td)
writer.Write("State:")
writer.RenderEndTag()
writer.RenderBeginTag(HtmlTextWriterTag.Td)
txtState.RenderControl(writer)
valState.RenderControl(writer)
writer.RenderEndTag()
writer.RenderEndTag()

' Create fourth row
writer.RenderBeginTag(HtmlTextWriterTag.Tr)
writer.RenderBeginTag(HtmlTextWriterTag.Td)
writer.Write("ZIP:")
writer.RenderEndTag()
```

```
            writer.RenderBeginTag(HtmlTextWriterTag.Td)
            txtZip.RenderControl(writer)
            valZip.RenderControl(writer)
            writer.RenderEndTag()
            writer.RenderEndTag()

            ' Close table
            writer.RenderEndTag()
        End Sub
End Class
```

3. Build the myCompositeControls project by selecting Build myCompositeControls from the Build menu.

Next, we need to create a separate project for testing our control:

1. Open the New Project dialog box by selecting New from the File menu and pointing to Project.

2. Select ASP.NET Web Application under Templates.

3. Select Add to Solution under Location.

4. Name the new project **TestCompositeControls** and click OK.

Next, we need to add the Address Form control to the Toolbox:

1. Add a new Web Form Page to your project named **TestAddressForm.aspx**.

2. Right-click the Toolbox under the General tab and select Customize Toolbox.

3. Select the .NET Framework Components tab.

4. Click the Browse button and browse to the following file:

```
My Documents\Visual Studio Projects\myCompositeControls\
➥myCompositeControls\bin\Debug\myCompositeControls.dll
```

5. Click OK.

After you complete these steps, the Address Form control should appear under the General tab. We are finally ready to test out the control:

1. Drag the Address Form control onto the TestAddressForm.aspx page.

2. Right-click the TestAddressForm.aspx page in the Solution Explorer window and select Build and Browse.

When the TestAddressForm.aspx page opens, you can enter address information into the control. Notice that each text box is validated with a RequiredFieldValidator. You can retrieve the entries in the Address Form control by using the Street, City, State, and Zip properties of the control.

> **NOTE**
>
> Notice that you can format the Address Form control from the Properties window. For example, you can modify its background color. We get these formatting properties automatically because the Address Form control derives from the base WebControl class.

Adding Designer Support to a Custom Web Form Control

The primary advantage of creating custom Web Form controls instead of Web User Controls is that custom Web Form controls provide better Designer support. You can add custom Web Form controls to the Toolbox, you can modify the properties of custom Web Form controls in the Properties window, and you can see the content rendered by custom Web Form controls during design time.

In this section, you'll learn how to take control over the appearance of custom controls in the Visual Studio .NET environment. First, we'll look at the special attributes that you can apply to a custom control. Next, we'll look at how you can customize the appearance of a custom control in the Toolbox. Finally, you'll learn how to take advantage of ControlDesigners to take control over the appearance of your control on the Designer surface.

Using Design-Time Attributes

There are a number of special design-time attributes that you can apply to your control. For example, you can use the DefaultProperty attribute to specify the property that is selected by default in the Properties window when you click a control. The following is a list of the most important design attributes that you can apply at the class, property, or event level:

- Bindable   Contains a Boolean value that indicates whether a property can be used for binding

- Browsable   Contains a Boolean value that determines whether a property or event appears in the Properties window

- Category   Contains a string value that determines the category associated with a property or event

- DefaultEvent   Contains a string value that specifies the default event associated with a control

- `DefaultProperty`   Contains a string value that represents the property that is selected by default in the Properties window

- `DefaultValue`   Contains an object that represents the default value for a property

- `Description`   Contains a string value that determines the help text associated with a property or event at the bottom of the Properties window

- `Editor`   Contains the name and type of the editor used for editing the value of a property in the Designer

- `ToolboxData`   Contains a string that specifies the tag generated for a control when the control is dragged onto the Designer surface

- `TypeConverter`   Contains a string or type that specifies a type converter used for converting the value of a property into a form that can be persisted

For example, the control in Listing 22.4 uses several of these attributes to determine its appearance in the Visual Studio .NET Designer.

LISTING 22.4.CS   myControl.cs

```
using System;
using System.Web.UI;
using System.Web.UI.WebControls;
using System.ComponentModel;

namespace myControls
{
  [DefaultProperty("Text"),
  ToolboxData("<{0}:myControl runat=server></{0}:myControl>")]
  public class myControl : System.Web.UI.WebControls.WebControl
  {
    private string text;

    [Bindable(true),
    Category("Appearance"),
    Description("The text this control displays")]
    public string Text
    {
      get
      {
        return text;
      }
```

LISTING 22.4.CS   Continued

```csharp
    set
    {
      text = value;
    }
  }

  protected override void Render(HtmlTextWriter output)
  {
    output.Write(Text);
  }
 }
}
```

LISTING 22.4.VB   myControl.vb

```vb
Imports System.Web.UI
Imports System.Web.UI.WebControls
Imports System.ComponentModel

<DefaultProperty("Text"), _
ToolboxData("<{0}:myControl runat=server></{0}:myControl>")> _
Public Class myControl
    Inherits System.Web.UI.WebControls.WebControl

    Private _text As String

    <Bindable(True), _
    Category("Appearance"), _
    Description("The text this control displays")> _
      Public Property Text() As String
        Get

            Return _text
        End Get

        Set(ByVal Value As String)

            _text = Value
        End Set
```

LISTING 22.4.VB   Continued

```
    End Property

    Protected Overrides Sub Render(ByVal output As HtmlTextWriter)
        output.Write(_text)
    End Sub
End Class
```

There is another design-time attribute that applies at the assembly level instead of the class, property, or event level. The TagPrefix attribute enables you to specify the tag that appears when your control is declared on a page.

By default, the first control added to a page appears with the tag prefix cc1, the second cc2, and so on. If you want to provide a more descriptive tag prefix, you need to assign a value to the TagPrefix attribute.

When you create a new Web Control Library project, a file is automatically added to your project named AssemblyInfo.cs or AssemblyInfo.vb. You need to add the TagPrefix attribute to this file. You can add the following attribute anywhere in this file:

C#

```
[assembly: System.Web.UI.TagPrefix("myControls","Super")]
```

VB.NET

```
<Assembly: System.Web.UI.TagPrefix("myControls", "Super")>
```

The first parameter, myControls, refers to the namespace. Typically, this will be the same name as your project. The second parameter, Super, is the tag prefix generated when you add a control to a page.

Controlling the Appearance of a Custom Control in the Toolbox

When you add a custom Web control to the Toolbox, it appears with an icon of a gear by default. You can create your own 16×16 pixel bitmap image to customize this icon.

1. Open the Image Editor by right-clicking the project that contains your custom control in the Solution Explorer window and selecting Add New Item from the Add menu. Select the Bitmap File template. *Make sure that you named the Bitmap image with the same name as your control* and click Open.

2. In the Properties window, set the Width and Height properties to the value **16**.

3. Use the Image Editor tool to draw an appropriate image for your control.

4. Click the Save button to save your image.

5. In the Solution Explorer window, select your image.

6. In the Properties window, assign the value **Embedded Resource** to the Build Action property.

7. Build your project by selecting Build *Project Name* from the Build menu.

After you complete these steps, you might need to remove and re-add the control to the Toolbox for the changes to appear.

Using the `ControlDesigner` Class

If you want your control to appear differently in the Visual Studio .NET Designer than it appears at runtime, you can use the `ControlDesigner` class to specify a design-time appearance for your control.

The `ControlDesigner` class has a method called `GetDesignTimeHtml()` that you can override to specify the design-time appearance of a control. This method simply returns a string that is used for rendering the control in the Designer. After you create a `ControlDesigner`, you associate it with a control by using the `Designer` attribute.

For example, the `ControlDesigner` in Listing 22.5 renders the text Hello World!.

LISTING 22.5.CS   myControlDesigner.cs

```
using System;
using System.Web.UI.Design;

namespace myControls
{
  public class myControlDesigner : ControlDesigner
  {
    public override string GetDesignTimeHtml()
    {
      return "Hello World!";
    }
  }
}
```

LISTING 22.5.VB   myControlDesigner.vb

```vb
Imports System.Web.UI.Design

Public Class myControlDesigner
    Inherits ControlDesigner

    Public Overrides Function GetDesignTimeHTML() As String
        Return "Hello World!"
    End Function
End Class
```

You can associate the ControlDesigner in Listing 22.5 with a control by adding the following attribute to the declaration of a control class:

C#

```csharp
[System.ComponentModel.Designer(typeof(myControlDesigner))]
public class myControl : WebControl, INamingContainer
{
  ...
}
```

VB.NET

```vb
<System.ComponentModel.Designer(GetType(myControlDesigner))> _
Public Class myControl
  ...
End Class
```

> **WARNING**
>
> The ControlDesigner class is part of the System.Web.UI.Design namespace. This namespace is located in an assembly that is not one of the default assemblies referenced in a project. You must add a reference to the System.Design.dll assembly before using the ControlDesigner class.

You can create a ControlDesigner for any type of control. However, you'll almost always want to associate a ControlDesigner class with a composite control because a composite control does not appear correctly in the Designer.

For example, earlier in this chapter, we created an Address Form composite control. To get the Address Form control to appear correctly in the Designer, do the following:

C# Steps

1. Add a new class to the myCompositeControls project named **AddressFormDesigner.cs**.

2. Add a new reference to the System.Design assembly to your project by right-clicking the References folder, selecting Add Reference, and selecting System.Design.dll.

3. Add a new class to your project named **AddressFormDesigner**.

4. Enter the following code for the AddressFormDesigner class:

```csharp
using System;
using System.Web.UI;
using System.Web.UI.Design;

namespace myControls
{
  public class AddressFormDesigner : ControlDesigner
  {
    public override string GetDesignTimeHtml()
    {
    ControlCollection AddressFormControls = ((Control)Component).Controls;
    return base.GetDesignTimeHtml();
    }
  }
}
```

5. Modify the AddressForm control by adding the following attribute before the class declaration:

```csharp
[System.ComponentModel.Designer(typeof(AddressFormDesigner))]
```

6. Rebuild the Solution by selecting Build Solution from the Build menu.

VB.NET Steps

1. Add a new class to the myCompositeControls project named **AddressFormDesigner.vb**.

2. Add a new reference to the System.Design assembly to your project by right-clicking the References folder, selecting Add Reference, and selecting System.Design.dll.

3. Add a new class to your project named **AddressFormDesigner**.

4. Enter the following code for the AddressFormDesigner class:

```
Imports System.Web.UI.Design
Imports System.Web.UI

Public Class AddressFormDesigner
    Inherits ControlDesigner

    Public Overrides Function GetDesignTimeHTML() As String
        Dim AddressFormControls As ControlCollection

        AddressFormControls = CType(Component, Control).Controls
        Return MyBase.GetDesignTimeHtml()
    End Function
End Class
```

5. Modify the AddressForm control by adding the following attribute before the class declaration:

```
<System.ComponentModel.Designer(GetType(AddressFormDesigner))> _
```

6. Rebuild the Solution by selecting Build Solution from the Build menu.

The important part of the AddressFormDesigner is the following line of code:

C#

```
ControlCollection AddressFormControls = ((Control)Component).Controls;
```

VB.NET

```
AddressFormControls = CType(Component, Control).Controls
```

The ControlDesigner class automatically creates the Component variable. It represents the AddressForm control. Consequently, this line of code retrieves the Controls collection from the AddressForm control.

When we created the AddressForm control, we overrode the Controls property to include a call to the EnsureChildControls() method. Therefore, because the AddressFormDesigner accesses the Controls collection, the AddressForm control is forced to create its child controls and render correctly in the Visual Studio .NET Designer.

Summary

In this chapter, you learned how to create custom Web Form controls that work in the Visual Studio .NET environment. In the first section, you learned how to create non-composite controls. We created a simple `Content Rotator` control that randomly retrieves content items from an XML file.

Next, we examined the topic of composite controls. You learn how to use composite controls to bundle together the functionality of existing controls in a new control. We create a simple `Address Form` composite control.

Finally, we looked at methods for controlling the appearance of a custom control in the Visual Studio .NET environment. You learned how to use design-time attributes, modify the appearance of a control in the Toolbox, and create a custom `ControlDesigner`.

Index

A

AccessKey property, Web controls, 105

Add Style Rule dialog box, 80

address Web User Control, 144-147

AddressForm control, 576-586

ADO.NET
 classes, 204
  specialized sets, 204
 Command object, 231
  parameters, 237-238
 data access models, DataSets compared to DataReaders, 205
 DataAdapters, overview, 208
 databases, connections, 206-207
 DataReaders, 220
  displaying database data, 220-223
 DataSets
  caching in memory, 223-228
  DataGrid control, 209-211
  displaying all rows, 211, 213
  DataViews, 218-219
  overview, 208
  Typed, 213-217
 OleCommand object
  creating, 235, 237
  parameters, 241-244
 relation views compared to XML views, 205
 SqlCommand object
  creating, 232-234
  parameters, 238-241

alignment
 Flow layout mode, 55
 Grid layout mode, 57-59

Allow Paging property (DataGrid control), 348

allowDefinition attribute (Machine.Config file), 410

AlternatingItemStyle (DataGrid control), 331

AlternatingItemTemplate, 291, 306

annotations, database diagrams, 196

application logic, adding to Web Form Pages, 85

Application State, 452-453

application tracing, 171-172

applications
 building
  overview, 153-154
  Release mode, 155
 configuration file, Machine.Config file, 396
 deployment
  checklist, 489-490
  overview, 487-489
  Web Setup Project, 490-493
  Web Setup Project, modifying properties, 493-494
  Web Setup Project, modifying user interface, 494-496
 Error event handling, 457-459
 errors, displaying, 157
 migrating to Visual Studio .NET, 14-15
 multi-tiered, creating, 518-521
 state
  Application State, 452-453
  Cookieless Session State, 450-451
  customizing View State, 443-444
  disabling View State, 441-442
  out-of-process Session State, configuring, 448
  out-of-process Session State, storing in SQL Server database, 449-450
  out-of-process Session State, storing in Windows service, 448-449

protecting View State, 444-445
Session State, 445-446
View State, 439-441
upgrading to Visual Studio .NET, 15-16

Application_AuthenticateRequest event handler (Global.asax file), 456

Application_BeginRequest event handler (Global.asax file), 456, 459-460

Application_End event handler (Global.asax file), 456

Application_Error event handler (Global.asax file), 456

Application_ResolveRequestCache event handler (Global.asax file), 464-466

Application_Start event handler (Global.asax file), 456

Application_UpdateRequestCache event handler (Global.asax file), 464-466

<appSettings> section (Machine.Config file), 397
 custom configuration information, 405-407

attributes
 text areas, 67
 WebMethod, 535

authentication
 compared to authorization, 414
 cookieless authentication modules, creating, 467-478
 Forms Authentication, 413
  cookies, 414
  custom roles, 434-437
  database tables and, 425-429
  enabling, 416-418
  login page, creating, 418-421
  registration pages, 430-434
  Sign Out link, creating, 422-423

usernames, retrieving, 421-422
Web.Config files, 414-416
FrontPage Server Extensions, 14
<authentication> section (Machine.Config file), 401
<authentication> section (Web.Config file), 414, 416
authorization
compared to authentication, 414
unauthorized users, redirecting, 415
<authorization> section (Machine.Config file), 401
<authorization> section (Web.Config file), 416
Auto Format dialog box, 308, 330
auto formatting, DataGrid control, 330-331
auto hide windows, enabling/disabling, 19
autoEventWireup attribute (Machine.Config file), 400
automatic code documentation, 43-44
automatic formatting, HTML View, 74-76
automatic statement completion, HTML View, 73
AutoPostBack property
list controls, 269-271
Web server controls, 101-102
Autos window, 160

B

BackColor property, Web controls, 105
background properties, HTML pages, 62-63
bin directory, making writeable, 156
BindGrid( ) method
caching records, 341
dividing records into pages, 346
sorting records, 339
Template Columns, 364
Block Format options, 61

bookmarks
adding to HTML pages, 65-66
Code and Text Editor, 35
BorderColor property, Web controls, 105
borders, DataList control, formatting, 307
BorderStyle property, Web controls, 105
BorderWidth property, Web controls, 105
breakpoints, adding, 158
Breakpoints window, 160
browser-dependent display of cached pages, 378-382
<browserCaps> section (Machine.Config file), 404
browsers
cookies, Forms Authentication, 414
HTML pages, specifying target, 50-51
buffer attribute (Machine.Config file), 399
Build and Browse option, 154
Build menu options, 89
building. See also compiling
Web Form Pages, 86
Web Forms applications overview, 153-154
Release mode, 155
button controls, 94-95
HTML pages, adding to, 69
Web Form Pages, adding to, 149-150

C

C# programming language
application logic, adding to Web Forms, 85
Code Editor, launching, 9
Cache object
DataSets and, 223-228
sorting records and, 341
caching
adding/removing items, 387-389
data objects, 386-387
expiration policies, 392-393
file dependencies, 389-392, 569

item priorities, 393
monitoring cache, 387
OutputCache directive, 374
specifying cache location, 382
VaryByCustom attribute, 380-382
VaryByHeader attribute, 378-380
VaryByParam attribute, 375-377
Page Output Caching, 373
enabling, 374-375
paging navigation (DataGrid control), 349-350
Partial Page Caching, 382
properties, 386
VaryByControl attribute, 385
Web User controls, 383-385
records, DataGrid control, 341-342
updating controls in cached pages, VaryByParam attribute, 377
Web method output, 552-553
camel casing, 397
CancelCommand event handler
Template Columns, 365
updating database tables, 353-354
capitalization, in Machine.Config file, 397
case sensitivity, Machine.Config file and, 397
check boxes, adding to HTML pages, 68
CheckBoxList control, 261
populating, 276
CheckPassword stored procedure, 429
child controls, adding to Repeater control, 297-301
classes
ADO.NET, 204
specialized sets, 204
compared to components, 503-505
HttpModule
cookieless authentication modules, 467-478
event handling, 466-467
performance logging modules, 478-485

OleDb compared to SqlClient, 204

Web services, 535

client-side script event handlers (HTML pages), 77-79

client-side scripts, debugging, 163-164

<clientTarget> section (Machine.Config file), 404

Clipboard Ring tab (Toolbox), 25

Code and Text Editor, 30

customizing, 36
  fonts, 37
  selecting Tabbed Documents or MDI mode, 36

documenting code automatically, 43-44

enabling full-screen mode, 39

enabling line numbering, 38

IntelliSense, 30-33

navigation
  bookmarks, 35
  definitions, 33
  line numbers, 33
  Navigation Bar, 33
  searching for text, 34

outlining code, 35-36

Task List window, 39, 41
  adding comments, 41-42
  adding shortcuts, 43
  adding user comments, 42
  displaying tasks, 41
  tracking code errors, 42

Code Editor, launching, 9

code files, opening, 30

code-behind files

compiling, 156-157

Web Form Pages, 86

cols attribute (text areas), 67

columns

DataGrid control, 331-333

hyperlinked, displaying with DataGrid control, 334-338

database tables, selecting for display, 329

Command class, 204

Command object, 231

parameters, 237-238

comments

adding to task lists, 41-42

user, adding to task lists, 42

CompareValidator control, 117, 124-126

compatibility

migrating applications to Visual Studio .NET, 14-15

upgrading applications to Visual Studio .NET, 15-16

Visual Database Tools, 177-178

compilation errors, 157

<compilation> section (Machine.Config file), 399

compiling. *See also* **building**

code-behind files, 156-157

projects, 9

Web Form Pages, 87-89

Web Forms applications, 153-154

components

compared to classes, 503-505

creating, 506-508
  database components, 514-516
  static/shared methods, 508-510

DataReaders and, 516-518

HttpContext object, accessing, 527-531

libraries, creating, 522-526

properties, 510-513

Toolbox, adding to, 526-527

usefulness of, 501-502

Components tab (Toolbox), 25

composite Web Form controls

AddressForm control, 576-586

ControlDesigner, 575

ControlDesigner class, 590-593

creating, 569-571

design-time attributes, 586-589

INamingContainer interface, 571-572

Render method, 572-575

Toolbox, adding to, 589-590

<configSections> section (Machine.Config file), 397

configuration

applying settings to particular files, 410-411

Machine.Config file
  custom configuration information, 405-409
  locking settings, 411-412
  overview, 396
  sections, 397-405

out-of-process Session State, 448

project file access, 13

settings, modifying for release, 155

target browser, 50-51

Windows registry, limitations of, 395

configuration errors, 157

Connection class, 204

creating database connections, 206-207

connection strings, configuration, 397

connections (database), creating, 206-207

Content Rotator control, 565-569

ContentRotator Web User Control, 141

Control Tree section, 168

ControlDesigner, 575

ControlDesigner class, 590-593

controls

adding to forms, pizza order form example, 255

event-bubbling, 312

grouping, 103, 105

Web Form
  AddressForm control, 576-586
  composite, 569-571
  Content Rotator, 565-569
  ControlDesigner class, 575, 590-593
  design-time attributes, 586-589
  HtmlTextWriter class, 562-565
  INamingContainer interface, 571-572
  non-composite, creating, 560-562
  overview, 559-560
  Render method, 572-575
  Toolbox, adding to, 589-590

Web Form compared to Web User, 557-558

ControlToValidate property, 118

cookieless authentication modules, creating, 467-478

Cookieless Session State, 450-451

cookies, Forms Authentication, 414

Copy Project command, application deployment, 488
Could Not Obtain Exclusive Lock on Database error, 181
Create Database dialog box, 181
CreateChildControls method, 569
csproj file, 11
CssClass property, Web controls, 105
custom page caching, 464-466
custom roles, 434-437
<customErrors> section (Machine.Config file), 400
customization, DataGrid control, 330
CustomValidator control, 117, 132-134, 136

D

data binding
  DataList control, 303-305
  Repeater control, 287
Data tab (Toolbox), 25
data type checks, Web Form validation, 127-129
DataAdapter class, 204
DataAdapters
  creating, 209
  overview, 208
database components, creating, 514-516
database data
  DataList control, binding to, 303-305
  displaying, list controls, 271-274
database diagrams, 191
  adding annotations, 196
  creating, 192-193
  creating tables, 193-194
  displaying tables, 194-195
  page breaks, 196
  relationships, 195-196
database objects, browsing with Server Explorer, 179-180
Database Projects
  creating, 197-198
  Database References, 198-199
  SQL queries, 200-201
  SQL scripts, 199-200

database tables, displaying, DataGrid control, 327-329
databases
  Command object, 231
    parameters, 237-238
  connections, creating, 206-207
  DataReaders, 220
    displaying database data, 220-223
  DataViews, 218-219
  deleting rows from, 357-358
  displaying data, DataGrid control, 209-213
  editing, Template Columns and, 359-369
  exposing data, Web services, 543-546
  interacting with, pizza order form example, 253, 255-258
  OleCommand object
    creating, 235, 237
    parameters, 241-244
  records, adding, 232
  Server Explorer
    adding data, 180
    creating, 181
    creating functions, 188-191
    creating stored procedures, 185-186
    creating tables, 182-183
    creating triggers, 187-188
    creating views, 183-185
    deleting data, 181
    editing data, 180
    retrieving data, 180
  SqlCommand object
    creating, 232-234
    parameters, 238-241
  storing usernames and passwords, 425-429
  Typed DataSets, 213-217
  updating, 350-353, 355-357
DataBind( ) method, 267, 303
DataBinder.Eval( ) method, 292
databinding
  adding items to list controls, 265-267
  expressions, 290
    formatting, 292-294
DataGrid control
  auto formatting, 330-331
  columns, 331-333

database tables, updating, 350-357
Delete button, 357-358
displaying database data, 209-211
  displaying all rows, 211, 213
  editing, Template Columns and, 359-365, 367-369
  functionality, 327-329
  hyperlink columns, displaying, 334-338
  records
    customizing paging user interface, 348
    dividing into pages, 344-348
    paging navigation with caching, 349-350
    sort order manipulation, 342-344
    sorting, 338-341
    sorting with caching, 341-342
  reloading pages, smart navigation, 359
  Style objects, 331
  View State, disabling, 329
DataKeys collection (DataList control), 316-319
DataList control
  database data, binding to, 303-305
  DataKeys collection, 316-319
  formatting
    auto formatting, 308-309
    borders, 307
  menus, creating, 312-316
  multicolumn, creating, 310-312
  Repeater control, using together, 320-324
  selected items, highlighting, 314
  templates
    adding, 305
    types of, 306
DataReader class, 204
DataReaders, 220
  compared to DataSets, 205
  components and, 516-518
  displaying database data, 220-223

DataSet class, 204

DataSets

  caching in memory, 223-228

  compared to DataReaders, 205

  creating, 209

    displaying data in list controls, 272

  DataGrid control, 209-211

    displaying all rows, 211, 213

  DataViews, 218-219

  overview, 208

  Typed, 213-217

DataSource property, DataList control, 303

DataTextField property, list controls, 273

DataValueField property, list controls, 274

DataViews, 218-219

dates (fields), validating, 127

debug attribute (Machine.Config file), 399

debugger

  breakpoints, adding, 158

  client-side scripts, 163-164

  exceptions and, 162-163

  SQL and, 164-165

  stepping through code, 159-160

  tracing, 166

    application, 171-172

    exceptions, 169-170

    message categories, 169

    programmatically enabling, 170-171

  tracing, page tracing, 166-169

  watches, adding, 161-162

  windows, 160

debugging, changing keyboard shortcuts, 159

declarations

  controls, 149

  Web service classes, 537

default list items

  adding, 279-281

  displaying, 281-282

default project access method, configuring, 13

default view, specifying, 49

default window layout (Visual Studio .NET), resetting to, 18

defaultLanguage attribute (Machine.Config file), 399

defaultRedirect attribute (Machine.Config file), 400

Delete button, DataGrid control, 357-358

DeleteCommand event handler, 357

dependencies, viewing, 154

deployment (applications)

  checklist, 489-490

  overview, 487-489

  Web Setup Project, 490-493

  Web Setup Project, modifying properties, 493-494

  Web Setup Project, modifying user interface, 494-496

Design View

  Global.asax file, adding components, 455

  HTML pages, 52

    adding bookmarks, 65-66

    adding buttons, 69

    adding check boxes, 68

    adding drop-down lists and list boxes, 68

    adding elements, 54-55

    adding file fields, 69

    adding form elements, 66

    adding framesets, 70

    adding hidden fields, 69

    adding hypertext links, 64

    adding images, 63-64

    adding password fields, 66

    adding radio buttons, 67

    adding tables, 69-70

    adding text areas, 67

    adding text fields, 66

    assigning pages to frames, 71

    background and margin properties, 62-63

    combining Flow and Grid layout modes, 60

    displaying a grid, 56

    element alignment, 57-59

    element layering, 59

    Flow layout mode, 55

    formatting text, 60, 62

    Grid layout mode, 56

    linking to pages in frames, 72-73

    modifying frameset properties, 73

    selecting layout modes, 53

    Snap to Grid, 56-57

    Repeater control, positioning, 289

    switching to HTML view, 29, 49

    Toolbox, adding elements to Web Form Pages, 8

design-time attributes (Web Form controls), 586-589

Designer, 29

development

  database diagrams, 191

    adding annotations, 196

    creating, 192-193

    creating tables, 193-194

    displaying tables, 194-195

    page breaks, 196

    relationships, 195-196

  Flow layout mode, 55

  Grid layout mode, 56

    displaying a grid, 56

    element alignment, 57-59

    element layering, 59

    Snap to Grid, 56-57

  HTML pages

    adding to projects, 48

    previewing, 49

  HTML View, 73

  layout modes, combining Grid and Flow, 60

  offline mode, 16-17

  production servers, copying projects to, 23-24

Direction property, Command object, 237

Document Outline, 76

documenting code automatically, 43-44

drop-down lists, adding to HTML pages, 68

DropDownList control, 261

  database tables, binding, 272

DTCs (Visual InterDev Design Time Controls), 16

dynamic compilation, 156

dynamic discovery files, referencing, 553-555

dynamically loading Web User Controls, 151-152

E

EditCommand event handler
Template Columns, 365
updating database tables, 352-353

editing Machine.Config file, 397

EditItemStyle (DataGrid control), 331

elements
form, adding in Design View, 66
HTML, adding in Design View, 54-55
locking (Design View), 59

email, Error event, sending to yourself, 457

Enabled property, Web controls, 105

enableSessionState attribute (Machine.Config file), 399

enableViewState attribute (Machine.Config file), 400

enableViewStateMac attribute (Machine.Config file), 400

EnsureChildControls method, 570

Error event (Global.asax file), 457-459

error handling, Web methods, 551-552

error messages, stored procedures, 245

errors
building code, viewing, 86
compiling problems, 88
configuring display of, 400
Could Not Obtain Exclusive Lock on Database, 181
displaying, 157
types of, 157
Web Setup Projects and, 492

event handlers
client-side scripts, HTML pages, 77-79
Global.asax file, 456
Application_BeginRequest method, 459-460
Application_ResolveRequest Cache method, 464-466
Application_UpdateRequest Cache method, 464-466
Error event, 457-459

Session_End method, 461-463
Session_Start method, 461-463
SortCommand, 340
sort order, 343

event handling
HttpModule class, 466-467
cookieless authentication modules, 467-478
performance logging modules, 478-485
Web controls, 107-110
Web Form Pages, 111-112
Page Load subroutine, 112-115
Web User Controls, 141, 143-144

event-bubbling (controls), 312

exceptions
debugger and, 162-163
page tracing and, 169-170

ExecuteNonQuery( ) method, 234

executionTimeout attribute (Machine.Config file), 398

expiration policies, 392-393

explicit attribute (Machine.Config file), 399

expressions, databinding, 290
formatting, 292, 294

F

file dependencies (caching), 389-392, 569

file fields, adding to HTML pages, 69

files
accessing project files, 12-14
code files, opening, 30
Global.asax
adding components in Design view, 455
Application_BeginRequest method, 459-460
Application_ResolveRequest Cache method, 464-466
Application_UpdateRequest Cache method, 464-466
cautions about modifying, 457

Error event handling, 457-459
event handlers, 456
Session_End method, 461-463
Session_Start method, 461-463
location, project creation, 11
password protecting, 417
projects, adding to, 21-22
Solutions, 12
Web Form Pages, 86-87
WSDL, 538

Flow layout mode, 55
combining with Grid layout mode, 60

folders, projects, adding to, 21-22

Font property, Web controls, 105

fonts, Code and Text Editor, 37

FooterStyle (DataGrid control), 331

FooterTemplate, 291, 306

ForeColor property, Web controls, 105

form elements, adding to HTML pages, 66

formatting
automatic, HTML View, 74-76
databinding expressions, 292, 294
DataGrid control, auto formatting, 330-331
DataList control
auto formatting, 308-309
borders, 307
text, Design View, 60, 62
Web control properties, 105-107

forms
creating, InsertPizzaOrders, 255
databases, interacting with, 253, 255-258
posting automatically, AutoPostBack property, 269-271

Forms Authentication, 413
cookies, 414
custom roles, 434-437
database tables and, 425-429
enabling, 416-418
login page, creating, 418-421
Machine.Config file and, 401
mapping files for, 415

registration pages, 430-434
Sign Out link, creating, 422-423
usernames, retrieving, 421-422
Web.Config files, 414-416
Fortune Web service example, 535
frames
assigning HTML pages to, 71
linking to HTML pages in, 72-73
framesets
adding to HTML pages, 70
properties, modifying, 73
FrontPage Server Extensions, configuring, 14
full-screen mode, Code and Text Editor, 39
functions
creating, Server Explorer, 188-191
SQL, debugging, 164-165

G

General tab (Toolbox), 25
Global.asax file
adding components in Design view, 455
event handlers, 456
Application_BeginRequest, 459-460
Application_ResolveRequest Cache, 464-466
Application_UpdateRequest Cache, 464-466
Error event, 457-459
Sesson_End, 461-463
Sesson_Start, 461-463
modifying, cautions about, 457
<globalization> section (Machine.Config file), 398
Grid layout mode, 56
combining with Flow layout mode, 60
displaying a grid, 56
element alignment, 57-59
element layering, 59
Snap to Grid, 56-57
grouping controls, 103, 105

H

HeaderStyle (DataGrid control), 331
HeaderTemplate, 291, 306
Height property, Web controls, 105
Hello World Web Form control, 560
hidden fields, adding to HTML pages, 69
highlighting selected items, DataList control, 314
HTML controls, 90-92
types of, 91
HTML pages
client-side script event handlers, 77-79
Design View, 52
adding bookmarks, 65-66
adding buttons, 69
adding check boxes, 68
adding drop-down lists and list boxes, 68
adding elements, 54-55
adding file fields, 69
adding form elements, 66
adding framesets, 70
adding hidden fields, 69
adding hypertext links, 64
adding images, 63-64
adding password fields, 66
adding radio buttons, 67
adding tables, 69-70
adding text areas, 67
adding text fields, 66
assigning pages to frames, 71
background and margin properties, 62-63
combining Flow and Grid layout modes, 60
displaying a grid, 56
element alignment, 57-59
element layering, 59
Flow layout mode, 55
formatting text, 60, 62
Grid layout mode, 56
linking to pages in frames, 72-73
modifying frameset properties, 73

selecting layout modes, 53
Snap to Grid, 56-57
Document Outline, 76
HTML View, 73
automatic formatting, 74-76
automatic statement completion, 73
validating documents, 76
previewing, 49
projects, adding to, 48
style sheets, 79
creating, 81-82
inline style attributes, 79
style blocks, 80-81
target browser, setting, 50-51
HTML tab (Toolbox), 25
HTML View
HTML pages, 73
automatic formatting, 74-76
automatic statement completion, 73
validating documents, 76
switching to design view, 29, 49
HtmlTextWriter class, 562-565
HttpContext object, accessing, 527-531
<httpHandler> section (Machine.Config file), 402
HttpModule class, event handling, 466-467
cookieless authentication modules, 467-478
performance logging modules, 478-485
<httpModule> section (Machine.Config file), 403
<httpRuntime> section (Machine.Config file), 398
Hyperlink dialog box, 64
hypertext links, adding to HTML pages, 64

I

<identity> section (Machine.Config file), 401
images, adding to HTML pages, 63-64

Immediate window, 160
impersonate attribute
    (Machine.Config file), 401
impersonation, enabling/
    disabling, 401
INamingContainer interface,
    571-572
initialization
    OleConnection/OleCommand
        objects, 235
    SqlConnection/SqlCommand
        objects, 232
    SqlParameter object, 240
inline functions, 190
Insert Image dialog box, 64
Insert method, Cache object, 224
Insert( ) method, caching, item
    priorities, 394
installation, SQL Server, 178
IntelliSense, 30-31
    disabling, 31
    keyboard shortcuts, 32
interface
    Code and Text Editor, 30
    Designer, 29
    Properties window, 29
    Query and View Designer, 184
    Server Explorer, 27-29
    Solution Explorer, 21
    Toolbox, 24-25
        adding items, 26-27
        adding tabs, 27
        selecting view, 26
    Visual Studio .NET
        Start Page, 20-21
        windows, 18
    Web Setup Projects, modifying,
        494-496
Internet Explorer, enabling
    debugging, 164
Invoke Web service, creating, 546
IsPostBack property, Page Load
    subroutine, 112-115
IsValid property, validation con-
    trols, 118
Items property, ListBox controls,
    99
ItemStyle (DataGrid control), 331
ItemTemplate, 290-291, 306

J-K

JavaScript, validation controls and,
    119

keyboard shortcuts
    changing, 159
    IntelliSense, 32
keywords, adding custom, task
    lists, 42

L

Label controls, 94
    displaying multiple items from
        list controls, 277
    list items, displaying currently
        selected, 267
    Web Form Pages, adding to,
        149-150
labels, adding to Web Form Pages,
    8
launching
    Code Editor, 9
    Solution Explorer, 21
    Start Page, 20
    Task List window, 41
    Toolbox, 24
layering elements, Grid layout
    mode, 59
layout modes
    combining Grid and Flow lay-
        out modes, 60
    Flow, 55
    Grid, 56
        displaying a grid, 56
        element alignment, 57-59
        element layering, 59
        Snap to Grid, 56-57
    selecting, 53
libraries, component, creating,
    522-526
line numbering, printing, 39
line numbers, Code and Text
    Editor, enabling, 38
LinkButton control, 313
list boxes, adding to HTML pages,
    68

List controls, 98-100, 261-262
    adding list items
        databinding, 265-267
        ListItem Collection Editor,
            262-263
        programmatically, 263-265
    AutoPostBack property, 269-
        271
    database data, displaying,
        271-274
    default items
        adding, 279-281
        displaying, 281-282
        interactivity between, creating,
            282-285
    multiple selected items, detect-
        ing and displaying, 277-278
    retrieving list items, 267-269
ListBox controls, 98, 261
    selecting multiple items, 275
ListItem Collection Editor, 99
    adding list items, 262-263
LoadControl( ) method, 152
loading Web User Controls
    dynamically, 151-152
Locals windows, 160
<location> tag, configuration set-
    tings and, 410-411
locking elements (Design View),
    59
login page, creating, 418-421
logs, performance logging mod-
    ules, creating, 478-485

M

MAC (Message Authentication
    Code), View State and, 444-445
Machine.Config file
    case sensitivity and, 397
    custom information, adding,
        405-409
    editing, 397
    locking settings, 411-412
    overview, 396
    sections, 397-405
<machineKey> section
    (Machine.Config file), 401
margin properties, HTML pages,
    62-63

master/detail pages, creating, 334-338

Math Web service, 536-538

maxRequestLength attribute (Machine.Config file), 399

MDI (Multiple Document Interface) mode (Code and Text Editor), 36

measurement units, 106

memory, caching DataSets, 223-228

memoryLimit attribute (Machine.Config file), 404

menus, creating, DataList control, 312-316

Message Authentication (MAC), View State and, 444-445

methods, Cache object, 224

migration, existing applications to Visual Studio .NET compatibility, 14-15

mode attribute (Machine.Config file), 400

Mode property (DataGrid control), 348

monitoring, data cache, 387

multi-tiered applications, creating, 518-521

N

name attribute, text areas, 67

name property, hidden fields, 69

names, Solutions, 12

namespaces, creating for Web services, 542

NameValueSectionHandler class, custom configuration information and, 409

navigating

DataGrid controls, smart navigation, 359

navigation, Code and Text Editor

bookmarks, 35

definitions, 33

line numbers, 33

Navigation Bar, 33

searching for text, 34

networks, connection configuration, 398

New Project in Existing Folder template, 15

Next page button text property (DataGrid control), 348

Numeric Buttons property (DataGrid control), 348

O

objects, custom, exposing through Web services, 546-550

offline mode, 16-17

OleCommand object

creating, 235, 237

parameters, 241-244

OleConnection object, initializing, 235

OleDb classes, compared to SqlClient classes, 204

OleDbConnection object, 242

opening. See launching

Options dialog box, HTML View, 74

OrderForm Web Form Page, 147

out-of-process Session State

configuring, 448

storing in SQL Server database, 449-450

storing in Windows service, 448-449

outlining code, Code and Text Editor, 35-36

output, Response output stream, reading, 466

output parameters (stored procedures), 250-253

OutputCache directive, 374

cache location, specifying, 382

Partial Page Caching, 383-385

VaryByCustom attribute, 380-382

VaryByHeader attribute, 378-380

VaryByParam attribute, 375-377

updating controls in cached pages, 377

P

page breaks, database diagrams, 196

page caching, implementing custom, 464-466

page headers, creating, 139-141

Page Load event, 111

Page Load subroutine, IsPostBack property, 112-115

Page Output Caching, 373

enabling, 374-375

OutputCache directive

specifying cache location, 382

VaryByCustom attribute, 380-382

VaryByHeader attribute, 378-380

VaryByParam attribute, 375-377

updating controls in cached pages, VaryByParam attribute, 377

page requests, rewriting, 459-460

Page Size property (DataGrid control), 348

page tracing, 166-169

exceptions, 169-170

message categories, 169

programmatically enabling, 170-171

<pages> section (Machine.Config file), 399

PageIndexChanged event, DataGrid control, 347

PagerStyle (DataGrid control), 331

Panel control, 103, 105

ParameterName property, Command object, 238

parameters

Command object, 237-238

OleCommand object, 241-244

output, stored procedures, 250-253

SqlCommand object, 238-241

parser errors, 157

Partial Page Caching, 382

Web User controls, 383-385

properties, 386

VaryByControl attribute, 385

Pascal casing, 397
password fields, adding to HTML pages, 66
passwordFormat attribute, 424
passwords
    password protecting files, 417
    storing in database table, 425-429
    storing in Web.Config file, 423-424
performance logging modules, creating, 478-485
Position property (DataGrid control), 348
positioning, Repeater control on Designer surface, 289
postbacks, form validation, 118-119
Precision property, Command object, 237
previewing HTML pages, 49
Previous page text button property (DataGrid control), 348
primary keys, displaying items, DataList control, 316-319
printing, line numbers with code, 39
priorities, setting for caching, 393
<processModule> section (Machine.Config file), 403
Products Web service, creating, 543
programmatically adding list items, 263-265
project folder, location, 11
projects
    accessing files, 12-14
    application deployment
        Web Setup Projects, 489-493
        Web Setup Projects, modifying properties, 493-494
        Web Setup Projects, modifying user interface, 494-496
    compiling, 9
    copies, 11
    copying to production server, 23-24
    copying/moving items, 22
    creating, overview, 11-12
    Database Projects
        creating, 197-198
        Database References, 198-199

SQL queries, 200-201
SQL scripts, 199-200
dependencies, viewing, 154
excluding pages temporarily, 88
files and folders, adding, 21-22
HTML pages
    adding, 48
    previewing, 49
offline mode, 16-17
showing all items, 23
Solutions, creating, 12
synchronization, 17
types, 10
Web Application, creating, 8
Web Forms, adding, 84
Web services, creating, 537
properties
    AutoPostBack, 101
    Command object parameters, 237
    CompareValidator control, 124
    components, adding to, 510-513
    DataGrid control, paging user interface, 348
    DataList control
        border appearance, 307
        multicolumn display, 310-312
    hidden fields, 69
    list controls
        AutoPostBack, 269-271
        DataTextField, 273
        DataValueField, 274
        SelectedItem, 267
    Partial Page Caching, 386
    project access, configuring, 13
    RangeValidator control, 122
    RequiredFieldValidator control, 120
    targetSchema, 50, 52
    validation controls, 118
    Web server controls, formatting, 105-107
    Web Setup Projects, modifying, 493-494
Properties Window, 18, 29
Property Builder (DataGrid control), controlling column display, 331, 333
Property Pages, database tables, 193
proxy classes, Web services, 540

Q-R

Query and View Designer, 184
    SQL queries, 200
QuickWatches, 162

radio buttons, adding to HTML pages, 67
RadioButtonList control, 261
RangeValidator control, 118, 122-124
records, DataGrid control
    customizing paging user interface, 348
    dividing into pages, 344-348
    paging navigation with caching, 349-350
    sort order manipulation, 342-344
    sorting, 338-341
    sorting with caching, 341-342
RedirectFromLoginPage( ) method, 421
referencing
    dynamic discovery files, 553-555
    Web services, 540
registration pages, creating, 430-434
registry. See Windows registry
RegularExpressionValidator control, 118, 129-131
relational views, compared to XML views, 205
relationships (database), database diagrams, 195-196
Release mode (building applications), 155
Remove method, Cache object, 224
Render method, 572-575
Repeater control
    child controls, adding, 297-301
    database data, binding to, 287
    DataList control, using together, 320-324
    positioning, Design View, 289
    templates, 287, 289
        loading dynamically, 294-297
        types of, 291-292
    Web Form Pages, adding to, 288

requests, rewriting page requests, 459-460

RequiredFieldValidator control, 118-122

Response output stream, reading, 466

Response.AppPathModifier( ) method, 452

Response.Write method, Web controls and, 563

ResponseWrite( ) statement, 166

return values (stored procedures), 248-250

rows attribute, text areas, 67

Run to Cursor command, 159

Running Documents window, 160

runtime errors, 157

S

scalar-valued functions, 189

Scale property, Command object, 237

scope, configuration settings, Machine.Config file, 396

scripts
client-side, debugging, 163-164
SQL, types of, 199

searching, Code and Text Editor, 34

section handler (Machine.Config file), creating custom sections, 407-409

security
authentication
compared to authorization, 414
configuration, 401
authorization, configuration, 401
configuration, locking settings, 411-412
form validation, pizza order form example, 257
Forms Authentication, 413
cookies, 414
custom roles, 434-437
database tables and, 425-429
enabling, 416-418

login page, creating, 418-421
registration pages, 430-434
Sign Out link, creating, 422-423
usernames, retrieving, 421-422
Web.Config files, 414-416
source code, production servers and, 488

<securityPolicy> section (Machine.Config file), 402

SelectCategory( ) method, Template Columns, 363

SelectedItem property, 267
List controls, 99

SelectedItemStyle (DataGrid control), 331

SelectionMode property, ListBox control, 275

SeparatorTemplate, 291, 306

Server Explorer, 18, 27-29
database diagrams
adding annotations, 196
creating, 192-193
creating tables, 193-194
displaying tables, 194-195
page breaks, 196
relationships, 195-196
database objects, browsing, 179-180
databases
adding data, 180
creating, 181
creating functions, 188-191
creating stored procedures, 185-186
creating tables, 182-183
creating triggers, 187-188
creating views, 183-185
deleting data, 181
editing data, 180
requerying, 234
retrieving data, 180

Server.Execute method, reading Response output stream, 466

servers, adding to Server Explorer, 28

session IDs, Response.AppPathModifier( ) method, 452

Session State, 445-446
Cookieless, 450-451
out-of-process
configuring, 448
storing in SQL Server database, 449-450
storing in Windows service, 448-449

Session_End event handler (Global.asax file), 456, 461-463

Session_Start event handler (Global.asax file), 456, 461-463

<sessionState> section (Machine.Config file), 402

Setup.exe files, application deployment and, 492

shortcuts, adding to task lists, 43

Show Navigation property (DataGrid control), 348

ShowCategory( ) method, Template Columns, 362

Sign Out link, creating, 422-423

Size property
Command object, 237
hidden fields, 69

smart navigation (DataGrid controls), 359

smartNavigation attribute (Machine.Config file), 400

Snap to Grid (Grid layout mode), 56-57

Solution Explorer, 18, 21
HTML pages, 48
project access, configuring, 13
projects
adding files and folders to, 21-22
copying to production server, 23-24
copying/moving items, 22
showing all items, 23
temporarily excluding pages from projects, 88
Web Form Pages, building, 86

Solutions, 12

SortCommand event handler, 340
sort order, 343

sorting records
DataGrid control, 338-342
sort order manipulation, 342-344

source code, production servers and, 488

SourceColumn property, Command object, 237

SourceVersion property, Command object, 237

SQL, debugging, 164-165

SQL commands, stored procedures, 244-245
  executing, 245, 247-248
  output parameters, 250, 252-253
  return values, 248-250

SQL queries, creating, 200-201

SQL scripts, creating, 199-200

SQL Server
  database connections, 206
  errors, Could Not Obtain Exclusive Lock on Database, 181
  installing, 178

SqlCommand object
  creating, 232-234
  parameters, 238-241

SqlConnection object, initializing, 232

SqlDbType/DbType property, Command object, 238

SqlParameters objects, 240

Start menu, compiling applications, 154

Start Page, 20-21

startup, modifying (Visual Studio .NET), 21

state, maintaining
  Application State, 452-453
  Cookieless Session State, 450-451
  customizing View State, 443-444
  disabling View State, 441-442
  out-of-process Session State
    configuring, 448
    storing in SQL Server database, 449-450
    storing in Windows service, 448-449
  protecting View State, 444-445
  Session State, 445-446
  View State, 439-441

Step Into command, 159

Step Over command, 159

stepping through code (debugging), 159-160

stored procedures
  creating
    pizza order form example, 255
    Server Explorer, 185-186
  error messages, 245
  SQL, debugging, 164-165
  SQL commands, 244-245
    executing, 245, 247-248
    output parameters, 250, 252-253
    return values, 248-250

strict attribute (Machine.Config file), 399

Style Builder dialog box, 79

Style objects
  DataGrid control, 331
  DataList control, 308-309

style sheets
  adding to HTML pages, 79
  creating, 81-82
  inline style attributes, 79
  style blocks, 80-81

synchronization, projects, 17

<system.diagnostics> section (Machine.Config file), 398

<system.net> section (Machine.Config file), 398

<system.web> section (Machine.Config file), 398

T

tab mode (Code and Text Editor), 36

Tabbed Documents mode (Code and Text Editor), 36

TabIndex property, Web controls, 105

table-valued functions, 190

tables, adding to HTML pages, 69-70

tables (database)
  creating
    pizza order form example, 254
    Server Explorer, 182-183
  database diagrams, 193-194
    table display, 194-195
  deleting rows from, 357-358

displaying, DataGrid control, 327-329
  updating, 350-353, 355-357

tags (HTML), converting to HTML controls, 91

targetSchema property, 50, 52

Task List window, 39, 41
  adding comments, 41-42
  adding shortcuts, 43
  adding user comments, 42
  displaying tasks, 41
  tracking code errors, 42
  viewing errors, 157

Template Columns, editing records and, 359-369

templates
  controls, adding, 298
  DataList control
    adding to, 305
    alternatives to, 309
    types of, 306
  New Project in Existing Folder, 15
  Repeater control, 287, 289
    loading dynamically, 294, 296-297
    types of, 291-292

testing
  Application_Error method, 458
  Page Output Caching, 374
  Web methods, 538
  Web services, 545

text areas, adding to HTML pages, 67

text fields, adding to HTML pages, 66

Text property, validation controls, 118

TextBox controls, 96-98
  Repeater control and, 298

This/Me window, 160

timeout attribute (Machine.Config file), 404

toolbox, 18, 24-25

Toolbox
  adding items, 26-27
  adding items to Web User Controls, 144-150
  adding tabs, 27
  components, adding, 526-527
  custom controls, adding, 589-590
  selecting view, 26

ToolTip property, Web controls, 106

Trace Information section, 168

<trace> section (Machine.Config file), 398

TraceWarn( ) statement, 166

tracing, 166
    application, 171-172
    page tracing, 166-169
        exceptions, 169-170
        message categories, 169
        programmatically enabling, 170-171

triggers
    creating, Server Explorer, 187-188
    SQL, debugging, 164-165

Typed DataSets, 213-217

U-V

unauthorized users, redirecting, 415

units of measurement, 106

Update command, Template Columns, 366

UpdateCommand event handler, updating database tables, 354-356

updating database tables, 350-357

upgrading existing applications to Visual Studio .NET compatibility, 15-16

user groups, custom roles, implementing, 434-437

user interface, paging navigation (DataGrid control), 348

user-defined functions, types, 188

userName attribute (Machine.Config file), 403

usernames
    retrieving, 421-422
    storing in database table, 425-429
    storing in Web.Config file, 423-424

users, unauthorized, redirecting, 415

validating documents, HTML View, 76

validation (forms), pizza order form example, 257

validation controls
    CompareValidator, 124-126
    CustomValidator, 132-134, 136
    data type checks, 127-129
    RangeValidator, 122-124
    RegularExpressionValidator, 129-131
    RequiredFieldValidator, 119-122
    ValidationSummary, 136-137
    Web Form Pages, 117-118
        JavaScript and, 119
        postbacks, 118-119

ValidationSummary control, 136-137

Value property
    Command object, 238
    hidden fields, 69

VaryByControl attribute, Partial Page Caching, 385

VaryByCustom attribute (OutputCache directive), 380-382

VaryByHeader attribute (OutputCache directive), 378-380

VaryByParam attribute (OutputCache directive), 375-377
    updating controls in cached pages, 377

VB.NET
    application logic, adding to Web Forms, 85
    Code Editor, launching, 9

vbproj file, 11

View State, 168, 439-441
    customizing, 443-444
    disabling, 329, 441-442
    principles of operation, 441
    protecting, 444-445

Visual Database Tools, support issues, 177-178

Visual InterDev Design Time Controls (DTCs), 16

Visual Studio .NET
    auto hide windows, 19
    default window layout, resetting to, 18

    interface, windows, 18
    migrating existing applications to, 14-15
    Start Page, 20-21
    Toolbox, 24-25
        adding items, 26-27
        adding tabs, 27
        selecting view, 26
    upgrading existing applications to, 15-16
    Visual Database Tools, support issues, 177-178

vs.targetSchema meta tag, modifying, 52

VSWebCache folder, 11

W

Watch windows, 160

watches, adding, 161-162

Web Application project, creating, 8

Web.Config file
    Forms Authentication, 414-416
        enabling, 416, 418
    releasing applications and, 155
    storing usernames and passwords, 423-424
    View State, disabling, 442

Web controls, event handling, 107-110

<webControls> section (Machine.Config file), 404

Web Form controls
    compared to Web User Controls, 557-558
    composite
        AddressForm control, 576-586
        ControlDesigner, 575
        ControlDesigner class, 590-593
        creating, 569-571
        design-time attributes, 586-589
        INamingContainer interface, 571-572
        Render method, 572-575
        Toolbox, adding to, 589-590
    HtmlTextWriter class, 562-565

non-composite
    Content Rotator, 565-569
    creating, 560, 562
    overview, 559-560
    Repeater control, adding to,
        297
    types of, 92-93
Web Forms applications
    building
        overview, 153-154
        Release mode, 155
    errors, displaying, 157
Web Forms Pages
    adding elements, 8
    application logic, adding, 85
    CompareValidator control,
        124-126
    compiling, 87-89
    components, 86-87
    controls
        buttons, 94-95
        labels, 94
        List, 98-100
        TextBox, 96-98
    creating, 8-9, 84-86
    CustomValidator, 132-134, 136
    data type checks, 127-129
    event handling, 107, 111-112
        Page Load subroutine,
            112-115
    HTML controls, 90-92
    overview, 83-84
    RangeValidator control,
        122-124
    RegularExpressionValidator,
        129-131
    Repeater control, adding, 288
    RequiredFieldValidator control,
        119-122
    uniform page headers, creat-
        ing, 139-141
    ValidationSummary, 136-137
    validation controls, 117-118
        JavaScript and, 119
        postbacks, 118-119
    Web server controls, adding,
        89
    Web services, adding, 541

Web Forms tab (Toolbox), 25
Web methods
    caching output, 552-553
    error handling, 551-552
    testing, 538
**Web server, project folder loca-
    tion, 11**
Web server controls
    adding to Web Form Pages, 89
    AutoPostBack property,
        101-102
    formatting properties, 105-107
**Web Server controls,
    targetSchema property, 51**
Web Service Help Page, 537
Web service proxy class, 540
Web services
    creating, 535-536
        Invoice Web service, 546
        Math Web service, 536-538
        Products Web service, 543
    custom objects, exposing,
        546-550
    databases, exposing data,
        543-546
    directory of (Web site), 534
    dynamic discovery files,
        553-555
    Fortune Web service example,
        535
    Global.asax file, event han-
        dlers, 457
    invoking, 540
    namespaces, creating, 542
    platform compatibility and,
        534
    support, 534
    testing, 545
    usefulness, 533-534
    Web Form Pages, adding to,
        541
    Web methods
        caching output, 552-553
        error handling, 551-552
**<webServices> section
    (Machine.Config file), 405**
**Web Setup Projects, application
    deployment, 489-493**
    modifying properties, 493-494
    modifying user interface,
        494-496

**Web sites, Web services directory,
    534**
Web User Controls
    adding Toolbox items, 144-150
    compared to Web Form con-
        trols, 557-558
    declaring, 149
    event handling, 141-144
    loading dynamically, 151-152
    Partial Page Caching, 383-385
        properties, 386
        VaryByControl attribute,
            385
    standard page headers, 139-141
webinfo file, 11
WebMethod attribute, 535
Width property, Web controls, 106
windows, debugger, 160
**Windows registry, limitations of,
    395**
wrap attribute, text areas, 67
**WSDL (Web Services Description
    Language), opening files, 538**

X-Y-Z

XCopy deployment, 487
**XML views, compared to rela-
    tional views, 205**